P U R E

Visual Basic®

Dan Fox

SAMS

Pure Visual Basic®

Copyright © 1999 by Sams Publishing

International Standard Book Number: 0-672-31598-X

Library of Congress Catalog Card Number: 98-89897

Printed in the United States of America

First Printing: August 1999

02   01   00   99   4   3

Trademarks

Warning and Disclaimer

EXECUTIVE EDITOR
Tim Ryan

DEVELOPMENT EDITOR
Songlin Qiu

MANAGING EDITOR
Jodi Jensen

PROJECT EDITOR
Heather Talbot

COPY EDITOR
Kate Talbot

INDEXER
Chris Barrick

PROOFREADERS
Mona Brown
Jill Mazurczyk

TECHNICAL EDITOR
Nick Dallett

TEAM COORDINATOR
Karen Opal

SOFTWARE DEVELOPMENT SPECIALIST
Dan Scherf

INTERIOR DESIGN
Karen Ruggles

COVER DESIGN
Aren Howell

COPY WRITER
Eric Borgert

LAYOUT TECHNICIANS
Steve Geiselman
Amy Parker

Overview

Contents

PART 2   TECHNIQUES REFERENCE   141

About the Author

Dan Fox is the Database Line of Business manager and a practice manager for Solutech, Inc., in Overland Park, Kansas. Solutech (www.solutechinc.com) is a leading Microsoft Partner and Solution Provider, with offices in 11 cities. Solutech provides consulting services to a wide range of clients and specializes in building digital nervous systems using Microsoft products. Solutech also offers a line of customizable intranet applications built with Microsoft technologies to jump-start development (www.webbizapps.com). As a Certified Technical Education Center, Solutech teaches the range of Microsoft official curriculum courses and specializes in development and Windows NT/2000 courses.

Dan is a Microsoft Certified Solutions Developer (MCSD), Systems Engineer (MCSE), and Trainer (MCT), who consults on and teaches Visual Basic, Visual InterDev, and SQL Server. In his role as a practice manager, Dan designs and builds solutions for Solutech clients and mentors other consultants.

Before joining Solutech in 1995, Dan worked for Chevron in Houston, Texas, and for the National Association of Insurance Commissioners in Kansas City, Missouri. Dan received his Bachelor of Science in computer science from Iowa State University.

Dan has been a frequent contributor to the *Visual Basic Programmer's Journal* and has co-authored a book on the Visual Basic 6 Distributed Exam (70-175) for Certification Insider Press. He has spoken at several Developer Days conferences and Microsoft events.

Dan lives with his beautiful wife, Beth, and daughter, Laura, in Overland Park, Kansas, where they root for the Cubs in the 91st year of the Cubs' rebuilding effort.

Dedication

To my parents, who always encouraged me to do my best and who gave me what I needed to succeed. I love you both.

Acknowledgments

First, I'd like to thank the Sams tag team executive editors on this project—Brian Gill and Tim Ryan. They both did a great job and made sure that the process went smoothly every step of the way. I'd also like to say a special thanks to Songlin Qiu, the development editor who read every chapter—some, more carefully than myself, I must admit—and made many suggestions that have served to make this a better book. Last, and certainly not least, thank yous are in order for Kate Talbot and Heather Talbot, whose gifted editing transformed many grammatically flawed sentences into plain English.

This book certainly wouldn't have been possible without all the support and help from the team at Solutech, Inc., for which I work. President Randy Schilling and Vice President Alan Groh's encouragement and investment in the project was instrumental to making it a success. To my co-workers in the Kansas City location, I'd like to say thanks, especially to Rick Kight, Joe McCloud, and Gail McDaniel, because Rick and Joe were patient during the writing of the book and Gail diligently read every word and provided valuable feedback.

Throughout the process, consultants and instructors from several of the Solutech locations took time from their busy schedules to read certain chapters and provide great advice and help. So to these talented people, I'm certainly indebted. Those who went the extra mile include Kevin Burkett, Allen Hackworth, Sue Van Gels, Susan Vegors, Eric Roland, John McCartan, Derek Lawless, and Jerome Dixon.

In addition, several other folks contributed and deserve a heartfelt thank you. Nick Dallett's outstanding technical editing made me rethink more than a few lines of code, for which I am very grateful. Early in the process, I received some valuable advice from Gus Miklos on style and content. And finally, during the development of the outline, Jeff Miller, John McCartan, Gail McDaniel, and Richard Roberts helped to extend and refine the content of the book.

Of course, this book could not have been written without the love and support of my lovely wife, Beth, and daughter, Laura. Beth's encouraging spirit and willingness to pick up the slack made the long hours and extra work much easier. Thank you, Beth, for always being there, and thank you, Laura, for reminding me of what's really important. I love you both more than I can say.

Tell Us What You Think!

As the reader of this book, *you* are our most important critic and commentator. We value your opinion and want to know what we're doing right, what we could do better, what areas you'd like to see us publish in, and any other words of wisdom you're willing to pass our way.

As an executive editor for Sams Publishing, I welcome your comments. You can fax, email, or write me directly to let me know what you did or didn't like about this book—as well as what we can do to make our books stronger.

When you write, please be sure to include this book's title and author as well as your name and phone or fax number. I will carefully review your comments and share them with the author and editors who worked on the book.

Fax: 317-581-4770

Email: tryan@mcp.com

Mail: Tim Ryan
            Executive Editor
            Sams Publishing
            201 West 103rd Street
            Indianapolis, IN 46290 USA

Introduction

Pure Visual Basic is a code-intensive reference designed for developers who need to get up to speed quickly on the tool and want to apply professional techniques to their projects. By *code-intensive*, I mean that this book focuses on the code as the primary means of conveying information. For developers, reading and analyzing code written by others often communicates concepts more quickly and efficiently than a long drawn-out explanation. As a result, I've attempted to add enough comments to the code to ensure that the meaning is understood without drowning the code in a sea of narration.

As a reference book, I intended the book to be more than simply lists of methods and functions with their calling syntax, but instead, a book that you will find worthy of including in your library as a primary reference for frequently used techniques implemented in your own projects.

The book is partitioned into three sections. Part I, "An Accelerated Introduction to Visual Basic," includes 10 chapters targeted at the developer who is new to Visual Basic but who has at least a rudimentary understanding of event-driven programming in the Windows environment. Although not a tutorial, this section takes you from an introduction to the IDE through compilation and distribution of a VB application. It is intended to be read sequentially because several of the discussions and examples build on information presented in earlier chapters.

Part II, "Techniques Reference," is the core of the book and includes nine chapters that present techniques you can reuse in your own development. Each chapter is intended to be read independently, although Chapter 15, "Using Object-Oriented Techniques," and Chapter 16, "Building ActiveX Components," comprise a more or less continuous discussion of techniques that exploit the COM-enabled nature of VB. In addition, because these techniques are devoted to building business applications in the corporate world, a large emphasis is placed on retrieving and manipulating data. To that end, the discussion on ActiveX Data Objects (ADO) in Chapter 14, "Using ADO for Data Access," provides a good foundation for its use throughout the book. Throughout this section, I've attempted to liberally include notes and tips directing you to other portions of this book or other sources where you can find more information.

The final section of the book, "Quick Reference," includes five chapters of reference material on ADO, VB functions and statements, and constants, as well as discussions on COM and sorting and searching algorithms. The first three chapters of this section are intended to be more of a classic reference to explain the basic purpose behind the methods, properties, events, functions, and constants discussed. These chapters are not meant to be your only source of information on the keywords discussed, but rather a jumping-off point into an exhaustive reference such as the online help.

The final two chapters on COM and sorting and searching algorithms are provided as supplemental information to get developers up to speed on the concepts underlying the Component Object Model (COM) and to provide a reference for commonly used algorithms to sort and search multidimensional arrays.

Throughout the book, the approach I've used is to introduce a concept or technique in a short discussion and then to provide a complete example that illustrates what is being discussed in one or more code listings. After the listing, you will often find a paragraph or more that explicates the details of the listing, using references to the particular function or variable names implemented. In addition, during the discussion, you may find code snippets inline with the explanation. These are primarily used to show how the code in the listing would be invoked or used. Typically, the code in listings—such as those in Chapter 13, "Using Win32 API Techniques"—can be extracted and reused without much modification. The code in the snippets, however, is more explanatory in nature and consequently will often have to be customized to your situation. That having been said, some listings depend on references to external components or controls referenced in the discussion. In these cases, you will have to create a project and reference the components or controls before the code can be used.

The code listings themselves can be downloaded from http://www.samspublish-ing.com/product_support. After entering this book's ISBN, you will be presented with a page where you can download all the listings from this book in a chapter-by-chapter zip file. Each chapter's listings are denoted using the naming convention LIS[*chap*][*listing*].TXT. For example, Listing 17.1 is in the file LIS1701.TXT. The code included in the listings was developed using the Enterprise Edition of Visual Basic 6 on Windows NT Server 4, and although the discussions in the book are not specific to version 6, I didn't shy away from using the latest features of the language. Still, in many instances you will be able to use the code listings unmodified in VB 5.0 and, to a lesser extent, VB 4.0.

All the code examples in the book that deal with manipulating relational databases (concentrated in Chapter 14) were developed using SQL Server 7 as the backend. I chose this combination because a large portion of Visual Basic development uses SQL Server. If you intend to use the code examples with other databases, such as Oracle, you will have to modify the code accordingly.

To some extent, the title *Pure Visual Basic* is a bit of a misnomer when talking about VB. In fact, the primary strength of the tool is its capability to act as the glue for building solutions by using prebuilt components. As a result, few applications that use Visual Basic are "pure" Visual Basic but are an amalgam of third-party and homemade components. Consequently, many of the discussions and code listings in the book do not deal only with the VB language itself, but rather with frequently used components, such as the ListView and TreeView controls (discussed in Chapter 12), Collaborative Data Objects (CDO) (discussed in Chapter 18), and ADO, used throughout the book. My intent was to write a book that shows VB at its best—as a tool for building business applications that leverage the component-based paradigm inherent in the tool. As noted earlier, some of the listings require these components to be added to the project before the listings will work.

What originally appealed to me about this project, and why I ultimately chose to write the book, is that in perusing the multitude of books published on VB, I noted that although there were plenty of books on specific topics such as database programming and using the Win32 API, there wasn't one that included a collection of relevant techniques in all these areas applicable to the professional developer. In this book, I've tried to focus on those techniques that developers will consistently use when putting together real-world solutions. Where appropriate, I've added a little more introduction to topics that not all corporate developers have yet had a chance to explore. This is especially true of the discussion on Microsoft Transaction Server (MTS) in Chapter 16, "Building ActiveX Components." In my experience as a Visual Basic instructor and consultant, I've seen many students who grasped the fundamentals of the tool but lacked the examples necessary to put their knowledge to work. I wrote this book primarily with those students in mind.

As a result, I hope that *we*'ve (because this was obviously a team effort) put together a book that will be a primary reference for you as you design and build business applications in Visual Basic. I look forward to and welcome your comments and suggestions. Please contact me at dfox@solutechinc.com.

Dan Fox
Overland Park, Kansas
July 1999

Conventions Used in This Book

This book uses various typefaces to differentiate between code and regular English and also to help you identify important concepts.

Occasionally, boldface type is used in a listing to highlight code that is discussed in the text.

Text that you type and text that should appear on your screen are presented in `mono-space type`.

```
It will look like this to mimic the way text looks on your screen.
```

Placeholders for variables and expressions appear in _monospace italic_ font. You should replace the placeholder with the specific value it represents.

This arrow (➥) at the beginning of a line of code means that a single line of code is too long to fit on the printed page. Continue typing all characters after the ➥ as though they are part of the preceding line.

NOTE

A Note presents interesting pieces of information related to the surrounding discussion.

TIP

A Tip offers advice or teaches an easier way to do something.

CAUTION

A Caution advises you about potential problems and helps you steer clear of disaster.

PART I

AN ACCELERATED INTRODUCTION TO VISUAL BASIC

If you are new to Visual Basic but have some familiarity with other programming environments and event-driven programming, Part I of this book is for you. Designed to be read sequentially, it starts by introducing you to the development environment in Chapter 1 and takes you through distributing your completed application in Chapter 10.

Although not a tutorial, this section of the book is intended to get you up to speed quickly so that you can begin to apply the techniques discussed in Part II, "Techniques Reference." I recommend reading each chapter and then applying what you've learned by attempting to develop your own sample programs, perhaps even using the listings from the chapter.

If you're new to Visual Basic, welcome, and by all means dig in!

CHAPTER 1

The Development Environment

Visual Basic is one of the most widely used development tools on the market today. Yet, as your reading of this chapter attests, new developers are joining the ranks daily. If you're already an experienced VB developer, you can safely skip this chapter (indeed, much of this first section) and jump right into the techniques presented, starting in Chapter 11, "Using Forms and Menus."

In this chapter, I'll discuss the basics of the development environment itself and show a simple application to familiarize you with the structure and components of a VB application.

Using the IDE

The Visual Basic Integrated Development Environment (IDE) has matured through the years to provide a host of features that make creating applications a straightforward process. At its most basic, the IDE provides the tools to edit various files that can be contained in the VB project. When the project is saved, the references to these files and any properties set in the IDE are saved in a .VBP file. Since version 5.0, the IDE has also had the capability to load multiple projects, called a *project group*. The definition of the project group can also be saved in a .VBG file so that the various projects can be reloaded as a group. Table 1.1 presents these files, their uses, and their extensions.

Table 1.1   The Types of Files That Can Make Up a Typical VB Project

Type	Extension	Description
Form	.frm, .frx	Used to create the user interface of an application. A form is a window.
MDI Form	.frm, .frx	Used when creating multiple document interface (MDI) applications. A window that can contain and organize child windows.
Module	.bas	Also called a *code module*. Used to contain procedures and variables used throughout the application. Contains no user interface.
Class Module	.cls	An object-oriented module that can contain methods and properties and is used as the basis for COM components.
User Control	.ctl	A module that provides the methods, properties, and user interface necessary to create an ActiveX control.
Property Page	.pag	Provides the user interface for property page dialogs used when creating ActiveX controls.
User Document	.dob	Provides the methods, properties, and user interface for an ActiveX document. Normally used in Internet Explorer.
Web Class	.dsr	Invokes a designer that assists in the creation of a Web interface to run in the context of the Active Server Page (ASP) engine on Internet Information Server (IIS).
Data Report	.dsr	Invokes a designer that assists with the creation of banded reports that can be embedded into the application.
DHTML Page	.dsr	Invokes a designer that assists with the creation of HTML pages that can utilize the dynamic HTML capabilities of Internet Explorer.
Data Environment	.dsr	Invokes a designer that encapsulates database connections and commands (in addition to code written in response to their events) so that they can be reused throughout the application.
Resource File	.res	A Windows resource file that can contain a string table, images, and other resources that can be loaded dynamically by the application.

Each of these file types has its place in one or more types of projects that can be created using VB. The remainder of this section discusses the types of projects and the layout of the IDE with its various windows.

Project Templates

Upon starting the IDE, the developer is presented with a dialog (shown in Figure 1.1) of the various types of projects that can be created. When selected, a project template can have the effect of loading one or more files into the project and setting the type of binary file (EXE or DLL) that will be created when the project is compiled.

Figure 1.1

The project templates dialog used to create a new project shown when starting VB.

NOTE

In addition to using the standard project templates, you can create your own. Simply put the .vbp file and any supporting files in the \Program Files\Microsoft Visual Studio\VB98\Template\Projects directory.

Table 1.2 presents the types of projects and their descriptions.

Table 1.2   The Types of Projects That Can Be Created in VB

Type	Description
Standard EXE	A standalone executable normally containing only forms and code modules.

continues

Table 1.2   continued

Type	Description
ActiveX EXE	An executable that can expose COM components (created as class modules and called *out-of-process components*) and act as an Automation client to other applications. Can run standalone.
ActiveX DLL	A DLL that exposes COM components (created as class modules) that are loaded in the same address space as the caller (*in-process components*).
ActiveX Control	A DLL compiled as an .OCX file that contains one of more user controls used by *containers* to provide prepackageduser interface functionality.
ActiveX Document DLL	A DLL that contains one or more user documents loaded in the address space of the caller. Normally loaded by Internet Explorer to provide a more robust user interface than simple HTML.
ActiveX Document EXE	An executable that exposes one or more user docu ments to another program. Can also run standalone.
DHTML Application	A DLL that encapsulates event handlers and other code for one or more Dynamic HTML (DHTML) pages and runs in-process with Internet Explorer. Provides the ability to create HTML pages that take advantage of DHTML using the Document Object Model (DOM).
IIS Application	A DLL that contains one or more Web classes and runs in-process on IIS. Takes advantage of the ASP object model.
Add-In	A DLL that can be loaded by the IDE itself (on the Add-Ins menu) to extend the functionality of the IDE.
Visual Basic Application Wizard	Not actually a type of project, but simply a wizard that asks a series of questions and creates a project template upon completion.
Visual Basic Wizard Manager	Adds the necessary forms and modules and a wizard designer to allow the creation of a wizard that can be invoked from the Add-Ins menu. Compiled as a DLL.

Window Layout

After you select a project template, the IDE presents a collection of windows (some dockable, some child windows) that are used to manipulate the project. The windows that are primarily used, shown in Figure 1.2, are the following:

- *Toolbox*—Contains icons representing the intrinsic and ActiveX controls available to the project. Controls can be added to the Toolbox by right-clicking on it or using the Project, Components menu. This window is dockable.

- *Project Explorer*—Contains references to all the files used by the project or projects currently loaded. New files can be added by right-clicking on the window and selecting Add. This window is dockable.
- *Properties*—Shows a property list for the object currently selected (accessed using F4). Properties can be set either by typing in the new value and using a drop-down list or by clicking a button that displays a dialog box. This window is dockable.
- *Object Browser*—Accessed from the View menu or by using the F2 key and shows all the methods, properties, and events for all components referenced by the project. Includes the language and IDE components of VB itself. This window is an MDI child window by default but may also be dockable.
- *Code Editor*—Accessed by right-clicking on a file in the Project Explorer or right-clicking on its graphical representation and selecting View Code. Allows editing of all the procedures associated with the file. The drop-down controls at the top of the window allow individual objects (on the left) and their procedures (on the right) to be selected. The code window can be split by dragging the splitter bar down from the upper-right corner above the scrollbar, allowing two procedures to be viewed simultaneously. This window is an MDI child window.
- *Interface Designer*—Accessed by right-clicking or double-clicking on a file in the Project Explorer. Used to create the user interface of the object by dragging controls from the Toolbox. This window is an MDI child window.

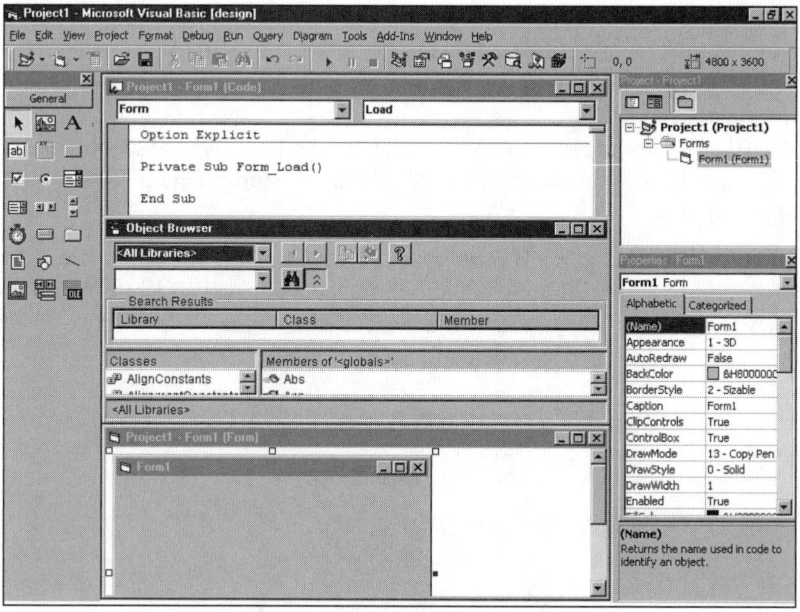

Figure 1.2

The VB IDE with its primary windows visible.

Hello World!

Typically, the process of building a VB application can be divided into the following steps. Keep in mind that application development is normally an iterative process and that the steps shown here simply represent the various tasks that must be completed.

1. *Adding the appropriate objects to the project.* This includes adding both files (such as forms, code modules, and class modules) and components (ActiveX controls and COM components).
2. *Creating the user interface.* This involves adding instances of controls from the Toolbox to the forms, user controls, or user documents and setting their properties for proper display. Each control instance is referred to with a unique name.
3. *Writing code to handle events.* After the interface has been created, code to respond to events raised by the interface must be handled. Typical events to be handled include mouse clicks and keystrokes that implement data validation and navigation.
4. *Writing application logic.* The key functionality of the project (its essential algorithms) will normally be abstracted from the user interface in code modules and class modules.
5. *Testing and debugging the project.* VB provides the ability to test the project before compilation by using the Run menu or the F5 key. This enables you to fully debug the program using line-by-line execution and variable inspection as required. Also, testing includes ensuring that the startup object and project properties are correctly set.
6. *Compiling the application.* After the project has been fully tested, it can be compiled into an EXE or DLL using the File item on the Make menu. The resulting dialog box allows you to specify compilation options and version information.
7. *Distributing the application.* VB ships with the Package and Deployment Wizard to allow you to create a redistributable setup program for the application.

To develop a feel for what a VB project comprises, consider the application shown in Figure 1.3. This example, although not as simple as your typical Hello World application, contains a simple user interface that accepts a filename in a `TextBox` control and a button that is used to load the file and display it in the `ListBox` control.

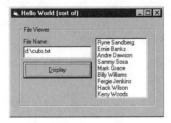

Figure 1.3

A simple VB application to load the contents of a file into a ListBox.

The application was developed by dragging instances of five controls (Frame, Label, CommandButton, ListBox, and TextBox) from the Toolbox onto the form. The properties of the controls were sized and manipulated using the Properties window, for example, by setting the Caption property of the CommandButton to "Display". The Click event of the CommandButton was then coded by double-clicking on the CommandButton and writing the following code:

```
Private Sub cmdOK_Click()

Dim arData As Variant
Dim i As Integer

    ' Load the array
    arData = GetFileData(txtFile.Text)

    ' Display the data in the ListBox
    For i = 0 To UBound(arData)
        lstData.AddItem arData(i)
    Next
End Sub
```

The code in this procedure loads an array with the data from a file using the GetFileData function. It then loops through the array and adds each element to the ListBox, lstData. The key point to note about this code is the call to the GetFileData function. This function contains the application logic of the project. To abstract this code from the user interface, a code module was added to the project, and in it was added a function written to open the file and load its contents into an array (shown in Listing 1.1).

Listing 1.1   The GetFileData Function Used to Open the File and Load Its Contents into an Array

```
Public Function GetFileData(ByVal pFileName As String) As Variant

Dim intFileNum As Integer
Dim arData As Variant
Dim flFirst As Boolean

intFileNum = FreeFile

' Open the text file
Open pFileName For Input Lock Read As intFileNum

' First time through
flFirst = True

' Load the array
Do While Not EOF(intFileNum)
```

continues

Listing 1.1   continued

```
    If Not flFirst Then
        ReDim Preserve arData(UBound(arData) + 1)
    Else
        ReDim arData(0)
        flFirst = False
    End If
    Line Input #intFileNum, arData(UBound(arData))
Loop

' Close the file
Close intFileNum

' Return the array
GetFileData = arData

End Function
```

NOTE

Obviously, the code shown here does not take into account data validation and error handling, which are covered in Chapter 9, "Debugging and Error Handling," and Chapter 11, "Using Forms and Menus."

Figure 1.4 shows the project as it exists in the IDE.

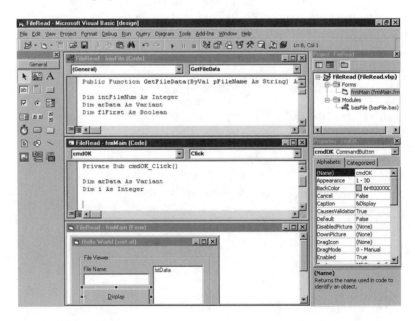

Figure 1.4

The Hello World project shown in the IDE.

Setting a Startup Object

Each VB project that is compiled into an executable file requires an entry point to begin execution. By default, the first form added to the project is selected as the startup object. This simply means that when the EXE is loaded, it will first load and display the chosen form. To change the default, you can invoke the Project Properties dialog, shown in Figure 1.5, from the *Project Name* properties menu item on the Project menu.

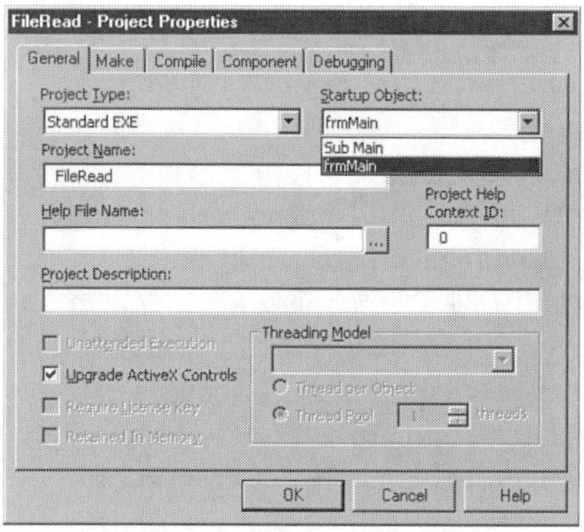

Figure 1.5

The Project Properties dialog box for the Hello World application showing frmMain as the startup object.

Optionally, you can specify Sub Main as the startup object. This allows the application to start with a procedure you can create in a code module as follows (analogous to the WinMain function required when writing Windows programs in C):

```
Public Sub Main()
    ' Startup code goes here
End Sub
```

> **TIP**
>
> Projects that build DLLs—such as ActiveX controls and ActiveX DLLs—can specify Sub Main, but not a form, as their startup object.

Configuring the IDE

As you begin working with the IDE, you will likely want to alter certain aspects of it. Many of these options can be found on the Options dialog invoked by the Tools, Options menu. The following list contains the key changes you can make:

- *Require Variable Declaration*—Found on the Editor tab and, when selected, ensures that the Option Explicit statement is present in all new modules added to the project. This statement does not allow variables to be declared on-the-fly within code (as the BASIC language normally would). Requiring variable declarations ensures that all variables are declared before they are used, which avoids errors due to mistyping the variable name. It is recommended that you always turn this on.

- *Auto Syntax Check*—Found on the Editor tab and instructs the IDE to display a dialog box each time a syntax error is discovered as a line of code is parsed. This can be annoying because often you will want to move around your code without completing a statement. In any case, lines with syntax errors are also colored red. It is recommended that you turn off this option.
- *IntelliSense*—Encompassed in the Auto List Members, Auto Quick Info, and Auto Data Tips options on the Editor tab. When turned on, these options provide a list of the methods, properties, and events, the calling syntax of procedures, and the values of variables during debugging, respectively. Normally, these are turned on to enhance productivity.
- *Full Module View* and *Procedure Separator*—When turned on in the Editor tab, these options display all procedures for a module within the code window and place a separator bar between them as a visual cue. This makes it simple to use the Page Up, Page Down and arrow keys to locate code in a module without having to resort to the drop-down list at the top of the window.
- *Fonts*—On the Editor Format tab, all the fonts, sizes, and colors can be modified.
- *Grid Settings*—On the General tab are several options for showing, sizing, and aligning controls on a grid. These options are useful for quickly placing controls on Forms and aligning them, although for more precise control, these options are turned off and the Format, Align menu is used.
- *Auto Save*—The Environment tab contains three radio buttons for determining what happens when a project in the IDE is put in run mode by selecting the Run, Start menu or pressing F5. By selecting Save Changes or Prompt to Save Changes, the project can be saved before being run. It is recommended that you select one of those two options to ensure that the project is saved in the event of a general protection fault or other system problem.
- *SDI Development Environment*—Finally, on the Advanced tab is an option that, when set, reconfigures the IDE the next time it is started to use a single document interface. This essentially returns the IDE to the way it worked before version 5.0 when all windows were independent (not dockable or MDI child windows).

Add-Ins

As mentioned earlier, the IDE can be augmented with functionality provided by add-ins. VB ships with a number of add-ins classified as wizards, builders, utilities, and simply add-ins. You can load these extensions using the Add-In Manager invoked from the Add-Ins, Add-In Manager menu shown in Figure 1.6. When you load the add-in using the check box, the add-in appears on the Add-Ins menu.

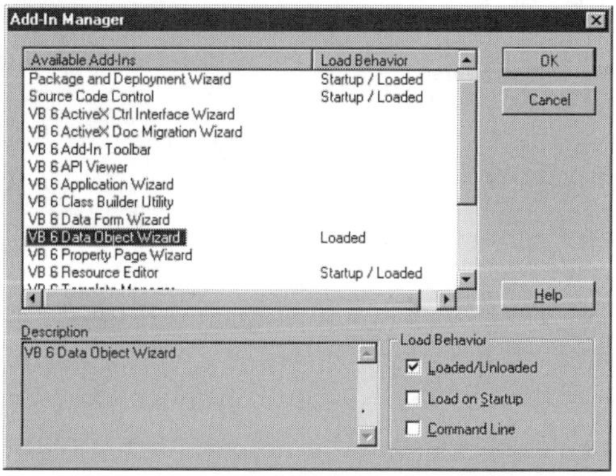

Figure 1.6

The Add-In Manager dialog box where you can load add-ins.

Although space prohibits a complete explanation of the extensions that ship with VB, keep in mind that you can create your own, using the tools provided with VB.

TIP

> To begin creating an add-in, see "Creating a Basic Add-In" in the online help or MSDN library.

Summary

This chapter covers the basics of the VB IDE, including the types of files and projects it can contain. In addition, I've shown a simple application to give you some perspective on how a VB project comes together. Finally, I discussed several ways the IDE is customized to suit your individual needs.

Now that you're familiar with the IDE as a whole, I'm going to start drilling down into what makes up a VB project. To begin this process, in the next chapter, you will look at controls and how they are used.

CHAPTER 2

Using Controls

Visual Basic became popular primarily because of its capability to allow developers to create Windows applications quickly. This success is due to two primary reasons. The first is that basing the product on the BASIC language (which is both flexible and simple to learn) provides immediate access to a large number of developers. However, equally important is the inclusion of standard graphical controls that enable developers to quickly build user interfaces without writing any code at all.

In all versions of VB, certain controls are added to the Toolbox automatically and are always available (called *intrinsic controls*), whereas others can be added to the Toolbox manually (simply called *ActiveX controls*). To add a control to the Toolbox, the control has to be created using the appropriate specification (COM, in the case of recent versions of VB) and be installed on the developer's machine. This architecture enables third-party vendors (and VB developers themselves) to create controls that can be plugged into the development environment. This mechanism is, in fact, how VB pioneered the use of component-based software.

In this chapter, I discuss the intrinsic and ActiveX controls that ship with VB, where to use them, and how.

Intrinsic Controls

In VB 6, the Toolbox always contains 20 intrinsic controls that you can use to build user interfaces. Table 2.1 gives their names and uses.

Table 2.1   *Intrinsic Controls and Their Uses*

Name	Description
PictureBox	Displays .bmp, .gif, .jpg, and .wmf files, among others. Also, supports a full range of events so that your code can detect when the control is clicked or dragged and dropped.
Label	Used to display static text and supports a full range of events.
TextBox	Used to allow data entry into a single-line or multiple-line control. Supports events that allow your code to inspect each keystroke and perform validation.
Frame	Acts as a grouping control to contain other controls for visual grouping and affects the scope of OptionButton controls.
CommandButton	Used to respond to Click events to kick off processes.
CheckBox	Can be used to let users select options that are binary (on or off).
OptionButton	Used in groups to allow the user to select one of several options. All OptionButtons within the same Frame control are in the same scope (only one can be selected). Outside a Frame, all OptionButtons operate at the same scope. Also referred to as radio buttons.
ComboBox	Used to drop down a list of choices. Using its Style property, it can allow editing or can restrict the selection to one of the items in the list.
ListBox	Used to display a list of items for the user to select from, by either highlighting the item or using a check box. Its MultiSelect property controls whether multiple items can be highlighted simultaneously.
HScrollBar and VScrollBar	Horizontal and vertical scrollbars used to display custom scrollbars and respond to events as the user manipulates them.

Name	Description
Timer	Used to set a timer on `Form` using its `Interval` property. At each interval, its `Timer` event fires. Can be used to create applications that periodically poll for some condition.
DriveListBox, DirListBox and FileListBox	Controls that read the current drive, current directory, and list of files in the current directory, respectively. Provides properties to change the current path and events that fire when the changes are made.
Shape	Graphic control that can draw and fill a rectangle, circle, square, or oval. Does not respond to events.
Line	Graphic control that draws a line. Does not respond to events.
Image	Displays .bmp, .gif, .jpg, and .wmf files, among others. More lightweight than the `PictureBox` control because it does not handle as many events or expose properties that allow it to be manipulated using the Win32 API.
DataControl	Utilizes the Data Access Object (DAO) component to create and make available recordsets to bound controls (most intrinsic controls can bind to data controls and display their data). Also, provides events that fire as the recordset is manipulated.
OLE	Encapsulates the functionality to display and manipulate OLE documents. Can be used to display spreadsheet or word processor documents, for example, in a VB application.

ActiveX Controls

In addition to the intrinsic controls that ship with VB, Microsoft also provides a number of ActiveX controls. To use these in an application, you must add them to the Toolbox using the Project, Components menu or by right-clicking on the Toolbox and selecting Components. Figure 2.1 shows the resulting dialog box.

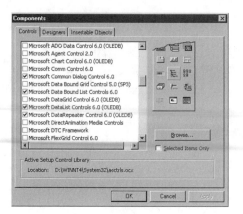

Figure 2.1

The Components dialog enables you to add controls to the Toolbox.

Table 2.2 describes the controls Microsoft ships with VB 6.

Table 2.2   ActiveX Controls and Their Uses

Name	Description
ADO Data Control	Similar to the intrinsic `DataControl` but is used to connect to OLE DB providers and created ActiveX Data Objects (ADO) recordsets.
Chart Control	Can be used to create charts from ADO recordsets or manually. You can find an example using this control in Chapter 16, "Building ActiveX Components."
Comm Control	Provides access to COM and LPT ports for writing applications that receive or transmit data through the ports.
Common Dialog Control	Provides access to the standard Color, Font, Printer, Save, and Open dialog boxes provided by the operating system. Can also invoke the help engine.
Data Bound Grid Control	A grid control that can be used independently or be bound to DAO or RDO (Remote Data Objects) data controls.
Data Bound List Controls	Contains the `DBList` and `DBCombo` controls that can be bound to DAO and RDO data controls to display a list of choices and update the recordset with the selection.

Name	Description
DataGrid Control	A grid that can be bound to an ADO `Recordset` or an ADO Data Control to display and update data.
DataList Controls	Analogous to the Data Bound List Controls but contains `DataList` and `DataCombo` controls to use with ADO recordsets instead of DAO or RDO.
DataRepeater Control	Can be used to display a specific control for each row returned by an ADO `Recordset`. Allows you to create a customized grid-type display.
FlexGrid Control	A grid control that can be used to display read-only data, including images. Also, allows columns or rows to be merged.
Hierarchical FlexGrid Control	A grid control that is similar to the `FlexGrid` control but can also display hierarchical recordsets created using the Microsoft Data Shape OLE DB provider and ADO 2.x.
Internet Transfer Control	A control that can communicate using HTTP, FTP, or Gopher protocols. Can be used to embed file transfer and Web communication into an application.
MAPI Controls	Contains `MAPISession` and `MAPIMessages` controls that allow an application to connect to and send and receive email messages from a MAPI provider. Does not provide the full functionality of CDO (discussed in Chapter 18, "Adding Professional Features").
Masked Edit Control	Like a `TextBox` but used to force the user to enter data in a specific format using its `Mask` property.
Multimedia Control	Used to manage media control interface (MCI) devices. It can play, stop, pause, move previous, move next, record, and eject.

continues

Table 2.2 continued

Name	Description
PictureClip Control	Used to store an image and extract regions of it for use within an application. Allows you to store several images in a single control rather than create multiple instances of the `PictureBox` control. The `ImageList` control provides much the same functionality.
RemoteData Control	Analogous to the intrinsic `DataControl` but used to create RDO recordsets.
Rich TextBox Control	Used to display and edit Rich Text Format (RTF) files.
Tabbed Dialog Control	Used to create a tabbed interface in dialog boxes (such as property dialogs). More full featured than the simple `TabStrip` control included in the Windows Common Controls library.
SysInfo Control	Exposes a collection of events that allow an application to respond to system events (`DisplayChanged`, `TimeChanged`), power status events (`PowerSuspend`, `PowerResume`), and plug and play events (`DeviceArrival`, `DeviceRemoveComplete`). Provides access to operating system properties (`OSVersion`).
Windows Common Controls	A collection of commonly used controls including `TabStrip`, `Toolbar`, `StatusBar`, `ProgressBar`, `TreeView`, `ListView`, `ImageList`, `Slider`, and `ImageCombo`. The `TreeView`, `ListView`, and `ImageList` are discussed in detail in Chapter 12, "Using `TreeView` and `ListView` Controls."
Windows Common Controls2	A second collection of commonly used controls, including `Animation`, `UpDown`, `MonthView`, `DTPicker`, and `FlatScrollBar`.
Windows Common Controls3	The third collection of commonly used controls. At this time, includes only the `CoolBar` control that can be used to create user-configurable toolbars such as those found in Internet Explorer.

Name	Description
Winsock Control	Provides access to TCP and UDP network services to enable developers to write applications that communicate using Winsock without having to understand the low-level Winsock APIs.

Figure 2.2 shows the Toolbox loaded with all the controls that ship with the Enterprise edition of VB, along with the intrinsic controls.

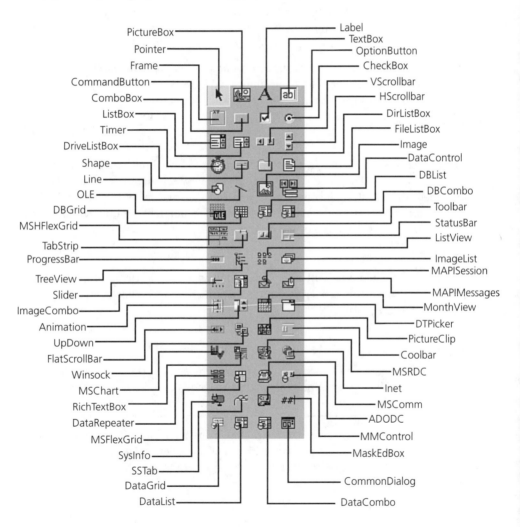

Figure 2.2

All the possible controls that ship with VB 6. The names of the controls are displayed by position, with the first two controls on the left and last two on the right in each row.

Graphically Manipulating Controls

To place instances of controls on a form, you can simply select the control using the cursor and then draw it onto the form. After placing the controls, you will want to address several issues, using the Properties window after selecting the control.

Naming

You will notice that the control is immediately given a name. By default, each instance is named with its classname followed by a number indicating how many instances of the control are now on the form. For example, the first instance of a CommandButton control on a form is named CommandButton1. Before coding, it's good practice to rename each control to something meaningful so that your code will be readable in the future. Refer to Chapter 6, "Coding Conventions," for a suggested naming convention.

The reason it is important to name your control first is that event procedures associated with the control have the control's name embedded in it. For example, the Click event of a CommandButton named cmdOK has the following declaration:

```
Private Sub cmdOK_Click()
End Sub
```

If you write code for a control (by double-clicking it to reveal the code editor window and the events exposed by the control) and subsequently rename the control, VB does not automatically transfer the code you've written to the new event procedure. In fact, VB places the old event procedure in the General Declarations section accessible by using the drop-downs at the top of the code window.

Tab Order

In addition to its name, you will likely want to change the TabIndex property of the controls on the Form. This property controls the order in which controls receive focus as the user presses the Tab key.

TIP

As controls receive and lose focus, their GotFocus and LostFocus events fire, respectively. Also, you can programmatically change the focus to a control by calling its SetFocus method.

By default, each control receives the next number in the tab sequence that starts at 0. To place a control in a different position within the tab sequence, you can simply assign it the proper TabIndex, and all other controls on the form will have their TabIndex property incremented automatically.

Tag

Each control on a form (and, indeed, forms themselves) can be assigned a Tag property, which is simply a string value that can be used by your application to store extra data. For example, you can use the Tag property to indicate which controls are required on a particular form by assigning the Tag property a value of R or Required.

ToolTips

Another property you might want to set at design time is ToolTipText. This property is used to provide a floating ToolTip for the control if the user pauses the mouse while over the control. Typically, ToolTipText is used to display a short help message that instructs the user about what to enter in the control. This property can also be manipulated programmatically, but often it is more efficient to simply define it at design time.

Providing Help

The final two properties you might want to set are HelpContextID and WhatsThisHelpID. Both these properties can contain a topic number for the help assigned by using the Project Properties dialog or the App.HelpFile property.

When the control has focus and a user presses the F1 key, the topic in the file specified by HelpContextID is displayed. For example, if you set the HelpContextID of a TextBox to 1050, place your cursor in the TextBox control, and then press the F1 key, the help file will be displayed and opened to the topic specified in the property.

If the HelpContextID is set to zero or not specified, VB will look in the form in which the control is placed to see whether a HelpContextID exists. If no ID is found in the container, the default topic in the help file is displayed.

The WhatsThisHelpID works slightly differently in that if you set the WhatsThisHelp property of the form to True, the F1 key will activate the help topic specified by the WhatsThisHelpID property instead of the HelpContextID. In addition, by setting the WhatsThisButton property of the form to True, the form will also display a button in the title bar. When clicked, this turns the cursor into a question mark that can be dropped on a control to activate the help topic. An example of this behavior can be seen in the Taskbar Properties dialog box shown in Figure 2.3.

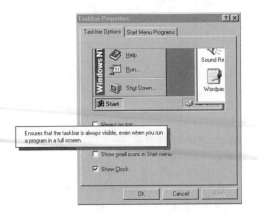

Figure 2.3

The Taskbar Properties dialog is a good example of using WhatsThisHelp. When you click on the question mark and drop it on a control, the help topic is displayed.

Manipulating Controls with Code

In most cases, after controls have been placed on a form and their design-time properties set, code must be written to manipulate the control at runtime. In this section, I discuss techniques for manipulating controls programmatically.

Using Dot Notation

The basic syntax for manipulating objects in VB (that is, controls, forms, and classes) is through *dot notation*. In this style, each method (procedure exposed by the object) or property (attribute of the object), together referred to as *members*, is called by appending the name of the member after the name of the object using a period in the form.

```
object.member
```

For example, to set the `Visible` property of a `ListBox` control named `lstPlayers` to `True`, you would use the syntax

```
lstPlayers.Visible = True
```

Similarly, to invoke the `SetFocus` method of the same control, you would simply use the syntax

```
lstPlayers.SetFocus
```

NOTE

Notice that in VB, if the method does not take any arguments and no return value is required, parentheses are not required after the method name. This is not the case in other languages, such as Java.

In addition, you can also use dot notation to drill down into an object that contains other objects as properties. For example, the `PictureBox` control contains a property named `Picture`, which is itself an object that contains members. To access the `Handle` property of a `PictureBox` named `picLogo`, you can use the syntax

```
lngHandle = picLogo.Picture.Handle
```

Default Values

Most controls have one property that is defined as its default property. As a result, this property can be accessed by simply referencing the name of the control. For example, the `Text` property of a `TextBox` control is the default, so to change the value displayed by the control, you can simply use the syntax

```
txtName = "Ernie Banks"
```

However, using this technique is not recommended because it makes your code less readable and actually does not perform as well as referencing the property explicitly.

Calling Multiple Members

As mentioned previously, you can explicitly reference methods and properties of a control using dot notation. However, in cases where you must set several properties in the same code block, a more efficient method is to use the `With...End With` syntax. Using this syntax makes your code more efficient—because only references to the control must be resolved—as well as more readable.

For example, to set three properties of a `CommandButton` and call its `SetFocus` method, you would execute the following code:

```
With cmdOK
    .Visible = True
    .Caption = "&OK"
    .Enabled = True
    .SetFocus
End With
```

Caching Frequently Used Properties

A similar technique to using `With...End With` to increase the performance of your code is to cache frequently used properties in local variables. A typical example of this, shown in the following code snippet, would be using a property value from a control in a loop that executes many times. In this case, the loop is calculating the principal amount for each payment in a 30-year mortgage and placing the results in an array. By referencing the amount of the loan directly from the `Text` property of the `TextBox` control inside the loop, VB will have to resolve the control and property each time.

```
For i = 1 to 360
    arData(i) = PPmt(0.075 / 12, i, 360, CDbl(txtLoan.Text))
Next
```

A more efficient technique would be to first read the Text property of txtLoan into a local variable and then pass the variable to the PPmt function. Note that this also spares VB from having to convert the loan value to a Double in each iteration of the loop.

```
Dim dblLoan as Double

dblLoan = CDbl(txtLoan.Text)

For i = 1 to 360
    arData(i) = PPmt(0.075 / 12, i, 360, dblLoan)
Next
```

Using Control Arrays

In addition to placing individual instances of controls on a form, you can also use control arrays. Basically, a *control array* is exactly what it sounds like, an array of controls that share the same name and are assigned an index value (the Index property). Any control in the array can be referenced using this index value, just as elements in an array. An array of TextBox controls that each display loan amounts can thus be referenced as

```
txtLoan(i).Text = arData(i)
```

In addition, control arrays share event procedures and consume fewer resources than creating each control individually.

There are two ways to create control arrays. One method is to simply place controls on a Form and then manually change the Name and Index properties using the Properties window. A faster approach is to first create a single control and name it appropriately. Then, copy the control to the Clipboard, and paste it back onto the Form. Seeing that the control already exists on the Form, VB will prompt you to create a control array.

When the controls are in an array, one of the advantages is the ability to code a single event handler for multiple controls. For example, OptionButton controls are used to allow the user to select one choice of several. By placing multiple OptionButton controls in a control array, a single handler for the Click event will be fired for all the controls in the array.

```
Private Sub optColors_Click(Index As Integer)
    ' Change the foreground color of the Form
    Select Case Index
        Case 0
            Me.ForeColor = vbRed
        Case 1
            Me.ForeColor = vbBlue
        Case 2
            Me.ForeColor = vbGreen
    End Select

End Sub
```

Notice that the event handler is passed in an argument that indicates the Index property of the control that was clicked. As shown, the normal way this is resolved is by using a Select Case statement.

TIP

The preceding code snippet uses the Me keyword. As discussed in Chapter 11, "Using Forms and Menus," this keyword is used to reference the form on which the control whose code is running is placed.

Adding New Controls

Another advantage of using control arrays is that controls can be added to the array using the Load statement. This is useful in cases where the number of controls necessary is not known at design time. For example, to add a new control to the txtLoan control array, you would use the syntax

```
Load txtLoan(txtLoan.UBound+1)
```

When a control array is created, it contains its own properties, including the number of items (Count), the lower bound (LBound), and the upper bound (UBound) of the array. By incrementing the upper bound using the Load statement, a new control is added to the array. The only caveat with this technique is that the array must be created at design time and include at least one element.

By default, the new control always takes on the properties of the first control in the array (element 0) and is invisible. To place and make the control visible, you could use the syntax

```
With txtLoan(txtLoan.UBound)
    .Top = 1
    .Left = 500
    .Visible = True
End With
```

Controls created with the Load statement can also be destroyed using the Unload statement.

```
Unload txtLoan(txtLoan.UBound)
```

VB 6 introduces a second technique for creating controls that do not have to be part of a control array, by using the Add method of the Controls collection. For example, to add a new CommandButton to a form, you would use the following code:

```
Form1.Controls.Add "VB.CommandButton", "cmdOk"
```

The first argument is the programmatic identifier of the ProgID of the control, and the second is the name of the new control. The ProgID can be discerned by using the Object Browser and appending the class of the control (in this case, CommandButton) to the name of the library, which is displayed as Member Of in the lower portion of the Object Browser window.

The control can then be referenced immediately by using the Controls collection. To set the properties of the newly created control, you can access it using the name of the control or its ordinal number:

```
Form1.Controls("cmdOk").Visible = True
```

Unlike control arrays, when controls are added with this technique, event handlers will not automatically be present. However, you might still have to handle various events that they fire. This is especially the case if you want to add dynamic CommandButtons or other controls that require an event handler to be useful.

In these cases, you must first declare an object variable using the WithEvents keyword to refer to the newly created control and then write code in events for that object variable. For example, to create a CommandButton and write code for its events, you would first declare a variable of type CommandButton in the General Declarations section of the form.

```
Private WithEvents cmdOK as CommandButton
```

This has the effect of creating event handlers for the cmdOK button that you can write code in. These will be fired after you've created the button with the Add method of the Controls collection using the cmdOK object variable.

```
Set cmdOK = Form1.Controls.Add("VB.CommandButton", "cmdOK")
```

However, going to all this work to capture events seems like a lot of trouble when you could simply place an instance of the control on the form at design time.

Using the Controls Collection

As controls are added to a form, they are placed in a global collection (conceptually similar to an array) of controls exposed as a property of the form. Using this collection, you can write code that loops through controls on the form using a For Each loop and changes their properties. For example, to automatically arrange all the TextBox controls on a form, you could execute the following code:

```
Dim objControl As Control

For Each objControl In Form1.Controls
    objControl.Visible = True
    objControl.Height = 350
    If TypeName(objControl) = "TextBox" Then
        objControl.Width = 3000
        objControl.Left = 1500
```

```
        lintTextTop = lintTextTop + 375
        objControl.Top = lintTextTop
    Else
        objControl.Left = 100
        lintLabelTop = lintLabelTop + 375
        objControl.Top = lintLabelTop
    End If
Next
```

Note that the `TypeName` function can be used to determine the type of the control and that the generic control instance can be referenced as `Control`.

Summary

In this chapter, I explained the various intrinsic and ActiveX controls included with Visual Basic and some common techniques used to manipulate them. I also provided some glimpses of how VB code handles flow of control through simple looping structures. The next chapter expands on these concepts by enumerating the flow of control structures that VB uses.

CHAPTER 3

Control of Flow Language

In this chapter, you will look at the key statements available in Visual Basic to control program flow. These statements fall into two categories: conditional statements and looping.

Conditional Statements

Conditional statements allow your code to make decisions based on the evaluation of a Boolean expression. Basically, you can employ four types of conditional statements.

If...Then

The If...Then statement is the most commonly used conditional statement and takes this form:

```
If expression Then
    statements
[ElseIf expression Then
    statements]...
[Else
    statements]
End If
```

Notice that both the ElseIf and Else keywords are not required (as denoted by brackets) and that ElseIf statements can be nested (denoted by the ellipses) to allow multiple expressions to be checked. In addition, the expressions themselves can be made up of multiple conditions that use the logical operators And, Or, and Not, for example,

```
If (x = 1 And y = 0) Or x = 0 Then
    y = 1
ElseIf x = 2 Then
    y = 2
ElseIf x = 3 Then
    y = 3
```

continues

```
Else
    y = 4
End If
```

> **TIP**
>
> Parentheses are not required for the expression to be evaluated, but they do explicitly specify the order of evaluation and make the code easier to read.

This statement also supports several shortcuts, for example, by not including the End If keywords and placing the statement directly after the Then keyword, you can make the code more compact.

```
If x = 0 Then y = 1
```

In fact, you can even include multiple statements in this way, by separating them with a colon.

```
If x = 0 Then y = 1: z = 3
```

This technique is not recommended, however, because it makes your code more difficult to maintain and debug.

You can use a second shortcut when evaluating Boolean variables. For example, to determine whether the variable flDone is True, you can simply execute the code

```
If flDone Then
    ....
```

which is equivalent to comparing flDone to True using an equal sign. Likewise, you can compare to False by using Not in front of the variable name. When not using actual Boolean variables, this syntax will evaluate to True if the variable is not zero. Conversely, by comparing the variable to True or False explicitly, its value must be -1 (True) or 0 (False).

Keep in mind that VB does not use any form of short circuit evaluation. Therefore, multiple conditions within an expression will all be evaluated even if the first condition makes evaluation of the remainder a moot point.

> **TIP**
>
> VB also supports a function named IIf (immediate If) that evaluates a single expression and returns one of two arguments passed into it. For example, the statement: IIf(intHR > 500, "500 Club", "None") returns 500 Club if the expression evaluates to True.

Select Case

Even though the If...Then statement allows nesting and the ElseIf keyword, using a Select Case statement is often more readable and logically simpler. This statement takes the following form:

```
Select Case testexpression
    [Case expression
        statements...]
    [Case Else
        statements]
End Select
```

Using this statement, each *expression* is evaluated against the *testexpression* specified at the beginning. If the evaluation returns True, the statements associated with it are executed. Unlike the If...Then statement, when the first *expression* evaluates to True, the remainder of the cases are not evaluated. The Case Else keywords are optional and act as a catch all if none of the expressions evaluates successfully against the *testexpression*.

The format of the *testexpression* is interesting because it can take on several forms, including a single value, a range (either numeric or alphabetical), or a logical expression. Listing 3.1 presents an example that highlights these options.

Listing 3.1   A Sample Select Case Statement That Uses Different Types of testexpressions

```
Dim intAge as Integer
Dim intMaxAge as Integer
Dim strMessage as String

Select Case intAge
    Case 0
        strMessage = "Invalid"
    Case 1, 2
        strMessage = "Infant"
    Case 3, 4
        strMessage = "Toddler"
    Case 5 To 12
        strMessage = "Elementary School"
    Case 13 Or 14 Or 15
        strMessage = "Junior High"
    Case 16 To 18
        strMessage = "High School"
    Case Is > 18, Is < intMaxAge
        strMessage = "Adult"
    Case Else
        strMessage = "Invalid"
End Select
```

TIP

There is also a function named `Switch`, which in a single statement will return a value based on expressions and values passed into it. It is conceptually similar to the `Select Case` statement. For example, the function
`Switch(strCity="Chicago", "Cubs",strCity="St. Louis","Cardinals",strCity="New York", "Mets")` returns the team name of the associated city. Note that the expressions are evaluated from left to right and the value returned is the one associated with the first one that evaluates to `True`.

Goto and Gosub Return

The `Goto` and `Gosub` statements have their roots deep in the BASIC language. Using these statements, your code can branch to a line label (also an original BASIC concept) and either continue execution at the line (`Goto`) or return to the statement following the branching when complete (`Gosub`). Line labels are defined by simply entering the line label, followed by a colon.

As a general rule, you should avoid these statements except when dealing with error handling (discussed in Chapter 9, "Debugging and Error Handling"). However, in some cases they are useful—such as when the code you want to execute is only a couple lines long, does not have to be used elsewhere in the program, and is also called in normal flow of execution. In these cases, the overhead of creating and calling a separate procedure, along with the increased readability, makes using these statements attractive. As an example, consider the code in Listing 3.2.

Listing 3.2 A Procedure Showing the Use of a Goto Statement

```
Private Sub ShowArray()

Dim i As Integer
Dim varPos As Variant

If Not IsEmpty(varPos) Then
    GoTo DisplayArray
End If

' Load the array here

DisplayArray:
    For i = 0 To UBound(varPos)
        lstData.AddItem varPos(i)
    Next

End Sub
```

The Gosub statement is similar to the Goto but is used when the code following the line label has to branch back to the line following the Gosub upon completion, using the Return statement. The code in Listing 3.3 illustrates the use of Gosub.

Listing 3.3   A Procedure That Utilizes the Gosub Statement to Load an Array from a ListBox

```
Private Sub ShowArray()

Dim i As Integer
Dim varPos As Variant

If IsEmpty(varPos) Then
    GoSub LoadArray
End If

' Display the array here

' Make sure that the procedure exits so that
' the following code does not run twice
Exit Sub
LoadArray:
    ReDim varPos(0)

    For i = 0 To lstData.ListCount - 1
        ReDim Preserve varPos(i)
        varPos(i) = lstData.List(i)
    Next

    Return

End Sub
```

On Goto and On Gosub

An extension of Goto and Gosub is the conditional branching possible by using the On statement.

```
On expression Gosub label1[, label2, label3...]
```

With this extension, you can provide a list of line labels that will be branched to, depending on the value of the numeric expression after the On statement. Position determines which label is executed. For example, the code in Listing 3.4 will branch to the Toddler label (position 2) and then return to execute the line following the On Gosub. Typically, this type of logic can be better represented as a Select Case statement.

Listing 3.4   An On Gosub Statement That Shows Conditional Branching

```
Dim intAgeRange As Integer
Dim strMessage As String
```

continues

Listing 3.4   Continued

```
intAgeRange = 2


On intAgeRange GoSub Infant, Toddler, School, Adult


Exit Sub

Infant:
    strMessage = "Infant"
    Return

Toddler:
    strMessage = "Toddler"
    Return

School:
    strMessage = "School"
    Return

Adult:
    strMessage = "Adult"
    Return
```

Looping Constructs

Visual Basic supports four looping constructs that allow your code to iterate through a series of instructions multiple times.

For...Next

The For...Next loop is useful for iterating when the number of executions of the loop is known. The basic syntax is as follows:

```
For counter = start to end [Step step]
    statements
    [Exit For]
Next [counter]
```

The loop will increment the counter variable with each iteration, based on the step value given. By default, the step will be 1 but can be specified using either a literal or a variable. The Exit For statement can be used to break out of the loop at any time and continue execution following the Next statement. The Next statement indicates the end of the loop and can optionally include a reference to the counter variable to make the code more readable.

For...Next statements are often nested. For example, to read the values from a multi-dimensional array passed in as an argument to a procedure and load them into a ListView control, you could execute the code in Listing 3.5.

Listing 3.5   Using Nested For...Next Loops to Load a ListView Control

```
Private Sub ShowList(pData as Variant)

Dim objItem As ListItem
Dim i As Integer
Dim z As Integer

' Load the ListView with data
    For i = 0 To UBound(pData, 1)
        ' Add the ListItem object
        Set objItem = lvListView.ListItems.Add(, , pData(i, 0))

        ' Add the SubItems
        For z = 1 To UBound(pData, 2)
            objItem.SubItems(z) = pData(i, z)
        Next z
    Next i

End Sub
```

For Each

A closely related looping structure to For...Next is the For Each loop. This syntax is used to loop through all the elements of a Collection object or an array. For example, to loop through all the items in a collection of Customer objects and place the names in a ListBox control, you could execute this code:

```
Dim objCustomer As clsCustomer
Dim Customers As Collection

For Each objCustomer In Customers
    lstName.AddItem objCustomer.Name
Next objCustomer
```

Do Loops

Do loops are useful when the number of iterations the loop will perform is not known at design time. There are basically two forms of the loop: one that checks the condition before each iteration and one that checks afterwards.

```
Do While ¦ Until condition
    statements
    [Exit Do]
Loop
```

Or

```
Do
    statements
    [Exit Do]
Loop While ¦ Until condition
```

Which one you use depends on whether the loop must be executed at least one time. In addition, the condition for performing the next iteration can be specified using the While keyword (when testing for changes in a value) or the Until keyword (for testing for a specific value). The following code is an example of using this type of loop to extract tokens from a semicolon-delimited string and load them in a ListBox control:

```
Dim strList As String
Dim intPos As Integer

strList = "Dan;Beth;Laura;Aaron;Dave;Tracy;Olivia;"

Do While Len(strList) > 0
    ' Find the position of the next delimiter
    intPos = InStr(1, strList, ";")
    If intPos > 0 Then
        ' Add the name to the list box
        lstData.AddItem Mid(strList, 1, intPos - 1)
        ' Truncate the string
        strList = Mid(strList, intPos + 1)
    End If
Loop
```

While...Wend

The final type of loop is the While...Wend loop. Basically, this is conceptually similar to a Do loop and will execute a series of statements as long as the provided condition is True.

```
While condition
    statements
Wend
```

I would recommend using a variation of the Do loop because it is more flexible by providing the capability to check the condition at the bottom of the loop and allowing execution to pass from the loop using the Exit Do statement.

Summary

This chapter examines the various methods VB programmers can use to control the flow of execution in their programs. These break down into conditional statements (If...Then, Select Case, Goto, and Gosub) and looping (For...Next, For Each, Do, and While...Wend).

To make these structures come to life, developers need access to a rich set of data types, variables, and scoping rules, all of which are presented in the next chapter.

CHAPTER 4

Data Types, Variables, and Constants

As with all programming languages, Visual Basic enables the developer to create variables that store the current state of the running program. Each variable points to a location in memory and is associated with a particular data type that determines how the data is represented.

In this chapter, you will look at the data types available to VB developers and how variables and constants are declared, scoped, and manipulated. In addition, I discuss user-defined types (UDTs) and the special structures for referencing data, including arrays.

Data Types

Data types are used in VB not only with variables but also to represent property values for objects and controls, as well as arguments for procedures. Table 4.1 gives the data types available in VB.

Table 4.1   VB Data Types with Their Sizes and Ranges

Data Type	Size (Bytes)	Description
Byte	1	Used to store a small number in the range of 0–255.
Boolean	2	Used to represent True (–1) and False (0) values. Defaults to False.

continues

Table 4.1   continued

Data Type	Size (Bytes)	Description
Integer	2	Used to store numbers in the range of –3,2768 to 3,2767.
Long	4	Used to store numbers in the range of –2,147,483,648 to 2,147,483,647.
Single	8	Used to store single-precision floating point numbers in the range of –3.402823E38 to –1.401298E-45 for negative values and 1.401298E-45 to 3.402823E38 for positive values.
Double	8	Used to store double-precision floating point numbers in the range of –1.79769313486232E308 to –4.94065645841247E-324 for negative values and 4.94065645841247E-324 to 1.79769313486232E308 for positive values.
Currency	8	Used to store monetary amounts in the range of 922,337,203,685,477.5808 to 922,337,203,685,477.5807.
Decimal	14	Used to store very large numbers from +/–79,228,162,514,264,337,593, 543,950,335 with no decimal point to +/–7.9228162514264337593543950335 with 28 places to the right of the decimal. At this time, the only way to create a Decimal variable is to declare a variable of type Variant and use the CDec function.
Date	8	Used to store dates (internally represented as numbers with date information on the left of the decimal point and time to the right) from January 1, 100 to December 31, 9999.
String	10+ length	Used to store variable-length strings from 0 to approximately 2 billion characters. Defaults to a zero-length string (" ").
String	Length of String	Used to store fixed-length strings from 1 to 65,400 characters. Defaults to a string with the number of spaces specified.

Data Type	Size (Bytes)	Description
Variant	16	Used to store Integer, Long, Single, and Double numeric values.
Variant	22+ length	Used to store a variable-length string.
Object	4	Used to store a pointer to a COM object class.
User- Defined Type	Varies	Used to encapsulate multiple values in a single variable. Similar to a structure in C or a record in Pascal.

Variants

The most interesting data type supported by VB is certainly the Variant. This data type can be used to store both numeric and string data. Internally, however, the Variant is actually representing the value as one of the standard data types, which can be determined using the VarType or TypeName functions.

When a value is assigned to a Variant, VB tries to use the representation that is most efficient—for example, when the variable varAge declared as Variant is set using the following code:

```
varAge = 12
```

VB internally represents varAge as an Integer. If the variable is subsequently assigned to a larger number or a string, the internal representation will change accordingly. Of course, the disadvantages to using variants are that they always consume at least 16 bytes of memory and incur a performance penalty because VB has to dynamically determine its data type. However, variants are often advantageous for use with multi-dimensional arrays (discussed later) and when you don't know at design time what the data type will be.

Variant Subtypes

As mentioned previously, you can use the VarType function to discover how a Variant is actually represented. This function returns a constant that represents the type, shown in Table 4.2.

Table 4.2   Variant Subtypes and the Constants Returned by the VarType Function

Data Type	Value	Constant
Empty	0	vbEmpty
Null	1	vbNull
Integer	2	vbInteger
Long Integer	3	vbLong

continues

Table 4.2   continued

Data Type	Value	Constant
Single	4	vbSingle
Double	5	vbDouble
Currency	6	vbCurrency
Date	7	vbDate
String	8	vbString
Object	9	vbObject
Error	10	vbError
Boolean	11	vbBoolean
Decimal	14	vbDecimal
Byte	17	vbByte
Array	8192	vbArray
Array of Variant	12	vbVariant
User-Defined Type	36	vbUserDefinedType

Notice that in addition to the standard types discussed earlier, variants can also be represented as empty or null. A Variant is empty if it has not been initialized. This condition can also be tested by using the IsEmpty function.

Variants can also be set to Null using the Null keyword and tested for this condition using the IsNull function. This is often useful in database applications when the values returned in a resultset may be Null or when the application must set the value to Null before saving it in the database. For example, if the user does not enter a value in the TextBox txtFName, the application might want to make this value Null in the recordset rsCustomers.

```
Dim varNull as Variant

If Len(txtFName.Text) = 0 Then
    varNull = Null
    rsCustomers("FName") = varNull
End If
```

NOTE

Because of the increases in processing power and available memory, some experts advocate using variants exclusively. Although using variants certainly makes your applications more flexible and reduces type mismatch errors at runtime, keep in mind that there is a price to pay. Specific problems include a performance penalty and possible logic, rounding, and parameter-passing errors. My own approach is that I am not at all hesitant to use variants (especially for multidimensional arrays and arguments that might change), but I also use specific data types when I'm certain that the variable or argument will always be represented correctly by the data type.

Strings

It is worth taking some time to discuss strings in VB. As noted in Table 4.1, strings can be of fixed or variable length. Although variable-length strings can store more data and perform better when using VB's string manipulation functions, fixed-length strings are good for minimizing memory usage and can be allocated and deallocated very quickly. To declare a fixed-length string, the following syntax

```
Dim strMyString As String * 15
```

is used; the length of the string is 15 characters. Typically, fixed-length strings are no longer used except when a large array of small strings has to be manipulated or when returning string data from Win32 API functions that require a preallocated string buffer. However, using fixed-length strings often means using string manipulation functions such as Trim$, RTrim$, LTrim$, Left$, and Right$ to remove extra spaces. As mentioned, these functions will convert the fixed-length string to a variable-length string. In addition, fixed-length strings are allocated even before they are assigned (unlike variable-length strings).

NOTE

Many of the string manipulation functions (Space, String, Right, LTrim, RTrim, and Trim) have two versions. Those with a $ at the end return strings, whereas those without return a Variant. The string versions perform better.

Empty Strings

By default, variable-length strings are assigned a zero-length string (" ") that can be referenced with the constant vbNullString. VB refers to this as an *empty* string (not to be confused with the empty value of an unassigned Variant). Unfortunately, VB mixes its terminology here, because a zero-length string is neither empty (because it has been assigned a value) nor null.

When assigning a zero-length string or doing comparisons, you can use an explicit " " or use the vbNullString constant. The latter choice is best because VB will not have to allocate a variable-length string for comparison. For example, use the syntax

```
strDescription = vbNullString
```

instead of

```
strDescription = ""
```

VB also supports a constant, vbNullChar, to represent a single null character (actually, Chr(0)). This constant can be appended to a string when an external DLL has to be passed a null-terminated string.

String Comparisons

In string comparisons, the default comparison method is *binary*, meaning that the characters are compared based on their binary representations. This can lead to some confusion because a comparison such as

```
Dim strName As String
Dim strName2 As String

strName = "beth"
strName2 = "Laura"

If strName < strName2 Then
    ' strName is first alphabetically?
End If
```

would not result in statements inside the If...Then clause being executed, because the binary value of *b* is actually greater than the value of *L*. As a result, you should use the Option Compare statement in the General Declarations sections of forms and modules to ensure that the comparisons are made correctly. By using this statement,

```
Option Compare Text
```

comparisons of strings will not be case sensitive and will be compared alphabetically (the default is actually Option Compare Binary). Of course, you could also use the UCase function to force the strings to uppercase before comparison, but this also incurs a performance hit.

NOTE

You can also use the StrComp function to perform string comparisons. With this function, you pass in the two strings to be compared and a constant specifying the comparison method to use (vbBinaryCompare, vbTextCompare, or vbDatabase). The result of the function will either be –1 (string1 < string2), 0 (string1 = string2), 1 (string1 > string2), or Null (one of the two strings is Null).

Variables

Variables in VB can be declared explicitly by using the Dim, Private, or Public keywords or implicitly by simply assigning a value to the variable. When declarations are made explicitly, the Dim statement is used inside a procedure to signify a local variable, whereas Private and Public are used in the General Declarations section of forms and modules to represent module-level data.

NOTE

Although the Dim statement can be used at the module level, it is equivalent to using Private and is included for backward compatibility with older versions of VB. The same can be said for Global, which is equivalent to Public.

To declare multiple variables, you can place them on separate lines or all on the same line:

```
Dim i As Integer, z As Integer, y As Integer
```

However, a similar syntax,

```
Dim i, z, y As Integer
```

will have the effect of creating i and z as Variant instead of Integer.

Variables can be declared implicitly by omitting the Option Explicit statement from the module and simply using the variable in a statement. Variables declared in this way will always be Variant. This is not recommended because simple typos will create multiple variables, causing errors that are difficult to track down.

Scoping

As previously mentioned, variables can be scoped at three levels in VB: local, module, and global. The scope controls the lifetime and visibility of the variable.

By declaring the variable with the Dim statement inside a procedure, it is local to the procedure and is reinitialized each time the procedure is executed. This rule is enforced except when the variable is declared using the Static keyword. Variables declared in this way can be used to persist data between invocations of a procedure, as in the Login procedure shown in Listing 4.1.

Listing 4.1   A Sample Procedure That Uses a Static Variable to Track the Number of Login Attempts

```
Public Function Login(ByVal pUser As String, ByVal pPw As String) As Boolean

Static intTries As Integer

' Determine whether maximum attempts have been made
If intTries = MAX_ATTEMPTS Then
    MsgBox "Maximum login attempts exceeded. Contact the administrator.", _
        vbCritical, "Login"
    Login = False
Else
    ' attempt the login...

    ' Increment the counter
    intTries = intTries + 1
End If

End Function
```

In this case, the variable intTries is used to track the number of times the Login procedure has been executed while the program has been running. If the number of attempts exceeds the constant MAX_ATTEMPTS, a message box is displayed to the user, and the procedure is exited.

Variables at the module level can be declared as `Private` or `Public`. Private variables in form, class, or code modules are accessible only to code within the module and are used for sharing data between procedures in the module. When used in form and class modules, private variables are allocated and deallocated, respectively, when the module is initialized, and they are set to `Nothing`. For code modules, private variables are simply available any time that code in the module is executed.

Public variables in form and class modules are treated as public properties and are accessible using dot notation. For example, consider the following code for a form named `frmMain`:

```
Option Explicit
Public flIsDirty As Boolean

Private Sub Save()
    ' Save the data
    If flIsDirty Then
        ' save the data
    End If
End Sub

Private Sub Form_Load()
    ' read data from the database
    ' load controls
End Sub
```

In this case, the variable `flIsDirty` can be accessed both within the module (as in the `Save` procedure) and outside the form using the syntax

```
frmMain.flIsDirty
```

Keep in mind that using a private variable in this example would probably be preferred because it would allow the form to hide its internal state. In fact, as a general rule, variables should be declared locally until you prove to yourself that form-level or global-level scope is required. This mindset will naturally produce code that is more maintainable and contains fewer dependencies. Chapter 15, "Using Object-Oriented Techniques," discusses this concept in more detail.

Global variables are created by declaring `Public` variables in code modules. These variables are available throughout the application and can be accessed by any procedures. Global variables should be reserved for data that can be handled in no other way, and as a general rule, your applications should contain zero or only a couple.

Converting Data

Frequently, data must be converted from one data type to another. VB provides two mechanisms to accomplish this: implicit and explicit conversion. Implicit conversion is simple and is invoked automatically when a value of one data type is assigned to a value of another. For example, the code

```
Dim intHR As Integer

intHR = txtHR.Text
```

will coerce a string value in the TextBox txtHR into an Integer. However, if the string entered in txtHR cannot be converted into an Integer, a trappable runtime error will be fired, as shown in Figure 4.1. As a result, code such as this can use the IsNumeric function to check for a valid entry:

```
Dim intHR As Integer

If IsNumeric(txtHR.Text) Then
    intHR = txtHR.Text
End If
```

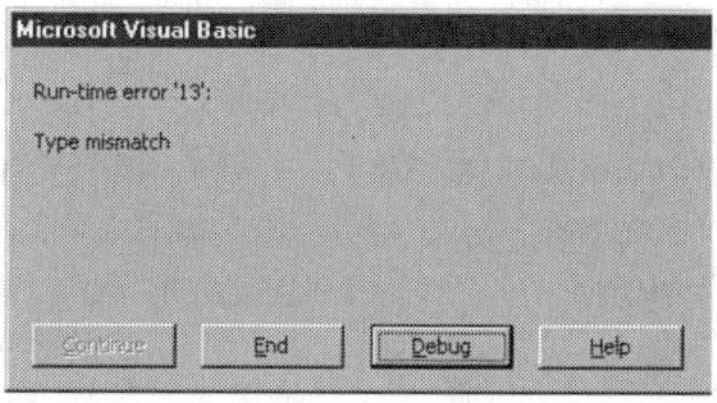

Figure 4.1

The default error dialog produced by VB when a type mismatch error occurs.

TIP

Techniques for restricting data entry (to only numbers in this case) are discussed in Chapter 10, "Compiling and Distributing."

VB also includes a number of functions that convert data explicitly. Table 4.3 lists the functions and their descriptions. If any of these functions encounter an error, the same trappable error shown in Figure 4.1 will be fired.

Table 4.3 Conversion Functions

Function	Description
CBool	Boolean. Can accept any valid string or numeric expression.
CByte	Byte. Can accept a number from 0 to 255.
CCur	Currency. Can accept any expression in the normal Currency range.
CDate	Date. Can accept a string or numeric expression that evaluates to a date.
CDbl	Double. Can accept any expression in the normal Double range.

continues

Table 4.3   continued

Function	Description
CDec	Variant of subtype vbDecimal. Can accept any expression in the normal Decimal range.
CInt	Integer. Can accept any expression in the normal Integer range.
CLng	Long. Can accept any expression in the normal Long Integer range.
CSng	Single. Can accept any expression in the normal Single range.
CStr	String. Can accept Boolean, date, numeric, Null, empty, and error expressions and returns strings containing True or False, the system's short date, a runtime error, a zero-length string, a string with the error number, or a string containing the number, respectively.
CVar	Variant. Like CStr, can accept multiple types of expression.
CVDate	Variant. Returns a Variant of subtype vbDate and is included only for backwards compatibility. It is recommended that you use CDate in VB 5.0 and higher.

Object Variables

In addition to standard data types, VB also supports the creation of both specific and generic object variables. Object variables can point to instances of forms, controls, classes, or external COM objects.

Declaring Object Variables

To declare a specific object variable, you can use the classname of the form, control, or class module, one of the intrinsic keywords Form, MDIForm, or Control, or the programmatic identifier (ProgID) of a COM object. For example, to declare an object variable that references an instance of a form named frmCustDetails, you can use the syntax

```
Dim objCustDetails As frmCustDetails
```

or

```
Dim objCustDetails as Form
```

The advantage to using the former syntax is that the IntelliSense features of the code window are activated, showing not only the standard form methods and properties but also any user-defined public procedures or variables.

To declare a generic object variable, you can use the data type Object. Although this is the most flexible method of referencing object variables because the class does not have to be determined until runtime, it also incurs the most overhead and does not allow any design-time type checking. All references to variables declared as Object are referred to as late-bound because the actual type will not be resolved until runtime. A more detailed explanation of early and late binding can be found in Chapter 23, "A COM Primer for Visual Basic Developers."

NOTE

For an example of using an argument declared as Object, refer to the discussion on printing in Chapter 18, "Adding Professional Features."

As a result, whenever possible, you should use the specific class name to create the object.

Instantiating Object Variables

After the object variable has been declared, it must be instantiated. Basically, you have a choice of three techniques.

The New Keyword in the Declaration

Using this technique, the New keyword is placed after the As keyword in the declaration itself. To create a new customer object from a class module, the syntax would be

```
Dim objCustomer as New Customer
```

This technique has the advantage of brevity but requires some extra processing each time the variable is referenced, to determine whether it has yet been instantiated. The actual object is not created until it is first referenced in the code.

The New Keyword with the Set Statement

This technique instantiates the object in a separate statement using its explicit class-name.

```
Dim objCustomer As Customer

Set objCustomer = New Customer
```

This method has the advantage of being highly efficient for classes internal to the application and is the recommended method.

CreateObject

This final technique uses the CreateObject function, which accepts the classname or ProgID as an argument.

```
Dim objCustomer As Customer
Set objCustomer = CreateObject("Customer")
```

This method has the advantage of being able to accept a string if the classname is not known at compile time or if the external COM object does not provide a type library.

Collections

A closely related topic to object variables is the use and manipulation of collections. Collections are conceptually the same as arrays and can store and reference a number of members. A variable declared as Collection exposes the Add, Item, and Remove methods, as well as a Count property.

VB developers often use collections to store other objects. For example, each time a new Customer object is created, it can be added to a Customers collection.

```
Dim objCustomer as Customer
Dim Customers as Collection

Set objCustomer = New Customer
Set Customers = New Collection

Customers.Add objCustomer, CStr(objCustomer.ID)
```

Notice that the Add method of the Collection object accepts an optional second argument of type String that can be used to reference an object in the collection by its key.

After items are in the collection, they can be referenced using the For...Each syntax discussed in Chapter 3, "Control of Flow Language," using a numeric index (starting at 1 and automatically assigned when the item is added to the collection) or using the key value provided during the Add method.

NOTE

The intrinsic Forms and Controls collections discussed in Chapter 2, "Using Controls," are 0-based.

For example, the name and address information for a customer can be retrieved by using the following key:

```
Private Sub DisplayCustomer(ByVal pID as Long)
    txtFName.Text =Customers(pID).FName
    txtLName.Text =Customers(pID).LName
    txtAddress.Text =Customers(pID).Address
End Sub
```

Dictionary Objects

Visual Basic 6 has seen a more sophisticated method of handling collections: the Dictionary object included in the Microsoft Scripting Runtime component SCRRUN.DLL. To use this object, you must set a reference to the Microsoft Scripting Runtime in the Project menu item on the References menu.

Like a Collection object, the Dictionary object stores members but also supports the methods and properties shown in Table 4.4.

Table 4.4 *Dictionary Object Methods and Properties*

Member	Description
CompareMode	Property that specifies the comparison mode to use when comparing key values in the dictionary. Options include vbBinaryCompare, vbTextCompare, vbDatabaseCompare (for Access only), and vbUseCompareOption (to use the setting in the Option Compare statement).
Count	Property that returns the number of members in the Dictionary.
Item	Property that specifies a member in the Dictionary, given its key value.
Key	Property that specifies a new key value for the given key. If the key is not found, a runtime error will occur.
Add	Method that adds an item to the Dictionary, given the key and the item. Note that these arguments are in the reverse order of the Collection object and that the key is not optional.
Exists Boolean.	Returns True if the given key exists in the Dictionary.
Items Variant.	Returns a Variant array containing all the members of the Dictionary.
Keys Variant.	Returns a Variant array containing all the keys for members in the Dictionary.
Remove	Removes an item from the Dictionary, given a key. Results in a runtime error if the key does not exist.
RemoveAll	Removes all members from the Dictionary.

Constants

Obviously, a closely related concept to variables is constants. Constants provide read-only data that is available to an entire module or application through a well-known name. Using constants not only makes your code more readable, maintainable, and efficient, but also prevents "magic numbers" (numbers that appear in code without any obvious explanation). VB provides many system constants, but you can also create your own constants using the Const statement.

As with variables, constants can be defined using a data type and the Private or Public keywords. For example, to declare the constant Pi, you could use the syntax

```
Private Const PI As Single = 3.141593
```

in a module. The general consensus is that user-defined constants should appear in all caps and that system-supplied constants are prefixed with vb and are mixed case.

Constants declared as Public within a code module are available to the entire application. You cannot declare Public constants in a form or class module.

Arrays

Like other languages, VB supports the ability to create and manipulate arrays. In VB, arrays can come in the form of static and dynamic arrays, as well as single and multi-dimensional arrays.

Static Arrays

A static array in VB is one whose upper and lower bounds are defined at compile time. Consequently, VB allocates space for the array at this time. The lower bound for all arrays by default is 0 but can be changed using the `Option Base` statement in the General Declarations section of a module.

To declare a static array, you can use the syntax

```
Dim arIDs(15) As Integer
```

In this case, the array will contain 16 elements, with the indexes running from 0 to 15. You can also explicitly specify the lower bound using the syntax

```
Dim arIDs(0 to 14) As Integer
```

As with any other type of variable, arrays can be scoped at the local, module, or global level using the `Dim`, `Private`, or `Public` keywords.

Dynamic Arrays

When the size of the array is unknown at compile time, it is often advantageous to use dynamic arrays. These arrays are declared without a specific number of elements and use the `ReDim` and `Preserve` keywords to subsequently allocate space.

As an example, consider the `LoadFile` function shown in Listing 4.2. This function loads the contents of an ASCII file to an array and periodically allocates 10 more elements to the array.

Listing 4.2   The LoadFile Illustrates Using a Dynamic Array
```
Public Sub LoadFile(ByVal pFile As String, pNames() As String)

Dim intFileNum As Integer
Dim i As Integer
Dim strName As String

' Get a free file number
intFileNum = FreeFile

' Open the text file as read-only
Open pFile For Input Lock Read As intFileNum

' Initialize the array
ReDim pNames(0)
```

```
' Load the array of names
Do While Not EOF(intFileNum)

    ' Add 10 elements to the array if divisible by 10
    If i Mod 10 = 0 Then GoSub RedimArray

    ' Read in the next line
    Line Input #intFileNum, strName

    ' Store it in the array and increment the counter
    pNames(i) = strName
    i = i + 1
Loop

' Resize the array to its final size
ReDim Preserve pNames(i - 1)

Close intFileNum

Exit Sub
RedimArray:
    ' Keep the existing data and allocate more space
    ReDim Preserve pNames(UBound(pNames) + 10)
    Return

End Sub
```

Notice that the code in Listing 4.2 uses the ReDim statement to dimension the array (passed in as an argument by reference) before it is first used and the ReDim Preserve statement to allocate new elements and to resize the array at the completion of the loop. The Preserve keyword ensures that any existing data in the array is retained.

The technique shown here is useful because allocating new space on an array is expensive. Allocating elements in blocks of 10 reduces the number of allocations that have to be performed.

NOTE

The Erase function can be used to deallocate an array and is useful for reclaiming memory after your application is finished working with the array.

The other interesting point to note is that the UBound and LBound functions can be used to programmatically determine the upper and lower bounds of the array.

Multidimensional Arrays

All the examples shown thus far have used arrays with a single dimension. VB also supports the ability to create multidimensional arrays by specifying a comma-delimited list of dimensions in the declaration. For example, to declare an array that could contain a table of information, you could use the syntax

```
Dim arData(15,15) As Integer
```

which would allocate space for 225 integers. Multidimensional arrays are often referenced using nested loops. To traverse all the elements in the preceding array, you could use the following code:

```
For i = 0 To 14
    objGrid.Row = i
    For j = 0 To 14
        objGrid.Column = j
        objGrid.Cell = arData(i,j)
    Next j
Next i
```

When you are using dynamic multidimensional arrays, it is possible with the ReDim statement to change both the number of elements in a dimension and the number of dimensions. However, if you want to preserve the existing data using the Preserve keyword, you can change the number of elements in the last dimension only.

TIP

Multidimensional arrays are often useful for storing data that was retrieved from relational database tables.

Variant Arrays

The final array topic to be discussed is Variant arrays. These arrays are especially interesting because they can contain elements of mixed data types (unlike the examples shown previously) and can contain nested arrays. In other words, the flexibility of using variants allows an element of a Variant array to be an array. In this way, you can store hierarchical information in a single variable.

NOTE

Unlike the other types of arrays discussed in this chapter, Variant arrays are also known as *ragged* arrays because each element of the array can contain a different number of bytes.

As an example of nested arrays, consider the code in Listing 4.3. The procedure shown here, LoadPlayer, uses a multidimensional nested array to store statistical information about players and their yearly totals.

Listing 4.3   A Procedure That Uses a Variant Array to Store the Career and Yearly Totals of Baseball Players

```
Public Sub LoadPlayer(pPlayers As Variant, pYearlyTotals As Recordset, _
    ByVal pName As String, ByVal pHR As Integer, ByVal pAVG As Single, _
    ByVal pRBI As Integer)

Dim i As Integer

' If the array has not been initialized,
' redimension it first
If Not IsArray(pPlayers) Then
    ReDim pPlayers(4, 0)
Else
    ' Find the upper bound of the last dimension
    ' and increment it by one
    i = UBound(pPlayers, 2) + 1
    ReDim Preserve pPlayers(4, i)
End If

pPlayers(0, i) = pName
pPlayers(1, i) = pHR
pPlayers(2, i) = pAVG
pPlayers(3, i) = pRBI

' Store the entire array returned by GetRows
' in the final dimension
pPlayers(4, i) = pYearlyTotals.GetRows

End Sub
```

Note that this procedure uses the `IsArray` function to test whether the `Variant` `pPlayers` has already been dimensioned as an array before initializing it. If the array has been initialized, the `UBound` function is used to discover the upper bound of the second dimension as denoted by its second argument. After placing the arguments in the first four elements of the first dimension, the `GetRows` method of the ADO `Recordset` object is called to return a `Variant` array containing all the yearly totals for the player (discussed in Chapter 14, "Using ADO for Data Access"). This array itself is stored in position 4 of the first dimension.

TIP

An alternative way to load a `Variant` array is to use the `Array` function and pass it a comma-delimited list of values.

User-Defined Data Types

Another popular method used to store a collection of data represented by different data types in a single variable is the user-defined type (UDT). UDTs can be declared at the module level using the Type keyword. For example, to rewrite the preceding example dealing with baseball statistics, a UDT could optionally be defined to hold the data as follows:

```
Type Player
    Name As String
    HR As Integer
    BAVG As Single
    RBI As Integer
    YearlyTotals As Variant
End Type
```

This type could then be used in the rewritten LoadPlayer function instead of the Variant array, as shown in Listing 4.4.

Listing 4.4   Using a UDT to Store Related Information
```
Public Function LoadPlayer(pYearlyTotals As Recordset, _
    ByVal pName As String, ByVal pHR As Integer, ByVal pAVG As Single, _
    ByVal pRBI As Integer) As Player

Dim recPlayer As Player

recPlayer.Name = pName
recPlayer.HR = pHR
recPlayer.BAVG = pAVG
recPlayer.RBI = pRBI

' Store the entire array returned by GetRows
' in the UDT
recPlayer.YearlyTotals = pYearlyTotals.GetRows

' Return the Type
LoadPlayer = recPlayer

End Function
```

Note that the UDT is used by simply declaring a variable using the name of the UDT. After it's declared, dot notation can be used to access the members of the UDT. Notice, too, that a member of the UDT can also be a Variant, so you can also store the yearly totals multidimensional Variant array.

NOTE

The rules for using UDTs have relaxed in VB 6. UDTs can now be used as arguments to procedures and as return values from functions, as shown in Listing 4.4. This allows them to be more useful than in previous versions. Keep in mind, however, that class modules (discussed in Chapter 7, "Using Class Modules") can perform the same function as UDTs and are much more flexible by allowing both methods and properties, as well as custom validation and data hiding.

Like other data types, UDTs can be used in arrays so that you could build a dynamic array of `Player` UDTs using the syntax

```
Dim recPlayers() as Player
```

When using UDT, you must adhere to several scoping rules, summarized in Table 4.5.

Table 4.5   Scoping Rules for UDTs

Module	Private	Public
Form	Yes (default)	No
Code	Yes	Yes (default)
Class	Yes	Only if the class module is a public class in an ActiveX DLL or EXE project (default)

To change the scope, you can simply use the `Private` or `Public` keywords. You can also declare a UDT as `Static`.

Summary

In this chapter, you've learned all the ways in which data is represented and stored in Visual Basic. However, to write efficient and maintainable applications, you must use procedures to manipulate the data. In the next chapter, you will learn the various types of procedures supported in VB and how to use them effectively.

CHAPTER 5

Using Procedures

If you've read the preceding four chapters, you've no doubt picked up on the fact that Visual Basic uses procedures (functions and subroutines) extensively. The benefits of using procedures in VB, as in other languages, include code reuse, maintainability, and encapsulation.

In this chapter, you will look at the basic structure and handling of those procedures in Visual Basic. This can be done by examining the types of procedures used by VB, how procedures are called, how parameters or arguments are passed, and finally, how external procedures in DLLs are declared and invoked.

Procedures Types

In VB, procedures are used to handle events (*event procedures*), user-defined properties (*property procedures*), and application-specific code written by developers (*user-defined procedures*). Each of these three types is categorized as either a Sub procedure or a Function procedure.

> **NOTE**
>
> Some languages differentiate between *functions*, which return values, and *procedures*, which don't. In VB, both are called *procedures* but are differentiated by the preface of Function or Sub.

Sub Procedures

A Sub procedure is a block of code that can take arguments but does not return a value. VB uses Sub procedures for the event handlers (procedures) of controls. For example, the MouseMove event of a form is created as a Sub procedure that passes in several arguments that determine the button on the mouse that was clicked, the state of the keyboard, and the coordinates of the mouse.

```
Private Sub Command1_MouseMove(Button As Integer, Shift As Integer, _
        X As Single, Y As Single)

End Sub
```

Each Sub procedure ends with an End Sub statement and can optionally include Exit Sub statements that will immediately end the procedure.

Function Procedures

Function procedures are essentially identical to Sub procedures, with the exception that they return a value to the calling procedure and can be exited using the Exit Function statement. An example might be a user-defined function procedure that calculates the number of runs created for a baseball player, given his batting statistics.

```
Public Function RunsCreated(ByVal pHits As Integer, pAB As Integer, _
    ByVal pHR As Integer, ByVal pDB As Integer, ByVal pTR As Integer, _
    ByVal pBB As Integer) As Single

Dim lngTotalBases As Long

    lngTotalBases = pHits + pDB + (pTR * 2) + (pHR * 3)

    RunsCreated = ((pHits + pBB) * lngTotalBases) / (pAB + pBB)

End Function
```

Notice that with function procedures, the data type returned by the function is specified using the As keyword directly after the argument list, whereas the value is returned by setting it equal to the name of the procedure.

Scoping Procedures

As with variables, you can scope procedures at the module and global levels using the Private and Public keywords. Public procedures in code modules are available throughout the application, whereas public procedures in form and class modules are available when an instance of the form or class is present. Like module-level variables, module-level procedures must also be invoked using dot notation.

VB implements all event handlers for forms and controls as private procedures inside the form. These event procedures are always titled with the name of the control, followed by an underscore and the name of the event.

Like variables, it is a good practice to declare procedures as `Private`, if possible, because this has the effect of hiding implementation details of modules from the rest of the application and subsequently creating fewer dependencies in your code.

TIP

When using public class modules, procedures can also be scoped using the `Friend` keyword. Doing so allows code in other modules within the application to invoke the procedure while hiding it from external applications.

In addition, procedures can be declared with the `Static` keyword if you want all variables declared inside the procedure to act as static variables, discussed in Chapter 4, "Data Types, Variables, and Constants." Although it is rarely used, the procedure declaration would look like the following:

```
Public Static Sub Login()

End Sub
```

To make it simple, new procedures can be created using the Add Procedure dialog (shown in Figure 5.1) invoked from the Tools, Add Procedure menu.

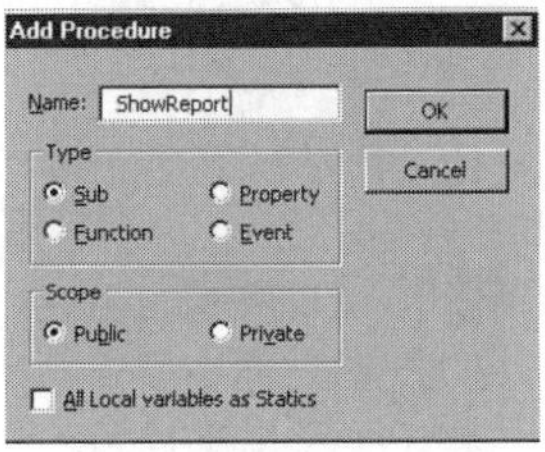

Figure 5.1

The Add Procedure dialog writes the declaration of the procedure.

Calling Procedures

Procedures can be invoked either automatically by VB in response to an event or programmatically using its name. To call a `Sub` procedure programmatically, you can use its name and pass it the parameters in a comma-delimited list. To call the `Sub` procedure `DisplayCustomer` (discussed in Chapter 4, "Data Types, Variables, and Constants"), you would use the following syntax:

```
Dim lngCustID As Long

' populate the customer id

DisplayCustomer lngCustID
```

Note that parentheses are not required when calling a procedure that does not return a value. An alternative syntax for calling this procedure is to use the `Call` statement and place parentheses around the arguments.

```
Dim lngCustID As Long

' populate the customer id

Call DisplayCustomer(lngCustID)
```

Calling `Function` procedures is similar, although setting one equal to the procedure name captures the return value. For example, to call the `Function` procedure `RunsCreated` discussed previously, you would use the following code:

```
Dim sngRC as Single

sngRC = RunsCreated(3283,10881,660,528,140,1015)
```

With VB 6, you can also use the `CallByName` function to invoke a procedure on an object, even if the procedure is unknown at compile time. This function takes arguments that specify the instance of the object, the name of the procedure, and the type of procedure being invoked (`vbGet`, `vbLet`, `vbSet`, and `vbMethod`). The arguments to the procedure are then passed as a comma-delimited list at the end of the call. The following example shows a call to a `RunsCreated` method of a class module named `clsPlayer`:

```
Dim sngRC As Single
Dim objPlayer As New clsPlayer
Dim strProc As String

strProc = "RunsCreated"
sngRC = CallByName(objPlayer, strProc, VbMethod, _
    3283, 10881, 660, 528, 140, 1081)
```

TIP

Obviously, this example is simplified because `strProc` is hard-coded. A technique you could use to populate this variable is to read it from the Registry (discussed in Chapter 18, "Adding Professional Features") or use a `Select Case` statement based on other data available to the application.

Unfortunately, the list of arguments must be known ahead of time unless the procedure is coded to accept a `Variant` array. In addition, this function works only for object variables and not for `Public` procedures in code modules.

TIP

To easily navigate to the declaration of procedure called in code, you can place your cursor on the procedure name and press Shift+F2. The code window containing the procedure will then be opened.

Parameter Passing

Most procedures accept arguments or parameters that are passed in from the calling code. These parameters can be passed in two ways, by value or by reference.

Using ByVal

Parameters can be passed by value using the ByVal keyword before the parameter name in the parameter declaration. This instructs VB to pass a copy of the value to the procedure, as opposed to its address. When parameters are passed by value, any changes made to the parameter inside the procedure are not reflected in the calling code. Although using ByVal is slower and less efficient for code running in the same process, it is a good practice because the procedure cannot make unwitting changes to variables that it was passed. However, using ByVal is more efficient when passing parameters to other processes running on the machine or across the network.

TIP

Since VB 4.0, implicit type coercion has been expanded to include not only assignment statements but also procedure calls. This can lead to problems because errors will not be detectable until runtime. In other words, if a procedure accepts an argument of type Integer and then is passed a String that contains a numeric value, all is well. However, if the String contains data that cannot be converted into an Integer, a trappable error will occur.

Using ByRef

Passing parameters by reference is the default mechanism used by VB and simply passes the address of the variable instead of a copy (similar to pointers in C). You can also explicitly pass an argument by reference using the ByRef keyword. Obviously, ByRef will be more efficient, especially for larger data types, but it has the effect of allowing the procedure to change the value. A developer can take advantage of this behavior to allow a procedure to return more than one argument. For example, the LoadFile procedure shown in Listing 4.2 (in Chapter 4) uses an array, pNames, as a parameter passed by reference to return a list of names read from an ASCII file.

As stated previously, keep in mind that passing parameters by reference is usually less efficient when the calling procedure is located in a separate process or on a separate machine. This is because each reference to the parameter from within the procedure will incur a round trip to and from the calling program where the address resides.

WARNING

When declaring ByRef parameters as Variant, keep in mind that the procedure may be passed a variable of an explicit type. In this case, the procedure can work with the variable only in the type that was passed. In addition, the procedure may force a change in the subtype of the Variant based on a calculation or assignment. As a result, you must make sure that code in the calling procedure can work with data of the new type.

To illustrate the former situation, the following procedure, PitchingStats, calculates hits per inning pitched. When an Integer is passed into the pHitsPer argument declared as Variant, the calculation will return an Integer, even though a Double would be preferred because a fractional number will be returned.

```
Public Sub PitchingStats(ByVal pInnings As Variant, _
    ByVal pHits As Variant, pHitsPer As Variant)
pHitsPer = (pHits / pInnings)
End Sub

Dim varHitsPer As Integer
PitchingStats 100.33, 98, varHitsPer
' variable varHitsPer returns 1!
```

Optional Parameters

In addition to specifying a list of arguments in the procedure declaration, you can also specify arguments that are not required, using the Optional keyword. To use optional arguments, the keyword must be placed before the ByVal or ByRef keyword and must be placed at the end of the argument list. Multiple arguments may be optional, but all of them must appear at the end of the declaration. To illustrate this, assume the PitchingStats procedure is modified to optionally accept arguments that calculate the earned run average (ERA) given the number of earned runs. These optional arguments can be placed at the end of the argument list as follows:

```
Public Sub PitchingStats(ByVal pInnings As Variant, ByVal pHits As _
    Variant, pHitsPer As Variant, Optional pER As Variant, _
    Optional pERA As Variant)

    pHitsPer = (pHits / pInnings)
```

```
If Not IsMissing(pER) And Not IsMissing(pERA) Then
        pERA = (pER / pInnings) * 9
End If
```

```
End Sub
```

Note that the IsMissing function can be used to determine whether the argument was supplied. This works only for Variant parameters, however. Other data types will be set to their default values if not supplied by the calling procedure. Optional arguments can also be given a default value if not supplied by the calling procedure within the declaration, using the syntax

```
Public Sub GetOrders(Optional ByVal pRefresh As Boolean = True)
```

Note that Boolean variables are False by default. This ensures that if the argument is not supplied, it will be set to True within the procedure. When using default values, the IsMissing function will always return False.

When optional arguments are used, it is sometimes beneficial to take advantage of specifying arguments by name rather than by position. For example, to call PitchingStats, you could also use the following syntax:

```
PitchingStats pInnings:=100.33, pHits:=98, pHitsPer:=varHitsPer
```

Using ParamArray

A second method for passing optional arguments to a procedure is to use the ParamArray keyword. This keyword automatically packages all arguments passed to a procedure to a Variant array that is passed by reference to the procedure. The arguments can then be extracted using normal array techniques and manipulated in the procedure. As an example, the RunsCreated function discussed previously has been rewritten to accept its arguments as a ParamArray in Listing 5.1.

Listing 5.1   Using ParamArray to Pass a Variant Array to a Procedure
```
Public Function RunsCreated(ParamArray Stats()) As Single

Dim lngTotalBases As Long
Dim pHits As Integer
Dim pAB As Integer
Dim pHR As Integer
Dim pDB As Integer
Dim pTR As Integer
Dim pBB As Integer

' Extract data from the parameter array
pHits = Stats(0)
pAB = Stats(1)
pHR = Stats(2)
```

continues

Listing 5.1   continued

```
pDB = Stats(3)
pTR = Stats(4)
pBB = Stats(5)

    ' Perform the calculation
    lngTotalBases = pHits + pDB + (pTR * 2) + (pHR * 3)
    RunsCreated = ((pHits + pBB) * lngTotalBases) / (pAB + pBB)

End Function
```

Although this technique looks promising, the calling procedure must enumerate all the arguments in a comma-delimited list, making it less flexible than it could be. A better approach might be to simply declare the parameter as Variant and create the array before passing it to the procedure.

Declaring External Procedures

Using Visual Basic, you can call not only procedures created in VB but also procedures that exist in external DLLs. To do so, you must use the Declare statement to provide VB with a declaration that specifies the location (referred to as the *library*), name, and arguments of the procedure to be called. The syntax of the Declare statement actually comes in two forms, as follows:

```
Declare Function publicname Lib "library" [Alias "aliasname"] _
    [([ByVal] variable [As type],...)] As Type
```

and

```
Declare Sub publicname Lib "library" [Alias "aliasname"] _
    [([ByVal] variable [As type],...)]
```

The difference is that the first version is used when the external procedure returns a value.

External procedures can be declared as either Private (in Form, code, and class modules) or Public (in code modules). In most instances, this statement will be used to call Windows API procedures that are not readily available in VB. (Chapter 13, "Using Win32 API Techniques," is devoted to this issue.) As an example, consider the following declaration, which allows a VB application to call the Win32 API FlashWindow to flash the title bar of the given window.

```
Public Declare Function FlashWindow Lib "user32" Alias "FlashWindow" _
    (ByVal hwnd As Long, ByVal bInvert As Long) As Long
```

The function can then be called from code within a form using the syntax

```
Dim lngRet as Long
lngRet = FlashWindow(Me.hWnd, 1)
```

The declarations for most Win32 API procedures can be found in the Win32API.txt file installed with VB and viewed with the API Viewer utility shown in Figure 5.2. The utility can be loaded as an add-in or executed from the Microsoft Visual Studio 6.0 folder.

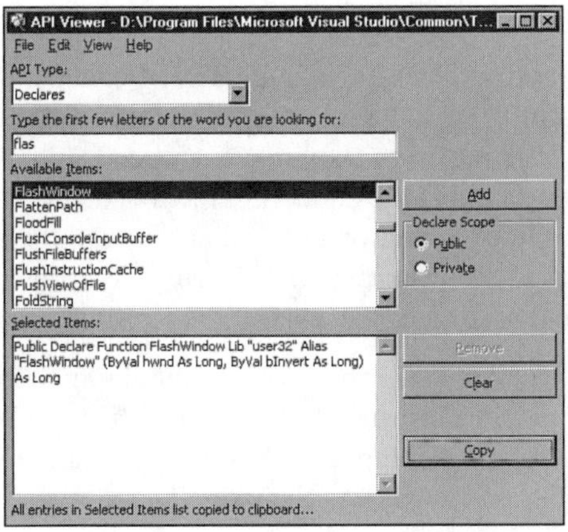

Figure 5.2

The API Viewer utility loads the Win32API.txt file.

Remember to save your project frequently when calling external procedures. If you pass the wrong data types to DLLs, bad things can happen that can cause general protection faults that shut down VB.

Aliasing

Occasionally, the name of a procedure in a DLL conflicts with an existing keyword in VB or uses characters that are illegal. In these cases, you can use the Alias keyword to refer to the actual name of the procedure as it exists in the DLL.

Another typical case is when the DLL exports two versions of the same procedure, although you want to hide the information about which one is being called from the program. The Win32 API uses this technique when dealing with procedures that accept strings as arguments. Because Windows NT can accept Unicode strings, each string function comes in A (ANSI) and W (Unicode) versions. To use the ANSI version of the GetWindowText API procedure, the following declaration uses the Alias to refer to the actual GetWindowTextA procedure:

```
Public Declare Function GetWindowText Lib "user32" Alias "GetWindowTextA" _
    (ByVal hwnd As Long, ByVal lpString As String, _
     ByVal cch As Long) As Long
```

Passing Parameters

As with user-defined procedures, external procedures can accept arguments. In most cases, the exceptions being arrays and structures, DLLs accept arguments passed by value. Two special cases worth noting are passing strings and using the keyword Any.

Passing Strings

In VB, strings are internally represented as something called a *BSTR*. A BSTR contains a header that includes information about the string itself, followed by a series of bytes and ending with a null character, as shown in Figure 5.3. When a BSTR is passed as a parameter by value, it references the address of the first actual byte of data in the string. This is what is normally expected of DLLs that take strings as arguments using the LPSTR type (a pointer to a null-terminated C string). For this reason, strings are typically passed using the ByVal keyword, even if they will be modified by the procedure.

For example, the GetWindowsDirectory API procedure that returns the location of the Windows directory, shown in Listing 5.2, is passed in a string buffer that it fills up and returns. Even though this would appear to require passing the string by reference, the characteristics of BSTR enable passing the string by value.

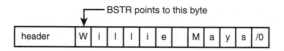

Figure 5.3

The internal structure of a BSTR in Visual Basic.

Listing 5.2   Calling the GetWindowsDirectory API Function Using a String
```
Private Declare Function GetWindowsDirectory Lib "kernel32" _
    Alias "GetWindowsDirectoryA" (ByVal lpBuffer As String, _
    ByVal nSize As Long) As Long
Public Function WinGetWindowsDirectory() As String

' Returns the Windows directory

Dim lstrBuffer As String
Dim llngRet As Long

' Create the buffer
lstrBuffer = Space(255)

llngRet = GetWindowsDirectory(lstrBuffer, Len(lstrBuffer))
```

```
If llngRet = 0 Then
    WinGetWindowsDirectory = vbNullString
Else
    WinGetWindowsDirectory = Left$(lstrBuffer, llngRet)
End If

End Function
```

Notice that the DLL procedure cannot actually allocate space on the string, so the string must be preallocated using the Space function and then trimmed using the Left$ function.

Using As Any

Some DLL procedures are written so that they can accept arguments of different types. In these cases, the parameters can be declared using the keyword Any to remove type checking. However, if you are certain that you're going to pass data of only a single type, it is a better practice to declare the parameter explicitly.

Summary

In this chapter, you have looked at the issues surrounding declaring and calling procedures both internal and external to Visual Basic. In addition, you have examined the way in which VB passes arguments to procedures.

Now that most of the VB syntax has been discussed, I can go back and discuss the issues of naming conventions and comments to ensure that the code you write is easy to maintain.

CHAPTER 6

Coding Conventions

An important part of any programming effort is not only the way the code works but also the way it looks. Writing professional code requires naming conventions that are descriptive, comments that are instructive, and a style (indentation and use of whitespace) that enhances readability. Don't fall into the trap of writing code with less care because Visual Basic is conceptually simpler to use than other programming languages.

When all three aspects are done well, your applications will not only be more maintainable (by you and others), but will also contain fewer bugs and consume less development time.

Naming Conventions

One of the most important aspects of coding professional programs is using a naming convention. Which convention you use is far less important than simply adopting one and sticking with it. I will say that yours should probably be based on the Hungarian notation because many VB developers use a modified form of it. When other developers look at your code, it will make sense even though a few specifics will differ.

The Hungarian notation, originally developed for programming in C, uses mixed-case qualifiers (generally of 20 characters or fewer) with no spaces or underscores. For example, the name of a procedure that invokes a dialog box showing a list of reports might be `ShowRptList`. Note that the name is made up of three words or abbreviations, each one capitalized, with no spaces or underscores between them.

You can apply this style of naming to variables, controls, and procedures.

Variables Names

When you must apply a naming convention most often is with the use of variables. The Hungarian style specifies not only qualifier rules but also the scope and data type placed in front of the qualifier.

The most frequently used convention is to prefix module-level and global-level variables with m and g, respectively. In most instances, local variables do not include a scope prefix. This is followed by a two-letter or three-letter base type, shown in Table 6.1.

Table 6.1 Base Types Used in Naming Variables

Base Type	Data Type
ar	Array
by	Byte
cur	Currency
dbl	Double
dec	Decimal
dt	Date
fl	Boolean
int	Integer
lng	Long
obj	Object
sng	Single
str	String
var	Variant

As a result, local variable declarations appear as

```
Dim intAge As Integer
Dim dtStart As Date
Dim arTitles() As String
Dim flRefresh As Boolean
```

whereas module-level variables include the scope prefix:

```
Private mflIsDirty As Boolean
Private mintTries As Integer
```

Note that most module-level variables will be declared as `Private` so that they cannot be manipulated from code outside the module. Finally, global variables declared as `Public` in a code module look like this:

```
Public gcnConnection As Connection
Public gstrConnect As String
```

Parameter Names

Parameters passed to procedures should also follow a naming convention. There are three popular ways of using the Hungarian convention with parameters. The first is to use the local naming convention, as just mentioned.

```
Public Sub GetCompany(ByVal lngCompID As Long, ByVal flRefresh As Boolean)
```

In this case, the parameters simply use the base type followed by the qualifier without any scope prefix.

A second technique is to use the scope prefix p to denote a parameter.

```
Public Sub GetCompany(ByVal plngCompID As Long, ByVal pflRefresh As Boolean)
```

This technique has the advantage of making sure that within the procedure it is clear that the variable has been passed as an argument. The downside is that it makes the parameter list longer and more complex.

The third technique, and the one I prefer, is to simply prefix the parameter with p and skip the base type.

```
Public Sub GetCompany(ByVal pCompID As Long, ByVal pRefresh As Boolean)
```

This is a trade-off between the first two and still makes it obvious that the variable is an argument, but it does not make the declaration quite so long. You will notice throughout the book that I've used both the first and third techniques, the third being more prevalent.

Automatic Declarations

Rather than declare variables explicitly using a naming convention, you can use two forms of automatic declarations: Def statements and type declaration characters.

Def Statements

The first form of automatic declaration is the Def statement, a feature similar to that found in FORTRAN. These statements, listed in Table 6.2, enable you to specify a range of letters that will be used for a data type.

Table 6.2   Def Statements

Statement	Data Type
DefBool	Boolean
DefByte	Byte
DefCur	Currency
DefDate	Date
DefDbl	Double
DefInt	Integer
DefLng	Long

continues

Table 6.2 continued

Statement	Data Type
DefObj	Object
DefSng	Single
DefStr	String
DefVar	Variant

These statements can be used in the General Declarations section of a module and will apply only to the module where they reside. For example, the code in Listing 6.1 has the effect of automatically declaring the variables in PopulateVars using the types defined in the Def statements. These are not simply variants that use the subtype. Notice that the DefStr statements use a range of letters. You can also use a comma-delimited list to specify discrete prefixes.

Listing 6.1   Using the Def Statements

```
Option Explicit

DefStr P-S
DefInt I
DefLng L

Public Sub PopulateVars()

Dim sName        'String
Dim qAddress     'String
Dim iAge         'Integer
Dim lSalary      'Long

sName = "Ralph"
qAddress = "Oak Street"
iAge = 55
lSalary = 7000

End Sub
```

Of course, you can override these defaults by explicitly declaring a variable using the Dim statement. Def statements are more appropriate if you use implicit declaration, although omitting Option Explicit leads to other errors, which makes Option Explicit unattractive. On the whole, I would not recommend using this feature.

Type Declaration Characters

The second method of automatic declaration involves using special characters appended to the variable names. Like Goto and Gosub, this technique has its roots at the dawn of BASIC. Type declaration characters have the effect of creating a data type of a specific type. Table 6.3 lists the characters and their associated data types.

Table 6.3   Type Declaration Characters

Symbol	Data Type
@	Currency
#	Double
%	Integer
&	Long
!	Single
$	String

NOTE

Not all data types have an associated type declaration character. This is because VB has not added any since version 3.

To use type declaration characters, you simply declare variables, like this:

```
Dim strName$
Dim intAge%

strName = "Dan"
intAge = 95
```

The rule is that if the variable is declared using the type declaration character, it can subsequently be referenced without the character. However, if you use implicit declaration, each subsequent reference to the variable must include the type declaration character.

As with `Def` statements, type declaration characters are most helpful when using implicit declaration but should be avoided because they make the code less readable.

Control Names

The other major aspect of a naming scheme is the name for an instance of a control. These names should also follow the Hungarian convention but do not include a scope prefix. Table 6.4 lists the base types for common controls.

Table 6.4   Base Types for Control Names

Base Type	Control
cb	ComboBox
cdc	CommonDialog
chk	CheckBox
cmd	CommandButton
drv, dir, fil	DriveListBox, DirListBox, and FileListBox
flx	FlexGrid

continues

Table 6.4   continued

Base Type	Control
grp	Frame
hflx	Hierarchical FlexGrid
img	Image
imgl	ImageList
lbl	Label
lst	ListBox
lv	ListView
msk	MaskedEdit
opt	OptionButton
pb	PictureBox
prg	ProgressMeter
sbr	StatusBar
scr	HScrollBar and VScrollBar
tab	TabStrip
tim	Timer
tlb	Toolbar
tv	TreeView
txt	TextBox

Using the naming convention leads to code that looks like the following:

```
txtName.Text = "Sammy Sosa"
chkRightHanded.Checked = True
imgAction = LoadPicture("c:\players\ssosa.jpg")
```

As with variables and parameters, the qualifier should be a name that describes how the control is used.

Procedure Names

Although procedure names do not employ scope prefixes or base types, many programmers have developed naming systems based on the usage of the procedure. For example, procedures that invoke a particular form are prefixed with Show; those that read from a disk file or database are prefixed with Load or Get; and procedures that insert data into a database or file are prefixed with Add.

Again, as long as a convention is used consistently and the procedure name is descriptive, the particular scheme you employ is not critical.

> ## TIP
>
> If you find that you have trouble deciding on a name for a procedure, it might be because the procedure is not well-defined. In other words, the procedure might be performing several functions instead of one that is well-defined. Procedures like these should be broken up.

Commenting

A key element of writing code that is maintainable and well thought out is commenting. In VB, you can essentially create only single-line comments, denoted by preceding the comment with a single quote. By default, the comments will appear green in the code window, although you can change this using the Options dialog invoked from Tools, Options.

Even though through syntax you can create only single-line comments, you can use the Edit toolbar to comment entire blocks of code. Figure 6.1 shows the Edit toolbar as the comment block button is about to be clicked to comment out the section of highlighted code. This can be very helpful for commenting out sections of code during debugging.

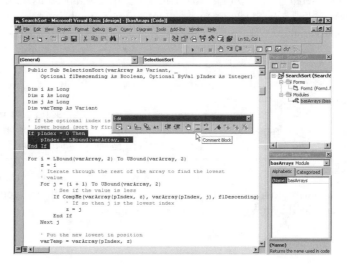

Figure 6.1

The Edit toolbar allows you to comment and uncomment blocks of code.

As a general rule, I advocate using comments before each major section of code within a procedure. Some people recommend creating a comment block at the top of each procedure, as shown in Figure 6.2, that includes data such as the author, the purpose, an argument list, and perhaps even modification dates and times. For most procedures, this is overkill and serves to make the code bulkier.

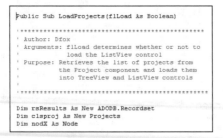

```
Public Sub LoadProjects(flLoad As Boolean)
'*****************************************************
' Author: Dfox
' Arguments: flLoad determines whether or not to
'            load the ListView control
' Purpose: Retrieves the list of projects from
'          the Project component and loads them
'          into TreeView and ListView controls
'
'*****************************************************
Dim rsResults As New ADODB.Recordset
Dim clsproj As New Projects
Dim nodX As Node
```

Figure 6.2

An example of a header comment block that describes the procedure.

A second technique sometimes advocated is placing comments after each variable dec-laration, like this:

```
Dim intAge As Integer    ' Age of the person
Dim strName As String    ' Name of the person
```

I don't typically use this technique because the names of the variables should ade-quately identify what the variable is for. This technique could be used, however, for Variant arrays where the declaration does not provide much information about the structure of the variable.

NOTE

A technique related to commenting declarations is that of placing comments at the end of lines containing code. I generally do not use this technique because it makes the code more difficult to edit and serves to lengthen the lines.

My preferred approach is to write out the algorithm in comments first and then fill in the procedure with code. This approach tends to guarantee that the comments are meaningful because they are not written as afterthoughts.

TIP

This is the key point. Comment *during* the code writing process, not after. Most comments written after the code has been written are useless.

Writing out comments in this way also enables you to gather your thoughts before you write code. Often, developers begin coding before they've thought about the algorithm, resulting in ugly code that is difficult to maintain and extend. Listing 6.2 gives an example of writing out the algorithm in comments first, and Listing 6.3 presents the fleshed-out procedure.

Listing 6.2 A Procedure Written in Comments Before the Process of Coding Has Begun

```
Private Sub LoadSkills(ByVal flLoad As Boolean)

' Create a new Skills object and retrieve the list of skills

    ' Get a reference to the Skills node of the TreeView control

    ' Remove all the nodes in the TreeView control

    ' If we're not in the initial load, also clear out the
    ' ListView control and set up the columns

    ' Loop through the skills

        ' Add a new node to the TreeView
        ' Add a new item to the ListView

End Sub
```

As you can see in Listing 6.2, each major step in the algorithm is spelled out before a single line of code is written. As a result, the procedure contains only a few comments, but each one is meaningful and direct.

Listing 6.3 The Fully Coded Procedure

```
Private Sub LoadSkills(ByVal flLoad As Boolean)

Dim rsResults As New ADODB.Recordset
Dim clsSkills As Skills
Dim nodX As Node
Dim itmX As ListItem

' Create a new Skills object and retrieve the list of skills
Set clsSkills = New Skills
Set rsResults = clsSkills.GetSkills

    ' Get a reference to the Skills node of the TreeView control
    Set nodX = tvTreeView.Nodes("skills")

    ' Remove all the nodes in the TreeView control
    Do While nodX.Children > 0
        tvTreeView.Nodes.Remove nodX.Child.Index
    Loop

    ' If we're not in the initial load, also clear out the
    ' ListView control and set up the columns
```

continues

Listing 6.3   continued

```
    If flLoad = False Then
        lblTitle(1).Caption = "Skills"
        lvListView.ListItems.Clear
        lvListView.ColumnHeaders.Clear
        lvListView.ColumnHeaders.Add , , "Skill"
        lvListView.ColumnHeaders.Add , , "ID"
    End If

    ' Loop through the skills
    Do While Not rsResults.EOF
        ' Add a new node to the TreeView
        tvTreeView.Nodes.Add "skills", tvwChild, "S" & rsResults("ID"), _
                rsResults("Skill"), "Skill"

        ' Add a new item to the ListView
        If flLoad = False Then
            Set itmX = lvListView.ListItems.Add(, , rsResults("Skill"), _
                    "Skill", "Skill")
            itmX.SubItems(1) = rsResults("ID")
        End If

        rsResults.MoveNext
    Loop
End Sub
```

Although some people advocate rules that specify a ratio for the number of comments per lines of code, I simply recommend commenting where appropriate. The end result is a procedure in which, if all the code were removed, someone could look at the comments and still understand what the procedure is supposed to do.

Style

The final issue to consider when writing code is the style you use. Basically, the style includes issues such as formatting, line continuation, and indentation. The fortunate aspect for VB developers is that the code editor ensures that all variables use the same case and that keywords have consistent capitalization. It even helps by placing the cursor at the same column as the previous line.

The only major style issue left to consider is that you ensure proper indentation. Every If...Then loop or other control structure is typically indented four spaces (the default) from the previous one, in what is commonly called a *pure block* (meaning that each beginning statement has an associated ending statement). Using this style always makes apparent which lines of code will execute within the control structure.

(**TIP**

> You can change the indentation amount by using the Options dialog found on the Tools menu.

For example, an `If...Then` statement that includes nested loops should be indented as follows:

```
If flLoad = True Then
    For i = 1 To lngRows
        flxLoans.Row = i
        For j = 1 To lngColumns
            If Not IsEmpty(varData(i, j)) Then
                flxLoans.Col = j
                flxLoans.Text = varData(i, j)
            End If
        Next j
    Next i
End If
```

Line Continuation

VB supports the underscore as a line continuation character for statements that span multiple lines. In this book, many examples use it so that the code fits on the printed page. Generally, you should avoid using line continuation because it makes the code harder to read and slows performance.

(**TIP**

> Many times, you will want to break a statement across lines when you have literal strings passed as arguments. A better approach would be to store these strings in a resource file and use the **LoadResString** function to retrieve a string from the file.

You can use the line continuation character anywhere within a statement where there is a natural breaking point. In other words, you cannot break the line in the middle of a keyword or literal string, but you can between keywords or arguments in a procedure call. In addition, there must be a space between the end of the last word and the line continuation character.

Summary

In this chapter, I have explained the issues surrounding the use of standard coding conventions in Visual Basic applications. Applying these standards, such as naming conventions and commenting, helps you write code that is more maintainable and readable.

One other feature you can use to write code that is maintainable and extensible is the class module. In the next chapter, you will learn the basics of creating and using class modules.

CHAPTER 7

Using Class Modules

With Visual Basic 4.0 came perhaps the most significant feature yet added to the product—class modules. The capability to use class modules meant that not only could VB be a consumer of objects, but it could also act as a creator of objects.

Although considerable debate exists over the extent to which class modules provide all the features associated with traditional object-oriented languages (see Chapter 15, "Using Object-Oriented Techniques"), they do allow an application to abstract functionality into classes that can be instantiated at runtime as objects. These classes can contain members (methods, properties, and events) that are invoked or trapped by the calling code. In many ways, classes can be thought of as replacements for code modules and UDTs because they are more flexible and reusable.

Perhaps the most interesting aspect of class modules is that, when used in certain types of projects, they can be compiled as COM (Component Object Model) components (also referred to as *ActiveX code components*) and made available to other applications by being published in the system Registry. This capability enables you to write applications that expose their functionality to not only applications running on the same machine through COM, but also those across the network through DCOM.

> **TIP**
>
> For a fuller explanation of the relationship between COM and VB, refer to Chapter 23, "A COM Primer for Visual Basic Developers."

This capability to abstract functionality both within an application and between applications allows the code to be reused either as source code or as one or more binary components.

To assist you in building class modules, VB includes several add-ins, including the Class Builder utility and Data Object Wizard. Both of these create class modules and write code based on selections you make. Figure 7.1 shows an example of using the Class Builder utility to create classes for an order entry application.

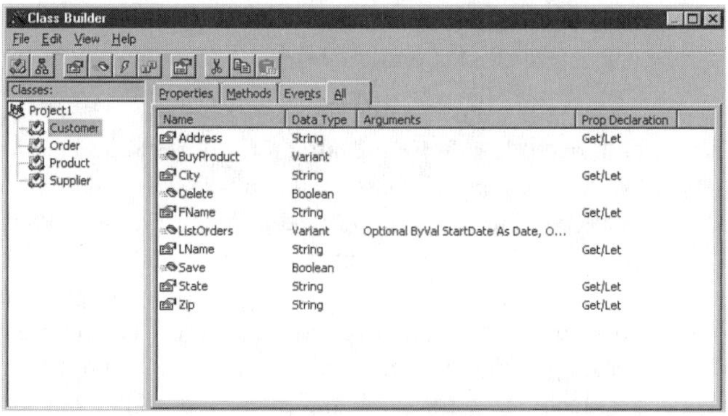

Figure 7.1

The Class Builder utility invoked from the Add-Ins menu allows you to define classes with their members.

Rather than use these code-writing tools, in this chapter you will look at the syntax behind class modules, including how to create properties and methods, use enumerated types, deal with events, set the properties of the class module, and reference class modules from a second project.

Creating Properties

The most basic member of a class module is a property. From the calling procedure's point of view, properties are exposed simply as variables that can be accessed using dot notation. However, internal to the class module, properties are implemented as a series of procedures. The property procedures are invoked automatically when the calling procedure manipulates the property. Typically, the property procedures store the internal state of the properties in Private variables within the class module. The advantage to this arrangement is that you can include code in the property procedures to perform validation or to call other procedures before returning control to the calling procedure.

The three types of property procedures you can code are Get, Let, and Set.

Property Get Procedures

Property Get procedures are invoked when the calling procedure retrieves the value of a property. For example, when a calling procedure instantiates the class module clsCustomer and retrieves the FName property, like this,

```
Dim objCust As clsCustomer
Dim strName As String


' Create a new instance of customer
Set objCust = New clsCustomer

' Retrieve a customer here

strName = objCust.FName
```

the property Get procedure for FName is called. This procedure has the syntax

```
Public Property Get LName() As String
LName = mstrLName
End Property
```

where mstrLName is a Private module-level variable declared in the General Declarations section of the class module. Notice that in actuality Get property procedures are function procedures that return a value.

TIP

Depending on how the class module will be used, the convention for naming is to prefix the class module with cls when the class will be a *concrete* class (a class that contains executable code) and I when it will act as a user-defined interface (discussed in Chapter 15, "Using Object-Oriented Techniques").

NOTE

It is possible to create a property by simply declaring a Public module-level variable in the class. Then, VB automatically stubs in the property procedure for you, although you lose the benefit of being able to tightly control access to the property. As a result, this technique is not recommended.

Property Let Procedures

Property Let procedures are invoked when the calling procedure uses an assignment statement to populate the property. For example, assume that a form contains a TextBox control used to collect the phone number for a customer. Code in the form can then populate the Phone property of a Customer object using the syntax

```
objCust.Phone = txtPhone.Text
```

This syntax is shorthand for using the traditional BASIC Let statement (Let objCust.Phone = txtPhone.Text). Behind the scenes, the property Let procedure for the Phone property is called, as shown in Listing 7.1.

Listing 7.1   The Phone Property Let Procedure
```
Public Property Let Phone(ByVal pPhone As String)

    ' Make sure that the phone is numeric
    If Len(pPhone) <> 10 Or Not IsNumeric(pPhone) Then
        Err.Raise E_PHONE_FORMAT, "Phone", E_PHONE_FORMAT_STR
    Else
        ' Has been edited
        mflIsDirty = True
        mstrPhone = pPhone
    End If

End Property
```

Notice that the property Let procedure is passed a parameter that is a copy of the value used in the calling procedure. This copy can then be validated. In this case, the phone number must be exactly 10 characters and must be able to be converted into a number (meaning that each character must be a digit). If one of these conditions is violated, an error is raised back to the calling procedure using an enumerated type (discussed next). However, if the value passes validation, the new value is used to populate the private variable mstrPhone.

The other interesting aspect of this property procedure is that it also sets the mflIsDirty private variable to True if the edit is successful. Using this technique, you can expose the Boolean variable as a property so that both the calling procedure and the class module itself can tell when the current Customer requires saving.

TIP

There are some properties you might not want the calling program to modify. In these cases, you can either delete the property Let or Set procedure (or don't create one at all), or raise an error using the Err.Raise method.

Property Set Procedures

The final property procedure is property Set. This procedure is invoked when the property is being populated with an object variable using the Set statement. For example, consider a class that exposes a property named ActiveConnection to reference an ADO Connection object. The calling procedure might use code such as the following to populate the property:

```
Dim objCust As clsCustomer
Dim cnConnect As New Connection

' Create a new instance of customer
Set objCust = New clsCustomer

' Code to open the connection object goes here

' Associate the connection with the customer
Set objCust.ActiveConnection = cnConnect
```

The property Set procedure invoked for ActiveConnection would look like the following code:

```
Public Property Set ActiveConnection(ByVal pConnection As ADODB.Connection)

    ' If the connection is closed, return an error
    If pConnection.State = adStateClosed Then
        Err.Raise E_CONNECTION, "ActiveConnection", E_CONNECTION_STR
    Else
        Set mcnConnection = pConnection
    End If

End Property
```

Keep in mind that only properties declared as an object variable or Variant can implement a Set property procedure.

TIP

Remember that property Set procedures will be invoked only when the calling procedure explicitly uses the Set statement. This can be somewhat confusing when your class exposes properties defined as Variant. Then, the calling procedure may place an object variable or a standard data type in the property. As a result, you have to provide both property Let and Set procedures for Variant properties.

UDTs as Properties

In version 6, VB added the capability to allow user-defined types (UDTs, as discussed in Chapter 4, "Data Types, Variables, and Constants") to be returned from function procedures. As a result, you can now represent properties as UDTs. This can be useful because it promotes efficiency by enabling you to package together several variables and pass them using a single parameter. This technique is also interesting because you can still use the property Let procedure to validate the individual variables included in the type. Unfortunately, this technique can be used only in class modules whose instancing property is not set to Private (discussed later in the chapter).

To use a UDT as a property, you must first declare the UDT as Public within the class module. The UDT can then appear as the return value from a function procedure. Listing 7.2 shows this technique; the UDT HittingStats is used as the data type for the property BattingStats in the clsPlayer class module.

Listing 7.2   The clsPlayer Class Module That Shows How to Use a UDT as the Data Type for a Property

```
Option Explicit

Public Type HittingStats
    AB As Integer
    Hits As Integer
    Runs As Integer
    DBL As Integer
    TR As Integer
    HR As Integer
    BB As Integer
    SO As Integer
    RBI As Integer
End Type

' Private variable to hold the stats
Private mrecBatting As HittingStats

Public Property Get BattingStats() As HittingStats
    BattingStats = mrecBatting
End Property

Public Property Let BattingStats(pBattingStats As HittingStats)

    'Note that you can still validate it
    If pBattingStats.Hits > pBattingStats.AB Then
        ' Raise Error
        Exit Property
    End If
```

```
If (pBattingStats.DBL + pBattingStats.TR + _
        pBattingStats.HR) > pBattingStats.Hits Then
    ' Raise Error
    Exit Property
End If

mrecBatting = pBattingStats

End Property
```

The class module can then be used in the calling procedure by declaring variables for both the class and the UDT (the reason it had to be declared as `Public`). After the UDT is populated, it can be used to set the property.

```
Dim objPlayer As Baseball.clsPlayer
Dim recBatting As Baseball.HittingStats

Set objPlayer = New Baseball.clsPlayer

' Populate recBatting here

objPlayer.BattingStats = recBatting
```

Creating Methods

The second type of member in a class module is the method. *Methods* are defined simply as function or `Sub` procedures declared within the class and contain actions to be performed. For example, the `clsPlayer` class discussed previously might contain a method named `Trade` that is implemented as a function procedure and accepts arguments that indicate the team being traded to and the terms of the deal.

As noted in the discussion on parameter passing in Chapter 5, "Using Procedures," the parameters of a method can be passed by value or by reference. When creating class modules that will be accessed across processes or across machine boundaries, keep in mind that passing variables by reference generally incurs more overhead than passing by value. This is because the actual memory address that will be manipulated will always be located on the calling procedure. Each reference to it will invoke a round trip from the method to the calling procedure.

Like properties, methods can be scoped at three levels: `Private`, `Public`, and `Friend`.

Private, Public, and Friend Scope

`Private` and `Public` scope work as with variables. Methods declared as `Private` can be accessed only from code within the class module, whereas methods declared as `Public` are added to the public interface of the module and can be accessed by any code that instantiates the class.

Methods and properties declared with the `Friend` scope are more interesting because they can be invoked from code within the project, but not from external procedures. In other words, if an ActiveX DLL project contains class modules `clsCustomer` and `clsOrder`, and the `clsCustomer` class contains the method `GetCustomerByOrder`,

```
Friend Function GetCustomerByOrder(ByVal pOrderID As Long) As Customer
```

it can be called only from code within `clsCustomer` or `clsOrder` and will not be added to the public interface of the `clsCustomer` class. The reason for doing this is to be able to allow class modules to communicate through a well-defined interface without publishing that interface to clients. This technique is often used when implementing object models.

Enumerated Types

To create class modules that are easy to use and that take advantage of the VB code window's IntelliSense technology, you can use a feature called *enumerated types*. These structures are similar to UDTs but define constants instead of variables. The enumerated type can then be used in both property procedures and parameters lists for methods within the class.

Like UDTs used in class modules, the enumerated type must be declared as `Public` so that the calling procedure can view the definition. For example, the class module `clsPlayer` exposes a property named `Position` that uses an enumerated type containing all the positions. Listing 7.3 presents the code for the module.

Listing 7.3   The clsPlayer Class Module Containing an Enumerated Type for Fielding Positions

```
Option Explicit

Public Enum bbFieldingPositions
    bbPitcher = 1
    bbCatcher = 2
    bbFirstBase = 3
    bbSecondBase = 4
    bbThirdBase = 5
    bbShortStop = 6
    bbLeftField = 7
    bbCenterField = 8
    bbRightField = 9
    bbDesignatedHitter = 10
End Enum

' Internal data
Private mintPos As Integer

Public Property Get Position() As bbFieldingPositions
    Position = mintPos
End Property
```

```
Public Property Let Position(ByVal pPos As bbFieldingPositions)
    ' Still need to validate it
    If pPos >= bbPitcher And pPos <= bbDesignatedHitter Then
        mintPos = pPos
    Else
        ' Raise an Error
    End If
End Property
```

Code in a calling procedure can then access the `Position` property of an instantiated `clsPlayer` object and will be presented with a drop-down list of the enumerated type (shown in Figure 7.2).

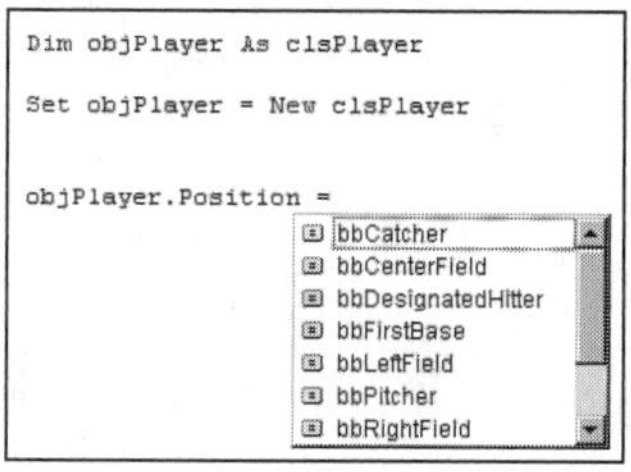

Figure 7.2

A calling procedure using an enumerated type is presented with an IntelliSense drop-down list.

Class Events

Each class module includes two events, `Initialize` and `Terminate`, that are fired when an object is instantiated from the class and when it is destroyed.

Initialize Event

The `Initialize` event is frequently used to open database connections or instantiate dependent objects, such as a `Customer` object that uses a `Collection` object to reference orders. The exact timing of these events differs, depending on how the object was created. For example, executing the code

```
Dim objPlayer As New clsPlayer

' Do other work here

objPlayer.Position = bbCenterField
```

will not cause the Initialize event of clsPlayer to execute until the Position property is referenced. On the other hand, the code

```
Dim objPlayer As clsPlayer
Set objPlayer = New clsPlayer

objPlayer.Position = bbCenterField
```

will invoke the Initialize event when the Set statement is executed.

TIP

A good technique to use during debugging is to place Debug.Print statements in the Initialize and Terminate events using a conditional statement to ensure that your objects are created and destroyed appropriately.

Terminate Event

The Terminate event is typically used to clean up objects created by the class module and perhaps save any modified data. The timing of this event is affected by when the object is destroyed. You can be assured that the event will fire when the object is set to Nothing as follows:

```
Set objPlayer = Nothing
```

However, if you fail to do this in your code, the object will be destroyed when it goes out of scope, causing the event to fire.

Instancing Property

Each class module included in a project can be assigned an instancing property (available from the Properties window) that controls where the class is visible and how it is instantiated. You can see the valid values for this property in Table 7.1.

Table 7.1   Valid Values for the Instancing Property

Value	Description
Private	Accessible only from within the project. Not created as a COM component.
PublicNotCreateable	Visible from code outside the project but cannot be created using the New statement or CreateObject function. Useful when creating an object model using dependent objects.
MultiUse	Can be created and manipulated from outside the project. Allows the client to create multiple objects within the DLL or EXE containing the class.

Value	Description
GlobalMultiUse	The same as MultiUse, but allows members of the class to be invoked as if they were global. When this setting is used, it is unnecessary to explicitly create the object.
SingleUse	Can be created and manipulated from outside the project, but each new instance loads a new copy of the DLL or EXE containing the class. Used in ActiveX EXE projects so that multiple clients do not block each other.
GlobalSingleUse	The same as SingleUse, but members of the class can be invoked as if they were global.

Not all instancing values are available, however, to all types of projects. For example, class modules within EXE projects must be instanced as private (in fact, the property does not even appear in the Properties window) that are not accessible from code outside the project. This is because the class modules in these projects are not compiled as COM components, so a type library is not generated and published in the system Registry.

Table 7.2 presents the complete list of project types and instancing values.

Table 7.2   Valid Values for the Instancing Property of a Class Module by Project Type

Project Type	Private	Public Not Createable	Multi Use	Global Multi Use	Single Use	Global Single Use
Standard EXE	Default	No	No	No	No	No
ActiveX EXE	Yes	Yes	Yes	Yes	Yes	Yes
ActiveX DLL	Yes	Yes	Yes	Yes	No	No
ActiveX Document DLL	Yes	Yes	Yes	Yes	No	No
ActiveX Document EXE	Yes	Yes	Yes	Yes	Yes	Yes
DHTML Project	Yes	Yes	Yes	Yes	No	No
IIS Application	Yes	Yes	Yes	Yes	No	No

Setting References

After a class module is compiled into a COM component (by using the appropriate instancing property and project type), it can be referenced by other applications. If the client program is a VB application, you can reference the component using the References dialog invoked from the Project, References menu. The resulting dialog, shown in Figure 7.3, displays a list of the type libraries for COM components installed on the machine. Notice that you can reference components created in VB, as well as components provided by Microsoft and other vendors. This ability to create software that can be plugged into applications is one of the biggest benefits of using class modules.

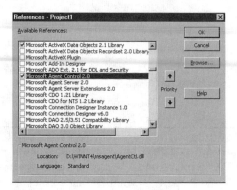

Figure 7.3

The References dialog allows a VB application to read the type libraries of COM components.

When you select one or more of the listed components, VB reads the interface definitions of the components from the type library. VB can then provide IntelliSense help on the members of the component, as well as perform early binding to make calls to the component more efficient.

Summary

Class modules allow VB to create and use objects within and between applications. In addition, they are a great way to abstract user interface code from code that performs business logic or data access.

In this chapter, you've learned how to create properties and methods and use them with enumerated types, as well as user-defined types. In addition, you've covered the `Initialize` and `Terminate` events and the various instancing options that can be employed.

In the next chapter, you will look at the ways VB can access both local and server-based data.

CHAPTER 8

Data Access

Since version 3.0, Visual Basic has been heavily used for accessing both local and remote databases. As the product has matured, VB developers have used three primary data access interfaces. In this chapter, I'll briefly discuss Data Access Objects (DAO), Remote Data Objects (RDO), and ActiveX Data Objects (ADO). In some detail, I'll explain the ADO Data Control and how to use it to query records from a database.

Data Access Interfaces

As already mentioned, VB supports DAO, RDO, and ADO. All three of these data access interfaces include an object model and ActiveX controls that allow both graphical and programmatic access to data. This section provides a brief overview of each of these and discusses their strengths and weaknesses.

DAO

Data Access Objects was the first data access interface, included with VB 3.0. Originally, DAO was designed to provide access to Microsoft Jet databases; later it was expanded to allow access to ODBC data sources. The version of DAO that ships with VB 6 is 3.51, although you will notice that VB also includes a 2.5/3.51 compatibility library that can be used when the code in a project was originally developed using the 16-bit DAO 2.5 library. The DAO 3.51 library contains 17 objects arranged hierarchically, as shown in Table 8.1.

Table 8.1   The Objects of the DAO Object Model

Object	Description
Connection	Used to make a connection to an ODBC data source when using an ODBCDirect workspace.
Container	Groups similar types of Document objects together in a Jet database. Examples include Databases, Tables, and Relations. Exposed through the Containers collection of the Database object.
Database	Used to refer to an open Jet database. Exposed through the Databases collection of the Workspace object.
DBEngine	Top-level object in the model used to control the Jet database engine.
Document	Used to refer to a Database, Table, QueryDef, or Relation saved in a Container in a Jet database.
Error	Encapsulates details of DAO errors encountered. Exposed through the Errors collection of the DBEngine object.
Field	Represents a column of data within a collection of Field objects exposed by a Recordset, Index, QueryDef, Relation, or TableDef.
Group	Represents a group of user accounts that have common permission in a Jet database. Exposed as a collection of Group objects by the Workspace object.
Index	Represents a data structure in a Jet database used to order records and provide efficient access to them. Exposed through the Indexes collection of the TableDef object.
Parameter	Represents a value supplied to a QueryDef object. Exposed through the Parameters collection of the QueryDef object.
Property	Represents a built-in or user-defined characteristic of a DAO object. All DAO objects except Connection and Error contain a Properties collection.
QueryDef	Represents a stored definition of a query in a Jet database or a temporary query in an ODBC workspace. Exposed through the QueryDefs collection of the Database object.
Recordset	Represents a resultset generated from a query or the records in a table. Exposed through the Recordsets collection of the Database object.
Relation	Represents a relationship between fields in a table or queries of a Jet database. Exposed through the Relations collection of the Database object.
TableDef	Represents the stored definition of a table in a Jet database. Exposed through the TableDefs collection of the Database object.

Object	Description
User	Represents a user account in a Jet workspace. Exposed through the Users collection of the Workspace object.
Workspace	Represents a named session for a user connected to either a Jet database or an ODBC data source. Provides collections of open Databases and Connections, as well as Groups and Users for Jet workspaces.

The DAO Data Control is included as an intrinsic control in VB and is used to provide a graphical way of creating recordsets by simply setting properties such as Connect, DatabaseName, and RecordSource. Typically, the data retrieved by a data control is displayed through bound controls. Several of the intrinsic controls, such as TextBox, CheckBox, and OptionButton, can act as bound controls by setting their DataSource and DataField properties to point to the data control and the column in the recordset, respectively. For example, the simple application shown in Figure 8.1 contains a data control and three bound TextBox controls to display records from the Customers table of the sample Northwind database that ships with VB.

NOTE

VB also ships with ActiveX controls, such as the Data Bound Grid control, that can act as bound controls. These controls are listed in Table 2.2 in Chapter 2, "Using Controls."

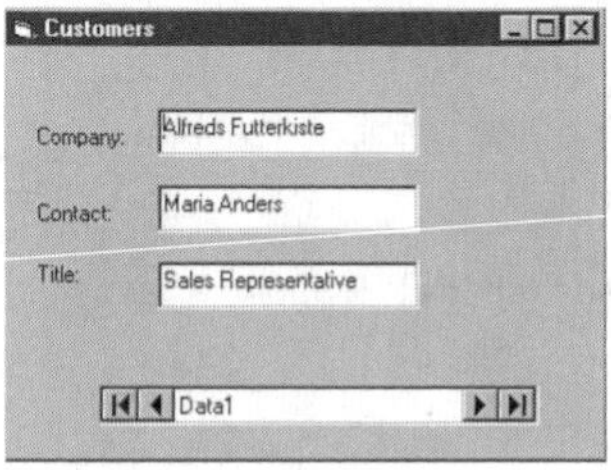

Figure 8.1

A simple form that contains a DAO Data Control with bound TextBox controls.

TIP

By adding a data control to a form in your application, VB automatically sets a reference to the DAO 3.51 library. If you want to use DAO programmatically, you yourself must set this reference, using the Tools, References menu.

If you want to use the DAO Object Model programmatically (without the data control), the advantage is that it provides direct and efficient access to Jet databases. In addition, you can manipulate features of Jet, such as validation rules, replication, security, object creation (DDL), and table-based index searches to provide additional functionality and performance. Listing 8.1 gives an example of using DAO programmatically.

Listing 8.1   Using DAO Programmatically to Populate a DBGrid Control

```
Option Explicit

Private mWks As Workspace
Private mDB As Database

Private Sub GetCustomers()

Dim rsProj As Recordset
Dim strSQL As String

' Build a SQL string
strSQL = "SELECT * FROM Customers"

' Open the recordset
Set rsProj = mDB.OpenRecordset(strSQL, dbOpenSnapshot)

' Set the recordset to the data control, which is in turn
' bound to the Data Bound grid using the DataSource property
Set dcProj.Recordset = rsProj

End Sub

Private Sub Form_Load()

' Create a workspace
Set mWks = DBEngine.CreateWorkspace("MyWks", "admin", _
    "", dbUseJet)

' Open up the Jet database
Set mDB = mWks.OpenDatabase("d:\program files\vs\vb98\nwind.mdb", _
    False, dbDriverNoPrompt)

' Display the customers
GetCustomers

End Sub

Private Sub Form_Unload(Cancel As Integer)

    ' Close the connection
    mDB.Close

End Sub
```

In Listing 8.1, the database is created in the `Load` event of a `Form` using a `Workspace` object with its `Type` property set to `dbUseJet` to instruct DAO to load the Jet database engine. The .MDB file is then opened using the `OpenDatabase` method in shareable mode. A user-defined procedure, `GetCustomers`, is then invoked to create the `Recordset` using the `OpenRecordset` method of the `Database` object. Finally, the `Recordset` property of the data control is populated with the list of customers.

TIP

By associating the data control with a Data Bound Grid control using the `DataSource` property, the records will display in the grid.

In the past, the primary weakness of DAO was its high overhead because the Jet DLLs (database engine) were always loaded by the VB application, even if the application used the ODBC pass through features of Jet to bypass DAO's parsing of queries sent to the database. However, with DAO version 3.0, the ODBCDirect feature was added to DAO to allow your application to decide which interface is to be used. By setting the `DefaultType` property of the DAO Data Control or `DBEngine` object to `dbUseODBC`, DAO will bypass loading the Jet database engine and will actually translate all data access calls to the RDO interface discussed next.

NOTE

For more information on using DAO, see the DAO Overview topic in the online MSDN help that ships with VB 6.

Generally, DAO should be reserved for legacy applications that are being maintained or that will use only Microsoft Jet as the backend and require access to some of the additional features, such as replication, that Jet provides.

RDO

The second data access interface VB supports is Remote Data Objects (RDO). RDO was developed to allow low overhead access to ODBC data sources and provides a simpler object model of just nine objects arranged hierarchically, as presented in Table 8.2.

Table 8.2 The Object in the RDO Object Model

Object	Description
rdoColumn	Represents a column of data in an `rdoResultset` or `rdoTable` object. Exposed through the `rdoColumns` collection of the aforementioned objects.
rdoConnection	Used to create a connection to a remote data source using ODBC. Exposed through the `rdoConnections` collection of the `rdoEnvironment` object.

continues

Table 8.2 continued

Object	Description
rdoEngine	Automatically created base object when RDO is first used in an application.
rdoEnvironment	Defines a logical set of connections for a particular user. Exposed through the rdoEnvironments collection of the rdoEngine object. The first item in the collection is created automatically.
rdoError	Represents an error returned by a database and exposed through the rdoErrors collection of the rdoEngine object.
rdoParameter	Represents a parameter associated with an rdoQuery object and exposed through the rdoParameters collection of an rdoQuery.
rdoQuery	Represents a SQL query that may return an rdoResultset object and contain a collection of rdoParameter objects. Exposed through the rdoQueries collection of the rdoConnection object.
rdoResultset	Represents a set of rows returned from a data source. Exposed through the rdoResultsets collection of the rdoConnection object.
rdoTable	Represents the definition of a table or view that resides in a data source. Exposed through the rdoTables collection of the rdoConnection object.

Like DAO, RDO also includes a data control named the RemoteData control that provides a graphical way of creating resultsets. Also, as with DAO, the same set of bound intrinsic and ActiveX controls can be used to display data.

For an example of what RDO code looks like, consider the code in Listing 8.2, used to query a SQL Server database to display all the rows in a Projects table given a starting date. The resultset created is then used to populate the Resultset property of a RemoteData control, which, in turn, populates a Data Bound grid control using its DataSource property. The populated grid is shown in Figure 8.2. Note that the DTPicker control is used to select the date to use in the query, and its Change event is fired when the user selects a new date.

Listing 8.2   Code That Uses RDO Programmatically to Create a Resultset and Populate a Grid Control

```
Option Explicit

Private mrdCon As rdoConnection

Private Sub GetProjects(ByVal pStartDate As Date)

Dim rdRs As rdoResultset
```

```
Dim strSQL As String

' Build a SQL string
strSQL = "SELECT * FROM Projects WHERE StartDate >= '" & pStartDate & "'"

' Open the resultsets
Set rdRs = mrdCon.OpenResultset(strSQL, _
        rdOpenKeyset, rdConcurRowVer)

' Set the resultset to the RemoteData control, which is in turn
' bound to the Data Bound grid using the DataSource property
Set rdcProj.Resultset = rdRs

End Sub

Private Sub dtpStartDate_Change()

    ' Call the form-level procedure and pass it the startinf date
    GetProjects dtpStartDate.Value

End Sub

Private Sub Form_Load()

' Create a new rdo Connection object
Set mrdCon = New rdoConnection

' Set its properties and establish the connection
With mrdCon
    .CursorDriver = rdUseOdbc
    .Connect = "DSN=ConTracker;uid=sa;pwd=;"
    .EstablishConnection rdDriverNoPrompt
End With

End Sub

Private Sub Form_Unload(Cancel As Integer)

    ' Close the connection
    mrdCon.Close

End Sub
```

Consulting Projects

Projects Starting After: Friday , January 01, 1999

Code	Description	Company	Contact	Phone
10815	Y2K Assesment	Payless Cashways	Carol Thomas	78523399
10076	A different Project	Solutech	Dan Fox	12345678
10061	Order Entry System	Intel	George Mason	91345187
10050	Billing System	Cherokee Market	Fred Flinston	12312312
10077	Information Center	Hertz	Fred Thompson	91332321
10078	Intranet Time System	USA Admin	Joe Blow	12312312
10079	Build a replication so	ACME Builders	Joe Blow	13212312
10080	SQL7 Replication (M	ACME	John Doe	13212312
10060	Online Travel Site	Microsoft	Bill Gates	44455512
10081	Project 2	ACME	John	12433242

Figure 8.2

The populated grid control using the code in Listing 8.1.

Notice that in Listing 8.2 the rdoConnection object is created in the form's Load event and opened using the ODBC cursor driver using an ODBC DSN. The adDriverNoPrompt constant passed to the EstablishConnection method instructs RDO not to prompt the user for a login id and password, even if they are not provided in the Connect properties connection string.

The Private procedure GetProjects is invoked by the Change event of the DateTimePicker control when the user selects a new date. The date value passed to GetProjects is used to build a SQL string to retrieve all the projects that are active for the specified date. The OpenResultset method of the rdoConnection object is used to create the updateable rdoResultset using a keyset cursor. The rdoResultset is then used to populate the DBGrid control rdcProj using its Resultset property.

RDO is extremely effective and is the most mature interface for developing applications that use ODBC data sources. RDO also supports features such as asynchronous processing and events to stop long-running queries from blocking your application.

Until recently, because of its success and the ubiquity of ODBC, Microsoft has touted RDO as its flagship data access interface. However, things change, and Microsoft has developed a new data access strategy based on COM that it has come to view as its strategic direction.

ADO

The third and newest data access interface that VB supports is ActiveX Data Objects (ADO). Because Chapter 14, "Using ADO for Data Access," and Chapter 20, "ADO Reference," are entirely devoted to this subject, suffice it to say that ADO, with its underlying OLE DB interface, is Microsoft's preferred method for connecting all its development tools to not only relational data sources such as SQL Server and Oracle but also nonrelational sources such as Exchange Server and the Windows 2000 Active Directory. The version of ADO that ships with VB 6 is 2.0, although version 2.1 was released with SQL Server 7 and Office 2000.

In addition to using ADO for traditional client/server applications, ADO has been extended to work in an Internet or intranet environment through Remote Data Services (RDS). (RDS is discussed in more detail in Chapter 17, "Building Web Applications.") RDS allows an ADO Recordset to be created on a Web server running Internet Information Server (IIS). This recordset can then be disconnected from its data source and transmitted via HTTP to a client PC and manipulated within a VB or browser-based application. This is a very popular method used in VB applications that must work in the occasionally connected Internet environment.

NOTE

RDS is distributed, along with ADO, in the Microsoft Data Access Components (MDAC) 1.5 (and higher) distributable package as well as Internet Explorer 4 and higher.

Because the programmatic aspects of ADO are covered in Chapters 14 and 20, in this section you will look at the Microsoft Visual Data Tools that ship with VB 6 and use ADO, as well the ADO Data Control, which provides graphical access to ADO recordsets.

Microsoft Visual Data Tools

The Microsoft Visual Data Tools are a collection of tools that can be plugged into development environments to allow developers to graphically view and manipulate a database using ADO. These tools are meant to be used during development to assist a developer in identifying which database objects to use by providing query and diagramming capability, as well as some administrative features such as table and stored procedure creation if the developer has been granted the appropriate security.

In VB, the Visual Data Tools are manifested in the Data View window. You can access this window using the View, Data View Window menu option or the icon on the standard toolbar. The Data View window contains folders for data links and data environment connections. Working with the data environment is discussed in Chapter 14, but essentially it provides connections and stored commands to your application at runtime. Conversely, data links provide connections at design time that can be used to manipulate a data source and populate a data environment.

After right-clicking on the Data Links folder and choosing Add a Data Link, you are presented with the Data Link Properties dialog, which allows you to choose or build an ODBC or OLE DB connection. When using ODBC, the drop-down box on the Connection tab allows you to select a previously defined ODBC DSN or create a DSN-less connection by specifying all the connection properties, shown in Figure 8.3.

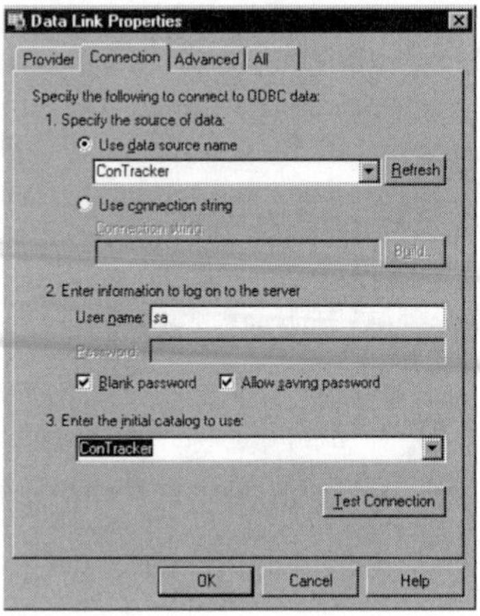

Figure 8.3

The Data Link Properties dialog allows you to specify the connection properties.

Once created, the new data link will appear in the folder and can be expanded to view database objects such as database diagrams, tables, views, and stored procedures.

NOTE

Depending on the ODBC driver or OLE DB provider you use, not all the folders and functionality might be available. For example, at this time, database diagrams are supported by SQL Server only.

When you double-click on an object, an editing window appears, where you can edit data or objects in the database. Note that, by right-clicking on an object, you can create new objects such as tables, views, or stored procedures. The screen shot in Figure 8.4 shows the IDE with the Data View window visible and editing windows open for a database diagram, table, and stored procedure, from left to right.

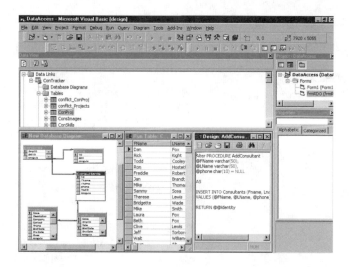

Figure 8.4

The Data View window and associated editing windows.

Using the ADO Data Control

The final topic in this chapter is the ADO Data Control. This control is analogous to the DAO Data Control and the RemoteData Control used with DAO and RDO, respectively. However, because it is new to VB 6, a short overview of its key members and events is warranted. Table 8.3 lists the key properties, methods, and events of the ADO Data Control.

Table 8.3   ADO Data Control Key Methods, Properties, and Events

Member	Description
Properties	
CommandTimeout	Specifies how long the control will wait for a single command to execute before returning an error.
CommandType	Specifies the format of the command that will be sent to the data provider. Options include the name of a table, stored procedure, or SQL statement.
ConnectionString	Specifies the connection information used to connect to the data provider.
ConnectionTimeout	Specifies how long the control will wait for the connection to the data provider before returning an error.
Mode	Specifies the permissions in use for modifying data returned by the control.

continues

Table 8.3   continued

Member	Description
Properties	
`Password`	Specifies the password to be sent to the data provider upon initiating a connection.
`Recordset`	Returns or sets a reference to the underlying recordset returned by the control.
`RecordSource`	Specifies the text of the command to be sent to the data provider. This may include a table name, stored procedure, or SQL statement.
Methods	
`Refresh`	Instructs the data control to refresh its recordset. This can be used after the `RecordSource` property is changed programmatically to repopulate the control.
`UpdateControls`	Restores the contents of all bound controls to their original values and is used when a user decides to cancel changes to the current record.
`UserName`	Specifies the username to be sent to the data provider upon initiating a connection.
Events	
`EndOfRecordset`	Fired when an attempt is made to move to a record that is past the end of the recordset.
`Error`	Fired when a data access error occurs and passes in arguments to determine the error number, description, and source, as well as an argument that can be used to suppress display of the error.
`WillChangeField` and `FieldChangeComplete`	Fired before and after the value o fone or more fields in the recordset changes. The events pass in information about the fields and their status, as well as a reference to the underlying recordset.
`WillChangeRecord` and `RecordChangeComplete`	Fired before and after one or more records in the recordset change in response to an `Update`, `Delete`, or `AddNew` operation. These events also pass in information about the status and reason for the change, as well as a reference to the recordset.

Member	Description
Events	
`WillChangeRecordset` and `RecordsetChangeComplete`	Fired before and after the underlying recordset changes in response to the `Requery`, `Resync`, `Close`, `Open`, or `Filter` methods. These events also pass in information about the status and reason for the change, as well as a reference to the recordset.

NOTE

The events exposed by the ADO Data Control are the same as those exposed by the ADO `Recordset` object discussed in Chapter 14, "Using ADO for Data Access," and enumerated in Chapter 20, "ADO Reference," with the exception of the `FetchComplete` and `FetchProgress` events, which are used for asynchronous processing and which the ADO Data Control does not support.

Even though the properties of the ADO Data Control are normally set at design time, the code in Listing 8.3 is provided to show an example of which properties must be set for the control to function. This example executes the same query as in Listing 8.2 to retrieve projects using an ADO Data Control named `acProjects`.

Listing 8.3   Using the ADO Data Control

```
Private Sub GetProjects(ByVal pStartDate As Date)

Dim strSQL As String

' Build a SQL string
strSQL = "SELECT * FROM Projects WHERE StartDate >= '" & pStartDate & "'"

' Set the properties of the ADO Data Control
With acProjects
    .CommandTimeout = 5
    .CommandType = adCmdText
    .ConnectionString = "Provider=SQLOLEDB;Server=SSOSA;Database=ConTracker"
    .Mode = adModeReadWrite
    .UserName = "sa"
    .Password = ""
    .RecordSource = strSQL
End With

' Open the recordset
acProjects.Refresh

End Sub
```

Like the other data controls, the ADO Data Control can be used as a data source for other controls to bind to. In addition to being able to bind to the intrinsic controls noted above, VB 6 also ships with ActiveX controls that can be bound to an ADO Data Control, including the `DataGrid`, `DataList`, `DataCombo`, `DTPicker`, `MonthView`, `Hierarchical FlexGrid`, `MSChart`, and `DataRepeater`.

Summary

Data access has always been central to Visual Basic, and the integration of database technology has increased dramatically in the most recent release of the product. VB's capability to connect to both local and remote, as well as relational and nonrelational, data sources makes it well suited for creating business applications in the corporate world.

In this chapter, I've reviewed the familiar DAO and RDO Object Models, as well as the new Visual Data Tools and ADO Data Control available in VB 6.

In the next chapter, I'll focus on debugging and handling errors that occur while developing VB applications.

CHAPTER 9

Debugging and Error Handling

Because no one is perfect (and I trust that you're not the exception), you will undoubtedly make mistakes when developing applications. These mistakes will manifest themselves in three types of errors: compile-time errors, runtime errors, and logic errors.

To assist you in catching compile-time and logic errors, the Visual Basic IDE includes a set of debugging tools that permit you to inspect and execute your code line by line to catch problems and correct them at design time.

In addition, when a user runs the application, conditions occur that simply cannot be anticipated during development. Typical examples of runtime errors include disk space shortages, network problems, and database crashes. For these reasons, VB also includes statements that allow runtime error handling. Using these statements, your application can catch and respond gracefully to conditions that would otherwise cause the application to end unexpectedly.

In this chapter, you will look first at the debugging tools used during development and then at the error handling schemes that can be employed.

Debugging

One of the often overlooked features of VB is the ease with which you can test your application in the IDE by pressing the F5 key or using the Run menu. This capability encourages iterative development, in which you make small changes and rerun your application to test those changes, rather than code most of the application before testing.

To assist you during iterative development, the IDE supports features such as breakpoints, watch variables, the Immediate window, and the Debug object.

Using Breakpoints

Pressing the F9 key or using the Debug, Toggle Breakpoint menu while in the code window places a breakpoint on the current line. After the application is started, VB will stop execution on the breakpoint and enter break mode. You can think of *break mode* as a point-in-time snapshot of the running application. While in break mode, the line about to be executed will be highlighted in yellow. By hovering the cursor over variables within the procedure, you pop up a ToolTip with the current value of the variable. Entire expressions can be evaluated by highlighting the expression with the cursor and hovering over it. Figure 9.1 shows a typical debugging session with the cursor hovering over an expression, causing a ToolTip to appear showing the expression's value.

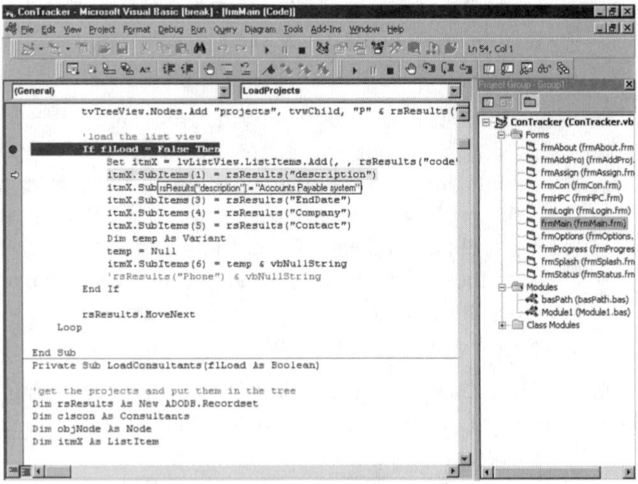

Figure 9.1

An application in break mode. The highlighted code line is about to be executed.

At this point, you can use any of the debugging tools available on the Debug menu to inspect the state of the program or continue execution line by line.

An easy way to access the debugging tools is through the Debug toolbar, shown in Figure 9.2. This toolbar contains menu items for stepping through the code line by line or opening one of the five debug windows. When stepping through the code, you can either step into, over, or out of the current procedure. Step Into (F8) executes each line in sequence. Step Over (Shift+F8) executes a procedure and then breaks at the line following the procedure call. Finally, Step Out (Ctrl+Shift+F8) breaks at the next line outside the current procedure. Variations on breaking at different lines can also be accomplished using the Debug menu options Run to Cursor and Set Next Statement.

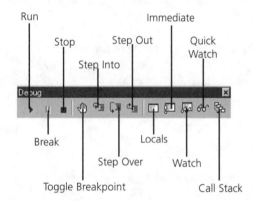

Figure 9.2

The Debug toolbar includes menu options for stepping through the code and viewing debug windows.

The Stop Statement

Unfortunately, breakpoints are not saved with the project when the project is closed. When you would like breakpoints to be saved, you can insert a Stop statement directly in the code. When encountered, the Stop statement causes the application to enter break mode.

TIP

Remember to take the `Stop` statements out of your code before compilation, because a `Stop` encountered in a executable will cause a dialog box to be displayed and the program to end.

Using the Debug Windows

You can use the various debug windows to obtain information about the running program, in addition to setting up conditions that will cause the application to enter break mode.

The Locals Window

The Locals window, shown in Figure 9.3, provides a hierarchical representation of all the variables in the current scope of the procedure. For object variables such as `rsResults` (see Figure 9.3), the window contains an expandable list of properties. Using this window, values can be changed by simply double-clicking on the value and typing in a new value.

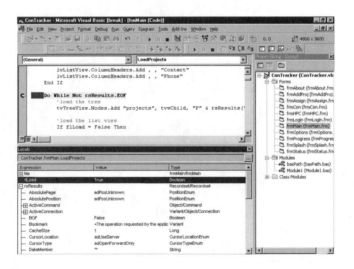

Figure 9.3

The Locals window docked in the lower-left corner of the screen.

The Immediate Window

The Immediate window is useful for evaluating expressions that are not present in the procedure. For example, using the Immediate window, you can use the question mark to print expressions to the window, as shown in Figure 9.4. This window can also be used to execute statements. Keep in mind that only variables in the current scope can be manipulated.

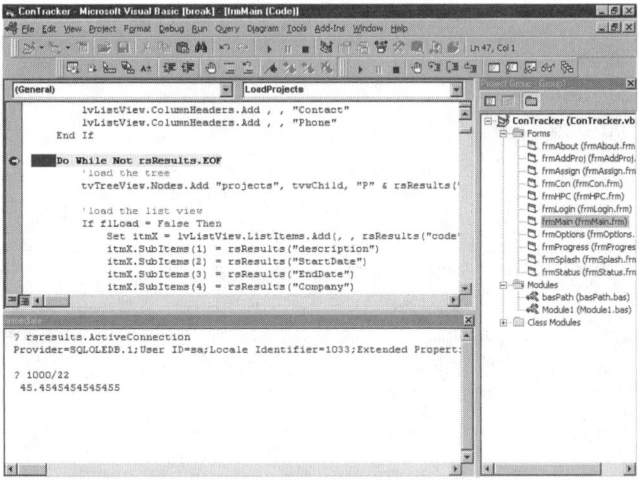

Figure 9.4

The Immediate window, in the lower-left corner of the screen, allows you to evaluate expressions or execute statements.

The Watch Window

The Watch window is used to view the values of variables or expressions throughout the run of the application. Variables can be added to the Watch window by dragging and dropping them into the window. They can also be set to automatically cause the application to enter break mode by right-clicking on the watch and selecting Edit Watch. The resulting dialog, shown in Figure 9.5, contains settings for breaking when the expression is True or whenever the value changes. The latter option makes it simple to track down bugs when a variable is inadvertently changed in the application.

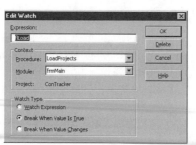

Figure 9.5

The Edit Watch dialog.

TIP

A second form of the Watch window is the Quick Watch window. It serves a similar purpose as the ToolTip shown when hovering over a variable. It simply displays the context, expression, and value of the currently highlighted variable and can be invoked from the Debug menu or by pressing Shift+F9.

The Call Stack

The call stack can be useful in determining the sequence of events that leads up to the current procedure being executed. In Figure 9.6, the procedures listed at the top were called most recently. As procedures finish executing, they are popped off the stack and disappear from the Call Stack window.

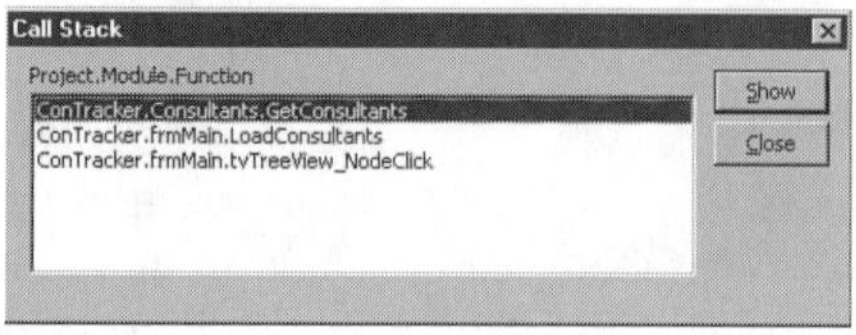

Figure 9.6

The call stack is used to display the procedures currently executing.

Using the Debug Object

A third debugging tool you can use is the Debug object. This object contains only two methods, Print and Assert. The Print method can be used to print values to the Immediate window while the application is executing in the IDE. For example, the following code will print out all the members of the ADO Command object's Properties collection to the Immediate window.

```
Dim objProp As Property

For Each objProp In cmCommand.Properties
    Debug.Print objProp.Name & " = " & objProp.Value
Next
```

This technique is often more beneficial than stopping the execution of the application using a breakpoint, which would mean interrupting or altering the sequence of events you are attempting to debug.

The `Assert` method is a tool familiar to C programmers and is used to test for invalid conditions in the application. When the expression passed to the method evaluates to `False`, the application enters break mode on the line that contains the `Assert` method. A typical use for `Assert` is to check for valid parameters—for example, a procedure that retrieves a set of records from a database, as in the following code:

```
Public Function GetOrders(ByVal pCustID As Long) As Variant
    Debug.Assert pCustID >= 0
    ' Get the orders here
End Function
```

In the event that a value of zero or less is passed to the procedure, the application will be suspended at the line containing `Debug.Assert`. Unlike the `Stop` statement discussed earlier, all references to the `Debug` object are automatically stripped out of your code when it is compiled.

TIP

Because references to `Debug.Assert` are stripped from the application at compile time, keep in mind that they should not be used as substitutes for proper error checking. Your code should still check for valid values and raise errors where appropriate.

Conditional Compilation

The final debugging technique that is sometimes used is to set a debug flag using conditional compilation and then use the flag to fire debugging code at runtime. To use this technique, a conditional constant is declared that determines whether debug mode is active. For example, in the General Declarations section of a module, the following line

```
#Const DEBUGVER = 1
```

would appear, indicating that the debugging code should be active. Note that the # indicates that the constant is conditional and can be used with the conditional #If Then directive. However, conditional constants can be referenced only from within the module in which they are declared. As a result, an application would have to contain constants in each module to use this technique. A second way to declare the conditional constant publicly for the entire project is to use the Make tab of the Project Properties dialog, shown in Figure 9.7. By creating the constant in this way, you make it available to all modules within the application.

NOTE

You can also specify conditional constants when compiling from the command line, using the syntax VB6.exe /make myproject.vbp /DEBUGVER=1.

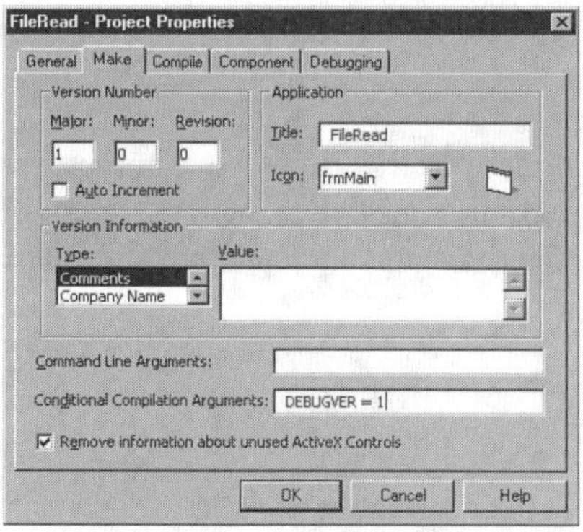

Figure 9.7

The Project Properties dialog contains the Conditional Compilation Arguments field for declaring conditional constants.

Code inside the project can then use the constant to conditionally compile debugging code into the executable. For example, the GetFileData function from Listing 1.1 could include the conditional #If Then directive to display a message box each time the loop is executed.

```
' Load the array
Do While Not EOF(intFileNum)
    If Not flFirst Then
        ReDim Preserve arData(UBound(arData) + 1)
    Else
        ReDim arData(0)
        flFirst = False
    End If
```

```
        Line Input #intFileNum, arData(UBound(arData))
        #If DEBUGVER = 1 Then
            MsgBox arData(UBound(arData)), , UBound(arData)
        #End If
Loop
```

By setting the constant to a value other than 1 before compilation, the VB compiler will skip the MsgBox statement, without affecting size or performance for the compiled executable.

NOTE

In version 4.0 of VB, conditional compilation is often used with the Win16 and Win32 constants to use a single code base for both types of executables. Because version 5.0 and higher supports only 32-bit Windows, the need for conditional compilation has lessened.

Error Handling

As mentioned previously, using debugging techniques enables you to correct compile-time and logic errors but does not deal with unanticipated or uncontrollable errors that occur at runtime. To handle these types of errors, you must use the error trapping and handling techniques discussed in this section.

Setting Error Traps

The mechanism VB uses to handle runtime errors is the error trap. Basically, *error traps* are sections of code within a procedure, denoted by a line label that can be executed when an error is fired. This is conceptually the same as raising exceptions in C++ and Java. By default, no error traps are enabled in an application, and any runtime error produces a less than informative dialog box that ends the application after it is dismissed (an example of which can be seen in Figure 9.8).

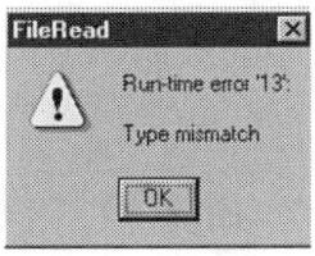

Figure 9.8

The default error dialog produced when an unhandled runtime error occurs.

To set an error trap, you use the On Error Goto statement followed by a line label. For example, to set an error trap in a click event in a command button, you would code the following handler:

```
Private Sub Command1_Click()
On Error Goto MyErr

' other code goes here

Exit Sub
MyErr:
    ' handle the error here
End Sub
```

In this case, any runtime errors that occur between the On Error statement and the Exit Sub will immediately redirect the flow of control to the MyErr line label. Note that the Exit Sub is required if you want to separate the error handling code from the normal flow of execution.

To disable the currently active trap (you can have only one active trap per procedure), you use the On Error Goto 0 statement. This might be desirable if you want to use inline error handling (discussed next) within the procedure. You may also skip all errors that occur in a procedure by using the On Error Resume Next statement, although this is recommended only for small procedures in which the possible trappable errors are well understood and insignificant.

Inside the error trap, you can use the Err object to view the Source, Description, and Number of the error using its properties.

Exiting an Error Trap

Once inside an error trap, you have a choice of five courses of action, presented in Table 9.1.

Table 9.1   Ways to Exit an Error Trap

Statement	Description
Resume	Forces program execution to continue at the statement that caused the error. For certain kinds of errors that the user can correct, this method is preferred. For instance, a runtime error occurs (error 71) when a floppy disk or CD-ROM is not ready for reading. By inserting the proper media, the statement can be re-executed successfully.
Resume Next	Forces program execution to continue with the statement following the one that caused the error. Useful when the statement can be safely bypassed without causing other errors.

Statement	Description
Resume *line*	Forces program execution to continue at a specific line label. This is often used to skip an entire section of a procedure and continue with a later section.
Err.Raise *number*	This statement raises an error from within the error handler so that it may be handled by another procedure. This technique is typically used by ActiveX code components to raise an error back to the calling program.
(Nothing)	By doing nothing in the error trap, the procedure will simply end after the error handler has finished executing. In many cases this is the desired action.

NOTE

When running your application in the IDE, you can affect when VB will enter break mode as runtime errors are encountered, using the General tab of the Options dialog invoked from Tools, Options. The three choices offered instruct VB to Break on All Errors, regardless of whether they've been trapped by an On Error statement; Break in Class Module for errors that occur within a class module; or Break on Unhandled Errors only (the default), which effectively mimics the behavior of a compiled application. Early in the development process, the first option is often chosen to make sure that your code is properly handling all error conditions.

Understanding Error Sequences

It is recommended that most procedures of any complexity, or in which errors are anticipated, contain an error handler. However, in the event that a runtime error is generated in a procedure that does not have an error trap set, VB will search the call stack to determine whether a procedure lower in the stack contains an error handler.

In other words, if procedure A calls procedure B, and procedure B generates a runtime error without an error trap set, the error trap in procedure A is called immediately, if it exists. This process continues until every active procedure has been checked. This functionality implies that not every one of your procedures must contain error traps, only those called directly from the user interface. However, in many instances you will still want to trap for specific errors in individual procedures.

Another key point to remember about the sequence of an error handler is that the Resume and Resume Next statements execute code only with the procedure in which the error handler is actually found. This means that in the example in the preceding paragraph, if the error handler in procedure A issues a Resume statement, the statement that is re-executed is actually the call to procedure B and not the actual statement in procedure B that initially caused the error. Likewise, if procedure A issues a Resume Next, the statement following the call to procedure B is executed.

Using Inline Error Handling

In some situations, it might be advantageous to bypass the error trapping mechanism and check for errors after each line of code is executed. This is referred to as *inline error handling* and can be done by first turning off all error traps using the On Error Resume Next statement. Errors are then detected by checking the Number property of the Err object.

As an example, consider a procedure that deletes a file using the following Kill statement. This procedure may use inline error handling to make sure that the file exists before deleting it.

```
Public Function DelFile(ByVal pFile As String) As Boolean

On Error Resume Next

Kill pFile
If Err.Number = 53 Then
    ' file not found
    DelFile = False
    Err.Clear
Else
    ' success
    DelFile = True
End If

End Function
```

Using Centralized Error Handling

A second technique for handling errors is to group error handlers in a central code module. This technique enables you to share error handling code not only within but also between projects. These centralized procedures can be coded to prompt the user and return the appropriate action to the procedure that generated the error.

Handling disk errors is a good example of when you can use a centralized error handler. The set of possible errors when dealing with disks and files can be checked within a centralized procedure. The procedure can then create a message to prompt the user and pass the appropriate action back to the calling procedure. Listing 9.1 presents the code for the DiskErrors procedure.

Listing 9.1 A Centralized DiskErrors Error Handling Procedure
```
Public Function DiskErrors() As Integer

Dim intMsgType As Integer
Dim strMsg As String
Dim intResponse As Integer

    Select Case Err.Number
        Case 68
```

```
            strMsg = "That device appears unavailable."
          Case 71
            strMsg = "Insert a disk in the drive "
          Case 57
            strMsg = "Internal disk error."
          Case 61
            strMsg = "Disk is full. Continue?"
          Case 76
            strMsg = "That path doesn't exist."
          Case 54
            strMsg = "Can't open your file"
          Case 55
            strMsg = "This file is already open."
          Case 53
            strMsg = "This file is not found."
          Case 62
            strMsg = "There was a problem with this file"
          Case Else
            DiskErrors = 1
            Exit Function
          End Select

       intResponse = MsgBox(strMsg, _
         vbExclamation + vbAbortRetryIgnore, "Disk Error")

       Select Case intResponse
        Case vbAbort
           DiskErrors = 1
        Case vbRetry
           DiskErrors = 2
        Case vbIgnore
           DiskErrors = 3
        End Select

End Function
```

The centralized procedure can then be called in the error handler for the DelFile procedure seen previously, rather than use inline error handling. The following is the rewritten procedure:

```
Public Function DelFile(ByVal pFile As String) As Boolean

On Error GoTo DelFileErr

Kill pFile

Exit Function
DelFileErr:
    Select Case DiskErrors
```

```
Case 1  'Abort
    Exit Function
Case 2  'Retry
    Resume
Case 3  'Ignore
    Resume Next
End Select

End Function
```

Summary

In this chapter, you've looked at the various techniques and tools available to minimize the compile-time, runtime, and logic errors in a Visual Basic application.

After the application is debugged, it must be compiled and distributed. In the next chapter, you will examine the various compilation options you need to consider, as well as the tools available to package and deploy your application.

CHAPTER 10

Compiling and Distributing

After an application is tested and debugged within the IDE, you will want to compile and distribute it so that it can be successfully installed and used. In this chapter, I will first discuss the various compilation options available. These include options for optimizing the compiled file and including descriptive information inside the file. Next, I'll run through the options for packaging and distributing the application using the Package and Deployment Wizard utility that ships with VB 6.

Compilation Options

The compilation options can be accessed from the File, Make *Project* or the Project, *Project* Properties menus. The former menu option first invokes a dialog where you can specify the name and location of the compiled project. In both cases, the options appear as two tabs in the dialog box.

The Make Tab

The Make tab in the Project Properties dialog (refer to Figure 9.7) includes options for specifying the version number, icon, and descriptive information, as well as the application title to be displayed in the Task Manager. Additional settings include any command-line arguments and conditional compilation arguments discussed in Chapter 9, "Debugging and Error Handling."

Perhaps the most important options on the Make tab are Version Number and Auto Increment. By selecting Auto Increment, VB will increment the revision number with each successive compilation of the project. This information is used by the Package and Deployment Wizard, discussed later in the chapter, to decide whether to overwrite a previous version of the application on a user's machine.

The Compile Tab

The second tab, shown in Figure 10.1, contains options that affect how the project is actually compiled. The main decision is whether to compile the project in p-code or native code. Compiling to p-code, or pseudo code, instructs VB to use an intermediate format for instructions that is between machine code instructions and the syntax typed into the code window. When the application is executed, these p-code instructions are translated into machine code instructions that can be executed on the processor. Compiling to native code eliminates this translation and thus can speed up execution of the application, especially when the code performs mathematical and code-intensive operations. However, p-code executables are generally smaller than those compiled in native code.

TIP

Even though you may choose native code for your application, the application still requires the runtime DLL MSVBM60.DLL (in the case of VB 6) to be distributed. This DLL includes the functionality for forms and intrinsic controls, as well as many built-in functions, among others.

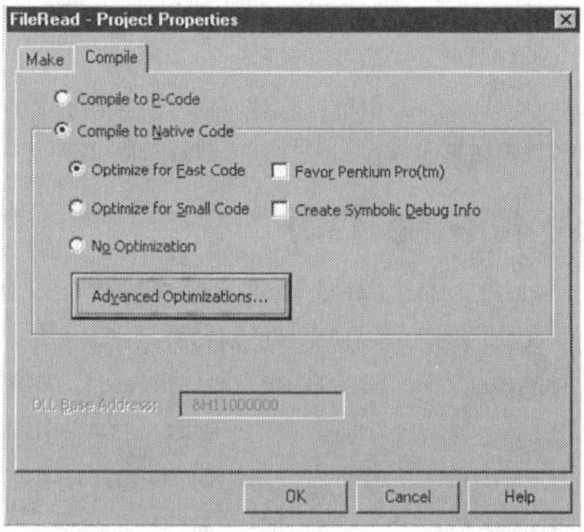

Figure 10.1

The Compile tab controls whether the project is compiled into p-code or native code.

If you choose Native Code, you can use a number of optimizations to create native code that is smaller and faster. On the initial screen, the most interesting option is Create Symbolic Debug Info. If this option is chosen, information will be written into a .PDB file so that the executable can be debugged using Visual C++ or any debugger that supports the CodeView style of debug information. Doing this allows you to seamlessly debug solutions created with multiple development tools. For example, a VB application that calls a COM component written in Visual C++ can be debugged line by line using this approach.

By pressing the Advanced Optimizations button, you are presented with six other options, listed in Table 10.1.

Table 10.1   Advanced Compilation Options for Native Code

Optimization	Description
Assume No Aliasing	Tells the compiler that your code does not refer to the same memory location using two names. As a result, the compiler can perform optimizations such as storing variables in registers. Aliasing does occur if you pass arguments using the `ByRef` keyword, so you should leave this option unchecked when using `ByRef`.
Remove Array Bounds Checks	Tells the compiler to remove the automatic check for the valid index and dimensions when accessing an array. Turning this option on can cause invalid memory locations to be accessed without warning but speeds up array manipulation.
Remove Integer Overflow Checks	Tells the compiler to turn off the automatic range check for `Byte`, `Integer`, `Long`, and `Currency` data types. Turning on this option will not cause errors and will speed up calculations, but you might get invalid results.
Remove Floating Point Error Checks	The same as the preceding option except for `Single` and `Double` data types. Also removes the check for division-by-zero errors.
Allow Unrounded Floating Point Operations	Tells the compiler not to round off the results of floating point calculations on `Single` or `Double` data types before making comparisons. Although this speeds up the comparison, it can result in comparisons between numbers of different precisions, causing two values that would normally be equal to compare as not equal.
Remove Safe Pentium FDIV Checks	Tells the compiler not to insert code to make floating point division safe on Pentium processors with the FDIV bug.

Registration

The final concept to be aware of when compiling your VB project is registration. ActiveX DLL (including DHTML and IIS Applications), EXE, Document EXE, Document DLL, and Control projects all contain class modules that will be compiled into COM components and require registration on the user's machine. Components packaged in EXEs will automatically register themselves the first time the executable is run, because VB inserts this self-registration code into the executable. Components in DLLs (referred to as *code components*), however, must be explicitly registered.

Although the various compilation options regarding code components are discussed in Chapter 16, "Building ActiveX Components," it is worth noting that VB automatically creates type library information for each component and registers it and the component in the system Registry upon compilation. However, if the component is moved to a different machine, it has to be reregistered. Deployment packages created by the Package and Deployment Wizard will perform this operation automatically, but it can be performed manually using the command-line regsvr32.exe utility. This utility is passed the name of the component and optional arguments to unregister the component, run silently, produce output to the console, or execute a supplied command. Figure 10.2 is a typical example of registering a component.

Figure 10.2

Running regsvr32 to register a code component.

Packaging and Deploying

The Package and Deployment Wizard is a utility that ships with VB and is used to create your distributable package. It can be invoked as a standalone utility from the Microsoft Visual Studio Tools program group, as an add-in, or through the PDCmdLine.exe at the command prompt—although using it as an add-in restricts you to creating packages for the currently opened project. The wizard creates one or more compressed cabinet (.cab) files and optionally a setup EXE that a user can invoke to install the application.

After the wizard is launched, you are prompted with the wizard's main window, shown in Figure 10.3. After selecting a VB project file using the Browse button, you can click the Package button to begin creating the package. If you've not compiled the executable or DLL for the project, the wizard will prompt you to do so before it can continue. After the project is compiled, the wizard presents up to three package types that may be created: the standard setup package, Internet setup package, and dependency file.

Figure 10.3

The Package and Deployment Wizard.

The Standard Setup Package

A standard setup package is one that can be used to create a setup.exe program to install the application, rather than have it downloaded through a browser.

As you navigate through the wizard, you will first be prompted for the location of the package. By default, this is a folder named Package that is created directly beneath the folder that contains the .vbp file for the project. However, you may also create the package directly in a different folder or on a network share or mapped drive.

Next, the list of files that will be distributed appears, shown in Figure 10.4. This list contains the files listed in Table 10.2, in addition to any components your application is using. For each component, a dependency file may exist that specifies which other files must be distributed with the component. For example, all the ActiveX controls that ship with VB also include dependency files so that if you redistribute them with your executable, the package will contain all the necessary files for their proper use.

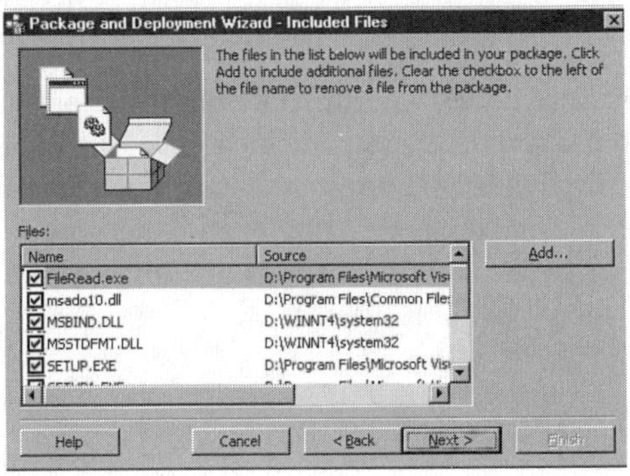

Figure 10.4

Files to be included in the package.

Table 10.2   Files Automatically Included in a Standard Setup Package

File	Description
SETUP.EXE	This is the bootstrap EXE first executed when the application is installed. It loads the actual setup program and prepares the program to be installed.
SETUP1.EXE	This is the main setup program for the application. This is a VB executable that may be customized by using the template in the Wizards\PDWizard\Setup1 folder. For more information about customizing the setup program, see "The Setup Toolkit" in the *Visual Basic 6.0 Programmer's Guide*.
ST6UNST.EXE	The application removal utility that allows users to remove your application from the Control Panel.
VB6 Runtime and OLE Automation	This includes all the runtime and support files for VB6.
VB6STKIT.DLL	The library that contains functions used by SETUP1.EXE.

TIP

Without the proper dependency information, the application may not work correctly when installed on a client computer. Dependency files are discussed later in this chapter.

The screen in Figure 10.4 also allows you to add any other files that should be distributed. Typically, this would include help files, utilities, INI files, or Jet database files.

After the files are selected, the wizard prompts for the compressed file (.cab) options and size. In this dialog, you can specify that the package should be created as a single .cab file or spread across multiple files. By choosing multiple files, you are given the option of choosing the disk size, using the standard floppy disk sizes. Keep in mind that this option affects which deployment options are available when you go to deploy the application. For example, if you choose a single .cab, you will not be given the option of performing a floppy disk–based deployment.

The remainder of the wizard gives you the opportunity to provide an installation title used by the setup program and the Start menu location of the application. These options do not affect functionality but are helpful to the user when installing and running your application. In addition, you can specify the location and properties of the files to be installed. The wizard provides a list of the files and gives you the option of choosing its install location, as shown in Table 10.3.

Table 10.3 *Installation Locations*

Location	Description
$(AppPath)	The application installation folder as chosen by the user during the setup program.
$(WinSysPath)	The \Windows\System folder in Win9x or the \Winnt\System32 folder in Windows NT.
$(WinPath)	The \Windows folder in Win9x or the \Winnt folder in Windows NT.
$(CommonFiles)	The Common files folder \Program Files\Common Files.
$(CommonFilesSys)	The Common system files folder \Program Files\Common Files\System.
$(ProgramFiles)	The \Program Files folder.
$(MSDAOPath)	The location where the Microsoft Data Access Object components are stored. Normally, you would not use this in your applications.
$(Font)	The \Windows\Fonts folder in Windows9x or the \Winnt\Fonts folder in Windows NT.

TIP

You can also use these paths as the starting point and then add to them by entering the values in the dialog box. For example, you can specify a directory tree beneath any of these directories using syntax such as `$(ProgramFiles)\MyAppDirectory\Bin`.

Finally, the wizard allows you to mark your files as shared files. Marking files as shared indicates that they may be used by other applications and should not automatically be removed when uninstalling the application. The operating system will keep a reference count for each of these DLLs and will increment it as new applications use the file and decrement it as they are uninstalled. When the reference count reaches zero, the user is prompted to remove the file completely.

As you select options in the wizard, a script that encapsulates all your choices is generated and can then be saved for later use. The package will be created in the Package folder chosen earlier and will contain the .cab files, the SETUP.EXE program, and a file named SETUP.LST. The .LST file is used by the setup program and contains the instructions regarding which files to install and where to install them. A Support folder is also created under the Package folder and includes uncompressed copies of all the files to be distributed. The two extra files in this folder that you will want to examine are the .ddf and .bat files. The .ddf file contains the instructions for rebuilding the .cab files, and the .bat file contains the command to re-create the installation package from the command line.

The Internet Setup Package

The Internet Setup Package is used to package components that will be installed through a browser. These components may be ActiveX controls, ActiveX code components, DHTML applications, or ActiveX documents.

This package does not include a traditional setup program but rather incorporates the setup information in a .cab file that is downloaded by the browser, unpacked, and installed. This process is called the *Internet Component Download* and is a feature of Internet Explorer (MSIE). Table 10.4 lists the files created by the wizard for this type of package.

Table 10.4   Internet Package Files

File Type	Description
.cab	A compressed cabinet file that contains the component(s) to be distributed (.dll or .ocx files), directions on how to install the component, and optionally the support files required.
.inf	An information file that specifies the files to be installed, their versions, and locations.
.ddf	Known as a *diamond directive file*, this file contains the directions for building the .cab file.
.htm	A sample Web page that provides instructions for download-ing the component using MSIE.

The .cab and .htm files are created in the Package folder, and the remaining files are placed in a Support folder beneath the Package.

The most important file created is the .inf file, which contains the instructions for installing the component. The .inf is structured much like an .ini file and contains sections for each file to be installed. For example, the section for an ActiveX control in the .inf file might look like the following:

```
[DataControl.ocx]
file-win32-x86=thiscab
RegisterServer=yes
clsid={D87DD03E-5C9C-11D1-A019-006008EB5F25}
DestDir=
FileVersion=1,0,0,0
```

Note that name/value pairs in this example imply that the .inf file may reference components that are not packaged in this .cab file or even components compiled for a specific platform. This allows the creation of a single .inf file that can be used to install versions of the component on different platforms and packaged in different .cab files.

The Internet Component Download

As mentioned earlier, the Internet Component Download feature allows MSIE to uncompress and install ActiveX components directly from .cab files. It also provides security mechanisms to check that the component is from a known source and that the component is safe to be used in a Web page.

To specify the component to be downloaded, the <OBJECT> tag is used in an HTML page. The sample .htm file created by the wizard will contain the appropriate tag for the component that was packaged. The <OBJECT> tag conveys three essential pieces of information to the browser: the name with which the component will be referenced (ID), the GUID of the component (CLASSID), and the location where the component may be downloaded (CODEBASE). The following is an example of an <OBJECT> tag:

```
<OBJECT ID="dcCustomerData"
CLASSID="CLSID:D87DD03E-5C9C-11D1-A019-006008EB5F25"
CODEBASE="DataControl.CAB#version=1,0,0,0">
</OBJECT>
```

When MSIE parses an <OBJECT> tag such as this, it performs the following steps:

1. Checks the Registry for the CLASSID in the tag. If the component is not registered, it refers to the CODEBASE attribute to find the location of the installation package. If MSIE does find the CLASSID, it compares the version of the component referred to in the Registry with the version in the CODEBASE to see whether it is current and proceeds with the download if it is not.
2. Downloads and uncompresses the appropriate .cab file. MSIE processes the .inf file associated with the .cab file. It then takes Registry settings, including those related to security (as I'll discuss shortly), if appropriate.
3. Checks whether all the necessary files or components are already installed as specified in the .inf file. If they are, it checks whether the files or components are current. If they are current, MSIE makes no changes to them. If they are not current, MSIE replaces them with a new copy that it downloads and extracts from the information found in the .inf file. Installs and registers the component.
4. Activates the component so that it is ready for use in the browser.

With the Internet package, you can also specify that the support files are downloaded from a site other than where the component resides. The wizard gives you the option of specifying your own URL for the file or the Microsoft site (www.activex. microsoft.com/controls) where the files are kept up-to-date.

All this information is stored in the .inf file created by the Package and Deployment Wizard. For example, by choosing the Microsoft site as the file source for the VB 6 runtime files, the .inf entry for the VB 6 runtime DLL MSVBVM60.DLL is

```
[msvbvm60.dll]
hook=msvbvm60.cab_Installer
FileVersion=6,0,81,76
```

```
[msvbvm60.cab_Installer]
file-win32-x86=http://activex.microsoft.com/controls/vb6/VBRun60.cab
run=%EXTRACT_DIR%\VBRun60.exe
```

TIP

One strategy you can employ for intranet applications is to provide a site accessible on the local network where the support and runtime files can be stored. This enables the download to be faster and more secure and gives your organization more control over the versions of these files that are installed. In addition, an Internet connection is not required. In either case, remember that these support and runtime files are downloaded only once for each client computer unless a component requires a later version.

TIP

If you specify a version of –1,–1,–1,–1 in the codebase of the <OBJECT> tag, MSIE will download the component every time, regardless of whether it is already registered on the machine. This is useful during development, when you are making frequent changes but don't always want to increment the version number.

Securing Components

Users downloading components from a Web site are naturally wary of the effects these components might have on their computers. To alleviate these concerns, you can take the following three steps:

- Use digital signatures to ensure that the code downloaded is from a trusted author and that it has not been tampered with. This process uses a technology called *Authenticode*.
- Mark the component *Safe for Scripting* to ensure that the component does not harm the user's computer when it is used in code running within the browser. Note that this does not change the functionality of the component but is a guarantee of sorts that a malevolent script using the component cannot erase or overwrite system files, insert unregulated information in the Registry, and perform similar actions that could be used to harm the machine.
- Mark the component *Safe for Initialization* to ensure that the component does not harm the user's computer when it is initialized with data by the HTML page. Like Safe for Scripting, this option is a nonbinding contract stating that any data passed into the component cannot be used to harm the user's machine.

Authenticode uses the cryptographic technique of public and private keys to create a digital signature for a piece of software. Basically, this key pair allows data to be encrypted with a private key and decrypted by the public key. As a result, the public key, as its name implies, must be widely distributed, whereas the private key is kept secret.

When a component is digitally signed, a special number called a *hash* is encrypted with the private key and inserted in the file with the component. After the component is downloaded, the browser decrypts and verifies the hash value using the public key. The browser can then be sure that the file was not tampered with during transmission.

In addition, the public key can be used to determine the identity of the author of the component. This is done by checking with the issuer of the key pair, provided with the public key—known as a *certificate authority*. The certificate authority then provides the identity of the author, using its own private key. In this way, MSIE can be certain that the component was authored by a verified source. Although this process does not fully protect a user's machine from malicious components, it does provide accountability.

Whereas digital signatures provide security for the transport and identification of components, the safety options are concerned with whether the component will be loaded by the browser. There are two ways to mark your component safe for initialization and scripting. The simplest method is to use the dialog box presented by the wizard.

By using the wizard to mark the control safe, instructions are added to the .inf file (in the AddToRegistry) section to add Registry settings to the user's computer when the control is installed. MSIE checks these settings against the security settings of the browser when the component is initialized. If the settings do not allow unsafe components to be loaded or scripted, an error message will result.

TIP

The version of the Package and Deployment Wizard that shipped with VB 6 included a bug that caused the AddToRegistry section to be omitted from the .inf file generated by the wizard. This has been fixed in Visual Studio Service Pack 3. The details and a workaround for previous versions is documented in Microsoft Knowledge Base article Q221541.

The second method for marking the component safe is to implement the IObjectSafety interface in the component (implementing interfaces is discussed in Chapter 15, "Using Object-Oriented Techniques"). This method, although more complicated, has the advantage of being encapsulated into the component and is therefore not dependent on the method used to install the component.

Dependency Files

The final type of package that can be created is not actually a package, but simply a dependency file with a .dep extension. This file lists all the runtime requirements of the project for which you are creating the package. This information is important for components you create that may be used in other projects.

> **NOTE**
>
> Dependency information is included for all components that ship with VB in either standalone .dep files or the VB6DEP.INI file.

Generally, you will want to create a dependency file for any component you create in VB that may be distributed with other applications. The wizard also includes an option for packaging the dependency information into a .cab file for deployment over the Web.

Deploying the Application

The Package and Deployment Wizard can use three methods to deploy applications after they have been packaged. Upon entering the deployment wizard by clicking the Deploy button on the main screen, you must choose one of the saved packages previously created by the packaging wizard. Packages can be deployed to a folder, a floppy disk, or a Web site.

Folder Deployment

Folder deployment simply copies the contents of the Package folder (not including the Support subfolder) to any location accessible by the computer running the wizard. This may include a local or network drive. Typically, this option is used for deploying the application to a share point on a file server. Optionally, you can deploy to a local drive and then copy the contents to a CD-ROM for duplication and distribution.

Floppy Disk Deployment

Floppy disk–based deployment is available only if you have chosen to package the application using multiple .cab files in the packaging wizard. This option gives you the choice of formatting diskettes before copying the contents.

Web-Based Deployment

Web-based deployment gives you the option of uploading the contents of the package to a URL on a Web server. This is especially convenient for components that will be used in HTML pages or IIS and DHTML applications created with VB.

Unlike the previous deployment options, this method provides dialogs that allow you to choose which files to upload to the Web server, including any files under the folder in which the project is located.

A screen in the wizard allows you to configure a Web publishing site. The site specifies the URL to upload to, the protocol to use (FTP or HTTP), and for some packages, whether to install the package on the Web server after the upload is complete. The wizard also gives you the option of saving this information so that it can be recalled the next time you want to deploy a package.

TIP

If Internet Information Server (IIS) is the Web server you want to publish to, you'll need to install the Posting Acceptor on the Web server. The Microsoft Knowledge Base articles Q192116 and Q192639 go into detail on setting up the Posting Acceptor to work with the Package and Deployment Wizard.

Summary

In this chapter, you've looked at the various options you will have to consider when compiling and distributing a project created in Visual Basic, including optimizations and the Package and Deployment Wizard. With that, you've covered all the basics of creating an application in VB.

In the next part, "Techniques Reference," you will drill down to advanced techniques for many of the topics discussed so far, beginning with forms and menus.

PART II

TECHNIQUES R

This section of the book introduces
most frequently used by the corp
implementing form-based validation
Chapter 11, to advanced ActiveX Data
Chapter 14, to building Web-based appli
this section of the book is designed to be
keep coming back to in order to refresh y
to implement a specific technique, in add
why.

Each chapter in this section is intended to
dently and for the most part can be read in an
cial attention to the notes and tips, which
places in the book to look for more informatio
cific topic.

Obviously, this is not an exhaustive list of te
focuses on those that provide the biggest bang f
when developing business applications in the corpo

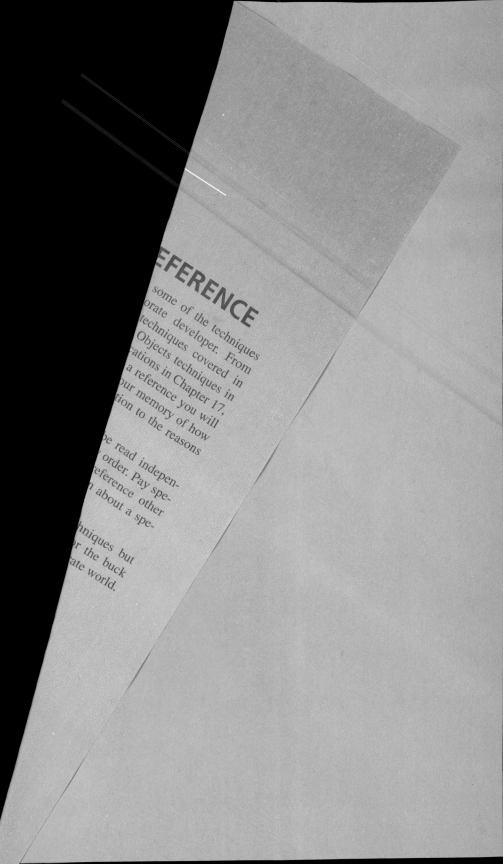

EFERENCE

some of the techniques
orate developer. From
techniques covered in
Objects techniques in
cations in Chapter 17,
a reference you will
our memory of how
tion to the reasons

be read indepen-
order. Pay spe-
reference other
n about a spe-

hniques but
or the buck
ate world.

CHAPTER 11

Using Forms and Menus

Although Visual Basic has broadened its reach by adding the capability to create UI-less components, ActiveX controls, and Web applications, it received its start as a rapid application development (RAD) tool for developing Windows applications. In this chapter, I discuss the two main elements that make up form-based applications: the Form object and the Menu object.

After general discussions of the behavior and use of these objects, I address some common techniques to manipulate these objects, including the following:

- Handling data validation
- Implementing a Most Recently Used list
- Using context menus
- Placing images on menus

Using the Form Object

Most VB projects contain more than one form. Consequently, developers spend much of their time writing code that manipulates the forms to deal with issues of navigation, communication, sizing, validation, and placement. Because this is the case, VB developers have to be intimately familiar with the way a Form object works.

In actuality, each Form object is a specialized class module that contains a user interface and exposes the standard methods, properties, and events shown in Table 11.1.

As a result, VB developers can deal with forms as if they were class modules by creating public procedures to expose methods and property procedures to expose properties, as well as using the Event statement to declare and raise events using RaiseEvent. One example of using this knowledge to fully encapsulate a form can be found in Chapter 15, "Using Object-Oriented Techniques."

Table 11.1   Key Properties, Methods, and Events of the Form Object (Note That the Members Are Presented in This Order)

Member	Description
Properties	
ActiveControl	Control. Property that returns the control that currently has focus. Controls may have focus even if the form is inactive or hidden.
Appearance	Property that specifies how controls on the form should be painted (0=Flat, 1=3D. 3D is the default).
AutoRedraw	Boolean. Property that specifies whether the form is automatically repainted. If set to False, Paint events occur on the form, and code is required to redraw elements of the form created, using the graphic methods (Circle, Cls, Line, Point, Print, and Pset).
BackColor ForeColor	Properties that specify colors for the form. Can be set using the RGB function or the system color constants (ColorConstants).
BorderStyle	Property that at design time specifies the style of the form. Can be set to 0=vbBSNone, 1=vbFixedSingle, 2=vbSizable, 3=vbFixedDouble, 4=vbFixedToolWindow, and 5=vbSizeableToolWindow.
Caption	String. Property that specifies the text displayed in the caption of the form.
ClipControls	Property that determines whether graphics methods in Paint events will repaint the entire form or only the newly exposed area and whether a clipping region is created by Windows. Normally, this should be set to False.
ControlBox MaxButton MinButton	Boolean. Properties that at design time determine whether the form will contain the control box, maximize, and minimize buttons. Can be used only on forms with their BorderStyle set to vbFixedSingle, vbSizable, or vbFixedDouble.

Member	Description
Properties	
Controls	Property that returns a collection of `Control` objects on the form. Useful for validation and checking the contents of controls.
CurrentX CurrentY	`Long`. Specifies the coordinates for the graphic method of the form. Units are determined by the `ScaleMode` property.
DrawWidth	`Long`. Specifies the width of lines drawn using the graphics methods in pixels, with the default being 1 pixel.
DrawStyle	`Long`. Specifies the style of the lines drawn using the graphics methods. If `DrawWidth` is greater than 1, this property is ignored. Valid settings are 0=`vbSolid`, 1=`vbDash`, 2=`vbDot`, 3=`vbDashDot`, 4=`vbDashDotDot`, 5=`vbInvisible`, and 6=`vbInsideSolid`.
DrawMode	Property that specifies the appearance of output from graphics methods. There are 16 options (`DrawModeConstants`) ranging from black to white, with 13=`vbCopyPen` as the default.
FillColor	`Long`. Specifies the `RGB` color value or VB constant to use when filling in shapes created with the graphics methods.
FillStyle	`Long`. Specifies the pattern used to fill in shapes created with the graphic methods. Most common settings are 0 = `vbFSSolid` and 1 = `vbFSTransparent`.
Font FontSize FontBold FontItalic FontStrikeThru FontUnderline FontName	Properties that set and change the properties of the current font that will be used to display text drawn on the form. Also used as the default for controls placed on the form.
FontTransparent	`Boolean`. Specifies whether text or graphics display behind text placed on the form using the graphics methods.
HasDC	`Boolean`. Specifies whether a unique display context is allocated to the form. If this property is set to `False`, you should not pass the `hDC` property to API calls.

continues

Table 11.1   continued

Member	Description
Properties	
hDC	Long. Returns a handle to the device context used by the operating system. Can be used in API calls to manipulate the image on the form.
Height	Long. Properties that specify the size of
Width	the form in twips, including the title bar and borders. These properties change as the user resizes the form.
HWnd	Long. Property that returns the window handle assigned to the form. Useful for working with the Windows API.
Icon	Property that specifies the icon display when the form is minimized. Can be set using LoadPicture or typically at design time.
Image	Long. Property that returns a handle to the image created by Windows when the form's AutoRedraw property is set to True. Can be used in Windows API calls.
KeyPreview	Boolean. When set to True, determines whether keystrokes are first handled by the form before being sent to the control that has focus. Useful for validation.
Left	Properties that specify the location of the form
Top	in twips. These properties change as the user moves the form.
LinkMode	Properties that specify the type of link used in a
LinkTopic	DDE conversation and the information necessary to set up the link, respectively. The mode may be 0=vbLinkNone or 1=vbLinkSource.
MDIChild	Boolean. Property that, when set at design time, determines whether the form will act as a child form inside an MDI parent.
MouseIcon	Property that specifies the icon to be displayed. Can be set using LoadPicture. Does not work with animated cursor files.
MousePointer	Property that specifies the type of built- in icon to be displayed. Of 15 built-in values, 0=vbDefault and 13=vbHourGlass are the most prevalent. A setting of 99 allows the custom icon specified in MouseIcon to be displayed.

Member	Description
Properties	
Moveable	Boolean. Specifies whether the form can be moved.
NegotiateMenus	Boolean. Specifies at design time whether the menus for the form will share space with menus of an activated OLE object. When set to True, individual menus can be manipulated using their NegotiatePosition property.
OLEDropMode	Property that specifies whether the form accepts dropped OLE objects (0=vbOLEDropNone) and whether the OLE drag-and-drop events occur (1=vbOLEDropManual, 2=vbOLEDropAutomatic). When set to automatic, the events do not occur.
PaletteMode	Specifies which, if any, palette is to be used on the form. Choices include the default HalfTone palette (0=vbPaletteModeHalfToneHalftone), the topmost control in the z-order (1=vbPaletteModeUseZOrder), or a custom palette (2=vbPaletteModeCustom). If custom is chosen, the palette is determined by the image referenced in the Palette property.
Picture	Specifies a graphic to be displayed on the form. Can be set using LoadPicture or the Clipboard function SetData. If specified at design time, the graphic is compiled into the application.
RightToLeft	Boolean. Returns True if the form is running on a bidirectional system, such as one that is using Arabic or Hebrew.
ScaleHeight ScaleWidth	Long. Specifies the horizontal and vertical coordinates to use for width and height when setting up a user-defined coordinate system. Changing these properties sets ScaleMode to user-defined.
ScaleLeft ScaleTop	Long. Specifies the horizontal and vertical coordinates to use for left and top when setting up a user-defined coordinate system. Changing these properties sets ScaleMode to user-defined.

continues

Table 11.1   continued

Member	Description
Properties	
ScaleMode	Long. Specifies the unit of measure to use. Most frequent settings are 0=vbUser, 1=vbTwips, 2=vbPoints, 3=vbPixels, 5=vbInches.
ShowInTaskBar	Boolean. Determines whether the form shows in the Windows 9x and NT 4 taskbar.
StartUpPosition	Property that, when set at design time, specifies the position of the Form when it is displayed (0=vbStartUpManual, 1=vbStartUpOwner, 2=vbStartUpScreen, and 3=vbStartUp WindowsDefault). Manual positions the form using the Top and Left properties, Owner centers the Form on the parent form, Screen centers it on the screen, and Default places the form in the upper-left corner of the screen.
Visible	Boolean. Specifies whether the form is visible.
WhatsThisButton	Boolean. Specifies whether the What's This help button is displayed. Will work only if the ControlBox property is True, BorderStyle is either Fixed Single or Sizable, or when BorderStyle is Fixed Dialog and the Minbutton and MaxButton properties are set to False.
WhatsThisHelp	Boolean. Determines whether context-sensitive help uses the What's This access techniques (True) or the F1 key to start Windows help. If True, the controls should specify a context ID in the WhatsThisHelpID property instead of HelpContextID.
WindowState	Property that specifies the visual state of the form (0=vbNormal, 1=vbMinimized, and 2=vbMaximized). Normal is the default.
Methods	
Circle	Graphic method that draws a circle, an ellipse, or arc, given coordinates, a radius, and color and aspect ratio.
Cls	Method that clears any graphics or text generated at runtime.

Member	Description
Methods	
Hide Show	Methods that make the form invisible (without unloading it) and visible.
Line	Graphic method that draws a line or rectangle, given the coordinates, the color, and a flag indicating whether a rectangle should be drawn and whether the rectangle is to be filled.
Move	Method that accepts arguments *left*, *top*, *width*, and *height* (in twips) and moves the form to the new location. Only *left* is required.
OLEDrag	Method that initiates an OLE drag operation on the form. The form can then be dropped on an OLE drop target.
PaintPicture	Graphic method that draws the contents of a graphic file, given the `Picture` property of a form or `PictureBox` and coordinates. Optionally supports clipping regions and bitwise operations using *width*, *height*, *coordinates*, and *opcode*.
Point	Method that, given the X and Y coordinates, returns the `RGB` value of the point on the form.
PopupMenu	Method that accepts a menu object, flags, X and Y coordinates, and the menu to bold in order to display a context menu. The flags indicate alignment of the menu and whether the left or right mouse button will cause the menus to react. Only the menu object is required.
PrintForm	Method that sends an image of the `Form` to the current printer. Graphics drawn on the form with the `AutoRedraw` property set to `True` will also print.
Pset	Graphic method that sets a single point, given the coordinates and a color.
Refresh	Method that forces a repaint of the form.
Scale	Method that resets the coordinate system, given coordinates that define the upper-left and lower-right corners of the coordinate system.
ScaleX ScaleY	Methods that convert width and height, respectively, from one `ScaleMode` to another, given a source and destination `ScaleMode`.

continues

Table 11.1   continued

Member	Description
Methods	
SetFocus	Method that causes the form to get the focus and be activated.
TextHeight TextWidth	Methods that, given a string, return the height and width of the text in the current ScaleMode.
WhatsThisMode	Method that causes the mouse pointer to change into the What's This pointer and causes the application to display help when a control is clicked.
ZOrder	Method that, when given a position, causes the form to be placed in the appropriate spot in the z-order. A setting of 0 causes the form to be brought to the front.
Events	
Activate Deactivate	Events that occur when the form gains and loses focus within the application as the user clicks on it or when its Show or SetFocus methods are called. These events occur only when the form is visible.
Click DblClick	Events that occur when the user clicks and releases a mouse button on an area of the form that does not contain controls or on a control that is disabled.
DragOver DragDrop	Events that occur as a VB object is dragged over the form and when it is dropped on the form. Both events supply arguments for the source control and X and Y coordinates. Additionally, DragOver supplies the state of the operation (0=Enter, 1=Leave, 2=Over).
GotFocus LostFocus	Events that occur as the form receives or loses the focus. These events occur only on forms that do not have controls and occur inside the Activate and Deactivate events.
Initialize Terminate	Events that occur when the form is loaded and removed from memory. Initialize occurs when a property or object of the form is referenced, using the Load function or calling its Show method. Terminate occurs when the form is set to Nothing.

Member	Description
Events	
KeyDown	Events that occur when the user presses
KeyUp	and releases a key if no controls are on the form or when the KeyPreview property is set to True. Supplies the keycode and the *shift state* of the keyboard. The shift state is a bitmask indicating whether the Shift (1=vbShiftMask), Ctrl (2=vbCtrlMask), or Alt (3=vbAltMask) keys are depressed.
KeyPress	Event that occurs when the user presses an ANSI key if no controls are on the form or when the KeyPreview property is set to True. Provides the key's ASCII value as an argument.
LinkOpen	Events that occur during the lifetime of a DDE
LinkExecute	conversation. In particular, LinkExecute
LinkError	supplies the command string and an argument
LinkClose	to cancel the command (when the form is the source in the conversation), and LinkError supplies the error code.
Load	Events that occur when the form is loaded
Unload	and unloaded. Load occurs when using the Load statement, when its Show method is called (if not previously loaded), or when a control or property of the form is referenced. Occurs after the Initialize event. Unload is fired when the Unload statement is used or the form is closed by a user or the operating system.
MouseDown	Events that occur when the user moves or
MouseUp	clicks and releases a mouse button while
MouseMove	on an unused area of the form. Each event supplies the mouse button, shift state, and X and Y coordinates. If the button is held, the form will receive all MouseMove events until it is released, even if the mouse moves over controls on the form.

continues

Table 11.1   continued

Member	Description
Events	
OLEDragOver OLEDragDrop	Events that occur as an OLE object is dragged over the form and when it is dropped on the form. Both events supply arguments for the data, the effects supported by the source, the state of the mouse buttons, the shift state of the keyboard, and the X and Y coordinates. Additionally, OLEDragOver supplies the state of the operation (0=vbEnter, 1=vbLeave, 2=vbOver).
OLEDragComplete	The final event that occurs in an OLE drag-and-drop operation. Supplies the *effect* argument, which indicates whether the source data is to be copied (1=vbDropEffectCopy) or moved (2=vbDropEffectMove) or whether the target cannot accept the data (0=vbDropEffectNone).
OLEGiveFeedback	Event that occurs after OLEDragOver and allows the form to adjust its display. Typical uses are to change the mouse pointer or to highlight an element of the form to provide visual feedback.
OLESetData	Event that fires when a target component attempts to get the data after the form has been dropped on the Target. Data is sent back to the target using the DataObject argument.
OLEStartDrag	Event that fires when the form's OLEDrag method is called or when OLEDragMode is set to automatic.
Paint	Event that fires when all or part of the form is exposed after being moved, being resized, or an overlapping window has been moved. Fires only when the AutoRedraw property is set to False and can be used to redraw graphics on the form.
QueryUnload	Event that fires when the form is closed by the user, when the Unload function is used, or when Windows shuts down. The event supplies a Cancel argument that can be used to stop the unloading of the form by setting it to a value other than 0. It also provides an *unloadmode* argument that indicates how the form was unloaded (0=vbFormControlMenu, 1=vbFormCode, 2=vbAppWindows, 3=vbAppTaskManager, 4=vbFormMDIForm, and 5=vbFormOwner).

Member	Description
Events	
Resize	Event that fires when the form is first displayed or when its size changes. Supplies the new height and width values as arguments.

In addition, all loaded form instances in a VB application are included in a global Forms collection available at runtime. Using this collection, you can write code to traverse the loaded forms in order to determine whether a particular form is loaded. For example, to unload all the loaded forms except the frmCompany form, you could write

```
Dim objForm As Form

For Each objForm In Forms
    If Not TypeOf objForm Is frmCompany Then
        ' Unload the form
        Unload objForm
    End If
Next objForm
```

You will notice that all form instances can be referenced using either the generic Form object or the actual reference variable (in this case, frmCompany). This characteristic allows you to write code that is reusable by creating procedures that accept arguments declared as Form instead of their actual classname. If your code must call one of the user-defined procedures or properties of the form, you can use the runtime-type inspection provided by the TypeOf statement to cast a variable of the actual type and subsequently call the method.

As an example, consider an application that displays multiple accounts in separate windows and may additionally display other windows containing different information. The Forms collection can be used to call the user-defined Print method on each loaded instance, like this:

```
Dim objForm As Form
Dim objfrmAccount As frmAccount

For Each objForm In Forms
    If TypeOf objForm Is frmAccount Then
        ' Print the account
        Set objfrmAccount = objForm
        objfrmAccount.Print
    End If
Next objForm
```

This also implies that multiple forms can be created using the same `Form` object. Not surprisingly, in this way, forms behave the same as class modules. To create an instance of `frmAccount`, you can simply use the `New` keyword.

```
Dim objfrmAccount as frmAccount

Set objfrmAccount = New frmAccount
objfrmAccount.Show
```

Keep in mind that if you create a form using its classname, in this case `frmAccount`, you are restricted to creating one instance of the form at runtime. Additionally, the ability to create multiple instances of a form at runtime leads to a problem if the form uses its classname in its code. For example, in the `Paint` method of `frmChart`, if a line is drawn as follows:

```
Private Sub Form_Paint()
    frmChart.Line (500, 500)-(1000, 2000)
End Sub
```

the code will cause a trappable error if the form is not created using the global reference variable `frmChart`. To alleviate this, you can use the intrinsic `Me` keyword inside a form to refer to itself. In this case, replace `frmChart.Line` with `Me.Line`.

WARNING

Be careful about the scope with which you declare variables used to create forms. If the variable goes out of scope before the form is closed, the form will remain open, but the variable your code was using to reference it will be unavailable.

Form Lifetime

In Visual Basic, forms go through several states during their lifetimes, as depicted in Figure 11.1. The key point is that forms can be initialized but not actually loaded. The difference being that when a form is initialized, its `Initialize` event fires, and all its user-defined members and form-level variables are available, but none of its standard members or controls are accessible. Forms can be initialized by simply using the `New` keyword or referencing a user-defined member.

When initialized, the form can be loaded by using the `Load` statement or referencing a standard member or control. When moved into this state, the form's `Load` event fires, and the form is fully functional, although it might be invisible. In the final stage, the form is made visible to the user using the `Show` method, and the `Activate` event is fired. Additionally, the `GotFocus` event may fire if no controls on the form automatically receive the focus.

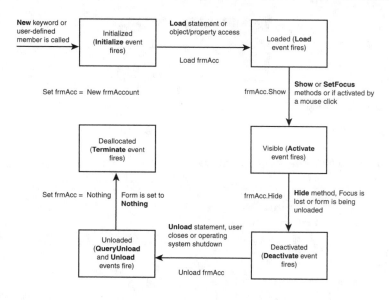

Figure 11.1

The key events in the lifetime of a Form object.

On the flip side, a form is unloaded using the Unload statement, which causes the QueryUnload and Unload events of the form to fire in succession. At this point, the form is unloaded, but its user-defined members and form-level variables are still available. Only by setting the form to Nothing does the Terminate event fire, and all data for the form instance is recovered.

VB developers can use this information to their advantage to make sure that forms are completely deallocated when memory constraints are tight or when data for the form should be completely destroyed. Conversely, techniques can be developed so that forms restore their user interface in the Load event using data stored in internal properties.

Listing 11.1 gives an example of the latter technique. A Find dialog, shown in Figure 11.2, has been implemented that retains the search strings typed in by the user throughout the run of the application. Because the user has the ability to unload the form by clicking the close button in the title bar, the form can save its state only by storing it in a form-level variable. In this case, the string array mSearchArray is used to store the search strings. The key element of this code is the For Next loop in the Load event of the form, which restores the array into the cbSearch ComboBox.

Figure 11.2

A Find dialog that reloads previous search strings when it is loaded.

Listing 11.1   The Code for the Find Dialog

```
Option Explicit

' private data used to store string searched on
Private mSearchArray() As String

Private Sub cmFind_Click()

    ' Code goes here to perform the search


    ' Add to the array of search strings
    AddString cbSearch.Text

End Sub

Private Sub Form_Load()
Dim i As Integer

On Error Resume Next

    ' Restore the state of the form by populating
    ' the combo box control
    For i = 0 To UBound(mSearchArray)
        cbSearch.AddItem mSearchArray(i)
    Next

End Sub

Private Sub AddString(ByVal pText As String)
Dim i As Integer

On Error GoTo RedimErr

    ' Add another element to the array
    ReDim Preserve mSearchArray(UBound(mSearchArray) + 1)
    mSearchArray(UBound(mSearchArray)) = pText
```

```
On Error Resume Next

    ' Check whether the text value is already
    ' in the combo box
    For i = 0 To cbSearch.ListCount
        If cbSearch.List(i) = pText Then
            Exit Sub
        End If
    Next

    ' If not already in, add it
    cbSearch.AddItem pText

Exit Sub
RedimErr:
    ' Dimension the array and try again
    ReDim mSearchArray(0)
    Resume

End Sub
```

MDI Versus SDI Applications

Visual Basic provides two types of forms. The second type is known as an MDIForm object and is used to create multiple-document interface–style (MDI) applications. Basically, the MDIForm object acts as the container for one or more (typically more) *child* forms (a regular form with its MDIChild property set to True). This style provides a simple way for the application to manage multiple open windows within a centralized framework. Child windows inside the container can be arranged and iconized within the container. Typically, MDI applications provide a menu named Window that displays a list of all the open child windows (VB menus provide a special property for this purpose).

The MDIForm object contains only a subset of the members of the Form object because controls cannot be placed on the container. However, it also contains several extra members, shown in Table 11.2, used to manage its child forms.

Table 11.2   Additional Properties and Method of the MDIForm Object

Member	Description
ActiveForm	Form. Property that returns a reference to the child form that currently has focus. Useful when code in a toolbar has to determine which form has focus.
AutoShowChildren	Boolean. Property that determines whether child forms are automatically displayed as soon as their Load event fires (even if the Show method has not been called).
Arrange	Method that arranges the child forms or icons (0=vbCascade, 1=vbTileHorizontal, 2=vbTileVertical, and 3=vbArrangeIcons).

Each VB project can contain only one `MDIForm` object, and any form with its `MDIChild` property set to `True` will always load within that container. When creating MDI applications, the ability to create multiple instances of a single form class, as discussed previously, comes in particularly handy. Overall, MDI applications are recommended for applications that fit naturally into a document-centric model. For example, a word processor such as Microsoft Word or spreadsheet application such as Microsoft Excel naturally work with multiple documents.

Many business applications, however, don't fit into the MDI model very well and, instead, opt for the single-document interface (SDI). SDI applications contain a single main window where users perform the majority of their work, with other windows being spawned as data is manipulated on the main window. For example, Outlook 98 is an SDI application that creates a separate window for each mail message displayed. Its main window contains an Explorer-style interface that uses a tree control to display folders on the left and a tabular view on the right. This style of application has become increasingly popular because of its direct interface and is used in the sample applications in this book. The danger of an SDI application comes when the user is allowed to open many windows and might have difficulty finding the appropriate one.

Choosing an appropriate interface style is not incidental to creating a successful VB application. Forethought about how a user will navigate through the application is essential to creating one that is both easy to use and efficient.

Handling Data Validation

Arguably, the primary activity of forms in VB applications is to collect and validate data entered by the user. To this end, you can employ several techniques to ensure that the data entered is correct and that the form provides sufficient visual cues to the user. To demonstrate these techniques, consider the form shown in Figure 11.3. In this example, the user is entering data for members of the 500 Homerun Club. Listing 11.2 presents the code for the form. Following this is a discussion of the techniques the form employs to validate the data.

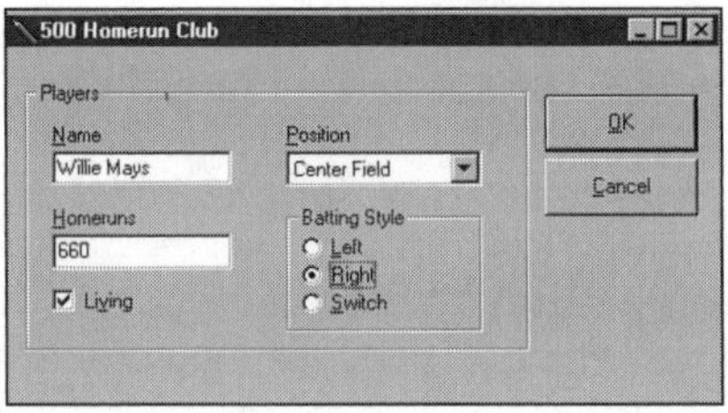

Figure 11.3

A data entry form that enforces required data, validates data, and prompts to save when closed.

Listing 11.2   The Code for the frmHomer Form

```
Option Explicit
' Flag that determines whether the form needs saving
Private mflIsDirty As Boolean

Private Sub cbPos_Change()
    mflIsDirty = True
End Sub

Private Sub Check1_Click()
    mflIsDirty = True
End Sub

Private Sub optBatting_Click(Index As Integer)
    mflIsDirty = True
End Sub

Private Sub cmdCancel_Click()
    Unload Me
End Sub

Private Sub cmdOK_Click()

    ' Save the data and unload the form
    If SaveData Then
        Unload Me
    End If

End Sub

Private Sub Form_KeyPress(KeyAscii As Integer)

Dim objControl As Control

    ' Set the dirty flag
    mflIsDirty = True

    ' Loop through all the controls and make sure
    ' that all required controls have text in them
    For Each objControl In Controls
        If objControl.Tag = "R" Then
            If Len(objControl.Text) = 0 Then
                cmdOK.Enabled = False
                Exit Sub
            End If
        End If
    Next
```

continues

Listing 11.2   continued

```
    ' Enable the ok button if required controls
    ' are filled
    cmdOK.Enabled = True

End Sub


Private Sub Form_Load()

' Populate the position drop-down
With cbPos
    .AddItem "First Base"
    .AddItem "Second Base"
    .AddItem "Third Base"
    .AddItem "Shortstop"
    .AddItem "Catcher"
    .AddItem "Right Field"
    .AddItem "Left Field"
    .AddItem "Center Field"
    .AddItem "Designated Hitter"
End With

cbPos.ListIndex = 1

End Sub

Private Sub Form_QueryUnload(Cancel As Integer, UnloadMode As Integer)
Dim intAns As Integer

If mflIsDirty And cmdOK.Enabled = True Then
    intAns = MsgBox("Do you want to save?", vbQuestion + _
        vbYesNoCancel, Me.Caption)

    Select Case intAns
    Case vbYes
        If Not SaveData Then
            Cancel = True
        End If
    Case vbNo
        ' Close without saving
    Case vbCancel
        ' Do not save or close
        Cancel = True
    End Select
End If


End Sub
```

```vb
Private Sub txtHR_GotFocus()
    ' Auto select the text in the control
    With txtHR
        .SelStart = 0
        .SelLength = Len(txtHR.Text)
    End With
End Sub

Private Sub txtHR_KeyPress(KeyAscii As Integer)
    ' Make sure that it will accept only numbers
    KeyAscii = ValidateText(KeyAscii, "0123456789", True)
End Sub

Private Sub txtHR_Validate(Cancel As Boolean)
    ' Homeruns must be greater than 500 or keep
    ' the focus on the control
    If Len(xtHR.Text) > 0 Then
        If CInt(txtHR.Text) < 500 Then
            Beep
            txtHR.ToolTipText = "Must be greater than or equal to 500"
            Cancel = True
        Else
            txtHR.ToolTipText = "Enter the number of homeruns hit"
        End If
    End If
End Sub

Private Sub txtName_GotFocus()
    ' Auto select the text in the control
    With txtName
        .SelStart = 0
        .SelLength = Len(txtName.Text)
    End With
End Sub

Private Function SaveData() As Boolean
    ' Code to save the data goes here
    SaveData = True
End Function

Private Sub txtName_KeyPress(KeyAscii As Integer)
    ' Make sure that it will accept only letters
    KeyAscii = ValidateText(KeyAscii, " abcdefghijklmnopqrstuvwxyz.", True)
End Sub
```

Enabling OK

The first technique is to ensure that the user cannot click the OK button or Save button before all the required data has been collected. This leads to forms that require less code when the data is actually saved and provides an additional visual cue to the user. Typically, this means keeping the OK button disabled until all the required controls have been populated.

A simple way to do this involves setting the KeyPreview property of the Form object to True and coding the KeyPress event to use the Controls collection to check all the required controls on the form. Note that the KeyPress event in Listing 11.2 loops through all the controls on the form, looking for Tag properties set to R, which stands for *required*. If the control is required, its Text property is inspected. If no value exists (Len function returns zero), the procedure disables the OK button and exits. If all required controls have values, the OK button is enabled.

WARNING

The code in Listing 11.2 assumes that all required controls will also have a Text property. If that were not the case, the code would have to use the TypeOf statement to determine the control class, cast objControl to a more specific variable, and check the appropriate property.

Restricting Data Entry

The second validation technique is to not allow users to type invalid characters in controls. This technique circumvents later errors by assisting the user in entering correct data the first time. Although you can use controls such as the Masked Edit control for special circumstances, it is often more convenient and flexible and requires less overhead to use the TextBox control. In this case, the txtName TextBox control should contain only letters and a period, and the txtHR TextBox control should contain only numbers.

TIP

Of course, to restrict data entry, another technique you should use (but it is often forgotten) is to set the MaxLength property of controls that support it. This is a good way to avoid truncation errors on string values and overflow errors on numeric values.

The KeyPress event can again be used to filter out the keystrokes not allowed by the controls. To reuse the code required to do the check, a public function can be created in a code module. The code in Listing 11.3 shows the function ValidateText, which takes the ASCII value of the pressed key, the allowable characters in the control, and a flag indicating whether the control is editable. The function simply uses the InStr function to determine whether the keystroke is allowed in the control. If not, the return value of the function is set to 0, which will suppress the keystroke when set to the KeyAscii argument of the KeyPress event. If the keystroke is allowed, the function returns it.

TIP

Although included in this example in the form module, the ValidateText function is one that could be placed in a code module and reused not only across forms but also across projects.

Note that the KeyPress events of both txtName and txtHR in Listing 11.2 use the function and pass in different allowable strings. See Listing 11.3.

Listing 11.3   The ValidateText Public Function Used Across Forms to Validate Keystrokes

```
Function ValidateText(ByVal pKeyIn As Integer, _
    ByVal pValidateString As String, _
    ByVal pEditable As Boolean) As Integer

Dim strValidateList As String
Dim intKeyOut As Integer

    ' If editable, include the backspace character
    ' Forces to uppercase so that case doesn't matter
    If pEditable = True Then
        strValidateList = UCase(pValidateString) & Chr(8)
    Else
        strValidateList = UCase(pValidateString)
    End If

    ' Check whether the key passed in is in the
    ' validation string
    If InStr(1, strValidateList, UCase(Chr(pKeyIn)), 1) > 0 Then
        ' If so, let it go through
        intKeyOut = pKeyIn
    Else
        ' If not, set to 0 to suppress
        intKeyOut = 0
        Beep
    End If

    ValidateText = intKeyOut

End Function
```

Validating Values

In addition to the techniques already discussed, Listing 11.2 also illustrates how to validate values. Even though keystrokes can be restricted, as shown previously, not all representations of the data can be validated in this fashion. For example, the txtHR TextBox control is restricted to only numbers. However, it must also be restricted to values that are 500 or above.

To perform this more sophisticated validation, VB developers have often attempted to use the LostFocus event to check the value and then act accordingly. For example, to validate the txtHR TextBox control, you might try code such as this in the LostFocus event:

```
If Cint(txtHR.Text) < 500 Then
    ' Display a message
    txtHR.SetFocus
End If
```

Unfortunately, code like this quickly leads to serious problems. Because the LostFocus event doesn't occur until the next control has already received focus, setting the focus back to txtHR using SetFocus causes the LostFocus event of the other control to fire. If that control contains similar validation code, the same sequence of events happens in reverse. This results in two controls essentially fighting over focus until a stack overflow error occurs. Although you can avoid this by creating a form-level variable that indicates when validation is in progress, the resulting code is not straightforward.

To avoid this scenario, Visual Basic 6 has introduced the CausesValidation property and the Validate event. This combination enables you to write code in the Validate event for a control that will be fired only if the CausesValidation property of the control about to receive focus is set to True. The Validate event also supplies a Cancel argument that, when set to True, will keep the focus on the control. The nice aspect of the CausesValidation property is that you can set it to False for controls that should not trigger Validate events, such as the Cancel button or a button that provides help. In Listing 11.2, the Validate event of txtHR ensures that the value is more than 500 and, if not, keeps the focus on the control and sets the ToolTipText property to an error message the user can view by hovering over the control.

TIP

In versions before Visual Basic 6, the best way to perform validation like this is to wait until the form is completed and do a form-level validation check before saving the data.

Using QueryUnload

The final technique often used with data entry forms is coding the QueryUnload event. This event fires before the form unloads and allows you to prompt the user if unsaved changes have been made. The Cancel argument, when set to True, keeps the form from being unloaded.

The technique used in Listing 11.2 uses a form-level private variable, mflIsDirty, to determine whether changes have been made to the form. This variable is then set to False in the Change events of various controls, in addition to the KeyPress event of the form. If the form requires saving and the cmdOK button is enabled (signifying that all required controls are filled in), a message box is displayed to the user, asking him how he wants to proceed. Convention dictates that answering Yes saves the data and closes the form, No closes the form without saving, and Cancel keeps the form open but does not save the data.

Using the Menu Object

When you are building the user interface of a VB application, perhaps the second most important object is the Menu object. In this section, I'll go over the basics and then present three frequently used techniques, including creating a Most Recently Used list, using context menus, and placing images on menus.

In VB, menus are created and associated with each Form object and are displayed beneath the title bar for the form. The exception to this rule is when a child form contains a menu and has focus inside an MDIForm. In this case, the child's menu displays in the MDIForm. Each top-level menu and submenu defined in a menu is represented as a Menu object and contains the properties and events shown in Table 11.3. The menu designer allows you to create menus that cascade up to four levels.

TIP

Especially when creating an MDI application, you will find that the creation of menus can become tedious because each Form requires its own menu, which is substantially like the others. If you're careful, you can create the menu one time and manually edit the .frm files to paste the menu definitions in subsequent forms.

You can discover the syntax for creating a menu by simply creating a menu on a form and viewing the .frm file in Notepad. A couple of points to remember are that the menu syntax must appear at the beginning of the file after the references to components and before the definition of the forms. Be sure to back up your original; a mistake will prevent VB from loading the form.

TIP

To create separator bars in the menu, use a hyphen. You must also assign a name, but because it won't be referenced by your code, you can use names such as mnuSep1, mnuSep2, and so on.

Table 11.3   Key Properties and Event of the Menu Object

Member	Description
Properties	
Caption	String. Property that specifies the text to be displayed in the menu. Using an ampersand (&) before a character in the caption causes an access key to be defined (an underlined key that will activate the menu by holding down Alt and pressing the key or simply pressing the key if the menu is open).
Checked	Boolean. Property that determines whether a check mark is displayed next to the menu caption.
Enabled	Boolean. Property that determines whether the menu can be selected by the user. If the menu has submenus, they will not be available when set to False.
Index	Integer. Specifies the Menu object when it is included in a menu array. Menu arrays allow multiple menus to share event procedures.
NegotiatePosition	Property that determines how a top-level menu is displayed if an OLE object is activated using in-place editing (0=Not displayed, 1=Left, 2=Middle, 3=Right).
Parent	Form. Returns a reference to the Form object on which the menu is sitting. Must be used when referencing a Form object created using the New keyword and a reference variable.
Shortcut	Property that at design time specifies the shortcut key(s) to activate the menu. When the form has focus, you can specify shortcut keys to immediately execute the menu. Typically, Ctrl+Alt key combinations are used, although functions keys may also be specified.
Visible	Boolean. Property that specifies whether the menu can be seen. If set to False, all submenus are also invisible.
WindowList	Boolean. Property used at design time to allow the menu to display all open child windows within an MDIForm. Used only on menus associated with child forms or on an MDIForm. Only one menu object on a form can have this property set to True.

Member	Description
Event	
Click	Event that fires when the user selects the menu by clicking on it, using shortcut or access keys, or pressing Enter.

Implementing a Most Recently Used List

One of the most common techniques used with menus is to create a Most Recently Used list. Typically, this takes the form of a list of files most recently opened by the user, although it could also be a list of accounts, queries, or any other application-specific information.

Implementing the list relies on the capability of menus to support menu arrays. To use menu arrays, you must define a Menu object using the menu editor and set its Index property to 0 at design time. At runtime, you can then use the Load statement to load new instances of the menu, which will appear below the first instance. When created, the Menu objects in the array can be accessed, using their Index property to set any properties or to respond to the Click event. Although a menu array can exist anywhere within the menu system, all its elements must be contiguous.

As an example, the code in Listing 11.4 shows a reusable procedure, LoadRecentList, that can be included in a standard module and reused across projects. It takes as arguments a Variant array that contains the filenames recently accessed by the user, a reference to the menu array, and optionally a reference to a separator menu that might have to be made visible after the menus have been created.

TIP

A good practice is to persist the list of Most Recently Used items in the system Registry. Chapter 18, "Adding Professional Features," discusses one technique for doing so.

Listing 11.4   The LoadRecentList Procedure
```
Option Explicit
Private Const MAX_FILE_LENGTH = 35

Public Sub LoadRecentList(ByVal pFileList As Variant, _
    pRecentMenu As Variant, Optional pSep As Menu)

Dim i As Integer
Dim strShortName As String

On Error GoTo RecentErr
```

continues

Listing 11.4   continued

```
    ' Load the array into the menu
    For i = 0 To UBound(pFileList)

        ' On first item, just make it visible
        If i = 0 Then
            pRecentMenu(i).Visible = True

            ' Check whether a separator was passed in
            If Not pSep Is Nothing Then
                pSep.Visible = True
            End If
        Else
            ' Create a new menu
            Load pRecentMenu(pRecentMenu.Count)
        End If

        ' If too long, truncate it
        If Len(pFileList(i)) > MAX_FILE_LENGTH Then
            strShortName = Left(pFileList(i), 3) & "..." & _
                Right(pFileList(i), MAX_FILE_LENGTH - 10)
        Else
            strShortName = pFileList(i)
        End If

        ' Change the caption and add an access key
        pRecentMenu(i).Caption = "&" & CStr(i + 1) _
            & " " & strShortName

        ' Store the actual path in the Tag
        pRecentMenu(i).Tag = pFileList(i)
    Next

Exit Sub
RecentErr:
    ' Array may have no items in it

End Sub
```

One of the key aspects of the code in Listing 11.4 is that on the first iteration through the array, the first element of pRecentMenu is already present. Therefore, the code simply makes the first element and the separator menu visible.

NOTE

One of the quirks of using both control and menu arrays in Visual Basic 5 and earlier is that the first element of the array has to be created before others can be added (hence, the need to create the menu array and make the first element invisible). In VB 6, this limitation does not exist for control arrays where a new control can be added by using the `Controls.Add` method.

The procedure then uses the `Load` statement to create a new element in the array. Note that menu arrays are zero-based, so the `Count` property can be used to indicate the next element to be added (because the `Count` property is 1-based).

After the menu is loaded, the procedure uses a simple algorithm to determine whether the path to the file is particularly long. If so, the first 3 characters of the name and the last 25 are concatenated with an ellipsis to stop the case where a long pathname would cause the menu to dominate the screen. Finally, the procedure modifies the `Caption` property of the menu and stores the actual file name in the `Tag` property. Figure 11.4 shows the resulting menu, complete with the Most Recently Used list.

Figure 11.4

A File menu with a Most Recently Used file list.

By storing the actual data in the `Tag` property, the `Click` event procedure on the `Form` that contains the menu can be easily coded to retrieve the data. For example, the code in the form could use the path stored in the `Tag` property to open the file, using a user-defined `GetMenuFile` procedure.

```
Private Sub mnuRecent_Click(Index As Integer)
    ' Get the file that was clicked on
    GetMenuFile mnuRecent(Index).Tag
End Sub
```

Using Context Menus

With the release of the new shell in Windows 9x and Windows NT 4, one of the menu techniques that became popular was the use of context menus. *Context menus* are simply menus activated by a right mouse click on the graphical item the user wants to manipulate. In most cases, the functionality provided by the context menu should also be located elsewhere because the user has no visual cue that a context menu is available. However, adopting this convention enables the user to more quickly and easily work with the application because it is more direct.

The key to creating a context menu (also called a *pop-up menu*) is to use the PopupMenu method of the Form object in the MouseDown event of a Form or a control. The PopupMenu statement accepts a Menu object that contains submenus, flags that determine alignment (defaulted to aligning on the left side of the coordinates), X and Y coordinates (defaulted to the current cursor location), and the Menu object that is to be highlighted, signifying the *default* action (what would normally happen if you double-click the Form or control).

The following is a typical example of creating a context menu:

```
Private Sub rxtDescription_MouseDown(Button As Integer, _
    Shift As Integer, X As Single, Y As Single)
If Button = vbRightButton And Shift = 0 Then
        PopupMenu mnuTextEdit, , , , mnuOpenFile
    End If
End Sub
```

In this case, the menu is shown when the user right-clicks on a RichTextBox control that includes menus for manipulating the text and loading and saving the current file.

Placing Images on Menus

The final technique regarding menus involves replacing the caption of a Menu object with an image. This is often useful when a picture of the menu item is more descriptive than simple text. A typical case would be a vehicle tracking application for a shipping company, allowing users to view various types of vehicles by placing graphics on the menu that represent the types.

To place images on menus, you must use several Win32 API functions because VB does not expose this capability natively. (Using the Win32 API is discussed in more detail in Chapter 13, "Using Win32 API Techniques.") The code in Listing 11.5 uses the ModifyMenu API call in the function AddMenuImage to place the image on the menu.

Listing 11.5   The AddMenuImage Function to Replace the Caption of a Menu Object with an Image

```
Public Declare Function WinGetMenu Lib "user32" Alias "GetMenu" _
    (ByVal hwnd As Long) As Long

Public Declare Function WinGetSubMenu Lib "user32" _
    Alias "GetSubMenu" (ByVal hMenu As Long, ByVal nPos As Long) As Long

Public Declare Function WinModifyMenu Lib "user32" _
    Alias "ModifyMenuA" (ByVal hMenu As Long, _
    ByVal nPosition As Long, ByVal wFlags As Long, _
    ByVal wIDNewItem As Long, ByVal lpString As Any) As Long
```

```
Public Const MF_BYPOSITION = &H400&
Public Const MF_BITMAP = &H4&


Public Function AddMenuImage(pForm As Form, ByVal pMenuNum As Long, _
    ByVal pMenuItemNum As Long, ByVal pImageHandle As Long) As Boolean

Dim lngMenuID As Long
Dim lngMenuHandle As Long
Dim lngSubMenuHandle As Long
Dim lngRet As Long

AddMenuImage = False

On Error Resume Next

' Get a handle to the form's menu
lngMenuHandle = WinGetMenu(pForm.hwnd)
If lngMenuHandle = 0 Then Exit Function

' Get a handle to the top-level menu using its position
lngSubMenuHandle = WinGetSubMenu(lngMenuHandle, pMenuNum)
If lngSubMenuHandle = 0 Then Exit Function

' Place the bitmap on the menu
lngRet = WinModifyMenu(lngSubMenuHandle, pMenuItemNum, _
        MF_BITMAP Or MF_BYPOSITION, 0, pImageHandle)
If lngRet > 0 Then
    AddMenuImage = True
End If

End Function
```

You will notice that AddMenuImage takes arguments, including the Form object on which the menu is sitting, the position of the top-level Menu object that will be modified (horizontally), the position of the Menu object on the top-level menu (vertically), and the handle of the image to be used. First, the procedure uses the GetMenu API function to retrieve a handle to the form's menu. This handle and the position of the menu are then used in the call to GetSubMenu to get the handle to the top-level menu. Finally, the handle to the top-level menu and the position of the menu to be modified are used in the call to ModifyMenu to place the image.

NOTE

After you've replaced the caption of a menu with an image, if you programmatically set the Menu object's Caption property, the image will not be displayed.

As you will also notice, the Win32 API relies on the position arguments because, under the covers, the Win32 API deals with individual Menu objects using their positions. The VB menu editor hides this by graphically displaying the position and making the appropriate API calls behind the scenes. Keep in mind that in windows, the first Menu object is always at position zero.

TIP

The code in Listing 11.5 is fully encapsulated so that it can be reused across projects. Chapter 13 presents two techniques for doing this, one using standard code modules and the other using a class module.

To place the images on the menu, a simple technique is to collect them in an ImageList control. This control (part of the Windows Common Controls component) can load images in various formats and make them available for other controls and code within the application. Each image added to the control can be referenced by the ListImages collection. The resulting ListImage object exposes a Picture property. This property, in turn, exposes the window Handle property that can be passed to AddMenuImage. For example, to place images in the first four Menu objects underneath the third top-level menu, you would write the following code:

```
Dim i As Integer

For i = 0 To 3
    AddMenuImage Me, 2, i, imgTrucks.ListImages(i + 1).Picture.Handle
Next
```

Figure 11.5 shows the resulting menu.

TIP

If you want to keep the caption and provide an image to the left of it, you should investigate using the SetMenuItemBitmaps API function.

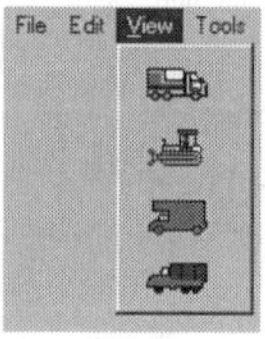

Figure 11.5

A menu populated with images of vehicle types.

Summary

Although Visual Basic has extended its reach to allow developers to use it for distributed and Web-based applications, it is still used primarily as a tool to develop Windows applications. The two fundamental components of these applications are forms and menus.

In this chapter, you examined the way in which windows (forms) are implemented in VB and how they behave. Because forms are primarily used for data entry and display, you also learned some techniques for validating data. In the discussion of menus, you looked at common techniques for creating a Most Recently Used list, using context menus, and placing images on menus.

Forms and menus can be thought of as the foundation for the application. Now that the foundation is laid, the next chapter focuses on two common controls, the TreeView and ListView, which you can use to build the user interface.

CHAPTER 12

Using TreeView and ListView Controls

One of the benefits of using Visual Basic has always been the productivity gained by using the controls that ship with the product. In fact, VB made popular the concept of component-based programming by allowing developers to focus on building their solutions without having to reinvent the wheel each time they wanted to display data to the user.

As the language has moved from 16-bit Windows to 32-bit Windows, the format of those controls has changed from .VBX files based on a proprietary interface to .OCX files based on the Component Object Model (COM). However, the way that VB programmers deal with controls hasn't changed significantly, even during this important shift in technologies. This, too, has contributed to VB's success.

This chapter focuses on two of the more advanced controls corporate developers have to work with to create modern professional-looking applications. These are the TreeView and ListView controls and, by association, the ImageList control. After presenting their basic structure and techniques for manipulating the controls, I explain methods for integrating the TreeView and ListView (because they are often used together) and for Web-enabling these controls to be used in a browser-based solution.

Using the TreeView Control

The `TreeView` control was first integrated into VB in version 5 and is primarily used to display information hierarchically in the now popular single document interface (SDI) Explorer-style applications. Along with its companion controls, `ImageList` and `ListView`, `TreeView` is a member of the Windows Common Controls component and in VB 6 is included in the MSCOMCTL.OCX file. (In version 5, it was included in COMCTL32.OCX and referenced COMCTL32.DLL.)

Although you will sometimes hear developers criticize the VB implementation of these common controls, keep in mind that these controls were designed to be easy to use while maintaining acceptable performance. To get the most out of the controls, however, you must be aware of the algorithms you use to manipulate them.

A reference to the component must be made using the Project, Components menu in your project before the control is visible in the Toolbox and an instance can be used on a form. You can see a typical example of using the `TreeView` control in Figure 12.1, which shows an application that tracks projects, consultants, and their skills for a consulting company.

TIP

> After adding a reference to the component, use the Object Browser, and select the MSComctlLib library to view the methods, properties, events, and enumerated types for all the controls included in the component.

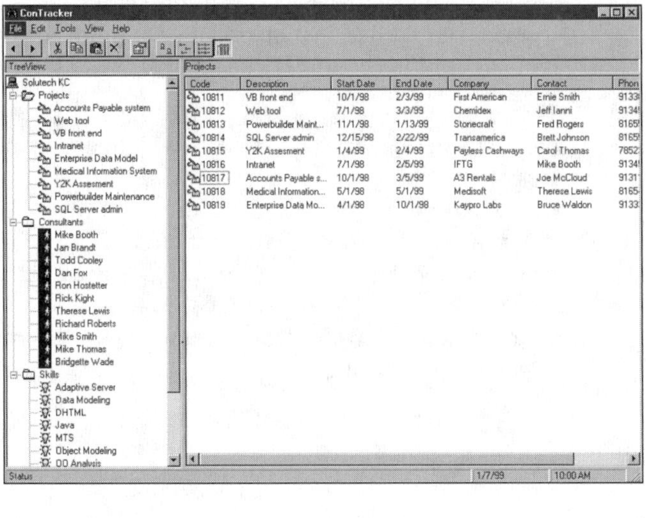

Figure 12.1

A typical example of using the TreeView and ListView controls together.

The companion `ImageList` control is used to store references to graphic files that represent the `Node` objects loaded into the control. Typically, developers store several graphics in the control and programmatically change the displayed image in response to the type of data loaded by the control or the state of the data. As you will see in the following section, the `ListView` control is also frequently used with the `TreeView` to display the tabular data associated with the `Node` currently selected by the user.

Table 12.1 lists the key methods, properties, and events of the `TreeView` control.

Table 12.1 Important Properties, Methods, and Events of the TreeView Control

Properties

Checkboxes	Boolean. Determines whether check boxes appear next to the Node. Useful for applications that require user selection of multiple items, such as a program to back up folders. New in VB 6.
DropHighlight	Node. Returns or sets a reference to the object that is highlighted when the cursor moves over it. It is used in conjunction with the HitTest method to display visual cues when performing drag-and-drop operations.
HotTracking	Boolean. Determines whether the text of the Node is highlighted when the mouse passes over the Node. New in VB 6.
ImageList	ImageList. Returns or sets a reference to the ImageList control used to store images for the TreeView.
LabelEdit	Integer. Determines whether the user can edit the label of the Node. 0=lvwAutomatic and 1=lvwManual.
Nodes	Nodes. Returns a reference to the collection of Node objects.
SelectedItem	Node. Returns a reference to the Node currently selected.
SingleSel	Boolean. Determines whether the Node is expanded or contracted when selected. New in VB 6.
Sorted	Boolean. Determines whether the Node objects are sorted by their text label.

Methods

GetVisibleCount	Returns the number of Node objects that can be seen in the visible area of the control.
HitTest	Returns a reference to the Node at the X and Y coordinates supplied as arguments to the method.
StartLabelEdit	Used to allow label editing when the LabelEdit property is set to lvwManual.

continues

Table 12.1 *continued*

Events

BeforeLabelEdit AfterLabelEdit	Fired before and after the user edits the label of the currently selected Node. Can be used to cancel the editing and inspect what the user has entered.
Collapse Expand	Fired when any Node in the control is collapsed or expanded. Returns a reference to the Node as an argument.
NodeCheck	Fired when the Checkboxes property is set to True and the check box is selected or cleared. New in VB 6.
NodeClick	Fired when a Node object is clicked (single or double). Returns a reference to the Node.

The Node Object and the Nodes Collection

Understanding the Node object and Nodes collection is the key to using the TreeView control effectively. Each item added to the control is represented as a Node object that contains its own methods and properties. The TreeView control then manages a collection of Node objects that expose methods for managing the collection (inserting, deleting, clearing, and traversing). Table 12.2 describes the most important properties and methods of both the Node object and collection.

Table 12.2 *Properties and Methods of the Node Object and Nodes Collection*

Member	Description
Properties	
Child	Node. Returns a reference to the first child of the Node object in the Nodes collection.
Children	Integer. Returns the number of children contained in the Node.
Expanded	Boolean. Determines whether the Node has been expanded.
ExpandedImage SelectedImage Image	Index. Specifies the index to the ImageList control that determines which images are loaded when the Node is expanded, selected, or unselected, respectively.
FirstSibling Next Previous LastSibling	Node. Returns a reference to the first, next, previous, or last Node on the same level as the given Node. Used to navigate through the TreeView.
FullPath	String. Returns the fully qualifiedpath to the Node using the PathSeparator property of the TreeView control.
Key	String. Property of the Node object that determines its unique identifier.

Member	Description
Properties	
Parent	Node. Returns or sets the parent Node in the hierarchy. Used to move Nodes.
Root	Node. Property of the Node object that returns a reference to the root Node of the control (the Node at the top of the hierarchy).
Selected	Boolean. Determines whether the Node is currently selected.
Text	String. Determines the text of the Node object to be displayed to the user.
Methods	
Add	Nodes collection. Used to add a Node to the Nodes collection. Takes arguments that represent the position, relationship, key, text, image, and selected image of the Node.
Clear	Nodes collection. Removes all the Nodes from the collection.
EnsureVisible	Scrolls or expands the control, as necessary, to make sure that the Node is visible.
Remove	Nodes collection. Removes the given Node from the collection.

Adding Nodes

To add Nodes to the Nodes collection of a TreeView control, you call the Add method of the Nodes collection. For example, to add the root folder and high-level folders for projects, consultants, and skills, shown in Figure 12.1, you would execute the following code:

```
Dim objNode As Node     ' Declare Node variable.

' First node with 'Root' as key.
Set objNode = tvTreeView.Nodes.Add(, , "r", "Solutech KC", "Solutech")
objNode.Expanded = True

' Load the first level
tvTreeView.Nodes.Add "r", tvwChild, "projects", "Projects", _
    "Closed", "Open"
tvTreeView.Nodes.Add "r", tvwChild, "consultants", "Consultants", _
    "Closed", "Open"
tvTreeView.Nodes.Add "r", tvwChild, "skills", "Skills", -
    "Closed", "Open"
```

The most confusing aspect of the Add method is the first three arguments. The first, relative, contains a reference to the index number or key of the Node object that will be related to the newly added Node. This relationship is determined by the second argument and can include first, last, next, previous, or child. The third argument contains the key value to associate with the new Node. The Key property is a string that must be unique within the TreeView control and is often used in code to determine which node was clicked or selected.

You can see that in this instance the root node has been assigned a Key of "r", and its relative and relationship have been left unassigned to denote that it is at the highest level. The three nodes that will contain projects, consultants, and skills all refer to the root node using its Key property of "r" and are denoted as children of that node, using the constant tvwChild. The Key properties of each of these three nodes are set to strings that can be easily remembered. The Key property is optional and may not be used when the node will not be manipulated in code.

The final three arguments set the Text, Image, and SelectedImage properties of the Node object. Note that in this example you're using the string value of the Key property of the images in the associated ImageList control. You may also use the integer value of the Index property, although assigning and using keys is recommended because they'll be easier to remember and can reflect the purpose of the image.

Deleting Nodes

Deleting a Node object from the Nodes collection is a simple operation that involves calling the Remove method of the Nodes collection and passing in the Key of the Node you want to remove.

A typical example is to create a pop-up menu that contains a Delete menu item which, when clicked, will delete the Node currently selected. A simple method to accomplish this is to create a private form-level DeleteNode procedure that takes as its argument the Node you want to delete. The procedure is called from the Delete menu, which is, in turn, called from the MouseDown event of the control using the PopupMenu statement. Listing 12.1 presents the complete code to implement this.

NOTE

The code block in Listing 12.1, beginning with Begin VB.Menu, is syntax generated by VB when a menu is placed on Form. It is reproduced here to show you the menu items placed on the Form, with their names. As mentioned in Chapter 11, "Using Forms and Menus," you can manually edit the .frm file to add the menu without using the menu editor.

Listing 12.1   Code to Implement the Deletion of a Node Object Using a Context Menu

```
Begin VB.Menu mnuContext
    Caption         =   "Context"
    Begin VB.Menu mnuInsert
       Caption         =   "Insert"
    End
    Begin VB.Menu mnuDelete
       Caption         =   "Delete"
    End
    Begin VB.Menu mnuRefresh
       Caption         =   "Refresh"
    End
    Begin VB.Menu mnuSep1
       Caption         =   "-"
    End
    Begin VB.Menu mnuProperties
       Caption         =   "Properties"
    End
End

Private Sub DeleteNode(objNode As Node)

Dim liRet

' Ask the user whether she is sure that she wants to delete
liRet = MsgBox("Are you sure you want to delete " & _
    objNode.Text & "?", vbYesNo + vbQuestion, Me.Caption)

' Delete the Node
If liRet = vbYes Then
    tvTreeView.Nodes.Remove objNode.Key
End If

End Sub

Private Sub mnuDelete_Click()

On Error Resume Next

' Call the DeleteNode private procedure passing the
' currently selected item

    DeleteNode tvTreeView.SelectedItem

End Sub
```

continues

Listing 12.1   continued

```
Private Sub tvTreeView_MouseDown(Button As Integer, Shift As Integer, _
    x As Single, y As Single)

' Check to make sure that the user clicked on the
' right mouse button and popped up the menu
If Button = vbRightButton Then
    Me.PopupMenu mnuContext, , , , mnuProperties
End If

End Sub
```

Populating from a Database

Because the majority of the applications that use the TreeView control display and manipulate data from relational databases, it is important to discuss the techniques used when dealing with databases.

When you are using a TreeView control with a database, the fundamental issues are abstraction, performance, and freshness of the data. *Abstraction* refers to making sure that the code used to manipulate the TreeView control is separated from the database access code. This ensures that the code will be more maintainable and easier to debug. *Performance* must be addressed because your control could potentially access hundreds or thousands of records from the database and this should be done in an efficient manner. *Freshness* of the data is an issue because you must make sure that the user is not left viewing stale data. These issues are not mutually exclusive, and sometimes you must choose between them when designing your application. The following discussion expresses my recommendations for using the TreeView control in an enterprise application.

Abstraction

The realization of the necessity to abstract the user interface code from code that implements business logic and data access is one of the most important shifts in the development model used by corporate developers in large applications over the past several years. Microsoft has made this shift easier by introducing products such as Microsoft Transaction Server (MTS) and enabling VB to produce COM components to support this abstraction.

NOTE

See Chapter 16, "Building ActiveX Components," for a more in-depth discussion of MTS and how it can be used from within VB.

In large applications, it is recommended that you create classes to encapsulate the business logic and data access (see Chapter 15, "Using Object-Oriented Techniques," for one technique). These classes can then be compiled within the application or as COM components and deployed using MTS. The location transparency provided by COM allows your client code to be written identically in either case.

For example, in the case of the consulting application (shown in Figure 12.1) that displays information about consultants, you would create a private form-level procedure named LoadConsultants. This procedure instantiates a business object implemented as a class module or compiled and referenced as a DLL named clsConsultants and invokes the method GetConsultants. This method in turn communicates with the database server to return an ADO Recordset object. The recordset is then loaded into the TreeView control using the techniques discussed previously. Listing 12.2 shows the code for LoadConsultants.

TIP

You will find the ADO techniques used to query information from data sources in Chapter 14, "Using ADO for Data Access." Listing 14.1 gives the particular example of the GetConsultants method.

Listing 12.2   The LoadConsultants Procedure Calls the Business Object to Populate the TreeView Control

```
Private Sub LoadConsultants()

Dim rsResults As Recordset
Dim objCon As Consultants
Dim objNode As Node

' Create the instance of the business object and invoke the method
Set objCon = New clsConsultants
Set rsResults = objCon.GetConsultants

   ' Get a reference to the parent node
   Set objNode = tvTreeView.Nodes("consultants")

   ' Delete the child nodes if they exist already
   Do While objNode.Children > 0
       tvTreeView.Nodes.Remove objNode.Child.Index
   Loop

   Do While Not rsResults.EOF
       ' Load the tree
       tvTreeView.Nodes.Add "consultants", tvwChild, "C" & _
           rsResults("ID"), rsResults("FName") & " " & _
           rsResults("LName"), "User"
```

continues

Listing 12.2   continued

```
        rsResults.MoveNext
    Loop

Set rsResults = Nothing
Set objCon = Nothing

' Indicate that the node has been loaded
objNode.Tag = "Loaded"

End Sub
```

The interesting aspect of the code in Listing 12.2 is the creation of the Key property for each Node added to the collection. Because the Key must be a string, you cannot simply assign the primary key of the database row to the property because this is normally a numeric value. In addition, the Key must be unique throughout the control. To address these concerns, the code in LoadConsultants creates the Key by appending the ID field of the table (the primary key) to the letter *C* to denote that the Node refers to a consultant. In this way, your code can not only determine which type of Node object was clicked but also retrieve the primary key if other database operations are required.

Performance

To address performance, you should keep in mind that users of the application will not necessarily traverse each Node in the control and expand its contents. Therefore, because every trip to the database requires a network roundtrip and resources on the database server (whether the call is made through a business object or directly), you should populate the lower levels of the TreeView only when the user clicks on them. In the example cited previously, you would call the LoadConsultants procedure from the Expand event when the user first clicks on the Consultants node, rather than when the form is loaded. The Tag property of the Node object can be used to determine whether the Node has been previously loaded.

```
Private Sub tvTreeView_Expand(ByVal Node As MSComctlLib.Node)

' Check whether the Node has already been loaded
If Node.Tag <> "Loaded" Then
    Select Case Node.Key
        Case "projects"
            LoadProjects
        Case "consultants"
            LoadConsultants
        Case "skills"
            LoadSkills
    End Select
End If

End Sub
```

Unfortunately, if you simply use this code, the load procedures will never be invoked, and the `TreeView` control will remain empty. This happens because the `Expand` event fires only when the current `Node` has children; in this case, none of the nodes have children yet. To work around this, you can use the technique of adding ghost nodes under the Consultants, Projects, and Skills nodes. In this way, the control will both display the visual cue indicating that children are present and fire the `Expand` event when it is clicked. The ghost nodes can be added when the control is initialized, as follows.

```
tvTreeView.Nodes.Add "projects", tvwChild
tvTreeView.Nodes.Add "consultants", tvwChild
tvTreeView.Nodes.Add "skills", tvwChild
```

Remember that these ghost nodes will then have to be cleaned up when the control is actually loaded, as in Listing 12.2.

Freshness

To address freshness, you can provide a Refresh context menu that the user can select to reload the contents of a `Node` object and all its children. The code takes advantage of the `Tag` property discussed previously, by setting it back to an empty string before firing the `Expand` event.

```
Private Sub mnuRefresh_Click()

' Reset the Tag on the currently selected node and refresh it
tvTreeView.SelectedItem.Tag = ""
tvTreeView_Expand tvTreeView.SelectedItem

End Sub
```

Implementing Drag and Drop

Implementing drag and drop inside a `TreeView` control, although not difficult, is a task that requires a little code and therefore is usually not easy to remember. The example in Listing 12.3 shows a technique for implementing drag and drop between two nodes in the `tvTreeView` control populated in the previous examples. For this application, a skill can be dropped onto a consultant, with the result that a business object is called to assign the skill to the consultant.

Listing 12.3   Implementing Drag and Drop Between Nodes in the Same TreeView Control
```
' Flag that signals a Drag Drop operation
Dim flDragging As Boolean
' Node that is being dragged
Dim nodX As Node

Private Sub tvTreeView_DragDrop(Source As Control, _
    x As Single, y As Single)
```

continues

Listing 12.3   continued

```
Dim objSkills As Skills

' If no Node is highlighted, get out
If tvTreeView.DropHighlight Is Nothing Then
        flDragging = False
        Exit Sub
Else
        ' If dropping on itself, get out
        If nodX = tvTreeView.DropHighlight Then Exit Sub

        ' Check to make sure that we're dragging a skill and
        ' dropping on a consultant
        If Mid(nodX.Key, 1, 1) = "S" And _
            Mid(tvTreeView.DropHighlight.Key, 1, 1) = "C" Then
            ' Assign a skill to a consultant
            ' using the business object clsSkills
            Set objSkills = New clsSkills
            If objSkills.Assign(Mid(tvTreeView.DropHighlight.Key, 2), _
                                Mid(nodX.Key, 2)) Then
                sbStatusBar.Panels(1).Text = "Skill assigned to consultant"
            End If
        End If

        Set tvTreeView.DropHighlight = Nothing
        flDragging = False
End If

End Sub

Private Sub tvTreeView_DragOver(Source As Control, x As Single, _
                                y As Single, State As Integer)

Dim objNode As Node

If flDragging = True Then
        ' Set DropHighlight to the mouse's coordinates only
        ' if the node is a consultant
        Set objNode = tvTreeView.HitTest(x, y)
        If Not objNode Is Nothing Then
            If Mid(objNode.Key, 1, 1) = "C" Then
                Set tvTreeView.DropHighlight = objNode
            End If
        End If
End If

End Sub

Private Sub tvTreeView_MouseDown(Button As Integer, Shift As Integer, _
                                x As Single, y As Single)
```

```
     ' Set the item being dragged
     Set nodX = tvTreeView.SelectedItem

End Sub

Private Sub tvTreeView_MouseMove(Button As Integer, Shift As Integer, _
                                 x As Single, y As Single)

Dim objNode As Node

' Signal a Drag operation.
If Button = vbLeftButton Then

        ' Only allow dragging if it is a skill
        Set objNode = tvTreeView.HitTest(x, y)
        If Not objNode Is Nothing Then
           If Mid(objNode.Key, 1, 1) = "S" Then
              flDragging = True ' Set the flag to true
              tvTreeView.Drag vbBeginDrag ' Drag operation
           End If
        End If
End If

End Sub
```

The key to the technique presented here is the DropHighlight property and the HitTest method. The DropHighlight property is used to hold a reference to, and visually highlight, the Node object that will receive the drop. It can be populated by the HitTest method that returns a reference to the Node object the cursor is over. Both are used in the DragOver event of the TreeView control. Notice that the code checks the Key property of the Node object in both the MouseMove and DragDrop events, only allowing a skill to be dropped onto a Consultant.

The other point to emphasize is that although the DropHighlight property indicates the receiver of the drop, there is no property to reference the source Node object. Therefore, you must declare a private form-level variable to hold this reference and populate it in the MouseDown event. Finally, a form-level Boolean variable is used to track when the drag operation is taking place.

NOTE

To reuse the code from Listing 12.3, you would have to place an instance of the TreeView control called tvTreeView on a form and remove the reference to the clsSkills business object. In addition, you would substitute your own code to check for the correct nodes to drop on by replacing the calls to Mid(nodX.Key, 1, 1).

Using the ListView Control

As mentioned previously, the `ListView` control is often used in conjunction with the `TreeView` control in applications that employ an SDI presentation style. The primary use of the control is to display, in one of four views, tabular data that can be easily sorted and manipulated by the user. Typically, this control is not used to edit data directly, as a grid control would be, but is used primarily for read-only data. This control is also supplied in the group of ActiveX controls contained in MSCOMCTL.OCX.

Internally, the `ListView` control contains collections of `ListItem` and `ColumnHeader` objects. Each `ListItem` object represents one row in the table, and each `ColumnHeader` can be used to label the data and provide a method to allow the user to sort the contents of the control. Like the `TreeView`, the `ListView` control can also use an instance of the `ImageList` control to provide images that are shown when the control is placed in different views. Table 12.3 presents the primary properties, methods, and events of the control.

Table 12.3   Properties, Methods, and Events of the ListView Control

Member	Description
Properties	
AllowColumnReorder	Boolean. Determines whether the user may reorder the columns. New in VB 6.
Arrange	Integer. Determines how the icons in the control are arranged when in Icon or SmallIcon view.
CheckBoxes	Boolean. Determines whether check boxes appear next to the `ListItem` objects. New in VB 6.
ColumnHeaders	ListItems. Returns a collection of `ColumnHeader` objects associated with the control.
ColumnHeaderIcons	ImageList. Determines which `ImageList` control will be used for images supplied to the `ColumnHeaders` collection.
DropHighlight	ListItem. Returns or sets a reference to the object that is highlighted when the cursor moves over it. It is used in conjunction with the `HitTest` method to display visual cues when performing drag-and-drop operations.
FullRowSelect	Boolean. Determines whether the entire row is selected instead of just the first column. New in VB 6.

Member	Description
Properties	
GridLines	Boolean. Determines whether the control displays gridlines when in Report view. New in VB 6.
HideColumnHeaders	Boolean. Determines whether ColumnHeader objects are hidden while in Report view.
HotTracking	Boolean. Determines whether the text of the ListItem object is highlighted when the mouse moves over it. Changes the cursor to an icon hand. New in VB 6.
HoverSelection	Boolean. Determines whether a ListItem object is selected when the mouse moves over it. New in VB 6.
Icons SmallIcons	ImageList. Determines the ImageList controls to use for displaying icons when in Icon or SmallIcon view.
LabelEdit	Integer. Determines whether the user can edit the label of the ListItem. 0=lvwAutomatic and 1=lvwManual.
LabelWrap	Boolean. Determines whether the labels will wrap when in Icon view.
ListItems	ListItems. Returns a collection of ListItem objects associated with the control.
MultiSelect	Boolean. Determines whether multiple ListItem objects can be selected.
SelectedItem	ListItem. Returns a reference to the ListItem currently selected.
SortKey	Integer. Determines which text to use to sort the control. If 0, it uses the Text property of the ListItem object. If >=1, it specifies the subitem whose index is specified. Note that the Sorted property must be set to True before this property is set.
Sorted	Boolean. Determines whether the ListItem objects are sorted.
SortOrder	Integer. Enumerated type that determines how the sort will be performed. 0=lvwAscending and 1=lvwDescending.

continues

Table 12.3   continued

Member	Description
Methods	
FindItem	Searches the control and finds the first reference to a ListItem object that matches the string passed to the method. It can begin the search at a specific location, do a partial search, and search on the ListItem's Text, SubItems, or Tag properties.
GetFirstVisible	Returns the first visible ListItem object when in List or Report view.
HitTest	Returns a reference to the ListItem at the X and Y coordinates supplied as arguments to the method.
StartLabelEdit	Used to allow label editing when the LabelEdit property is set to lvwManual.
Events	
BeforeLabelEdit AfterLabelEdit	Fired before and after the user edits the label of the currently selected ListItem. Can be used to cancel the editing and inspect what the user has entered.
ColumnClick	Fired when a ColumnHeader object is clicked when in Report view. An argument passed into the event references the ColumnHeader object.
ItemClick	Fired when a ListItem object is clicked. An argument passed into the event references the ListItem object.

The ColumnHeader Object and the ColumnHeaders Collection

The ColumnHeaders collection contains ColumnHeader objects associated with the ListView control. The population of ListItem objects in the control has the effect of creating one ColumnHeader object in the collection that represents the ListItem object. Subsequent ColumnHeader objects in the collection map to elements in the SubItems array of the ListItem object.

The object itself contains properties to align and position the ColumnHeader, as well as to specify the text and the icon to display. Table 12.4 describes the properties and methods.

Table 12.4 Properties and Methods of the ColumnHeader Object

Member	Description
Alignment	Integer. Enumerated type that aligns the text or image of the object. 0=lvwColumnLeft, 1=lvwColumnRight, and 2=lvwColumnCenter.
Icon	Icon. Specifies the image Key or Index from an ImageList control to be displayed in the ColumnHeader object.
Key	String. Determines the unique identifier of the ColumnHeader object in the collection.
Position	Integer. Specifies the visual position of the ColumnHeader object.
SubItemIndex	Integer. Returns the index of the element from the ListItem object's SubItems property, which is associated with the ColumnHeader.
Text	String. Determines the text to be displayed to the user.
Methods	
Add	ColumnHeaders collection. Adds a ColumnHeader to the collection of the control. Takes arguments that represent the index, key, text, width, alignment, and icon of the ColumnHeader.
Clear	ColumnHeaders collection. Removes all the ColumnHeader objects from the collection.
Remove	ColumnHeaders collection. Removes the given ColumnHeader from the collection.

The ListItem Object and the ListItems Collection

Each ListView control is made up of a collection of ListItem objects. Each object represents one row in the control, when displayed in List or Report view, and can contain an array of SubItems that will be displayed as columns beneath the ColumnHeader objects. The ListItem and ListItems collection are quite simple and contain the important properties and methods shown in Table 12.5.

Table 12.5   Properties and Methods of the ListItem Object and ListItems Collection

Member	Description
Properties	
Bold	Boolean. Determines whether the Text of the ListItem appears as bold.
Checked	Boolean. Determines whether a check box appears if the CheckBoxes property of the ListView control is set to True.
ForeColor	Long. Determines the color of the text in the ListView control, using a color constant or the RGB function.
Ghosted	Boolean. Determines whether the ListItem object appears disabled.
Icon SmallIcon	Integer. Specifies the index into the ImageList control that determines which images are loaded. SmallIcon is used when the control is displayed using the SmallIcon view. Icon is used in all other views.
Key	String. Determines the unique identifier of the ListItem object in the collection.
Selected	Boolean. Determines whether the ListItem is currently selected.
SubItems	Array. Specifies an array of strings that is associated with the ListItem object. Each element of the array corresponds to a ColumnHeader object. The array is 1-based.
Text	String. Determines the text to be displayed to the user.
Methods	
Add	Used to add a ListItem object to the ListItems collection of the control. Takes arguments that represent the position, key, text, icon, and small icon of the ListItem.
Clear	ListItems collection. Removes all the ListItem objects from the collection.
CreateDragImage	Creates a drag image using a dithered version of the icon associated with the ListItem.
EnsureVisible	Scrolls the control, as necessary, to make sure that the ListItem is visible.
Remove	ListItems collection. Removes the given ListItem from the collection.

Adding ListItems

Adding ListItem objects to a ListView control is a fairly straightforward process. Essentially, three tasks must be performed: populating the ColumnHeaders collection, populating the ListItems collection, and populating the SubItems array for each ListItem if multiple columns have to be displayed. For example, the code in Listing 12.4 shows a procedure named LoadConsultantsList, which, when passed an ADO Recordset, clears and then reloads a ListView control with the appropriate data.

Listing 12.4   The LoadConsultantsList Procedure That Populates the ListView Control with an ADO Recordset

```
Private Sub LoadConsultantsList(rsResults as Recordset)

Dim objItem As ListItem

' Clear the existing data in the control
  lvListView.ListItems.Clear
  lvListView.ColumnHeaders.Clear

' Add three columns for Name, Email, and Phone
  lvListView.ColumnHeaders.Add , , "Name"
  lvListView.ColumnHeaders.Add , , "EmailAddress"
  lvListView.ColumnHeaders.Add , , "Phone"

' Load the ListView with data
    Do While Not rsResults.EOF

        ' Add the ListItem object
        Set objItem = lvListView.ListItems.Add(,"C" & _
            rsResults("ID"), rsResults("FName") & " " _
            & rsResults("LName"), "User", "User")

        ' Add the SubItems
        objItem.SubItems(1) = rsResults("EmailAddress")
        objItem.SubItems(2) = rsResults("Phone") & vbNullString

        rsResults.MoveNext
    Loop

End Sub
```

Note that NULL values are not allowed in the SubItems array. By appending the constant vbNullString to fields in the database that allow NULL values, such as Phone, a run-time error will not be encountered. Once again, the primary key of the consultant record is being stored in the Key property of the ListItem object. This technique allows the primary key to be extracted if the application must manipulate the underlying database record.

As discussed previously, this control is typically used to display data from a database. Therefore, issues such as abstraction, performance, and freshness also apply to adding ListItem objects to the ListView control. To address these issues when the application must display several sets of data, you can follow two popular approaches. These include caching the data and managing multiple ListView instances.

Because managing multiple instances of the control consumes extra resources and presents additional challenges related to sizing and visibility, I recommend caching multidimensional variant arrays or ADO recordsets in either form-level variables or client-side business objects. The code in Listing 12.3 (discussed previously) can then be used to clear and populate the ListView control on demand. The LoadConsultantsList procedure can also be called from the LoadConsultants procedure (refer to Listing 12.2) when the consultants Node on the TreeView control is clicked. In this way, roundtrips to the database server are reduced while consuming little additional memory.

Deleting ListItems

The technique for deleting ListItem objects is the same as deleting Node objects from the TreeView control. The code in Listing 12.1 can be slightly modified to support calling the Remove method of the ListItems collection.

Sorting ListItems

In most instances, sorting ListItems is accomplished by the user clicking on the header of the column he or she wants to sort by. This may be accompanied by functionality to allow the user to toggle the sort order by reclicking on the column. In addition, you typically want to visually indicate to the user which column has been sorted on and whether it was in ascending or descending order. Listing 12.5 presents the code to implement this functionality.

Listing 12.5   The ColumnClick and SortList Procedures to Sort the ListView Control

```
Private Sub lvListView_ColumnClick(ByVal ColumnHeader As _
  MSComctlLib.ColumnHeader)

' Sort the ListView
SortList ColumnHeader

End Sub

Private Sub SortList(ByVal ColumnHeader As MSComctlLib.ColumnHeader)

Dim objCol As ColumnHeader

' Clear the icons
For Each objCol In lvListView.ColumnHeaders
    objCol.Icon = 0
Next
```

```
' Check whether the column is the same as was clicked on
' previously. If so, toggle the sort order
If lvListView.SortKey = ColumnHeader.SubItemIndex Then
    If lvListView.SortOrder = lvwAscending Then
      lvListView.SortOrder = lvwDescending
    Else
      lvListView.SortOrder = lvwAscending
    End If
Else
    ' Otherwise, set up the sort using the SortKey
    lvListView.SortKey = ColumnHeader.SubItemIndex
End If

' Assign the appropriate Icon
If lvListView.SortOrder = lvwAscending Then
    ColumnHeader.Icon = "Ascending"
Else
    ColumnHeader.Icon = "Descending"
End If

' Set Sorted to True to sort the list.
lvListView.Sorted = True

End Sub
```

Inside the SortList procedure in Listing 12.5, the icons for each existing ColumnHeader are first cleared before the SortKey property is set. You will notice that you can simply set the SortKey to the SubItemIndex of the ColumnHeader because SortKey points to the element in the SubItems array that is to be sorted on. Because the ColumnClick event of the ListView control does not pass in the shift state of the keyboard, you cannot easily detect a keystroke at the time the column is clicked. As a result, an alternative method shown here is to toggle the sort if the user clicks on the same column as was previously sorted. The ColumnHeader icon is then set before the sort is actually performed, by setting the Sorted property to True.

Integrating TreeView and ListView

As mentioned previously, in many applications the TreeView and ListView controls are used together to display data retrieved from a database. Because this is such a common usage, it will improve your productivity as a developer if you develop code that can be reused without having to dig down into the particulars of the Node and ListItem objects each time.

To make this process easier, I've developed two reusable class modules that can be added to an existing project or compiled and referenced as an ActiveX DLL. Essentially, these classes handle the population of a ListView control from data that is supplied and cached when the user clicks on a TreeView control. Handling these issues inside the class modules makes it much simpler to write applications that do not access the database each time the control is refreshed. It also shields the developer from the internals of the ListView and TreeView controls.

The heart of the technique is the Explorer class module shown in Listing 12.6. This class exposes properties to reference ListView and TreeView controls and controls when data to be displayed is read from the cache. It also exposes two events that are raised when the controls are clicked. In the case of the TreeView, the TreeViewClicked event will fire when the data for the ListView control is not already cached or the ReadFromCache property is set to False. This event gives you the opportunity to pass back variant arrays that contain the data and headers to display. The ListViewClicked event will fire when the user clicks on the ListView control, passing back the key value of the ListItem that was clicked.

The most work of the Explorer class is done in the LoadListView private procedure called from the NodeClick event of the TreeView control declared inside the class. This procedure traverses the variant arrays to load the data and headers passed to it. Note that it also automatically reads data from the cache if the variant array of data is not passed to the procedure.

TIP

The final section of code in LoadListView uses a Win32 API technique to instruct the ListView control to automatically size its columns based on the data that was loaded. This technique is documented in the February 1999 edition of *101 Tech Tips for VB Developers*. For more information on sending messages to controls, see Chapter 13, "Using Win32 API Techniques."

Listing 12.6 The Explorer Class Integrates the TreeView and ListView Controls and Allows Data to Be Cached

```
Option Explicit

Private Declare Function SendMessage Lib "user32" _
    Alias "SendMessageA" (ByVal hwnd As Long, _
    ByVal wMsg As Long, ByVal wParam As Long, _
    lParam As Any) As Long

Private Const LVM_SETCOLUMNWIDTH = &H1000 + 30
Private Const LVM_USEHEADER = -2

Private WithEvents mtvTreeView As TreeView
Private WithEvents mlvListView As ListView

Private mflCached As Boolean
Private mCache As New Collection
```

```
Event TreeViewClicked(ByVal vKey As Variant, _
    varListData As Variant, varListHeader As Variant, _
    strIcon As String, strSmallIcon As String)
Event ListViewClicked(ByVal vKey As Variant)

Public Property Get ListView() As ListView
    Set ListView = mlvListView
End Property

Public Property Let ListView(ByVal vNewValue As ListView)
    Set mlvListView = vNewValue
End Property

Public Property Get TreeView() As TreeView
    Set TreeView = mtvTreeView
End Property

Public Property Let TreeView(ByVal vNewValue As TreeView)
    Set mtvTreeView = vNewValue
End Property

Public Property Get ReadFromCache() As Boolean
    ReadFromCache = mflCached
End Property

Public Property Let ReadFromCache(ByVal vNewValue As Boolean)
    mflCached = vNewValue
End Property

Private Sub mlvListView_ItemClick(ByVal Item As MSComctlLib.ListItem)

' Raise the event back to the ListView control
' passing back the parsed key
RaiseEvent ListViewClicked(Mid(Item.Key, 2))

End Sub

Private Sub mtvTreeView_NodeClick(ByVal Node As MSComctlLib.Node)

Dim lvarListData() As Variant
Dim lvarListHeader() As Variant
Dim lstrIcon As String
Dim lstrSmallIcon As String

' Load from the cache if the property is set
' and the data is already cached
If mflCached And IsPresent(Node.Key) Then
    LoadListView Node.Key
Else
```

continues

Listing 12.6   continued

```
    ' Otherwise, raise an event back to the client
    RaiseEvent TreeViewClicked(Node.Key, lvarListData, _
        lvarListHeader, lstrIcon, lstrSmallIcon)
    LoadListView Node.Key, lvarListData, _
        lvarListHeader, lstrIcon, lstrSmallIcon
End If


End Sub


Private Sub LoadListView(strNodeKey As String, _
    Optional varListData As Variant, Optional varListHeader As Variant, _
    Optional strIcon As String, Optional strSmallIcon As String)


Dim i As Integer
Dim z As Integer
Dim itmX As ListItem
Dim objExpData As ExplorerData


' Clear the listview
mlvListView.ListItems.Clear
mlvListView.ColumnHeaders.Clear


' Read from the cache if available
If IsMissing(varListData) Then
    varListData = mCache(strNodeKey).DataArray
    varListHeader = mCache(strNodeKey).HeaderArray
    strIcon = mCache(strNodeKey).Icon
    strSmallIcon = mCache(strNodeKey).SmallIcon
Else
    ' Create and populate an object to hold
    ' the cached data
    Set objExpData = New ExplorerData
    With objExpData
        .DataArray = varListData
        .HeaderArray = varListHeader
        .Icon = strIcon
        .SmallIcon = strSmallIcon
    End With

    ' Remove and re-add if already in the cache
    If IsPresent(strNodeKey) Then
        mCache.Remove (strNodeKey)
    End If

    ' Add the data to the collection
    mCache.Add objExpData, strNodeKey
End If
```

```
' Load the headers
For i = 0 To UBound(varListHeader)
    mlvListView.ColumnHeaders.Add , , varListHeader(i)
Next i

' Load the data
For i = 0 To UBound(varListData, 1)
    ' Add the first item
    Set itmX = mlvListView.ListItems.Add(, "K" & CStr(varListData(i, 0)), _
        CStr(varListData(i, 1)), strIcon, strSmallIcon)
    ' Add the columns
    For z = 1 To UBound(varListData, 2) - 1
        If Not IsNull(varListData(i, z + 1)) Then
            itmX.SubItems(z) = CStr(varListData(i, z + 1)) & ""
        End If
    Next z
Next i

' Size the widths of the columns automatically
For i = 0 To mlvListView.ColumnHeaders.Count - 1
    SendMessage mlvListView.hwnd, LVM_SETCOLUMNWIDTH, _
        i, LVM_USEHEADER
Next i

End Sub

Private Function IsPresent(strNodeKey As String) As Boolean

' Check whether the Node is present in the collection
On Error GoTo IsPresentErr

    If Not IsEmpty(mCache(strNodeKey)) Then
        IsPresent = True
    Else
        IsPresent = False
    End If

Exit Function
IsPresentErr:
    IsPresent = False

End Function
```

The `Explorer` class uses a `Collection` object, `mCache`, and a simple class named `ExplorerData` to cache the data, headers, and icon settings in variant arrays, shown in Listing 12.7.

Listing 12.7   The ExplorerData Class Is Used Internally in a Collection by the Explorer Class to Store Data to Be Displayed by the ListView Control

```
Option Explicit

Private mDataArray As Variant
Private mHeaderArray As Variant
Private mstrIcon As String
Private mstrSmallIcon As String

Public Property Get DataArray() As Variant
    DataArray = mDataArray
End Property

Public Property Let DataArray(ByVal vNewValue As Variant)
    mDataArray = vNewValue
End Property

Public Property Get HeaderArray() As Variant
    HeaderArray = mHeaderArray
End Property

Public Property Let HeaderArray(ByVal vNewValue As Variant)
    mHeaderArray = vNewValue
End Property

Public Property Get Icon() As String
    Icon = mstrIcon
End Property

Public Property Let Icon(ByVal vNewValue As String)
    mstrIcon = vNewValue
End Property

Public Property Get SmallIcon() As String
    SmallIcon = mstrSmallIcon

End Property

Public Property Let SmallIcon(ByVal vNewValue As String)
    mstrSmallIcon = vNewValue
End Property
```

A client program simply needs to create an instance of the Explorer class, set its properties to reference instances of TreeView and ListView controls, and then write code that responds to the two events discussed previously. When the client program passes data to the Explorer class, it should be done in variant arrays, with the primary key of the data in the first position. A good technique to do this is to accept an ADO

Recordset generated by a business object and call its GetRows method to save the data in a variant array. The headers for the data can be generated using the Fields collection of the recordset.

Web-Enabling the TreeView Control

One of the features introduced in Visual Basic 5 is the addition of the ActiveX control template. This template provides a UserControl object that allows developers to create ActiveX controls using a combination of code, intrinsic controls, and third-party controls (in this context, termed *constituent* controls). The ActiveX control project can then be compiled in an .OCX file and distributed for use in containers (other development environments) that can act as a host site for ActiveX controls.

NOTE

> More information on creating ActiveX controls can be found in Chapter 16, "Building ActiveX Components."

One of the most profitable uses of this technology for corporate developers is to use the UserControl object to encapsulate the combinations of controls and code they want to use in multiple projects or in multiple development environments. With the increase in the need to develop intranet applications that contain the visual robustness of native Windows applications, this technique has been used to create user interface elements that can be instantiated by Internet Explorer (MSIE) and manipulated using client-side script in HTML. With the introduction of Dynamic HTML (DHTML), the need for this technique has lessened somewhat but is still useful for applications containing more sophisticated user interfaces.

The TreeView control works well in this type of environment to display hierarchical information in a browser-based application. However, to do this efficiently, code must be written to download the data that is to be displayed by the control and provide a method so that data is read incrementally and asynchronously to increase performance.

Using AsyncRead and AsyncReadComplete

The key to encapsulating the TreeView control to be used in a browser-based application is the AsyncRead method of the UserControl object. This method allows the ActiveX control to download data from a URL asynchronously. When the data has been downloaded, the AsyncReadComplete event will fire. The event passes in an argument of type AsyncProperty that specifies the location of the data on the local machine, which can then be manipulated by the control.

In the case of the UserControl shown in Listing 12.8, the AsyncRead method is used in the NodeClick event of the constituent TreeView control and the user-defined Refresh method. In both instances, a URL is used (defined by the user-defined property SourceURL) to call AsyncRead and download data that is loaded into the control. When a Node is clicked, a query string identifying the Key property of the Node that was clicked is appended to the URL. In this way, server extensions on the Web server can parse the query string to determine which data to deliver to the browser.

The downloaded data, named TreeItems, is stored in an array inside the control. TreeItems is an array that contains elements defined using the user-defined type (UDT), TreeData. The TreeData UDT stores browser-related information such as the URL, the frame, and the text to be displayed in the control. This technique highlights another method for caching data after it has been retrieved.

Listing 12.8   The UserControl Object That Encapsulates a TreeView Control to Load Data Incrementally from URLs

```
Option Explicit

Private TreeItems() As TreeData
Private mstrURL As String

' Type declaration for tracking
Private Type TreeData
    Caption As String
    Key As String
    Parent As String
    URL As String
    Frame As String
    Folder As Boolean
    NodeIndex As Long
End Type

Private Sub tvTreeView_NodeClick(ByVal Node As MSComctlLib.Node)

Dim strFrame As String
Dim strURL As String
Dim strTarget As String

strTarget = mstrURL & "?Key = " & Node.Key

' Check to make sure that the control is in run mode
If Ambient.UserMode = True Then
    ' If not already loaded and not a leaf, load
    If Node.Tag <> "Loaded" And Node.Image <> "Leaf" Then
        AsyncRead strTarget, vbAsyncTypeFile, _
            "filename", vbAsyncReadForceUpdate
        Node.Tag = "Loaded"
    Else
        ' Get the node's associated properties and navigate
        strFrame = TreeItems(Node.Index - 1).Frame
        strURL = TreeItems(Node.Index - 1).URL

        If strURL <> "" Then Hyperlink.NavigateTo strURL, , strFrame
    End If
```

```
End If

End Sub

Private Sub UserControl_AsyncReadComplete(AsyncProp As AsyncProperty)
    LoadTree AsyncProp.Value
End Sub


Private Sub LoadTree(pstrFileName As String)

Dim intFileNum As Integer
Dim strData As String
Dim i As Integer
Dim nodx As Node
Dim strImage As String
Dim strSelectedImage As String
Dim intRelationship As Integer
Dim strRelative As String
Dim intFirst As Integer
Dim strItems() As String

intFileNum = FreeFile
intFirst = -1

' Open the text file
Open pstrFileName For Input Lock Read As intFileNum

' Load the array of structures
Do While Not EOF(intFileNum)
    On Error GoTo ReDimErr
    ReDim Preserve TreeItems(UBound(TreeItems) + 1)
    If intFirst = -1 Then intFirst = UBound(TreeItems)

    On Error GoTo LoadTreeErr
    i = UBound(TreeItems)
    Line Input #intFileNum, strData

    ' Parse the file data into a string array
    ' Note that this is a new VB 6.0 function
    strItems = Split(strData, "~")

    With TreeItems(i)
        .Caption = strItems(0)
        .Key = strItems(1)
        .Parent = strItems(2)
        .URL = strItems(3)
```

continues

Listing 12.8   continued

```
        .Frame = strItems(4)
        .Folder = strItems(5)
    End With
Loop

Close intFileNum

' Load the tree
For i = intFirst To UBound(TreeItems)
    If TreeItems(i).Folder = True Then
        strImage = "Closed"
        strSelectedImage = "Open"
    Else
        strImage = "Leaf"
        strSelectedImage = "Leaf"
    End If

    ' If there is no parent, this is the root
    If TreeItems(i).Parent = "" Then
        Set nodx = tvTreeView.Nodes.Add(, , TreeItems(i).Key, _
            TreeItems(i).Caption, strImage, strSelectedImage)
        nodx.Expanded = True
    Else
        intRelationship = tvwChild
        strRelative = TreeItems(i).Parent
        Set nodx = tvTreeView.Nodes.Add(strRelative, intRelationship, _
            TreeItems(i).Key, TreeItems(i).Caption, _
            strImage, strSelectedImage)
    End If

    ' Populate the Node Index so that they are in sync
    TreeItems(i).NodeIndex = nodx.Index

Next i

Exit Sub
ReDimErr:
    ReDim TreeItems(0)
    Resume Next
    Exit Sub

LoadTreeErr:
    MsgBox "An error occurred while loading the tree." & _
        Err.Description, vbExclamation

End Sub
```

```
Public Property Get SourceURL() As String
    SourceURL = mstrURL
End Property

Public Property Let SourceURL(ByVal vNewValue As String)
    mstrURL = vNewValue
End Property

Public Sub Refresh()

' Reset the Tree and get the first set of data
tvTreeView.Nodes.Clear
Erase TreeItems

' Check to make sure that the control is in run mode
If Ambient.UserMode = True Then
    AsyncRead mstrURL, vbAsyncTypeFile, _
        "filename", vbAsyncReadForceUpdate
End If

End Sub

Private Sub UserControl_Resize()

On Error Resume Next

' Resize to the full size of the user control
tvTreeView.Top = 1
tvTreeView.Left = 1

tvTreeView.Width = UserControl.Width
tvTreeView.Height = UserControl.Height

End Sub
```

The LoadTree private procedure is invoked by AsyncReadComplete to open the downloaded file and populate the nodes in the TreeView control and elements in the TreeItems array.

TIP

Even though VB 6 supports the newer FileSystemObject to open a read text file (see Chapter 18, "Adding Professional Features "), I've chosen the older technique of using intrinsic statements so that the Scripting Runtime component will not have be compiled and distributed to the end user's computer.

When a Node object of the TreeView control is clicked, the URL is retrieved from the TreeItems array. The Hyperlink object of the UserControl is then used to invoke the NavigateTo method that displays the URL of the item in the appropriate frame.

Instantiating the Control

Using the control shown in Listing 12.8, data is loaded and displayed incrementally as nodes are clicked, which reduces wait time as the data is downloaded. To use the new control, you must reference it in the <OBJECT> tag of an HTML page. Additionally, client-side VBScript can be written to populate the SourceURL property and call the Refresh method as the page is loaded using the Window_OnLoad event. For an example, look at Listing 12.9.

Listing 12.9   A Web Page Used to Instantiate the Control and Download Data to Be Displayed

```
<HTML>
<HEAD>
<META NAME="GENERATOR" Content="Microsoft Visual InterDev 6.0">
<META HTTP-EQUIV="Content-Type" content="text/html; charset=iso-8859-1">
<TITLE>Web Tree Sample</TITLE>
</HEAD>

<!-- Now add the client-side script to load the initial folders -->
<SCRIPT Language="VBScript">
Sub Window_OnLoad()
    WebTree1.SourceURL = "http://ssosa/stateu/solutech.asp"
    WebTree1.Refresh
End Sub
</SCRIPT>

<BODY>

<!-- Now instantiate the webtree control -->
<OBJECT ID="WebTree1" WIDTH=150 HEIGHT=300
  CLASSID="CLSID:9ACE6B4F-2855-11D1-8504-08005A497BFD"
  CODEBASE="WebTree.cab#version=1,0,0,0">
</OBJECT>

</BODY>
</HTML>
```

Figure 12.2 shows the resulting Web page loaded in Internet Explorer.

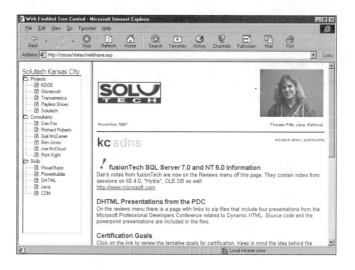

Figure 12.2

A Web-enabled tree control that incrementally downloads data from the Web server.

Sourcing from ASP

It is possible to use the control discussed in this section with Web servers other than Internet Information Server (IIS). However, Active Server Pages (ASP) provides a way to generate the required data dynamically. Although this procedure is beyond the scope of this book, you can use ASP script to instantiate business objects or ADO `Recordsets` and subsequently create a data stream that is returned to the browser when the `AsyncRead` method is called. Note that the `SourceURL` property in Listing 12.9 is set to an ASP page that will return the initial set of data to be displayed.

The format of the required data stream expected by the `LoadTree` procedure as implemented in Listing 12.8 is as follows:

```
Projects~Proj~~~topic~true
Consultants~Cons~~~topic~true
Skills~Skills~~~topic~true
```

Note that the `-~` is used to delimit the data representing the caption, key, parent, URL, and frame, and whether the item should be displayed as a folder. If no data is required for the field, it is simply omitted, as in the case of the parent for the items shown in the previous code snippet. When the Consultants node is clicked, the following data stream is downloaded:

```
Dan Fox~dfox~Cons~users.asp?id=1~topic~false
Richard Roberts~rroberts~Cons~users.asp?id=2~topic~false
Gail McDaniel~gmcd~Cons~users.asp?id=3~topic~false
Ben Jones~benj~Cons~users.asp?id=4~topic~false
Joe McCloud~jmcc~Cons~users.asp?id=5~topic~false
Rick Kight~rkight~Cons~users.asp?id=6~topic~false
```

Summary

This chapter focuses on techniques for manipulating and integrating the `TreeView` and `ListView` controls. Much of the discussion is centered on using these controls when interacting with a database in form-based and Web applications because this is their primary use in corporate applications. Knowing how to intelligently work with these controls can make your applications more responsive and easier to maintain and debug.

CHAPTER 13

Using Win32 API Techniques

If you have been developing Visual Basic applications for any length of time, you realize that using the rapid development capability of a tool involves trade-offs. Normally, you recognize these limitations after pouring through the documentation, trying to duplicate some feature or function you've seen in a different application, only to find out that it's impossible in VB. Many of these advanced features can be implemented using only the Win32 API. Luckily, VB makes taking advantage of many API calls fairly straightforward.

TIP

As in all discussions of VB and the Win32 API, I recommend obtaining a copy of Dan Appleman's *Visual Basic 5.0 Programmer's Guide to the Win32 API* (ISBN: 1562764462, published by Ziff-Davis Press). Although some examples might not be applicable to the corporate developer, the book as a whole is a great reference on the entire topic.

In this chapter, you will take a look at some of the most widely used techniques that rely on the Win32 API, for the corporate developer. These include

- Encapsulating API calls
- Creating floating windows
- Playing waveform sounds
- Enhancing the TextBox control
- Putting an application's icon in the system tray
- Printing a document from the shell

- Creating a searchable `ComboBox` control
- Creating a multithreaded application
- Accessing the Internet

Although you might have seen some of these techniques before or tried them on your own, I've included them here for reference when you're scratching your head trying to remember how you implemented a feature. First, I talk about some general principles for using the Win32 API and about one technique commonly used for encapsulating the API calls in your applications.

Using Encapsulation Techniques

Because using the Win32 API is usually a code-intensive proposition, two standard techniques have been developed for reusing declarations, constants, types, and any code required to set up the API calls—using standard modules to wrap commonly used API calls and using class modules to develop an API class library.

Wrapping API Calls

This method of encapsulating access to the Windows API using code (standard) modules has a long history and is the traditional method for accomplishing this. Typically, the idea is to group a number of related declarations, constants, and types into a central module and then create wrapper functions that call the API. Not all API functions require wrappers, but those that require some code to set up the arguments are good candidates.

To give you an example of this type of reuse, consider the five VB procedures that encapsulate calls to the Win32 API listed in Table 13.1 and implemented in the standard module in Listing 13.1.

Table 13.1   Common Operating System Path Functions Encapsulated as Public Visual Basic Procedures

Procedure	Description
`WinGetShortPathName`	Given a path to a file, it returns the DOS 8.3 path using the `GetShortPathName` API function.
`WinGetSystemDirectory`	Returns the path to the system directory (c:\winnt\system32) using the `GetSystemDirectory` API function.
`WinGetTempFileAndPath`	Returns a complete unique temporary file and path, given a three-character prefix (often application specific). Uses the `GetTempPath` and `GetTempFileName` API functions.
`WinGetWindowsDirectory`	Returns the path to the windows directory (c:\winnt) using the `GetWindowsDirectory` API function.
`WinSetCurrentDirectory`	Given a path, it sets the current directory in the operating system using the `SetCurrentDirectory` API function.

Listing 13.1   Wrapping API Calls in a Standard Module

```
Option Explicit

Private Declare Function GetShortPathName Lib "kernel32" _
    Alias "GetShortPathNameA" (ByVal lpszLongPath As String, _
    ByVal lpszShortPath As String, ByVal cchBuffer As Long) As Long

Private Declare Function GetSystemDirectory Lib "kernel32" _
    Alias "GetSystemDirectoryA" (ByVal lpBuffer As String, _
    ByVal nSize As Long) As Long

Private Declare Function GetTempFileName Lib "kernel32" _
    Alias "GetTempFileNameA" (ByVal lpszPath As String, _
    ByVal lpPrefixString As String, ByVal wUnique As Long, _
    ByVal lpTempFileName As String) As Long

Private Declare Function GetTempPath Lib "kernel32" Alias _
    "GetTempPathA" (ByVal nBufferLength As Long, _
    ByVal lpBuffer As String) As Long

Private Declare Function GetWindowsDirectory Lib "kernel32" _
    Alias "GetWindowsDirectoryA" (ByVal lpBuffer As String, _
    ByVal nSize As Long) As Long

Private Declare Function SetCurrentDirectory Lib "kernel32" _
    Alias "SetCurrentDirectoryA" (ByVal lpPathName As String) As Long

' Maximum size of file paths
Private Const MAX_PATH = 260

Public Function WinGetShortPathName(ByVal pstrPath As String) As String

' Returns the DOS 8.3 name for the given path

Dim lstrBuffer As String
Dim llngRet As Long

' Create the buffer
lstrBuffer = Space(MAX_PATH)

llngRet = GetShortPathName(pstrPath, lstrBuffer, Len(lstrBuffer))
If llngRet = 0 Then
    WinGetShortPathName = vbNullString
Else
    WinGetShortPathName = Left(lstrBuffer, llngRet)
End If

End Function
```

continues

Listing 13.1   continued

```
Public Function WinGetSystemDirectory() As String

' Returns the Windows system directory

Dim lstrBuffer As String
Dim llngRet As Long

' Create the buffer
lstrBuffer = Space(MAX_PATH)

llngRet = GetSystemDirectory(lstrBuffer, Len(lstrBuffer))
If llngRet = 0 Then
    WinGetSystemDirectory = vbNullString
Else
    WinGetSystemDirectory = Left(lstrBuffer, llngRet)
End If

End Function

Public Function WinGetTempFileAndPath(ByVal pstrPrefix As String) As String

' Returns a unique temporary filename and path

Dim lstrBuffer As String
Dim llngRet As Long
Dim lstrTempPath As String

' Create the buffer
lstrBuffer = Space(MAX_PATH)

llngRet = GetTempPath(Len(lstrBuffer), lstrBuffer)
If llngRet = 0 Then
    WinGetTempFileAndPath = vbNullString
    Exit Function
Else
    lstrTempPath = Left(lstrBuffer, llngRet)

    ' Re-create the buffer
    lstrBuffer = Space(MAX_PATH)
    llngRet = GetTempFileName(lstrTempPath, pstrPrefix, 0, lstrBuffer)
    If llngRet = 0 Then
        WinGetTempFileAndPath = vbNullString
    Else
        ' Return the path using the length of the hex representation
        ' of the unique value placed in the temporary file
        WinGetTempFileAndPath = Left(lstrBuffer, Len(lstrTempPath) + _
            3 + Len(Hex(llngRet)) + 4)
```

Listing 13.1   continued

```
    End If
End If

End Function

Public Function WinGetWindowsDirectory() As String

' Returns the Windows directory

Dim lstrBuffer As String
Dim llngRet As Long

' Create the buffer
lstrBuffer = Space(MAX_PATH)

llngRet = GetWindowsDirectory(lstrBuffer, Len(lstrBuffer))
If llngRet = 0 Then
    WinGetWindowsDirectory = vbNullString
Else
    WinGetWindowsDirectory = Left(lstrBuffer, llngRet)
End If

End Function

Public Function WinSetCurrentDirectory(ByVal pstrPath As String) As Boolean

' Sets the current directory in the operating system

Dim llngRet As Long

llngRet = SetCurrentDirectory(pstrPath)
If llngRet = 0 Then
    WinSetCurrentDirectory = False
Else
    WinSetCurrentDirectory = True
End If

End Function
```

You will notice that the approach taken in Listing 13.1 is to declare the API functions as `Private` in the module and to prefix the `Public` VB function with `Win` to signify that an API call is taking place behind the scenes. These functions are good candidates for encapsulation because they require string buffers to be passed to the function. In the case of `WinGetTempFileAndPath`, the VB procedure actually encapsulates two API calls to build the path and filename for a temporary file.

The other particular to note in this approach is that although API functions often return long integers indicating the size of a buffer or 0 if an error occurred, the encapsulated VB functions hide this from the user by translating the return value to a Boolean (in the case of WinSetCurrentDirectory) or a null string, as appropriate.

The primary advantage to using this method is flexibility because the module can be added to any project and customized where appropriate. In addition, as the language changes over time, you can update these standard modules to take advantage of those changes without changing the calling convention of the procedures. Finally, some developers might simply be more comfortable using this procedural method when dealing with the API.

The disadvantage, of course, is that the binary code cannot be shared among projects because the source code is compiled into each project. This adds to the footprint of the application and does not provide a straight "black box" approach.

Using an API Class Library

The other major approach to using the Windows API is to encapsulate the calls in class modules to provide a more object-oriented approach. Each API call roughly maps to a method in the component; sets of constants and error messages are defined as enumerated types; and each type or structure becomes its own class module, with properties that expose the variables within the structure.

To understand this technique, consider the class module APIWin that encapsulates some of the most commonly used API manipulations done on windows using the handle of the window. Table 13.2 lists the exposed methods and their API equivalents, whereas Listing 13.2 shows the implementation of the class module.

Table 13.2 Methods Exposed in the APIWin Class Module to Manipulate Windows in the Operating System

Method	Description
WinEnableWindow	Given the window handle and a flag, it enables or disables keyboard and mouse interaction with a window. Uses the EnableWindow API function and can be used to disable the use of windows or controls within the current application or even in different applications, typically for a short period of time.
WinFindWindow	Long. Given the window class and/or window name, it returns the window handle, using the FindWindow API function. Useful for getting a handle to a window in a different application.
WinGetActiveWindow	Long. Returns the handle of the window currently active, using the GetActiveWindow API function.
WinGetWindowText	String. Given the handle of the window, it returns the caption or text, using the GetWindowText API function.

Method	Description
`WinIsWindowEnabled`	`Boolean`. Given the handle of the window, it returns a `Boolean` indicating whether the window is enabled (`True`) or disabled (`False`), using the `IsWindowEnabled` API function.
`WinLBAddItem`	`Boolean`. Given a handle to a `ListBox` control and a string to add, it uses the `SendMessage` API function and the `LB_ADDSTRING` message to add the item. Used to load a large number of items in a `ListBox` when the `ListBox` is not being redrawn (previously set using `WinSetReDraw`).
`WinMoveWindow`	`Boolean`. Given a window handle and new coordinates and sizes (in pixels), it moves the window in relation to either the screen or its parent. It automatically forces a repaint of the window and uses the `MoveWindow` API function. Useful for cutting down on the number of `Resize` events that fire on a form when you are doing a lot of resizing.
`WinOpenIcon`	`Boolean`. Given the handle of the window, it restores it and makes it active. Uses the `OpenIcon` API function.
`WinSetForeground Window`	`Boolean`. Given the handle of the window, it moves the window to the foreground using the `SetForeGroundWindow` API function. Useful for automatically switching between applications.
`WinSetReDraw`	`Boolean`. Given a window handle and a flag, it enables or disables redraws of the window or control. Uses the `SendMessage` API function to send `WM_SETREDRAW` messages to the window or control. Used to stop VB from redrawing the window or control every time something is changed on it (note that it does not work with all controls, and hence, the need for `WinLBAddItem`).

Listing 13.2 *Using a Class Module, APIWin, to Encapsulate API Calls Provides an Object-Oriented Approach*

```
Option Explicit

'Type safe declaration
Private Declare Function SendMessageNum Lib "user32" _
    Alias "SendMessageA" (ByVal hwnd As Long, _
    ByVal wMsg As Long, ByVal wParam As Long, _
    ByVal lParam As Long) As Long

'Type safe declaration
Private Declare Function SendMessageString Lib "user32" _
    Alias "SendMessageA" (ByVal hwnd As Long, _
    ByVal wMsg As Long, ByVal wParam As Long, _
    ByVal lParam As String) As Long
```

continues

Listing 13.2   continued

```
Private Declare Function EnableWindow Lib "user32" _
    (ByVal hwnd As Long, ByVal fEnable As Long) As Long

Private Declare Function FindWindow Lib "user32" _
    Alias "FindWindowA" (ByVal lpClassName As String, _
    ByVal lpWindowName As String) As Long

Private Declare Function GetActiveWindow Lib "user32" () As Long

Private Declare Function GetWindowText Lib "user32" _
    Alias "GetWindowTextA" (ByVal hwnd As Long, _
    ByVal lpString As String, ByVal cch As Long) As Long

Private Declare Function IsWindowEnabled Lib "user32" _
    (ByVal hwnd As Long) As Long

Private Declare Function OpenIcon Lib "user32" _
    (ByVal hwnd As Long) As Long

Private Declare Function SetForegroundWindow Lib "user32" _
    (ByVal hwnd As Long) As Long

Private Declare Function MoveWindow Lib "user32" (ByVal hwnd As Long, _
    ByVal x As Long, ByVal y As Long, ByVal nWidth As Long, _
    ByVal nHeight As Long, ByVal bRepaint As Long) As Long

' Constants
Private Const WM_SETREDRAW = &HB
Private Const LB_ADDSTRING = &H180
Private Const LB_ERR = (-1)
Private Const LB_ERRSPACE = (-2)

' Types
Public Enum APIWinErrors
    NO_WINDOW_ACTIVE = vbObjectError + 600
    WINDOW_NOT_FOUND = vbObjectError + 601
    WINDOW_NOT_MOVED = vbObjectError + 602
    REDRAW_NOT_SET = vbObjectError + 603
    LB_ADDITEM_FAILED = vbObjectError + 604
End Enum


Public Sub WinEnableWindow(ByVal pHwnd As Long, _
    ByVal flEnable As Boolean)

' Enables or disables a window from receiving mouse and
```

```
' keyboard input
Dim llngRet As Long
Dim llngEnable As Long

' Translate the argument
If flEnable Then
    llngEnable = 1
Else
    llngEnable = 0
End If


llngRet = EnableWindow(pHwnd, llngEnable)

End Sub

Public Function WinFindWindow(ByVal pstrClass As String, _
    ByVal pstrName As String) As Long

' Return the handle of the window given the class or
' text in the title bar. Return 0 if not found.
Dim lstrClass As String
Dim lstrName As String
Dim llngRet As Long

' Translate the arguments
If Len(pstrClass) = 0 Then
    lstrClass = vbNullString
Else
    lstrClass = pstrClass
End If

If Len(pstrName) = 0 Then
    lstrName = vbNullString
Else
    lstrName = pstrName
End If

llngRet = FindWindow(lstrClass, lstrName)

' Check the return value and raise an error
' if no window was found
If llngRet = 0 Then
    WinFindWindow = 0
    Err.Raise APIWinErrors.WINDOW_NOT_FOUND, "WinFindWindow", _
        "No window of that class or name was found."
    Exit Function
Else
    WinFindWindow = llngRet
End If
```

Listing 13.2   continued

```
End Function

Public Function WinGetActiveWindow() As Long

' Returns the handle of the active window
' or zero if there is none
Dim llngRet As Long

llngRet = GetActiveWindow

If llngRet = 0 Then
    WinGetActiveWindow = 0
    Err.Raise APIWinErrors.NO_WINDOW_ACTIVE, "WinGetActiveWindow", _
        "No Window is active"
    Exit Function
Else
    WinGetActiveWindow = llngRet
End If

End Function

Public Function WinGetWindowText(ByVal pHwnd As Long) As String

' Retrieves the caption of a window or text of a control
Dim lstrBuffer As String
Dim llngRet As Long

' Create the buffer
lstrBuffer = Space(255)

llngRet = GetWindowText(pHwnd, lstrBuffer, Len(lstrBuffer))
If llngRet = 0 Then
    WinGetWindowText = vbNullString
    Err.Raise APIWinErrors.NO_WINDOW_ACTIVE, "WinGetWindowText", _
        "No window is active."
    Exit Function
Else
    WinGetWindowText = Left(lstrBuffer, llngRet)
End If

End Function

Public Function WinIsWindowEnabled(ByVal pHwnd As Long) As Boolean

' Determines whether a window is enabled
Dim llngRet As Long
```

```
llngRet = IsWindowEnabled(pHwnd)
If llngRet = 0 Then
    WinIsWindowEnabled = False
Else
    WinIsWindowEnabled = True
End If

End Function

Public Function WinOpenIcon(ByVal pHwnd As Long) As Boolean

' Restores a minimized program and activates it
Dim llngRet As Long
Dim llngEnable As Long

llngRet = OpenIcon(pHwnd)
If llngRet = 0 Then
    WinOpenIcon = False
    Err.Raise APIWinErrors.WINDOW_NOT_FOUND, "WinOpenIcon", _
        "Window not restored."
    Exit Function
Else
    WinOpenIcon = True
End If

End Function

Public Function WinSetForegroundWindow(ByVal pHwnd As Long) As Boolean

' Sets the window to the foreground window of the system
Dim llngRet As Long
Dim llngEnable As Long

llngRet = SetForegroundWindow(pHwnd)
If llngRet = 0 Then
    WinSetForegroundWindow = False
    Err.Raise APIWinErrors.WINDOW_NOT_FOUND, "WinSetForegroundWindow", _
        "Window not set to the foreground."
    Exit Function
Else
    WinSetForegroundWindow = True
End If

End Function

Public Function WinMoveWindow(ByVal pHwnd As Long, pLeft As Long, _
```

continues

Listing 13.2   continued

```
        ByVal pTop As Long, ByVal pWidth As Long, _
        ByVal pHeight As Long) As Boolean

' Moves a window to a specified location and resizes it
Dim llngRet As Long

llngRet = MoveWindow(pHwnd, pLeft, pTop, pWidth, pHeight, 1)
If llngRet = 0 Then
    Err.Raise APIWinErrors.WINDOW_NOT_MOVED, "WinMoveWindow", _
        "The Window was not moved."
    WinMoveWindow = False
Else
    WinMoveWindow = True
End If

End Function

Public Function WinSetReDraw(ByVal pHwnd As Long, _
    ByVal flRedraw As Boolean) As Boolean

' Sets the redraw on or off for the window
Dim llngRet As Long

llngRet = SendMessageNum(pHwnd, WM_SETREDRAW, flRedraw, 0)
If llngRet = 0 Then
    WinSetReDraw = True
Else
    Err.Raise APIWinErrors.REDRAW_NOT_SET, "WinSetRedraw", _
        "Window redraw has not been set."
    WinSetReDraw = False
End If

End Function

Public Function WinLBAddItem(ByVal pHwnd As Long, _
    ByVal pstrItem As String) As Boolean

' Adds an item to a listbox (to be used when the
' redraw is set to False on the ListBox)
Dim llngRet As Long

llngRet = SendMessageString(pHwnd, LB_ADDSTRING, 0, pstrItem)
If llngRet = LB_ERR Or llngRet = LB_ERRSPACE Then
    Err.Raise APIWinErrors.LB_ADDITEM_FAILED, "WinLBAddItem", _
        "Item has not been added."
    WinLBAddItem = False
Else
```

```
        WinLBAddItem = True
End If

End Function
```

One major difference in the approach used in Listing 13.2 as opposed to Listing 13.1 is error handling. When abstracting the API calls in a class module, it is good practice to use the error handling convention of COM components, namely, to raise errors back to the calling program using an enumerated type in the range above `vbObjectError+512`. This allows client programs to catch the errors in an error trap and use the enumerated type to interrogate their values. The code in Listing 13.3 shows how a client program would use the `APIWin` class to discover whether an application is running (in this case, the Calculator) and subsequently invoke it using the intrinsic `Shell` function if `WinFindWindow` returns a trappable error.

TIP

If you set the `Instancing` property of the `APIWin` class to `GlobalMultiUse`, client code does not have to specifically instantiate the class module before calling its methods.

Listing 13.3   Client Code That Uses the APIWin Class Module
```
Dim objAPI As New APIFunctions.APIWin

On Error GoTo LoadErr
Dim lngHwnd As Long

' Find the handle to the Calculator
lngHwnd = objAPI.WinFindWindow(vbNullString, "Calculator")

' Bring it to the foreground
objAPI.WinSetForegroundWindow lngHwnd

Exit Sub
LoadErr:
    If Err.Number = APIWinErrors.WINDOW_NOT_FOUND Then
        ' Open it up because it is not open
        Shell "calc.exe", vbNormalFocus
    End If
```

The benefit of using an API class library is that compiling the class into a DLL and referencing it among projects will reuse the binary code. The primary drawbacks, however, are that it requires more overhead, resulting in slower performance, and it introduces dependencies and versioning issues if you have to modify the class. Keep in mind that you can still take advantage of the object orientation of class modules by adding the class directly to your project. As with standard modules discussed previously, this results in larger executables if you do not pare down the classes.

Creating Floating Windows

One of the most common requirements of VB programs is to create windows that float either on top of all other windows on the system or on top of windows within their own application. The former effect is necessary for applications that are continually updating their display or are used for reference, such as an application that monitors database statistics. The latter technique is often used for creating a floating tool palette or a search dialog such as that found in Microsoft Word.

Neither effect can be created using the mechanisms inherent in VB. However, both can be accomplished with simple API calls.

Keeping a Window on Top

The ability to float a window on top of all other windows requires only a call to the SetWindowPos API with the HWND_TOPMOST constant in the placement order argument and passing it the requisite constants. Likewise, passing the constant HWND_NOTOPMOST will release the window from staying on top. The code in Listing 13.4 has been extracted from the APIWin class in Listing 13.2 and is just the code necessary to perform this function.

Listing 13.4   Code Extracted from the APIWin Class to Float a Window on Top of All Other Windows

```
Private Declare Function SetWindowPos Lib "user32" _
    (ByVal hwnd As Long, ByVal hWndInsertAfter As Long, _
    ByVal x As Long, ByVal y As Long, ByVal cx As Long, _
    ByVal cy As Long, ByVal wFlags As Long) As Long

Private Const SWP_NOMOVE = &H2
Private Const SWP_NOSIZE = &H1
Private Const HWND_NOTOPMOST = -2
Private Const HWND_TOPMOST = -1

Public Function WinSetFloating(ByVal pHwnd As Long, _
    ByVal flOnTop As Boolean) As Boolean

' Sets a window to float or releases it
Dim llngRet As Long
Dim llngMess As Long

If flOnTop = True Then
    llngMess = HWND_TOPMOST
Else
    llngMess = HWND_NOTOPMOST
End If

llngRet = SetWindowPos(pHwnd, llngMess, 0, 0, 0, 0, _
    SWP_NOMOVE Or SWP_NOSIZE)
```

```
If llngRet = 0 Then
    Err.Raise APIWinErrors.FLOATING_NOT_SET, "WinSetFloating", _
        "Windows has not been set on top."
    WinSetFloating = False
Else
    WinSetFloating = True
End If

End Function
```

NOTE

Using this technique keeps the window on top while the window is not minimized. Minimizing the window has the effect of resetting the position. To keep the window on top, you can call the `WinSetFloating` method again in the `Resize` event of the form.

Keeping a Child Window on Top

The second instance of creating a floating window is useful inside an application to keep a form on top of its parent form, even when the form does not have focus. A typical use for this technique is to create a modeless Find dialog that allows users to work with a document while keeping the attributes of the search in a floating window.

The code in Listing 13.5, again extracted from APIWin, uses the SetParent API function to assign the window to change the parent of the form that should float.

Listing 13.5   Code Extracted from the APIWin Class to Create a Modeless Floating Window in an Application

```
Private Declare Function SetParent Lib "user32" _
    (ByVal hWndChild As Long, _
    ByVal hWndNewParent As Long) As Long

Private Const GWL_HWNDPARENT = (-8)

Public Function WinSetModeless(ByVal pHwnd As Long, _
    ByVal pHwndParent As Long) As Long

' Sets the parent window
Dim llngRet As Long

llngRet = SetParent(pHwnd, pHwndParent)

If llngRet = 0 Then
    Err.Raise APIWinErrors.MODELESS_NOT_SET, "WinSetModeless", _
        "Windows has not been set on top."
    WinSetModeless = 0
```

continues

Listing 13.5   continued

```
Else
    ' Return the handle to the previous parent
    ' used to restore before the modeless window is closed
    WinSetModeless = llngRet
End If

End Function
```

This technique also requires that the floating window restore the handle of the original parent window (VB Form) before it is closed. The WinSetModeless method in APIWin returns the original handle so that it can be saved in a form-level variable. Restoring the original handle should be done in the Unload event of the floating window, like this:

```
Option Explicit

Private mlngOrgParent As Long

Private Sub Form_Load()

Dim objAPI As New APIFunctions.APIWin

' Set the window to float on Form1
mlngOrgParent = objAPI.WinSetModeless(Me.hWnd, Form1.hWnd)

End Sub

Private Sub Form_Unload(Cancel As Integer)

Dim objAPI As New APIFunctions.APIWin

' Restore the original parent handle
objAPI.WinSetModeless Me.hWnd, mlngOrgParent

End Sub
```

An example of using the technique shown in Listing 13.5 appears in Figure 13.1. A floating tool palette is created using the FixedToolWindow BorderStyle new in VB 6.

TIP

You can also create a floating window by using the optional OwnerForm parameter of the Show method of the Form object and passing a reference to the form that will act as the parent.

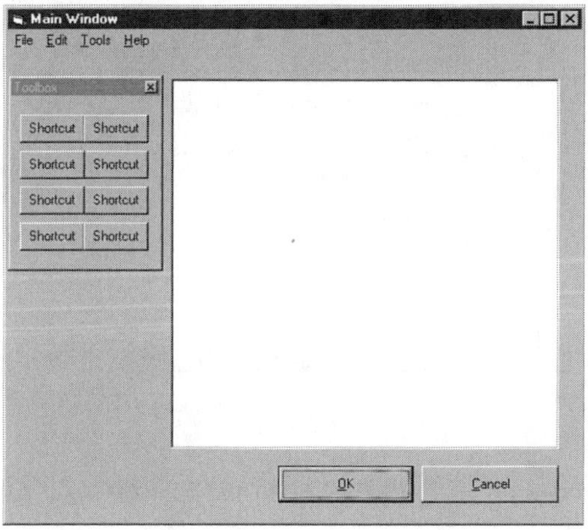

Figure 13.1

A floating tool palette window created using the SetParent API function.

Playing Waveform Sounds

Although most business applications are not known for their glitzy multimedia appeal, at times your application might require the capability to store and play audio. This form of feedback can be useful in providing additional cues and as a form of online help (as long as it is not overused).

You can play sounds through VB in several ways, the most familiar being the sndPlaySound API function. This function, when passed the path to a file or the name of a system sound, plays the sound based on a set of constants passed as the second argument. This technique has proved useful but is limited because it plays only from files and always returns False if another sound is playing.

A more flexible approach is to use the newer PlaySound API function, also included in the winmm.dll library. By default, this function attempts to stop playback if a sound is currently playing and can also play the sound directly from a resource file. This is a particularly useful behavior because VB 6 now sports a resource editor that allows you to easily incorporate .WAV files into a resource file that is compiled into the .EXE or .DLL. By doing this, you can avoid distributing multiple .WAV files by adding all the sounds needed by your application into a resource file. Figure 13.2 shows the resource editor with several included .WAV files.

TIP

> For the PlaySound function to see the .WAV resource, it must be added with a type of "WAVE", and its name must be a string (denoted by double quotes). In addition, the resource will not be found when the application is run in the development environment.

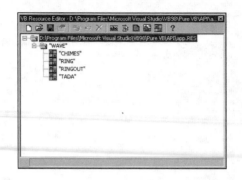

Figure 13.2

The resource editor included with VB 6 can be used to add .WAV files to a resource file.

In Listing 13.6, the class APIMM encapsulates PlaySound.

Listing 13.6   Code from the APIMM Class That Encapsulates the PlaySound API

```
Option Explicit

Private Declare Function PlaySound Lib "winmm.dll" _
    Alias "PlaySoundA" (ByVal lpszName As String, _
    ByVal hModule As Long, ByVal dwFlags As Long) As Long

Private Const SND_FILENAME = &H20000   ' name is a filename
Private Const SND_ASYNC = &H1          ' play asynchronously
Private Const SND_RESOURCE = &H40004   ' name is a resource id
Private Const SND_SYNC = &H0           ' play synchronously

Public Enum MMApiErrors
    WAVE_NOT_PLAYED = vbObjectError + 700
End Enum

Public Function WinPlaySound(ByVal pSound As String, _
    ByVal flFile As Boolean, _
    ByVal flAsync As Boolean) As Boolean

' Plays a wave file directly from a resource file
' or from a disk file
Dim llngRet As Long
Dim llngMode As Long

If flAsync = True Then
    llngMode = SND_ASYNC
Else
    llngMode = SND_SYNC
End If
```

```
If flFile = True Then
    llngRet = PlaySound(pSound, 0, _
        SND_FILENAME Or llngMode)
Else
    llngRet = PlaySound(pSound, App.hInstance, _
        SND_RESOURCE Or llngMode)
End If


' Note that this function will return True
' if the default system sound is played
If llngRet = 1 Then
    WinPlaySound = True
Else
    Err.Raise MMApiErrors.WAVE_NOT_PLAYED, "WinPlaySound", _
        "Wave sound not played"
    WinPlaySound = False
End If

End Function
```

Note that `WinPlaySound` allows the sound to be played synchronously or asynchronously and includes a flag that specifies whether the `pSound` argument is a resource identifier or the name of a file.

Enhancing the TextBox

Certainly, the control most often used in data entry applications is the `TextBox`, although as most VB developers know, it is not as flexible as it could be. For example, it does not automatically respond to the Esc key to undo the last change and does not contain a property to track whether the contents of the control have changed.

Providing these features is simply a matter of sending the appropriate messages to the `TextBox` using the `SendMessage` API function. I've encapsulated several of these messages in the `APITextBox` class module whose methods are discussed in Table 13.3. Listing 13.7 shows the implementation of the class module.

Table 13.3 Methods Exposed in the APITextBox Class Module to TextBoxes in an Application

Method	Description
WinTxtClearUndo	Given the `TextBox` handle, it empties the undo buffer using the `EM_EMPTYUNDOBUFFER` message. This can be used to prevent the user from undoing a change.
WinTxtHasChanged	Given the `TextBox` handle, it returns `True` using the `EM_GETMODIFY` message if the modified state of the control is `True`. Used when attempting to determine whether a control was changed during a save operation.

continues

Table 13.3 Continued

Method	Description
WinTxtSetChanged	Given the `TextBox` handle and a flag, it sets the modified flag of the control to `True` or `False` using the `EM_SETMOD-IFY` message. This is useful for flagging each control as modified in the `Changed` event so that it can be skipped during a save operation and reset after the save is successful.
WinTxtUndo	Given the `TextBox` handle, it sends the `EM_UNDO` message to the control, forcing it to populate the `Text` property with the contents of the undo buffer.

Listing 13.7   The APITextBox Class Module That Encapsulates Message Calls to Enhance the Intrinsic TextBox Control

```
Option Explicit

Private Declare Function SendMessageNum Lib "user32" _
    Alias "SendMessageA" (ByVal hwnd As Long, _
    ByVal wMsg As Long, ByVal wParam As Long, _
    lParam As Long) As Long

Private Const EM_CANUNDO = &HC6
Private Const EM_EMPTYUNDOBUFFER = &HCD
Private Const EM_GETMODIFY = &HB8
Private Const EM_SETMODIFY = 185
Private Const EM_UNDO = &HC7

Public Sub WinTxtUndo(ByVal pHwnd As Long)
    ' Undo the last change to the textbox
    SendMessageNum pHwnd, EM_UNDO, 0, 0
End Sub

Public Sub WinTxtSetChanged(ByVal pHwnd As Long, _
    ByVal flChanged As Boolean)

' Sets the modified flag of the text box
If flChanged = True Then
    SendMessageNum pHwnd, EM_SETMODIFY, 1, 0
Else
    SendMessageNum pHwnd, EM_SETMODIFY, 0, 0
End If

End Sub

Public Function WinTxtHasChanged(ByVal pHwnd As Long) As Boolean

' Returns whether the textbox has changed
```

```
Dim llngret As Long

llngret = SendMessageNum(pHwnd, EM_GETMODIFY, 0, 0)
If llngret = 1 Then
    WinTxtHasChanged = True
Else
    WinTxtHasChanged = False
End If

End Function

Public Sub WinTxtClearUndo(ByVal pHwnd As Long)
    ' Empty the undo buffer so that future undos
    ' revert the current value
    SendMessageNum pHwnd, EM_EMPTYUNDOBUFFER, 0, 0
End Sub
```

To use these enhanced features to undo changes, you would write some code in the KeyDown event of the TextBox. In the following example, the KeyDown event is coded to respond to the Esc key being depressed in one of the TextBox controls in a control array (as long as neither the Alt, Ctrl, or Shift keys are depressed) and to call the WinTxtUndo method.

```
Option Explicit
Dim objAPI As New APIFunctions.APITextBox


Private Sub txtData_KeyDown(Index As Integer, _
    KeyCode As Integer, Shift As Integer)

' If no special keys are depressed and the
' Esc key is pressed, undo
If Shift = 0 And KeyCode = vbKeyEscape Then
    objAPI.WinTxtUndo txtData(Index).hwnd
End If

End Sub
```

Working with the Shell

One of the most significant, and certainly the most noticeable, features added to Windows 95/98 and NT 4 is the new shell. The shell not only includes the graphical user interface but is also accessible to programs that want to use its services. Two of the most popular services that can be accessed by VB are the system tray and automatic execution.

Using the System Tray

Perhaps the most interesting feature of the shell is the ability to place your application's icon in the system tray. This is normally appropriate for applications that run in the background or are used to modify properties of the system (such as a virus scanner or the volume control). Corporate applications can also find uses for this feature, for example, to display an updated list of scheduled tasks on a server or to view the status of data in a database.

The key to getting an icon in and out of the tray is the Shell_NotifyIcon API function in shell32.dll. This function is passed an action and a structure of type NOTIFYICONDATA that specifies the icon, ToolTip text, and an optional message number that the tray will use to notify a window when the user performs an action, such as double-clicking on the icon.

The code in Listing 13.8 implements the necessary code in a standard module to put an icon in the tray and take it back out again, using two public functions PutInTray and TakeOffTray.

Listing 13.8   A Standard Module Used to Add and Remove an Application from the System Tray

```
Option Explicit

Private Declare Function Shell_NotifyIconA Lib "shell32" _
    (ByVal dwMessage As Long, _
    lpData As NOTIFYICONDATA) As Integer

Private Declare Function SetWindowLong Lib "user32" _
    Alias "SetWindowLongA" (ByVal hwnd As Long, _
    ByVal nIndex As Long, ByVal dwNewLong As Long) As Long

Private Declare Function CallWindowProc Lib "user32" _
    Alias "CallWindowProcA" (ByVal lpPrevWndFunc _
    As Long, ByVal hwnd As Long, ByVal Msg As Long, _
    ByVal wParam As Long, ByVal lParam As Long) As Long

' Used by Shell_NotifyIconA
Private Type NOTIFYICONDATA
    cbSize As Long
    hwnd As Long                  ' Handle that receives messages
    uID As Long                   ' App-defined identifier of the taskbar icon
    uFlags As Long                ' Flags
    uCallbackMessage As Long ' App-defined message identifier
    hIcon As Long                 ' Handle to an icon
    szTip As String * 64          ' Tool text display message
End Type

Private Const WM_USER = &H400

' Build a private message to respond to events
Private Const WM_TRAYMESSAGE = WM_USER + 1024

Private Const NIM_ADD = 0
```

```
Private Const NIM_MODIFY = 1
Private Const NIM_DELETE = 2

Private Const NIF_MESSAGE = 1
Private Const NIF_ICON = 2
Private Const NIF_TIP = 4
Private Const GWL_WNDPROC = (-4)

Public Enum TRAY_EVENTS
    TRAY_RIGHT_MOUSE_DOWN = 516
    TRAY_RIGHT_MOUSE_UP = 517
    TRAY_LEFT_MOUSE_DOWN = 513
    TRAY_LEFT_MOUSE_UP = 514
    TRAY_DOUBLE_CLICK = 515
End Enum

Private plngOldProc As Long

Public Function PutInTray(frmForm As Form, _
    ByVal pTip As String) As Boolean

' Fill in the structure and put the application
' in the tray. Also, subclass so that you can respond
' to events.

Dim lnd As NOTIFYICONDATA
Dim llintRet As Integer

    ' Fill the nd structure.

    lnd.cbSize = Len(lnd)
    lnd.hwnd = frmForm.hwnd
    lnd.uID = vbNull
    lnd.uCallbackMessage = WM_TRAYMESSAGE
    lnd.hIcon = frmForm.Icon
    lnd.uFlags = NIF_MESSAGE Or NIF_ICON Or NIF_TIP
    lnd.szTip = pTip & Chr$(0)

    ' Add it to the Tray
    llintRet = Shell_NotifyIconA(NIM_ADD, lnd)
    If llintRet = 0 Then
        PutInTray = False
        Exit Function
    Else
        PutInTray = True
    End If
```

continues

Listing 13.8   continued

```
' Subclass the window so that it is notified of tray events
plngOldProc = SetWindowLong(Form1.hwnd, GWL_WNDPROC, _
    AddressOf TrayWindowProc)

End Function


Public Function TakeOffTray(ByRef frmForm As Form) As Boolean

' Take the icon out of the tray
Dim lnd As NOTIFYICONDATA
Dim lintRet As Integer

    lnd.cbSize = Len(lnd)
    lnd.hwnd = Form1.hwnd
    lnd.uID = vbNull
    lnd.uCallbackMessage = vbNull
    lnd.uFlags = NIF_MESSAGE Or NIF_ICON Or NIF_TIP

    ' Delete the Icon
    lintRet = Shell_NotifyIconA(NIM_DELETE, lnd)

    If lintRet = 0 Then
        TakeOffTray = False
    Else
        TakeOffTray = True
    End If
End Function

Public Function TrayWindowProc(ByVal hwnd As Long, _
    ByVal lMsg As Long, ByVal wParam As Long, _
    ByVal lParam As Long) As Long

If lMsg = WM_TRAYMESSAGE Then
    ' Application-specific code to call a handler
    Form1.ProcessTray lParam
Else
    ' Continue with default processing
    TrayWindowProc = CallWindowProc(plngOldProc, _
        hwnd, lMsg, wParam, lParam)
End If

End Function
```

Although most of the code in Listing 13.8 is straightforward, the capability to respond to user events such as mouse clicks requires the more advanced technique of subclassing. Simply put, subclassing a window or control allows a VB program to respond to messages for which VB does not provide event handlers. Normally, this is done to allow VB to see standard Windows messages.

The idea in this case, however, is slightly different. The uCallBackMessage and hwnd variables in the NOTIFYICONDATA structure hold the message identifier for a Windows-specific message, not a standard Windows message, and the window handle to send the message to. In the declarations section, the message has been defined using the constant WM_TRAYMESSAGE.

NOTE

Private Windows messages such as WM_TRAYMESSAGE should be created in the range from WM_USER (1024) through &H7FFF (32767). Numbers outside this range are reserved for the operating system, for communication between applications, and for future use.

For the program to "see" this message, it must be subclassed using the SetWindowLong API function. This function is passed the address of the new procedure to handle events for the window using the AddressOf operator. The TrayWindowProc VB procedure then responds to messages with the WM_TRAYMESSAGE identifier by calling an application-specific procedure (in this case, ProcessTray) and allows the rest of the messages to be processed normally, using the CallWindowProc API function.

NOTE

Note that the lParam argument passed into TrayWindowProc has been encapsulated in an enumerated type to allow client programs to test for them more easily.

To allow an application to place its icon in the tray, here is the code required in the form module:

```
Private Sub Form_Load()
    PutInTray Me, "Server Viewer"
End Sub

Private Sub Form_Unload(Cancel As Integer)
    TakeOffTray Me
End Sub

Public Sub ProcessTray(ByVal pMess As TRAY_EVENTS)

' Receive the event and take the appropriate action
Select Case pMess
Case TRAY_EVENTS.TRAY_DOUBLE_CLICK
    Me.Show
```

continues

```
Case TRAY_EVENTS.TRAY_RIGHT_MOUSE_DOWN
    PopupMenu mnuTray
End Select

End Sub
```

WARNING

If you do not call `TakeOffTray` in the `Unload` event of the form or if the program ends abruptly, the icon will remain in the tray even when the program is no longer running. This can cause duplicate icons to appear the next time your program is run. Not to worry, though. If the user clicks on the orphaned icon, the tray will notice that its application is no longer running and will remove it. Alternatively, by closing the second instance of the program, both icons will be unloaded.

Printing from the Shell

One of the other nice features in the shell is the capability to emulate the functionality users have when right-clicking on a document in Windows Explorer. The context menu that users see is populated dynamically from the Registry with a list of verbs that specify the action to be taken when the menu item is selected. Common verbs include Open, New, and Print.

Using the `ShellExecute` API function, your VB program can also activate files using these verbs. A particular instance of this is to instruct the shell to print a file. The code in Listing 13.9 encapsulates this function to print a file, given its name and directory.

Listing 13.9   A Standard Module That Encapsulates the Automatic Printing of a File from the Shell in the WinShellPrint Function

```
Option Explicit
Private Declare Function ShellExecute Lib "shell32.dll" _
    Alias "ShellExecuteA" (ByVal hwnd As Long, _
    ByVal lpOperation As String, ByVal lpFile As String, _
    ByVal lpParameters As String, _
    ByVal lpDirectory As String, _
    ByVal nShowCmd As Long) As Long

Public Function WinShellPrint(ByRef frmForm As Form, _
    ByVal pFile As String, _
    ByVal pDirectory As String) As Boolean

Dim llngRet As Long

' Execute the file using the "print" verb
' The window handle is used to specify which
```

```
' window should own any dialog boxes that are returned
llngRet = ShellExecute(frmForm.hwnd, "print", pFile, _
    vbNullString, pDirectory, 0)
' Error codes are also returned that can
' be passed along
If llngRet > 32 Then
    WinShellPrint = True
Else
    WinShellPrint = False
End If

End Function
```

As you will note in Listing 13.9, the WinShellPrint function accepts arguments that include the form that owns any dialog boxes produced from the operation, the filename, and the directory of the file. These arguments are passed to the ShellExecute Win32 API function along with the verb *print* to instruct the shell to open the given file and print it. The fourth argument passed to the function as vbNullString can include optional parameters that may be passed if the file represents an executable file. The final argument controls how the application is to be displayed. In this case, setting the argument to 0 hides the application during printing. Although the function can return 1 of 15 different error numbers, all return codes greater than 32 indicate success.

> **TIP**
>
> Other verbs you can use include *edit, explore, open,* and *properties*. In fact, if you specify the *open* verb with a URL, the default browser will be used to navigate to the URL using the syntax ShellExecute(0, "http://www.solutechinc.com/", vbNullString, vbNullString, 1).

Creating a Searchable ComboBox

One of the more common user interface techniques found in commercial applications is the searchable ComboBox. This type of control scans the items in the list as the user types. When a match is found, the combo or list box is scrolled to the correct entry, and the selected text is set to the remainder of the matched item.

This technique cannot be implemented solely by the Win32 API but can be done using a combination of VB code and the API. As with the TextBox discussed earlier, the ComboBox, as implemented by VB, does not provide event handlers for all the messages it can respond to. One of the key messages that are not included is CB_FINDSTRING. When sent to a ComboBox, along with the item at which to begin the search and the string to search for, this message returns the index of the first matching item in the control. This information can be used to scroll the ComboBox appropriately and set the selected text, using the ComboBox properties SelStart and SelLength.

NOTE

Note that in addition to the `WinCBFindString` method, I've also included the `WinCBShowDropDown` method that sends the message `CB_SHOWDROPDOWN` to a `ComboBox`. This method can be used in the `GotFocus` event to automatically instruct the `ComboBox` to drop down its items. If you allow users to type into the `ComboBox`, however, this technique has side effects that make it difficult to retain the text typed in by the user.

Listing 13.10 presents the code to encapsulate the sending of the message in a class module.

Listing 13.10   A Class Module That Encapsulates Message Calls to a ComboBox Control

```
Option Explicit

Private Declare Function SendMessageStr Lib "user32" _
    Alias "SendMessageA" (ByVal hwnd As Long, _
    ByVal wMsg As Long, ByVal wParam As Long, _
    lParam As String) As Long

Private Const CB_FINDSTRING = &H14C
Private Const CB_SHOWDROPDOWN = &H14F
Private Const CB_FINDSTRINGEXACT = &H158

Public Function WinCBFindString(ByVal pHwnd As Long, _
    ByVal pSearch As String, ByVal flExact As Boolean) As Long

Dim llngMess As Long

If flExact Then
    llngMess = CB_FINDSTRINGEXACT
Else
    llngMess = CB_FINDSTRING
End If

WinCBFindString = SendMessageStr(pHwnd, _
    llngMess, -1, ByVal pSearch)

End Function

Public Function WinCBShowDropDown(ByVal pHwnd As Long) As Boolean

Dim llngRet As Long

llngRet = SendMessageStr(pHwnd, CB_SHOWDROPDOWN, 1, vbNull)

If llngRet = -1 Then
```

```
        WinCBShowDropDown = False
    Else
        WinCBShowDropDown = True
    End If

End Function
```

You will notice that the method `WinCBFindString` also includes a flag that toggles which message is actually sent to the control. If `True`, the method sends `CB_FIND-STRINGEXACT`, which returns the index only if there is an exact match with the string passed in. This allows you to write code in the `LostFocus` or `Validate` events of the `ComboBox` to check whether the text currently in the `ComboBox` has an exact match in the control. If a match is not found, you can prompt the user to add the item to the control.

Listing 13.11 gives the code to implement the searchable combo box, with the optional capability to add items dynamically.

Listing 13.11   Form-Level Code to Implement the Searchable ComboBox, with the Capability to Dynamically Add Items the User Has Entered

```
Option Explicit

Private objTxt As New APIFunctions.APITextBox

Private Sub Combo1_KeyPress(Index As Integer, KeyAscii As Integer)

Dim llngRet As Long
Dim lstrFind As String

' Filter out unprintable keys
If KeyAscii >= 33 And KeyAscii <= 126 Then
    ' Assign the text to be found
    ' Note that Combo1.Text does not include the
    ' key just typed.
    If Combo1(Index).SelLength = 0 Then
        lstrFind = Combo1(Index).Text & Chr(KeyAscii)
    Else
        lstrFind = Left(Combo1(Index).Text, _
            Combo1(Index).SelStart) & Chr(KeyAscii)
    End If

    ' Is the text found?
    llngRet = objCB.WinCBFindString(Combo1(Index).hwnd, _
        lstrFind, False)
    If llngRet <> -1 Then
        ' If so then select the text and scroll the combo
        Combo1(Index).ListIndex = llngRet
        Combo1(Index).SelStart = Len(lstrFind)
```

continues

Listing 13.11   continued

```
            Combo1(Index).SelLength = Len(Combo1(Index).Text) - _
                Combo1(Index).SelStart
            ' Throw away the key because we just included it in
            ' the selected text
            KeyAscii = 0
        End If
    End If

End Sub

Private Sub Combo1_LostFocus(Index As Integer)

' If there is text in the control, do an exact match and
' add the text if not found
If Len(Combo1(Index).Text) > 0 Then
    If objCB.WinCBFindString(Combo1(Index).hwnd, Combo1(Index).Text, _
            True) = -1 Then
        ' May put a dialog here and perform
        ' processing to add the item
        If MsgBox("Add this item to the list of choices?", _
                vbQuestion + vbYesNo, Me.Caption) = vbYes Then
            Combo1(Index).AddItem Combo1(Index).Text
        Else
            ' Do not leave the existing text there if the
            ' user does not want to add it. If you want focus
            ' to remain, you should put this in the Validate
            ' event.
            Combo1(Index).Text = ""
        End If
    End If
End If

End Sub
```

> **TIP**
>
> Because this technique is code intensive, you should use control arrays when you want to add this functionality to multiple controls. Although not as widely used, an analogous function can be performed on `ListBox` controls using the `LB_FIND-STRING` and `LB_FINDSTRINGEXACT` messages. In fact, by adding an argument and some conditional logic to the `WinCBFindString` method (not to mention a name change), it could handle both types of controls.

Creating Multithreaded Applications

Since the addition of the `AddressOf` operator in version 5.0, VB developers have been looking for ways to take advantage of it. In fact, you've already looked at several techniques that take advantage of it to subclass a window. Unfortunately, one of the first things developers noticed is that the `CreateThread` API function can take the address of a procedure that is used as the entry point for the new thread. As a result, many developers have tried to make their applications multithreaded using this approach. Many of these same developers soon discovered that this technique destabilized their applications and caused a number of mysterious problems that are difficult to debug.

TIP

Although `CreateThread` can be used safely, (see *Ingenious Ways to Implement Threads in Visual Basic 5.0, Part I* in the August 1997 issue of the *Microsoft Systems Journal* by John Robbins), it requires diligence, not to mention more code, and should be used only when the application can justify the development effort.

It turns out that in VB there's a simpler and safer method for creating and using multiple threads in form-based applications.

For several years, VB has had the capability to create ActiveX Servers containing classes that can be externally created by client programs. In addition, these out-of-process servers themselves are standalone executables that can be invoked by a user and can contain a graphical form-based interface. The interesting aspect of this type of application is that the Project Properties dialog box, shown in Figure 13.3, contains the option Thread per Object. When set, this option instructs the server to pass external class creation requests to the COM Service Control Manager (SCM). The SCM creates the object from the class, placing it in its own single-threaded apartment (STA).

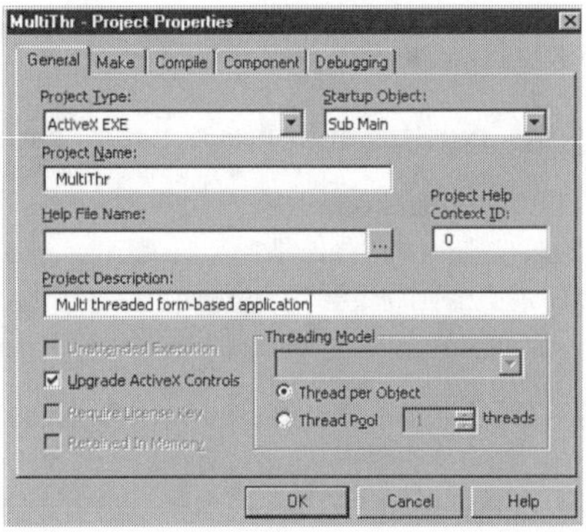

Figure 13.3

The Project Properties dialog box contains the Thread per Object option when you create an ActiveX Server application.

NOTE

An *apartment* is simply the term used to describe the execution environments in which COM objects run. COM objects run in either STAs (single-threaded apartments) or MTAs (multithreaded apartments).

STAs serialize all inbound requests for objects in the apartment through a single thread (hence the name) and use a message queuing mechanism to service incoming requests. As a result, no two objects loaded in the same apartment can execute simultaneously. This can reduce concurrency when multiple requests are made for objects in the same STA, but it allows developers to not have to worry about the thorny issues of multithreading, such as synchronization and critical sections. More information about threading models can be found in Chapter 16, "Building ActiveX Components."

When COM objects run in an MTA, a pool of threads is created that can service requests on multiple objects within the apartment simultaneously. At this time, VB does not support the creation of COM objects that can run in MTAs (commonly referred to as *free-threaded components*), but they can be built using Visual C++. As a final note, the option Thread Pool, shown in the dialog box in Figure 13.3, does not refer to an MTA but simply a pool of STAs.

The end result is that ActiveX Server applications can create multiple objects, each on its own thread.

The creation of objects in their own STAs works well and was designed for applications that are serving up objects for clients to use (such as the case of a distributed server application providing data to clients on the network). However, you can also take advantage of this ability to create multiple threads from within a single application by understanding when and how the SCM creates STAs.

The four keys to creating this type of multithreaded application are

- Make sure that the STA is created.
- Stop the main thread of the program from blocking the new STAs.
- Implement notification functionality from the new STA.
- Handle multiple invocations of the Sub Main procedure.

To illustrate these four concepts, consider the sample ActiveX EXE application whose class module, form module, and code module are shown in Listings 13.12, 13.13, and 13.14, respectively. The code in Listing 13.12 implements a file search class, clsFileSearch, which will be created in its own thread. This class contains the methods FindFilesAsync and FindFilesSync, which recursively search for files matching the given specification and starting in the given path.

Listing 13.12   Code for the clsFileSearch Class

```
Option Explicit

Private objFileSystem As New FileSystemObject
Private objFilesFound As New Collection
```

```vb
' Events that will be used to notify the main thread
Public Event SearchComplete(colRes As Collection)
Public Event SearchErr(ByVal SearchError As ErrObject)


Public Sub FindFilesAsync(ByVal pFileName As String, _
        ByVal pStartPath As String)
    ' Async method calls the public function to
    ' start the search
    RequestCallback Me, pFileName, pStartPath
End Sub

Public Sub FindFilesSync(ByVal pFile As String, _
    ByVal pStartPath As String)

Dim objFolder As Folder
Dim objSubFolder As Folder
Dim objFile As File

On Error GoTo FindFileErr

' Check for the existence of the starting path
If Not objFileSystem.FolderExists(pStartPath) Then
    RaiseEvent SearchErr(Err)
    Exit Sub
End If

' Get a reference to the starting folder
Set objFolder = objFileSystem.GetFolder(pStartPath)

' Search the folders recursively
SearchFolder objFolder, pFile

' Return the collection of file objects using the event
RaiseEvent SearchComplete(objFilesFound)
Exit Sub
FindFileErr:
    RaiseEvent SearchErr(Err)

End Sub

Private Sub SearchFolder(ByVal objFolder As Folder, _
    ByVal strFileName As String)

Dim objSubFolder As Folder
Dim objFile As File
```

continues

Listing 13.12   continued

```
' Traverse the subfolder in the given folder
For Each objSubFolder In objFolder.SubFolders
    ' Call this procedure recursively
    SearchFolder objSubFolder, strFileName
Next

' Traverse the files in the folder and look for matches
For Each objFile In objFolder.Files
    If Mid(objFile.Name, 1, Len(strFileName)) = strFileName Then
        ' Match! Add it to the collection
        objFilesFound.Add objFile
    End If
Next

End Sub
```

NOTE

The file search class uses the `FileSystemObject` and associated objects introduced in VB 6. For a more complete explanation of their functionality and use, see Chapter 18, "Adding Professional Features." For an all-Win32 API approach, you could also use the `FindFirstFile` and `FindNextFile` functions.

WARNING

The VB debugger can be used to debug applications developed with this technique, although the application will always be single threaded. The same cannot be said of applications developed using the `CreateThread` API. You can, however, compile the project with the Create Symbolic Debug Info option turned on and debug the multithreaded VB application in Visual C++.

Creating the STA

To make sure that the SCM is used to create the object, you must use the `CreateObject` function and pass it the name of the class to be created. Essentially, the SCM calls back into the application and creates the new STA when `CreateObject` is used. To make sure that the SCM is called, the object is created like this (extracted from Listing 13.13):

```
Set objFileAsync = CreateObject("MultiThr.clsFileSearch")
```

rather than

```
Set objFileAsync = New clsFileSearch
```

Using the second method always creates the object in the main thread of the application. The code for the application's main form is shown in Listing 13.13. Note that `Command1` creates a new object in the main thread and performs the search synchronously while `Command2` creates a new STA to perform the search asynchronously.

Listing 13.13   The Code Behind the Application's Main Form

```
Option Explicit

Private WithEvents objFileAsync As clsFileSearch
Private WithEvents objFileSync As clsFileSearch

Private Sub Command1_Click()
 ' Run synchronously
 Set objFileAsync = New clsFileSearch
 objFileAsync.FindFilesSync "auto", "c:\"
End Sub

Private Sub Command2_Click()
 ' Run asynchronously
 Set objFileAsync = CreateObject("MultiThr.clsFileSearch")
 objFileAsync.FindFilesAsync "auto", "c:\"
End Sub

Private Sub objFileAsync_SearchComplete(colRes As Collection)

Dim lItem As Variant
Dim i As Integer

' Load the results in a ListBox
For i = 1 To colRes.Count
    List1.AddItem colRes(i)
Next

Set objFileAsync = Nothing

End Sub

Private Sub objFileAsync_SearchErr(ByVal SearchError As ErrObject)
    MsgBox SearchError.Description
    Set objFileAsync = Nothing
End Sub

Private Sub objFileSync_SearchComplete(colRes As Collection)

Dim lItem As Variant
Dim i As Integer

' Load the results in a ListBox
For i = 1 To colRes.Count
    List2.AddItem colRes(i)
Next

Set objFileSync = Nothing
```

continues

Listing 13.13   continued

```
End Sub

Private Sub objFileSync_SearchErr(ByVal SearchError As ErrObject)
    MsgBox SearchError.Description
    Set objFileSync = Nothing
End Sub
```

Stopping the Blocking

The second concern is to ensure that the main thread of the program does not block the new thread. By simply calling a method on the object, the new STA will block the main thread, causing the method to perform synchronously. The key to overcoming this behavior is to use the SetTimer API function to create an asynchronous entry point for the method.

The SetTimer API function is one that uses the callback mechanism of the Win32 API to call back into the program at regular intervals. To do this in VB, you pass the address of a VB public standard module procedure into the function using the AddressOf operator. Other API functions that use this mechanism include the enumeration functions, such as EnumWindows, EnumFontFamilies, and EnumPrinters, each of which calls back into the program multiple times to enumerate a list of items.

To make a method asynchronous (releasing the main thread), the class module can call SetTimer, passing it the address of a procedure that will be used to call the actual method that performs the work. In this way, the method acts as a kind of proxy. For example, in Listing 13.12, the method FindFilesAsync calls the public procedure RequestCallback, passing along the arguments it was given, in addition to a reference to the object itself:

```
Public Sub FindFilesAsync(ByVal pFileName As String, _
        ByVal pStartPath As String)
    RequestCallback Me, pFileName, pStartPath
End Sub
```

RequestCallback then stores the arguments in module-level variables and invokes the SetTimer API function:

```
Private objFile As clsFileSearch
Private mstrFile As String
Private mstrStart As String

Public Sub RequestCallback(obj As clsFileSearch, _
    ByVal pFile As String, ByVal pStartPath As String)
  mstrFile = pFile
  mstrStart = pStartPath
  Set objFile = obj
  mlngTimerID = SetTimer(0, 0, 1, AddressOf TimerCallback)
End Sub
```

Note that `SetTimer` passes in the address of the public procedure `TimerCallback` with an interval of 1 millisecond. After the timer has been set, the main thread is released and may continue to process other requests. Windows then calls back into the program to invoke `TimerCallback`. This procedure simply stops the timer (because it is used for a one-time notification) and invokes the appropriate method on the cached file search object using the module-level variables:

```
Public Sub TimerCallback(ByVal hWnd As Long, ByVal uMsg As Long, __
    ByVal idEvent As Long, ByVal dwTime As Long)
  KillTimer 0, mlngTimerID
  objFile.FindFilesSync mstrFile, mstrStart
  Set objFile = Nothing
End Sub
```

Although it might seem confusing, keep in mind that the module-level variables and all global variables are copied into each STA that is created. In other words, each STA has its own copy of `mstrFile`, `mstrStart`, and `objFile`. This makes sharing data between STAs somewhat difficult, but for this application it is not required. The complete code module that implements the callback can be seen in Listing 13.14.

Listing 13.14   The Standard Module That Implements the Callback Functionality and the Sub Main Procedure
```
Option Explicit

' Constant that holds the caption of the main form
Public Const MAIN_FORM_CAPTION = "Form1"

Declare Function FindWindow Lib "user32" Alias _
    "FindWindowA" (ByVal lpClassName As String, _
    ByVal lpWindowName As String) As Long

Public Declare Function SetTimer Lib "user32" _
    (ByVal hWnd As Long, ByVal nIDEvent As Long, _
    ByVal uElapse As Long, ByVal lpTimerFunc As Long) As Long

Public Declare Function KillTimer Lib "user32" _
    (ByVal hWnd As Long, ByVal nIDEvent As Long) As Long

Private mlngTimerID As Long ' ID of the timer
Private objFile As clsFileSearch ' Private Search object

Private mstrFile As String
Private mstrStart As String

Public Function IsMainFormLoaded() As Boolean

' Determines whether the main form has been loaded.
```

continues

Listing 13.14   continued

```
' If it has, return True; otherwise, return false.
If FindWindow(vbNullString, MAIN_FORM_CAPTION) = 0 Then
    IsMainFormLoaded = False
Else
    IsMainFormLoaded = True
End If

End Function

Public Sub RequestCallback(obj As clsFileSearch, _
    ByVal pFile As String, ByVal pStartPath As String)

' Called from the class that is to be run asynchronously
  mstrFile = pFile
  mstrStart = pStartPath

' Set the object to call back into and set up the timer
  Set objFile = obj

  mlngTimerID = SetTimer(0, 0, 1, AddressOf TimerCallback)
End Sub

Public Sub TimerCallback(ByVal hWnd As Long, ByVal uMsg As Long, _
    ByVal idEvent As Long, ByVal dwTime As Long)

' Kill the timer
KillTimer 0, mlngTimerID

' Invoke the call synchronously, but because it
' is on a different thread, it is really asynchronous
objFile.FindFilesSync mstrFile, mstrStart

' Set the reference to Nothing
Set objFile = Nothing

End Sub

Public Sub Main()

If App.PrevInstance = True Then
    MsgBox "Cannot run more than one instance of this app"
    Exit Sub
End If

' Check whether the main form has been loaded.
' If not then load it.
```

```
If Not IsMainFormLoaded() Then
  Form1.Show
End If

End Sub
```

Implementing Notification

After the method in the new STA has been invoked, some notification mechanism must be available back to the main thread. One easy way to do this is to implement events in the class module. In the example of clsFileSearch (in Listing 13.12), two events, SearchComplete and SearchError, have been defined:

```
Public Event SearchComplete(colRes As Collection)
Public Event SearchErr(ByVal SearchError As ErrObject)
```

These events are raised when the FindFilesSync method either completes its search or encounters an error. Note that SearchComplete also passes back a collection of File objects that were found. To make sure that the main thread is notified, you must declare the object variable using the WithEvents keyword in the form.

```
Private WithEvents objFileAsync As clsFileSearch
```

Dealing with Sub Main

The final issue that must be addressed is handling the code in the Sub Main procedure. By necessity, an ActiveX Server application must use the Sub Main procedure as its startup object. Unfortunately, each time a new STA is created, the code in Sub Main is executed. This can lead to multiple instances of your main form being opened.

To stop this behavior, you can use a simple Win32 API technique to search for the main window's caption in the list of windows using the FindWindow function. If the window is found, the code does not show the main form. I've encapsulated the call to FindWindow in a public procedure (in Listing 13.13):

```
Public Sub Main()
  If App.PrevInstance = True Then
    MsgBox "Cannot run more than one instance of this app"
    Exit Sub
  End If

  If Not IsMainFormLoaded() Then
    Form1.Show
  End If
End Sub
```

Note that Sub Main can also check the PrevInstance property of the App object to stop the user from invoking multiple instances.

Should You Multithread?

Obviously, implementing multithreaded applications requires a good understanding of what VB is doing under the covers, as well as making the application more complex to code and debug. Therefore, it is recommended that you consider multithreading only when your application's design calls for it. Performing tasks such as logging, printing, and database work are all good candidates in designs where this activity would normally cause the user to wait.

Accessing the Internet

As Internet protocols have been integrated more fully into the operating system, developers have been looking for techniques to exploit this functionality in their applications. As you may be aware, much of the functionality of MSIE is available through the WinInet and URLMon DLLs that began shipping with MSIE 3. In this section I'll cover one of the most basic techniques for determining whether the computer on which your application runs has access to the Internet.

A quick check of the documentation for WinInet reveals that there is an `InternetGetConnectedState` function available that will return an indicator as to whether the computer is connected via modem, LAN, proxy server, or is running in offline mode. Unfortunately, this function is not foolproof and does not return a value that can be used unquestioningly. For example, cases where the computer thinks the Internet connection is available but the LAN or modem connection has been severed may not be detected.

A more reliable approach is to use the `InternetGetConnectedState` function in combination with the `InternetOpen` and `InternetOpenURL` functions to open a connection to the Internet and attempt to access a URL. If the operation succeeds you can be assured that an Internet connection exists and can be subsequently used.

To illustrate this technique consider the class module `clsWinInet` shown in Listing 13.15. This class module contains a single method, `IsConnected`, which is passed a URL used when checking for the connection. Obviously, a well-known and reliable URL should be used.

Listing 13.15   The clsWinInet Class Module Used to Check for the Existence of an Internet Connection

```
Option Explicit

' Constants used to determine the state of the connection
' and how a connection should be established
Private Const INTERNET_CONNECTION_MODEM = 1
Private Const INTERNET_CONNECTION_LAN = 2
Private Const INTERNET_CONNECTION_PROXY = 4
Private Const INTERNET_CONNECTION_MODEM_BUSY = 8
Private Const INTERNET_CONNECTION_OFFLINE = 32

' Open the connection using settings from the registry
```

```
Private Const INTERNET_OPEN_TYPE_PRECONFIG = 0

' Flags for InternetOpenURL
Private Const INTERNET_FLAG_RELOAD = &H80000000
Private Const INTERNET_FLAG_NO_CACHE_WRITE = &H4000000

' API functions from the WinInet DLL
Private Declare Function InternetGetConnectedState Lib "wininet" _
    (lpdwFlags As Long, ByVal dwReserved As Long) As Long

Private Declare Function InternetOpen Lib "wininet" Alias _
    "InternetOpenA" (ByVal lpszAgent As String, _
    ByVal dwAccessType As Long, ByVal lpszProxyName As String, _
    ByVal lpszProxyBypass As String, ByVal dwFlags As Long) As Long

Private Declare Function InternetOpenUrl Lib "wininet" Alias _
    "InternetOpenUrlA" (ByVal hInternet As Long, _
    ByVal lpszUrl As String, ByVal lpszHeaders As String, _
    ByVal dwHeadersLength As Long, ByVal dwFlags As Long, _
    ByVal dwContext As Long) As Long

Private Declare Function InternetCloseHandle Lib "wininet" _
    (ByVal hInternet As Long) As Long

Public Function IsConnected(ByVal pURL As String) As Boolean

Dim lngInet As Long
Dim lngFlags As Long
Dim lngURL As Long

' Assume disconnected until otherwise known
IsConnected = False

' First check to see if we're online
InternetGetConnectedState lngFlags, 0
If (lngFlags And INTERNET_CONNECTION_MODEM) Or _
    (lngFlags And INTERNET_CONNECTION_OFFLINE) Then
    ' Either in directly connected offline mode or using a dial up
    ' which is not connected
    Exit Function
End If

' Now try to open up the URL and return True if successful

' First get an Internet handle
lngInet = InternetOpen("APIInet", INTERNET_OPEN_TYPE_PRECONFIG, _
    vbNullString, vbNullString, 0)
```

continues

Listing 13.15   continued

```
' Now try to open the connection
If lngInet > 0 Then
    ' Don't write it to the cache and read from the Internet
    ' even if the page is cached
    lngURL = InternetOpenUrl(lngInet, pURL, vbNullString, 0, _
        INTERNET_FLAG_NO_CACHE_WRITE Or INTERNET_FLAG_RELOAD, 0)
    If lngURL > 0 Then
        ' Clean up
        InternetCloseHandle lngURL
        IsConnected = True
    End If
    ' Clean up
    InternetCloseHandle lngInet
End If

End Function
```

As you can see in Listing 13.15, the `IsConnected` function first calls `InternetGetConnectedState` to determine the status of the connection. If the resulting flags indicate a modem connection or offline mode, an Internet connection does not currently exist.

NOTE

Additional functions are available, such as `InternetAutoDial`, that can be used to initiate a modem connection.

If the flags indicate a modem busy, LAN, or proxy connection, the `InternetOpen` function is used to return a handle used in subsequent WinInet functions. The `InternetOpenURL` function is then called to attempt to open the URL passed in as the argument to `IsConnected`. Flags passed to `InternetOpenURL` specify that the page is not to be cached, and it should be accessed from the Internet rather than from cache. The `InternetCloseHandle` function is then used to clean up both the connection to the URL and the Internet session itself.

The `IsConnected` method can then be called from client code using the following syntax:

```
Dim objAPIInet as APIInet.clsWinInet

If objAPIInet.IsConnected("http://www.solutechinc.com") Then
    ' Do some other operation here
End If
```

Summary

As you can probably guess, you have an almost unlimited number of opportunities for using the Win32 API to enhance your applications. However, the key point to remember is that although it is possible to duplicate some of the features seen in commercial applications, you have to weigh the development time and effort against the benefit to the end user. Because they add complexity and reduce maintainability, features such as multithreading and subclassing should be used with care. Because VB is primarily a tool for rapid application development, this is an especially important consideration. For the corporate developer, the focus should be on providing the core functionality and using the Win32 API only when it is required.

CHAPTER 14

Using ADO for Data Access

The primary activities of most corporate applications involve data access of one sort or another. Whether the target is a relational database running on a remote server, as in the case of Oracle and SQL Server, or a local Jet database, much of the coding and debugging involves connecting, retrieving, and updating data. As a result, this chapter is devoted to taking an in-depth look at using ActiveX Data Objects (ADO) in VB applications that are designed to run on the desktop or are distributed across the network.

I decided to focus on ADO exclusively in this book because, as you will see shortly, it is clearly Microsoft's strategic direction. Therefore, for new development, ADO is certainly the recommended starting place. In addition, VB 6 makes connecting to ADO and using it much simpler than previously, when in fact, VB was not aware that ADO even existed.

After a brief introduction to the architecture and objects of ADO, I go over the basics of recordsets, cursors, and locking before drilling down into some general techniques and recommendations when using ADO. Included in these techniques are

- Using the `Command` object
- Using prepared statements
- Calling stored procedures with parameters
- Calling data modification stored procedures
- Calling stored procedures with return values
- Using the Data Environment
- Populating controls with reference data
- Loading the `MSFlexGrid` control
- Working with BLOBs

- Implementing asynchronous processing with ADO events
- Distributed application considerations
- Understanding connection pooling
- Using disconnected recordsets
- Performing batch updates
- Persisting resultsets on the client

Much of the discussion and many of the examples in this chapter focus on using remote data providers and Microsoft SQL Server 7, in particular, because it is arguably the primary database VB developers use. However, many techniques discussed here can be duplicated using other data providers.

An Overview of OLE DB and ADO

As most developers in the corporate world know, useful data resides in many formats throughout the organization. At one time or another, most developers have attempted to interface with relational database management systems (RDBMSs), spreadsheets, directory services, email engines, and ISAM files such as Access or Paradox. The only common denominator in these attempts is that each requires a different API and the time to figure out how to do the job.

Early on, Microsoft recognized this difficulty in dealing with relational databases and developed ODBC to address the issue. ODBC provides an abstraction layer between the database and the application code by injecting drivers and a cursor library that communicates with the database, using its native protocol and optionally managed records returned by the database. Microsoft has applied the same concept, Windows Open Services Architecture (WOSA), to other data sources such as email (MAPI), telephony (TAPI), and even financial services (WOSA/XFS).

NOTE

The term *WOSA* has had a long and confused life. At various times, it has been called *Windows Open Systems and Services Architecture*, *Windows Open Systems Architecture*, and *Windows Open Services Architecture*.

Although this technique works well for relational databases, the model does not apply to data that is not easily represented in a tabular format. Once again, Microsoft analyzed the problem and in 1996 came up with its *Universal Data Access (UDA)* strategy.

At the core of UDA are a series of COM interfaces, dubbed *OLE DB*. These interfaces allow developers to build *data providers* that flexibly represent data stored in various formats. Although this is similar in concept to ODBC, the difference is in the flexibility of OLE DB when you are accessing more than simply tabular data. In addition, OLE DB defines interfaces for building *service components*, which are components that manipulate data, such as cursor and sorting engines.

OLE DB is great for C++ programmers, but because it requires manipulation of interface pointers, VB programmers cannot access it directly. This is where ADO comes in.

ADO was developed as an object interface to OLE DB, accessible by automation clients. Now, VB developers can use OLE DB through ADO to communicate with data providers. Figure 14.1 shows the resulting architecture.

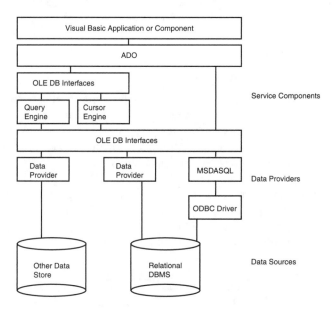

Figure 14.1

The Universal Data Access architecture.

NOTE

ADO has been through releases 1.0, 1.5, 2.0, and 2.1 (which is used in this discussion). Briefly, 1.0 was introduced in 1996 for use with Internet Information Server (IIS) 3.0 and Active Server Pages (ASP); 1.5 in 1997 allowed VB developers to get into the act and expanded the core set of features; 2.0 in 1998 added asynchronous processing, events, and a more sophisticated cursor library; and 2.1 in 1999 refines 2.0 to add advanced searching and custom control of updates to recordsets created using a JOIN. ADO 2.0 shipped with VB 6, and 2.1 shipped with SQL Server 7 and Office 2000.

Note that databases for which an ODBC driver exists can still be used with OLE DB. This is because ADO ships with the Microsoft OLE DB Provider for ODBC Drivers (MSDASQL), which transparently uses an ODBC driver by specifying a DSN when connecting. In fact, the default behavior of ADO is to use MSDASQL. That having been said, Microsoft is hoping that OLE DB data providers will be written by data source vendors to take advantage of features of OLE DB and increase performance. Microsoft ships several providers, including those for Oracle, Microsoft SQL Server,

Jet, Microsoft Site Server, Microsoft Index Server, Active Directory Services Interface, and Microsoft OLAP Services.

Because UDA is a key part of Microsoft's strategic direction and is integral to so many of its products, Microsoft has created a separate group and distribution point for the ADO and OLE DB software. All the data access software is now bundled in the Microsoft Data Access Components (MDAC) and can be downloaded from www.microsoft.com/data.

The ADO Object Model

Perhaps the most striking features of the ADO object model are its simplicity and non-hierarchical nature. The arrangement of the model, shown in Figure 14.2, highlights the fact that, of the seven objects (Connection, Command, Recordset, Parameter, Property, Error, and Field) in the model, four of them (Connection, Recordset, Command, and Parameter) can be created and manipulated independently of the others. These objects can then be associated with others at runtime via the properties (ActiveConnection and ActiveCommand) shown in Figure 14.2 or, in the case of the Parameter object, by appending it to the collection of Parameter objects for the Command. The figure also highlights which methods (Execute, CreateParameter) can be used to create one object from another object.

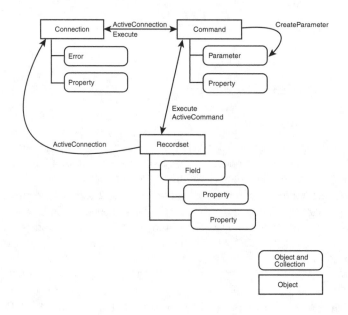

Figure 14.2

The ADO object model is not strictly hierarchical and contains fewer collections than its predecessors.

TIP

In Figure 14.2, even though it appears that the three primary ADO objects are totally independent, this is not strictly the case.

ADO does occasionally create objects implicitly, even if you do not create them explicitly. For example, a `Recordset` object always requires a `Connection` object when used to retrieve data from a data source. When the `Recordset` is opened by passing a connect string, instead of a `Connection` object, to the `Open` method, ADO will create an invisible `Connection` object before the `Recordset` is opened. The code for this would be

```
Dim rsADO As Recordset

Set rsADO = New Recordset

rsADO.Open "SELECT * FROM authors", & _
    "provider=SQLOLEDB;server=ssosa;" & _
    "database=pubs;uid=dfox;pwd=dfox1"
```

This also has the side effect of creating multiple connections to the data source each time code such as this is executed. As a result, it is recommended, especially for fat client applications, that a `Connection` object be explicitly created and reused to preserve precious server connections.

The same rules about implicit creation also apply to the `Error`, `Recordset`, and `Field` objects in similar scenarios.

The other three objects (`Field`, `Error`, and `Property`) represent collections of objects that are dependent on their immediate ancestor. The other feature of ADO, which differentiates it from other Microsoft data access technologies such as DAO and RDO and makes it more lightweight, is the lack of collections. RDO and DAO both keep collections of recordsets, queries, and connections, increasing the complexity and resources required. In ADO, you create these objects individually and deallocate them when you're finished.

TIP

If you're interested in comparing ADO to RDO and DAO, you can check out my article, *ADO 2.0 Adds Performance, Flexibility* in the July 1998 issue of the *Visual Basic Programmer's Journal*. It compares the code necessary to perform six common techniques, using each of the three data access interfaces.

With the introductions out of the way, it's time to drill down into how to leverage ADO in real applications.

Cursors and Locking

Before looking at specific techniques using ADO, you should have a thorough understanding of the concepts of cursors and locking. Oftentimes, understanding which cursor options to choose makes the difference between an application that performs well and one users will reject.

At the simplest level, a *cursor* is a collection of pointers to a resultset returned by the data source and code that allows the pointers to be manipulated. Cursors can support features such as the abilities to scroll forward and backward, to update the recordset, and to view data as it is changed by another user. However, with these features comes a price. The more features you ask for, the more resources are consumed by either the data source, ADO, or both. In some cases, using these cursor features will also slow performance because more server round trips might be incurred.

Basically, ADO supports two cursor locations (client and server), five cursor types (forward only, dynamic, keyset, static, and firehose), and four types of locking (pessimistic, optimistic, batch, and read-only). The interplay of these settings is where it becomes confusing. First, you will look at the cursor locations.

Cursor Locations

ADO supports the creation of cursors on both the client (adUseClient) and the server (adUseServer). In this context, *client* can refer to either a client workstation running a VB application or a COM component running in MTS. *Server* refers to a cursor supplied by the OLE DB provider or ODBC driver for a specific data source. In other words, client-side cursors bring rows down to the client machine to be manipulated, whereas server-side cursors usually implement some technique for manipulating rows directly on the data source.

The location can be specified by setting the CursorLocation property of either the Connection or Recordset object before a recordset is created. Because applications rarely perform best when one option is used ubiquitously, it is recommended that before each recordset is created, the cursor location be chosen explicitly. Server-side cursors are the default in ADO.

Keep in mind that not all data sources (in fact, most) support both methods. For example, starting with version 6.0, SQL Server supported server-side cursors by creating the resultset in its TempDB database on the server. The resultset is stored on the server, and rows are accessed via system stored procedures (such as sp_cursoropen and sp_cursorfetch) called by the OLE DB provider or ODBC driver. Issues you should understand when choosing a cursor location include round trips, resources, and functionality.

Round Trips

Obviously, when server-side cursors are employed, the client application will make multiple trips to the data source to work with rows from the resultset because they are, by definition, managed by the data source. The number of trips is affected by the CacheSize property of the Recordset object, which indicates how many rows the data provider will keep in its cache with each call to the data source. The default CacheSize of 1 will force ADO to make a trip to the data source for each row and, in almost all cases, hurts performance. This is especially true when the communication is occurring on a slow local area network or across a wide area network.

Alternatively, when client-side cursors are employed, the entire resultset is sent to the client using one SQL statement, with the rows being managed by client-side cursor code. As a result, when considering network traffic, client-side cursors are generally more efficient because they incur fewer round trips to the data source.

That having been said, server-side cursors can be more efficient when an application is likely to address only a small percentage of the rows in the resultset. Fewer round trips to the data source will be required. You should note, however, that applications should be designed to ask for only those rows required by the client. An application should not attempt to create large resultsets when only a few rows will be viewed by the client.

Resources

A second point to consider is the consumption of resources on the client and server. When server-side cursors are used in the case of SQL Server, the server must maintain resultsets for each user of the application. In applications that support more than 50 users, this can quickly bog down most server installations.

However, client-side cursors require that a cursor library be loaded on the client to manage the resultset. When using a native OLE DB provider (such as those shipped with ADO for Oracle, SQL 7, and Jet) and client-side cursors, ADO loads the ADO Cursor Library to manage the rows. This cursor library is relatively fast and supports features such as disassociated recordsets, background population, and batch updating.

As mentioned previously, MSDASQL can be used to access data through an ODBC driver. In MDAC 2.0, MSDASQL loads the ODBC Cursor Library to manage the resultset. Historically, the ODBC Cursor Library has been branded as inefficient and does not support the features in the ADO Cursor Library, such as background population. In cases where batch updating is required when using MSDASQL, both the ADO Cursor Library and the ODBC Cursor Library are loaded. With version 2.1, it appears as if MSDASQL uses the ADO Cursor Library exclusively.

Functionality

The final consideration regarding cursor location is the level of functionality required by the application. Although both types of cursors can be updateable, server-side cursors can dynamically reflect changes made by other users. This can be important when the application has to know immediately about changes made by other users. This type of functionality requires more overhead but may be justified, depending on the requirements. Conversely, client-side cursors cannot dynamically reflect changes made by other users but can, for example, work with statements that return multiple resultsets and perform offline modifications and batch updates. This allows the application to accumulate changes to the resultset and post them to the server in groups.

The specific functionality supported by either client-side or server-side cursors is determined by the type of cursor selected.

Cursor Types

When creating a recordset, you determine the type of cursor by setting the `CursorType` property of the `Recordset` object either before the recordset is created or as the recordset is opened using the `Open` method. Table 14.1 describes the cursor types supported.

Table 14.1   ADO Cursor Types

Constant	Description
adOpenDynamic	Fully scrollable cursor where all changes made by other users are immediately visible. Can be updateable. Normally, this option is not supported when using client-side cursors.
adOpenForwardOnly	Default cursor type that allows the resultset to be traversed in a forward-only direction. This is ideal when the results are to be traversed once, such as loading into a `ComboBox`. Changes made by other users to the resultset are not visible. Can be updateable.
adOpenKeyset	Fully scrollable cursor where a key for each row is retrieved into the cursor. Can be updateable. Additions made by other users are not visible, but deletions and changes are visible if the row is changed before it becomes the current row in the cursor. Normally, this option is not supported when using client-side cursors.
adOpenStatic	Fully scrollable cursor where all the columns in the resultset are copied into the cursor. This cursor can be updateable, but changes made by other users are not visible.

As alluded to earlier, the fifth option, not shown in Table 14.1 since it cannot be set explicitly, is the cursorless resultset, or *firehose cursor*. In this instance, and if the provider supports it, ADO does not use a cursor library at all but reads rows directly out of the network buffers into the `Recordset` object.

NOTE

In SQL Server terminology, a firehose cursor is also referred to as using the *default resultset*.

Firehose cursors usually provide the best performance because the rows are not maintained by the server (increasing scalability), nor are they loaded into a client-side cursor library (reducing memory requirements on the client). Firehose cursors allow the application to obtain the data more quickly at the cost of leaving issues such as update-ability and scrollability up to the client code. In addition, firehose cursors do not support other features of the `Recordset` object, such as the `RecordCount` property, and always set it to –1.

TIP

When using firehose cursors, you should always fetch all the rows from the result-set and close it by looping through the `Recordset` using the `MoveNext` method or by copying the data directly to a buffer using the `GetRows` or `GetString` methods discussed later. Not doing so can prevent the `Connection` object from doing other work, resulting in trappable errors or the provider opening up multiple connections to the data source. In addition, locks may be held at the data source until all the data is retrieved.

To generate a firehose cursor, you must use a server-side, forward-only, read-only cursor with a cache size of 1.

```
Dim cn as Connection
Dim rs as New Recordset

' Generate a firehose cursor
With rs
    .CursorLocation = adUseServer
    .CursorType = adOpenForwardOnly
    .LockType = adLockReadOnly
    .CacheSize = 1
    .Open strSQL, cnn
End With
```

Note that firehose cursors are the default and, as I explain later, are particularly effective in cases where the resultset can be read-only because updates will be done through stored procedures or when loading lookup data.

TIP

Although the documentation explicitly states that the `CacheSize` must be set to 1 for a firehose cursor to be created, my tests and information from a member of the MDAC team revealed (at least against SQL Server 7) something different. A firehose cursor will still be created if the `CacheSize` is set to a value greater than 1, all other properties being equal. In fact, doing so will instruct OLE DB to pull records from the network buffers in larger groups, thereby increasing performance at the cost of allocated memory (as discussed previously).

Obviously, there is an endless number of permutations of the cursor types, locations, and functionality supported, based on the OLE DB Provider and data source you are using. However, as a general rule, ADO and its cursor library support the cursor types and locations shown in Table 14.2.

Table 14.2   ADO Cursor Types and Locations Supported by Default

Type	Client	Server	Update-able	Fully Scrollable
Dynamic	No (defaults to Static)	Yes	Can be	Yes
Firehose	No (defaults to Static)	Yes	No	No
Forward-Only	No (defaults to Static)	Yes	Can be	No
Keyset	No (defaults to Static)	Yes	Can be	Yes
Static	Yes	Yes	Can be	Yes

You will notice that the ADO Cursor Library does not support dynamic, keyset, or forward-only cursors and simply defaults to using a static cursor in those instances.

Locking and Isolation

The last major properties to consider when creating a cursor are `LockType` and `IsolationLevel`. Like `CursorType`, `LockType` can be set either on the `Recordset` object before the `Open` method is called or in the `Open` method itself as an argument. Table 14.3 lists the lock types supported by ADO.

Table 14.3   ADO Lock Types

Constant	Description
adLockBatchOptimistic	When used with client-side static cursors, it enables `Recordsets` to be disconnected, modified, reconnected, and then updated using the ADO Cursor Library. When used with server-side cursors, it disables immediate updates on the server as the rows are modified. Used with the `UpdateBatch` and `CancelBatch` methods of the Recordset.
adLockOptimistic	Instructs the provider to lock rows at the data source only as they are updated. This ensures greater concurrency but less consistency because multiple users may have changed data. When using this option, the application must be prepared to handle failed updates and refresh the data using the `Resync` or `Requery` methods of the `Recordset` object.

Constant	Description
adLockPessimistic	Instructs the provider to lock rows at the data source as they are edited. This ensures greater consistency but less concurrency because other users may be blocked while the row is locked.
adLockReadOnly	This is the default and disallows changes to the data explicitly by using the Update or UpdateBatch methods of the Recordset or implicitly by moving off a modified row.

Keep in mind that once again not all lock types are supported by the various providers. For example, the supported lock types and cursor locations when using the OLE DB Provider for SQL Server (SQLOLEDB) can be seen in Table 14.4.

Table 14.4 *Supported Locking Options When Using SQLOLEDB*

Lock Type	Client	Server
Batch Optimistic	Yes	Yes
Optimistic	Yes	Yes
Pessimistic	No (defaults to Batch Optimistic)	Yes (but rows are locked as they are traversed)
Read-Only	Yes	Yes

A setting related to the lock type is the IsolationLevel property of the Connection object. This property tells the provider which locks to apply, or not apply, during a transaction. For example, by default SQL Server attempts to put share locks at the row or page level as rows are read or updated by a user. Unfortunately, if those rows are in the process of being updated by another user, an exclusive lock will have been placed on them until the changes are committed. As a result, SQL Server will make the connection, attempting to obtain the share lock wait until the exclusive lock has been released. Normally, this is the correct behavior because you don't want to have users reading data that is in the process of being updated but not yet committed. However, in some circumstances—such as a monitoring application that you want to make sure does not lock data being processed by a high-volume transaction processing system—you would always want the data to be queryable, regardless of its committed state. Again, this is a trade-off between increased concurrency and decreased consistency.

Table 14.5 describes the options for setting the isolation level.

Table 14.5 Valid ADO Isolation-Level Settings

Constant	Description
`adXactBrowse` or `adXactReadUncommitted`	Allows the application to read rows that have been modified but are not committed.
`AdXactCursorStability` or `adXactReadCommitted`	Allows the application to only read data that has been committed, but releases locks when the data is no longer being accessed.
`adXactIsolated` or `adXactSerializable`	Allows the application to only read data that has been committed, but holds locks for the duration of the transaction.
`adXactRepeatableRead`	Allows the application to only read data that has been committed, but holds locks for the duration of the transaction. In addition, it allows new rows to be added to the resultsets if it refreshed using the `Requery` method.
`adXactUnspecified`	Indicates that ADO cannot determine what isolation level is being used.
`adXactChaos`	Indicates that the transaction cannot overwrite pending changes from a higher isolation transaction. In SQL Server, this is the same as `adXactReadUncommitted`.

An Example Using Cursors

A typical example of creating and using a cursor can be seen in Listing 14.1. In this example, a two-tier VB application contains a class module, `clsConsultants`, that includes a method that returns a `Recordset` object containing all the consultants in the database. Because this application requires that the consultant records be scrollable (so they can be cached in the private variable `mrsCon`) but not updateable, a client-side static and read-only cursor was created.

TIP

There are three documented ways to create recordsets using ADO. You can use the `Open` method of the `Recordset` object (as shown in the example), the `Execute` method of the `Connection` object, or the `Execute` method of the `Command` object. Only the first method allows you to customize the `CursorLocation`, `CursorType`, and `LockType` for each `Recordset` created. The latter two options always create firehose cursors if the `Connection` object's `CursorLocation` is set to `adUseServer` (the default, if not otherwise specified). They create static, read-only cursors if set to `adUseClient`.

The `GetConsultants` method takes an argument that determines whether the server is requeried for the results. Note that the method checks for the existence of a valid connection and creates a new one if one does not exist. In this way, the class can provide a method that disconnects the client application from the data source if it remains unused for some time and does not connect until it is absolutely necessary. `GetConsultants` then returns a reference to the client-side recordset in the argument.

Listing 14.1   The clsConsultants Class Module Containing the GetConsultants Method

```
Option Explicit

Private cnADO As Connection
Private Const DATABASE = "Database=ConTracker"

' Variables used to connect and populated from
' the Registry, user prompt, or properties
Private mstrServer As String
Private mstrUID As String
Private mstrPWD As String
Private mrsCon As Recordset


Public Sub GetConsultants(pCon as Recordset, Optional ByVal flRefresh _
    As Boolean)

On Error GoTo GetConErr

' If the recordset was created, simply pass it back
If Not mrsCon Is Nothing And flRefresh = False Then
    mrsCon.MoveFirst    'reposition to the front
    Set pCon = mrsCon
    Exit Sub
Else
    ' Create the recordset and set its properties if it does not exist
    If mrsCon Is Nothing Then
        Set mrsCon = New Recordset
        With mrsCon
            .CursorLocation = adUseClient
            .CursorType = adOpenStatic
            .LockType = adLockReadOnly
            .CacheSize = 25
        End With
    Else
' Close the recordset if it is still open
If mrsCon.State = adStateOpen Then
    mrsCon.Close
End If
```

continues

Listing 14.1   continued

```
      End If
End If

' Create the Connection object if it doesn't exist
If cnADO Is Nothing Then
      Set cnADO = New Connection
      ' Set the Connection properties
      With cnADO
          .Provider = "SQLOLEDB"
          .CommandTimeout = 7
          .ConnectionTimeout = 10
          .IsolationLevel = adXactReadCommitted
      End With
End If

' Connect if not already connected
If cnADO.State = adStateClosed Then
      ' Connect to the database
      cnADO.Open "server=" & mstrServer & ";" & DATABASE, mstrUID, mstrPWD
End If

' Retrieve the data
mrsCon.Open "SELECT * FROM Consultants ORDER BY LName", cnADO

' Return the data to the caller
Set pCon = mrsCon

Exit Sub
GetConErr:
      ' Raise an error and deallocate
      Err.Raise vbObjectError + 800, "GetConsultants", Err.Description
      Set mrsCon = Nothing
      Set pCon = Nothing

End Sub
```

To call the GetConsultants method, code such as the following would be used in a
form module or in a procedure such as LoadConsultants (refer to Listing 12.2 of
Chapter 12, "Using TreeView and ListView Controls"):

```
Option Explicit
Dim objCon As New clsConsultants

Private Sub cmdShowCon_Click()

Dim rsCon As Recordset
```

```
' Retrieve the consultant list and refresh it
objCon.GetConsultants rsCon, True

' View the consultants in a ListView control
LoadConsultants rsCon

Set rsCon = Nothing

End Sub
```

General ADO Techniques

Before delving into specific techniques for building form-based (fat client) applications and distributed (thin client) applications, I will explain some basic techniques for dealing with reusable commands and stored procedures.

Included here are examples that show how to encapsulate SQL statements in Command objects, how to use prepared statements, and how to call stored procedures using arguments and return values.

Using Command Objects

One of the most useful concepts in ADO is the Command object. With an instance of this object, a developer can encapsulate all the properties and behaviors of a statement into an object that can be freely associated with Connection objects at runtime.

To encapsulate a command, the minimum properties that must be set are CommandText, CommandType, and ActiveConnection. The command can then be run using the Execute method. The CommandType property is particularly important because it instructs ADO about the nature of the command being executed. Table 14.6 presents the valid values for CommandType.

Table 14.6   ADO Command Types

Constant	Description
adCmdFile	Evaluates CommandText as the name of a file that has been persisted. Used when an application has to read data from files saved using the Save method of the Recordset object.
adCmdTable	Evaluates CommandText as the name of the table in the data source. Provider generates a simple SELECT * FROM table-name statement. Useful for small tables.
adCmdTableDirect	Evaluates CommandText as the name of a table and instructs the provider to use a more efficient OLE DB interface (IOpenRowset) to open the table directly. Some providers, such as Jet, can utilize this.
adCmdText	Evaluates CommandText as a text command to be sent to the data source. Used with SQL statements generated on the client.

continues

Table 14.6   continued

Constant	Description
adCmdStoredProc	Evaluates `CommandText` as the name of a stored procedure.
adCmdUnknown	This is the default and means that the `CommandText` is of an unknown type.

To understand the use of a `Command` object, examine the code in Listing 14.2. This is a modified version of the `clsConsultants` class in Listing 14.1, with the differences highlighted. This version uses a module-level `Command` object to encapsulate the `SELECT` statement that retrieves consultants. This code also illustrates the technique of creating the `Command` object and the `Connection` object in the `Initialize` event of the class. This might be preferable if the user interface code intends to create an instance of the class module that is module-level or global in scope. The `Command` object, `mcmCon`, can then be associated with a `Connection` object and executed using the `Execute` method.

Listing 14.2   Using the ADO Command Object to Encapsulate a SQL Statement

```
Option Explicit

Private cnADO As Connection
Private Const DATABASE = "Database=ConTracker"

' Variables used to connect and populated from
' the Registry, user prompt, or properties
Private mstrServer As String
Private mstrUID As String
Private mstrPWD As String
Private mrsCon As Recordset
Private mcmCon As Command

Public Sub GetConsultants(pCon as Recordset, Optional ByVal flRefresh _
    As Boolean)

On Error GoTo GetConErr

' If the recordset was created, simply pass it back
If Not mrsCon Is Nothing And flRefresh = False Then
    mrsCon.MoveFirst     'reposition to the front
    Set pCon = mrsCon
    Exit Sub
Else
    ' Create the recordset and set its properties if it does not exist
    If mrsCon Is Nothing Then
        Set mrsCon = New Recordset
        With mrsCon
            .CursorLocation = adUseClient
            .CursorType = adOpenStatic
            .LockType = adLockReadOnly
```

```
                    .CacheSize = 25
              End With
       Else
' Close the recordset if it is still open
If mrsCon.State = adStateOpen Then
   mrsCon.Close
End If
       End If
End If


' Connect if not already connected
If cnADO.State = adStateClosed Then
      ' Connect to the database
      cnADO.Open "server=" & mstrServer & ";" & DATABASE, mstrUID, mstrPWD
End If


' Set the ActiveConnection and Execute the command
mcmCon.ActiveConnection = cnADO
mrsCon.Open mcmCon


' Return the data to the caller
Set pCon = mrsCon


Exit Sub
GetConErr:
      ' Raise an error and deallocate
      Err.Raise vbObjectError + 800, "GetConsultants", Err.Description
      Set mrsCon = Nothing
      Set pCon = Nothing

End Sub



Private Sub Class_Initialize()

' Create the Command object
Set mcmCon = New Command

' Initialize its properties
With mcmCon
      .CommandText = "SELECT * FROM Consultants ORDER BY LName"
      .CommandType = adCmdText
      .Name = "ListConsultants"
End With

' Create the Connection object
Set cnADO = New Connection
```

continues

Listing 14.2   continued

```
' Set the Connection properties
With cnADO
     .Provider = "SQLOLEDB"
     .CommandTimeout = 7
     .ConnectionTimeout = 10
     .IsolationLevel = adXactReadCommitted
End With

End Sub
```

Using Prepared Statements

Although Command objects allow you to create reusable objects on the client, they do not provide for any reuse at the data source. By default, each time a Command object is executed, the text of the command in the CommandText property is sent to the data source. Depending on the characteristics of the data source, what typically occurs is that the data source must parse, optimize, and compile the command before executing it and returning the resultset. Most data sources then throw this information away, only to repeat the process when the next statement is processed. This additional overhead can slow performance, especially for those commands that are complex and executed multiple times within a single run of the application.

To allow for this, the Command object exposes a Prepared property. When set to True, ADO instructs the data provider to attempt to save a compiled version of the command for later use, even before it is first executed.

In the case of SQL Server, SQLOLEDB executes the sp_prepare system stored procedure to create a temporary stored procedure and sp_execute to execute it. When the connection is closed, sp_unprepare is called to drop the procedure. In the case of the clsConsultants class discussed previously, the code in the Initialize event could be changed to prepare the command:

```
' Initialize its properties
With mcmCon
     .CommandText = "SELECT * FROM Consultants ORDER BY LName"
     .CommandType = adCmdText
     .Name = "ListConsultants"
     .Prepared = True
End With
```

Note that only when the command will be executed multiple times does creating a prepared statement make sense. In addition, keep in mind that prepared commands can be reused only if the Command object is executed on the same connection it was initially created on. In fact, setting the ActiveConnection property of the Command object to Nothing signals the provider to release the prepared command (in the case of SQLOLEDB, it calls sp_unprepare). This makes prepared commands unattractive for server components that want to take advantage of connection pools.

Of course, when dealing with stored procedures, using a prepared command is unnecessary because stored procedures are, in essence, permanently prepared commands.

Using Stored Procedures

Perhaps the most prevalent use of Command objects is to execute stored procedures. Stored procedures are popular because they are commonly used to abstract SQL and the underlying database structure from the client program. Also, stored procedures increase performance because they are precompiled, and they can be used to provide secure access to the underlying database objects. In fact, for Microsoft SQL Server, using stored procedures for almost all data access is recommended.

When dealing with stored procedures, you must consider essentially three issues: invoking procedures with parameters, invoking procedures that simply modify data and do not return resultsets, and invoking procedures that contain output parameters or return values.

Invoking Stored Procedures with Parameters

Most stored procedures, except those that are very simple, accept arguments that allow the resultset to be customized. To accommodate this, ADO exposes a collection of Parameter objects for each Command object. There are two primary methods for creating and populating the parameters.

Using the Refresh Method

After a command has been created and its CommandText, CommandType, and ActiveConnection properties set, the Refresh method of the Parameters collection of the Command object can be invoked. Doing so will instruct the data provider to discover the appropriate parameters for the stored procedure. In most cases, this will initiate a round trip to the data source to return the parameters. After the collection has been populated, individual parameters can be set by accessing the Value property of the parameter. As discussed previously, this is one time when ADO automatically creates ADO objects (in this case, Parameter objects).

The following code snippet presents this approach by calling a stored procedure, ConByProj, which returns all the consultants assigned to a particular project. The project code is contained in the variable pCode, ostensibly passed in as an argument to the method that contains the code.

```
Dim lrsCon As New Recordset
Dim lcmCon As Command

' Create the Command
Set lcmCon = New Command
With lcmCon
    .CommandText = "ConByProj"
    .CommandType = adCmdStoredProc
    .ActiveConnection = cnADO
    ' Refresh the parameters collection and populate it
```

```
    .Parameters.Refresh
    .Parameters(1).Value = pCode
End With

' Execute the command
lrsCon.Open lcmCon
```

Listing 14.3 presents the ConByProj stored procedure, written in SQL Server's Transact SQL.

Listing 14.3   The ConByProj Stored Procedure—Note That It Takes One Argument and Returns a Resultset
```
Create Procedure ConByProj
@code varchar(15)
As
SELECT b.ID, b.FName + ' ' + b.LName AS Name, c.Description,
       c.Company, a.StartDate, a.EndDate, a.Rate
FROM ConProj a INNER JOIN Consultants b ON a.EmpId = b.ID
    INNER JOIN Projects c ON a.Code = c.Code
WHERE a.Code = @code
ORDER BY LName, FName
```

Using the CreateParameter Method

The other technique, the more efficient of the two, is to use the CreateParameter method of the Command object to explicitly create, define, and append the parameters to the Parameters collection. By providing all the information, you ensure that the data provider does not have to query the data source to retrieve it.

The following code snippet is functionally the same as the one to call the stored procedure ConByProj, shown in Listing 14.3:

```
Dim lrsCon As New Recordset
Dim lcmCon As Command

' Create the Command
Set lcmCon = New Command
With lcmCon
    .CommandText = "ConByProj"
    .CommandType = adCmdStoredProc
    .ActiveConnection = cnADO
End With

' Create and append the parameter
lcmCon.Parameters.Append lcmCon.CreateParameter("@code", adVarChar, _
    adParamInput, Len(pCode), pCode)

' Execute the command
lrsCon.Open lcmCon
```

Note that when using the `CreateParameter` method, you must give ADO the data type, direction, size, and value for the parameter. In this case, `@code` is an *input parameter*, meaning that it is passed by value into the stored procedure. The trickiest aspect of this technique is ensuring that the data type and size are correct. Mapping the 40 ADO data types to the data types supported by the data source can take some research. Incorrectly specifying either can cause the execution to fail with unpredictable results. You must also add parameters to the collection in the same order as they were specified in the stored procedure.

TIP

Although you probably don't want to use the `Refresh` method in production code, you can use it during development to discover what ADO thinks the proper data types and directions are for your parameters. Although this isn't foolproof, it will give you a place to start.

As an alternative, the parameter can be set using the collection syntax

```
lcmCon.Parameters("@code") = pCode
```

before execution and simply omitting the final argument of `CreateParameter`. As if these options aren't enough, you can also pass all the values for the parameters in a variant array when using the `Execute` method of the `Command` object. For example, assume that a `Command` object accepted parameters for the project code, minimum rate, and starting date. All three parameters could be passed in the `Execute` method.

```
Set lrsCon = lcmCon.Execute( , Array(pCode,pRate,pStartDate))
```

Note that the intrinsic `Array` function returns a variant array when passed a series of comma-delimited values to insert into the array.

Invoking Data Modification Stored Procedures

Another particularly good use for stored procedures is to perform data modifications. By allowing stored procedures to be the gatekeepers of the data, you can enhance security and introduce some business logic or data validation at the data source. Again, the primary benefit is that the client code running on a user's workstation or on a distributed server does not have to generate SQL or understand the database schema.

`Command` objects do a good job of supporting this paradigm because they can be used to execute to stored procedures with parameters to perform the update. Rather than create updateable cursors in ADO, this technique is preferred, especially when you are using SQL Server, because it allows the timing and nature of updates to be precisely controlled, in addition to the benefits of performance and security noted previously.

To understand this approach, examine Listing 14.4, which contains the code to implement the `AssignConsultant` method of the class module `clsConsultants`.

Listing 14.4   The AssignConsultant Method of the clsConsultants Class

```
Public Function AssignConsultant(ByVal pCode As String, _
    ByVal pConID As Long, ByVal pRate As Currency, _
    ByVal pStart As Date, ByVal pEnd As Date) As Boolean

Dim lcmCon As Command
Dim lngAffected As Long


On Error GoTo AssignConErr


' Connect if not already connected
If cnADO.State = adStateClosed Then
    ' Connect to the database
    cnADO.Open "server=" & mstrServer & ";" & DATABASE, mstrUID, mstrPWD
End If


' Create the Command
Set lcmCon = New Command
With lcmCon
    .CommandText = "AssignConsultant"
    .CommandType = adCmdStoredProc
    .ActiveConnection = cnADO
End With


' Create and append the parameters
lcmCon.Parameters.Append lcmCon.CreateParameter("@code", _
    adVarWChar, adParamInput, Len(pCode), pCode)
lcmCon.Parameters.Append lcmCon.CreateParameter("@ID", _
    adInteger, adParamInput, 4, pConID)
lcmCon.Parameters.Append lcmCon.CreateParameter("@rate", _
    adCurrency, adParamInput, 4, pRate)
lcmCon.Parameters.Append lcmCon.CreateParameter("@startdate", _
    adDate, adParamInput, 4, pStart)
lcmCon.Parameters.Append lcmCon.CreateParameter("@code", _
    adDate, adParamInput, 4, pEnd)


' Execute the command
lcmCon.Execute lngAffected, , adExecuteNoRecords


' Deallocate
Set lcmCon = Nothing


' Return True if a consultant was assigned
If lngAffected = 1 Then
    AssignConsultant = True
Else
    AssignConsultant = False
End If
```

```
Exit Function
AssignConErr:
    ' Raise an error and deallocate
    Err.Raise vbObjectError + 805, "AssignConsultant", Err.Description
    AssignConsultant = False

End Function
```

The key points to note in Listing 14.4 are that the command is executed with the constant adExecuteNoRecords and that the local variable lngAffected is passed by reference to the Execute method. The constant adExecuteNoRecords instructs ADO not to create a Recordset object when executing the command, thereby saving memory. The variable passed as the first argument to the Execute method is populated with the number of rows affected by the command. In this case, it will contain the number of rows inserted into the ConProj table.

TIP

Commands that contain multiple parameters, such as the one shown in Listing 14.4, are also good candidates to be cached in module-level variables to avoid incurring the overhead of reconstructing the **Parameters** collection with each invocation.

In Listing 14.5, note that the Transact-SQL stored procedure AssignConsultants not only performs the insert into the ConProj table (which records the assignments of consultants) but also does a data validation check to ensure that the date range the consultant is assigned to the project falls within the scope of the project.

Listing 14.5   The AssignConsultant Stored Procedure
```
CREATE Procedure AssignConsultant
@code varchar(15),
@ID integer,
@rate numeric,
@startdate smalldatetime,
@enddate smalldatetime
As

DECLARE @start smalldatetime
DECLARE @end smalldatetime

SELECT @start = StartDate, @end = EndDate
FROM Projects
WHERE Code = @code

-- Check that the date range is valid
IF NOT ((@startdate BETWEEN @start AND @end) AND
  (@enddate BETWEEN @start AND @end))
```

continues

Listing 14.5   continued

```
BEGIN
    RAISERROR('Assignment date range is invalid.',14,1)
    RETURN
END

-- Insert the new assignment
INSERT INTO ConProj
VALUES (@code,
@ID,
    @rate,
    @startdate,
    @enddate)
```

Invoking Stored Procedures That Return Values

The final technique to address when dealing with stored procedures is dealing with output parameters and return values. In both cases, this is information, other than a result-set, returned by the stored procedure. Both kinds of information are handled through the Parameters collection of the Command object.

Handling Output Parameters

To understand dealing with output parameters, examine the Transact-SQL stored procedure in Listing 14.6. The stored procedure RevByWeek is used to calculate an estimate of revenue for a week when passed in the date on which Monday of the week falls. Basically, the estimate is calculated by searching the ConProj table containing consultant assignments and by multiplying the number of days during the week consultants are on the project by their rate. Because consultants might not be assigned to a project for the entire week, separate calculations are used for each of the four overlap scenarios. Obviously, this is a rough estimate because it assumes 5-day, 40-hour weeks and does not take into account vacation, holidays, and other time off. However, it can be used by a manager or salesperson to forecast potential future revenue.

That being said, the interesting aspect of the stored procedure is that it returns two parameters: one containing the revenue estimate and the other the number of assignments considered, both as output parameters.

Listing 14.6   The RevByWeek Stored Procedure Highlighting the Use of Output Parameters in Transact-SQL

```
Create Procedure RevByWeek
@startdate smalldatetime,
@total numeric OUTPUT,
@totcon integer OUTPUT

AS

DECLARE @enddate smalldatetime
DECLARE @val1 integer
```

```
DECLARE @val2 integer
DECLARE @val3 integer
DECLARE @val4 integer
DECLARE @num1 integer
DECLARE @num2 integer
DECLARE @num3 integer
DECLARE @num4 integer

--Revenue estimator per week
--This proc assumes 5-day, 40-hour weeks
--It also assumes that you pass it the Monday the week started

IF DATEPART(dw,@startdate) <> 2
BEGIN
    RAISERROR('The date provided is not a Monday',14,1)
    RETURN
END

-- Find the last day of the week
SELECT @enddate = DateAdd(d,5,@startdate)

--Calculates four values ,depending
--on amount of billable time per week the consultant had


--start later end later
SELECT @val1 = SUM((DATEDIFF(dd,StartDate,@enddate)+1) * 8 * Rate),
       @num1 = COUNT(*)
    FROM ConProj
    WHERE @startdate < StartDate
        AND (StartDate < @enddate
        AND @enddate < EndDate)


--start earlier end earlier
SELECT @val2 = SUM((DATEDIFF(dd,@startdate,EndDate)+1)*8*Rate),
       @num2 = COUNT(*)
    FROM ConProj
    WHERE @startdate > StartDate
        AND (EndDate < @enddate
        AND EndDate > @startdate)

--start later end earlier
SELECT @val3 = SUM((DATEDIFF(dd,Startdate,@endDate)+1)*8*Rate),
       @num3 = COUNT(*)
    FROM ConProj
    WHERE @startdate < StartDate
        AND @enddate > EndDate
```

continues

Listing 14.6   continued

```
--total overlap assume a 40 hour week
SELECT @val4 = SUM(rate*40),
       @num4 = COUNT(*)
    FROM ConProj
    WHERE @startdate >= StartDate
       AND @enddate <= EndDate


-- Compute the total
SELECT @total = CONVERT(integer,COALESCE(@val1,0)+COALESCE(@val2,0)+
       COALESCE(@val3,0)+COALESCE(@val4,0))

SELECT @totcon = CONVERT(integer,COALESCE(@num1,0)+COALESCE(@num2,0)+
       COALESCE(@num3,0)+COALESCE(@num4,0))
```

As previously noted, output parameters are handled through the `Parameters` collection and are analogous to arguments passed by reference in other programming languages. According to convention, the code to call the `RevByWeek` stored procedure is in the `GetRevByWeek` method of the `clsConsultants` class, shown in Listing 14.7.

Listing 14.7   Calling the RevByWeek Stored Procedure from the GetRevByWeek Method

```
Public Sub GetRevByWeek(ByVal pStart As Date, _
    pRevenue As Currency, pAssignments As Integer)

Dim lcmRev As Command

On Error GoTo GetRevErr

' Connect if not already connected
If cnADO.State = adStateClosed Then
    ' Connect to the database
    cnADO.Open "server=" & mstrServer & ";" & DATABASE, mstrUID, mstrPWD
End If

' Create the Command
Set lcmRev = New Command
With lcmRev
    .CommandText = "RevByWeek"
    .CommandType = adCmdStoredProc
    .ActiveConnection = cnADO
End With

' Create and append the parameters, both input and output
lcmRev.Parameters.Append lcmRev.CreateParameter("@startdate", _
    adDate, adParamInput, 4, pStart)
lcmRev.Parameters.Append lcmRev.CreateParameter("@total", _
```

```
    adCurrency, adParamOutput, 4)
lcmRev.Parameters.Append lcmRev.CreateParameter("@totcon", _
    adInteger, adParamOutput, 4)

' Execute the command
lcmRev.Execute , , adExecuteNoRecords

' Read the output parameters
pRevenue = lcmRev.Parameters("@total")
pAssignments = lcmRev.Parameters("@totcon")

' Deallocate
Set lcmRev = Nothing

Exit Sub
GetRevErr:
    ' Raise an error and deallocate
    Err.Raise vbObjectError + 807, "GetRevByWeek", Err.Description

End Sub
```

Again, the stored procedure is executed with the `adExecuteNoRecords` constant because only parameters, and not a resultset, are returned. The main difference in using output parameters is that the parameters are created using the `adParamOutput` constant in the `CreateParameter` method. After execution, they can be read using the `Parameters` collection and referencing them by name or ordinal number. In this case, the VB procedure passes the output parameters back to the calling code by reference.

TIP

If a stored procedure would return a single-row, single-column resultset or a single row with only a couple columns, it would be more efficient to return those results in output parameters than as a `Recordset` object (provided you use `adExecuteNoRecords`) because no `Recordset` would have to be built and maintained on the client.

Handling Return Values

The other type of value that can be returned from a stored procedure is the return value. In the case of SQL Server, for example, all stored procedures return a long integer indicating the execution status of the procedure. This value can also be used to return data required by the client application.

A typical example of using return values is when you are dealing with self-incrementing columns in a relational database. In SQL Server, these columns are created with the IDENTITY data type and given a seed and increment from which to assign values. A column is then automatically populated each time a row is inserted. These columns are termed *identity values* and are often used to assign a system-generated, unique number to a row in the table. Generally, this value will be used as the primary key.

To illustrate this, the following is a typical stored procedure, AddConsultant:

```
CREATE PROCEDURE AddConsultant
@FName varchar(50),
@LName varchar(50),
@phone char(10) = NULL

AS

INSERT INTO Consultants
VALUES (@FName, @LName, @phone)

RETURN @@identity
```

Here, the primary key of the Consultants table is ID, an identity value that is automatically assigned during the INSERT statement. Note that after the stored procedure performs the INSERT, the RETURN statement is used to pass back the global variable @@identity. This variable is populated by SQL Server and represents the last identity value inserted by the connection. By using this technique, the stored procedure always returns the primary key of the new consultant. This is normally important information for the client program so that it can manipulate the consultant by its key value, if necessary.

To handle the return value, you simply create and add a Parameter to the collection using the constant adParamReturnValue in the first position, referenced as ordinal 0.

NOTE

When using the Refresh method of the Parameters collection, discussed previously, the return value will automatically be added to the collection in the first position.

Listing 14.8 does not duplicate all the code for the InsertConsultant method, but abstracts only the setup and execution of the Command object.

Listing 14.8   Code to Call a Stored Procedure That Returns a Value—Abstracted from the InsertConsultant Method

```
' Create the Command
Set lcmCon = New Command
With lcmCon
    .CommandText = "AddConsultant"
    .CommandType = adCmdStoredProc
    .ActiveConnection = cnADO
End With

' Create and append the parameters, both input and output
lcmCon.Parameters.Append lcmCon.CreateParameter("RETURN_VALUE", _
    adInteger, adParamReturnValue, 4)
lcmCon.Parameters.Append lcmCon.CreateParameter("@FName", _
```

```
    adVarChar, adParamInput, Len(pFName), pFName)
lcmCon.Parameters.Append lcmCon.CreateParameter("@LName", _
    adVarChar, adParamInput, Len(PLName), PLName)
lcmCon.Parameters.Append lcmCon.CreateParameter("@phone", _
    adVarChar, adParamInput, Len(pPhone), pPhone)

' Execute the command
lcmCon.Execute , , adExecuteNoRecords

' Read the output parameters
InsertConsultant = lcmCon.Parameters("RETURN_VALUE")
```

ADO Techniques with Form-Based Applications

The previous section describes techniques used in both form-based and distributed applications and more or less lays the groundwork for ways to use ADO to return resultsets and modify data. This section, however, deals only with techniques that are useful when using ADO in a form-based VB application. Topics covered in this section include

- Using the Data Environment
- Populating controls used for reference data
- Loading the MSFlexGrid control
- Working with BLOBs
- Implementing asynchronous processing

Using the Data Environment

One of the nicest features for form-based applications added to VB 6 (and all of Visual Studio 6) is the Data Environment (DE). This utility includes a graphical design tool and exposes programmatic access at runtime. Essentially, by using the DE, a developer can encapsulate ADO Connection and Command objects into a single object that can then be manipulated at runtime through methods, properties, and events. You can think of the DE as an object wrapper for all the ADO-related activities of an application.

To add an instance of the (DE) to the project, you simply right-click on the project in the Project Explorer and select Add, Data Environment. This adds a new DE object under the Designers folder. Adding connections and commands to the DE is straightforward. By right-clicking on the appropriate folder in the designer, you can add a new connection or command or can view the code (events).

Creating a Connection

By default, the DE contains a single Connection object, Connection1, that does not yet connect to a data source. To configure the connection, right-click on it and select Properties. The resulting dialog box, shown in Figure 14.3, allows you to set all the properties of the Connection object, including ConnectionString, Provider, and

`ConnectionTimeout`. After the properties are set, you can rename the connection by right-clicking on it and selecting Rename.

You can create multiple `Connection` objects that are exposed in the `Connections` collection of the DE.

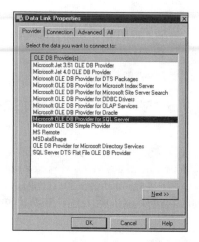

Figure 14.3

The Data Link Properties dialog box used to configure Connection objects encapsulated in a DE object.

Creating a Command

Commands can beadded in much the same way as connections. By right-clicking on the Commands folder, you can select either Add Command or Insert Stored Procedures. Both options create commands, but the first is more versatile because it can be used to create each of the command types discussed in Table 14.6, with the exception of file-based commands.

> **TIP**
>
> The preceding procedure works if the Arrange by Objects toolbar button is depressed. If Arrange by Connections is selected, you have to use the Add Command toolbar button to add a new command.

As with connections, `Command` objects are exposed in a `Commands` collection of the DE.

The resulting dialog box, shown in Figure 14.4, allows you to choose a command type and stored procedure or optionally build or type in a SQL statement. In this case, the `GetConByProj` command encapsulates the call to the `ConByProj` stored procedure. From previous discussions, it should be obvious that the `ActiveConnection`, `CommandType`, and `CommandText` properties are being populated.

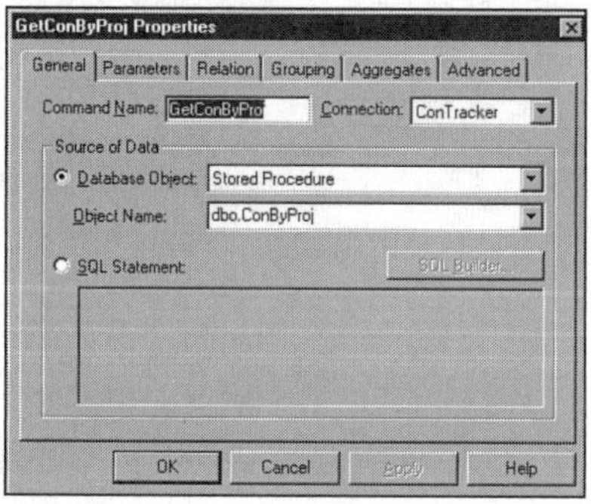

Figure 14.4

The Properties dialog box for the GetConByProj command of the DE object.

One of the other important tabs of the Properties dialog box is the Advanced tab. The properties exposed here (see Figure 14.5) allow the developer to set the CursorType, CursorLocation, CacheSize, and MaxRecords properties of the Recordset to be returned, in addition to the Prepared and CommandTimeout properties of the Command object. Also, note that the adExecuteNoRecords constant is exposed through the "Recordset Returning" checkbox.

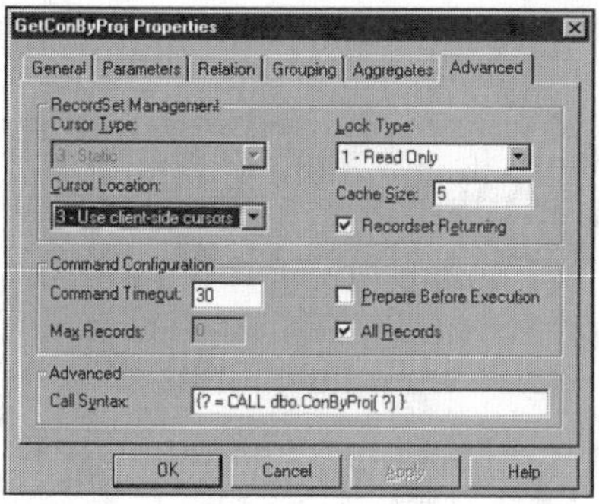

Figure 14.5

The Advanced tab of the Properties dialog box for the GetConByProj command of the DE object.

Finally, the Parameters tab of the dialog box allows you to specify all the information normally specified in the CreateParameter method of the Command object. Figure 14.6 shows the tab from the GetRevByWeek command.

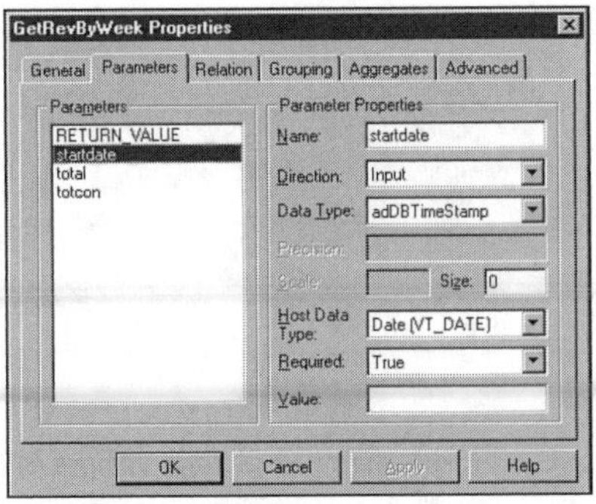

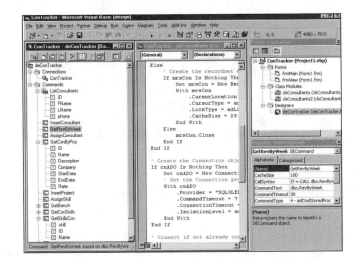

Figure 14.6

The Parameters tab of the Properties dialog box for the GetRevByWeek command of the DE object.

Because the information in this tab is collected by ADO using the `Refresh` technique (if the command is associated with an appropriate connection) discussed earlier, you will want to make sure that the parameter direction and data type arguments are correct. Even though ADO incurs the overhead of the additional round trip when the command is first created at design time, it does not do so when it is executed at runtime.

After creating all the commands at design time, the DE will be populated with connections and commands, as shown in Figure 14.7.

Figure 14.7

The populated DE.

Invoking a Command Programmatically

After the DE has been fully populated, you can write code to invoke the commands. You handle commands that return resultsets, such as `GetConByProj`, differently than those that do not return results, such as `GetRevByWeek`.

Listing 14.9 gives an example of invoking a command that returns resultsets. The `ShowConsultantsProj` form-level procedure uses the exposed `GetConByProj` method of the form-level DE object (`objDE`) to pass the project code parameter and execute the command. The DE then exposes a property for each `Recordset` object returned by a command, prefacing it with `rs`. In this case, the `rsGetConByProj` property can be used to retrieve the recordset. The remainder of the procedure loads a `ListView` control with the results, similar to the technique given in Chapter 12.

Listing 14.9 Executing a DE Command That Accepts Parameters and Returns a Recordset

```
Option Explicit
Private objDE As New deConTracker

Private Sub ShowConsultantsProj(ByVal pCode As String)

Dim rs As Recordset
Dim objItem As ListItem

On Error GoTo ShowConErr

' Load the consultants for this project in a ListView control

' Pass the parameter to the DE object
objDE.GetConByProj pCode

' Create the recordset from the DE
Set rs = objDE.rsGetConByProj

' Populate the control

' Clear the existing data in the control
    lvListView.ListItems.Clear
    lvListView.ColumnHeaders.Clear

' Add three columns for Name, Email, and Phone
With lvListView
    .ColumnHeaders.Add , , "Name"
    .ColumnHeaders.Add , , "Start Date"
    .ColumnHeaders.Add , , "End Date"
    .ColumnHeaders.Add , , "Rate"
End With
```

continues

Listing 14.9 continued

```
' Load the ListView with data
    Do While Not rs.EOF
        ' Add the ListItem object
        Set objItem = lvListView.ListItems.Add(, "C" & _
            rs("ID"), rs("Name"))

        ' Add the SubItems
        With objItem
            .SubItems(1) = Format(rs("StartDate"), "mm/dd/yyyy")
            .SubItems(2) = Format(rs("EndDate"), "mm/dd/yyyy")
            .SubItems(3) = Format(rs("Rate"), "Currency")
        End With

        rs.MoveNext
    Loop

' Deallocate
Set rs = Nothing

Exit Sub
ShowConErr:
    MsgBox Err.description, vbExclamation, Me.Caption

End Sub
```

Two key points to remember here are that the command is actually sent to the data source when the parameters are passed to the command, even though the code might not inspect the recordset property associated with the command until some time later. The second point is that the connection to the data source is not made until it is required by a DE command. In other words, if ShowConsultantsProj was the first procedure executed that required a DE command, the connection would not be made until the GetConByProj method is called. You can control when the connection is made by programmatically calling the Open method of the appropriate Connection object in the DE object's Connections collection.

Some DE commands do not return recordsets, so they are called by simply invoking the DE method for the command and passing it any required parameters. The following code snippet is used to call the GetRevByWeek command (discussed earlier) that takes one input parameter and returns two output parameters. The resulting values are then placed in Label controls for display.

```
Private objDE As New deConTracker

Private Sub ShowRevByWeek(ByVal pStart As Date)

Dim curTotal As Currency
Dim lngAssignments As Long
```

```
objDE.GetRevByWeek pStart, curTotal, lngAssignments

lblTotRev.Caption = curTotal
lblTotAssign.Caption = lngAssignments

End Sub
```

Populating Controls Used for Reference Data

Every application that allows data to be edited requires some support for reference data. Typically, this takes the form of lists of values used to populate the foreign keys of a table. For example, when you add a consultant to the database (using the data I've been discussing), each consultant is associated with one or more skills and a job position. This type of data, the list of skills and positions, is called *reference data* because it is normally used only for reference and, itself, is not updated.

Because reference data is normally static by definition, you should employ techniques to cache the data in local storage, rather than retrieve it from the data source each time it is required. ADO includes three features that make retrieving reference data more efficient: firehose cursors, referencing multiple resultset commands, and the GetRows method of the Recordset object. Using these three features allows your application to retrieve read-only, nonscrollable resultsets efficiently (firehose cursors), bundle several requests for lookup data in a single stored procedure or command, and then load the reference data into variant arrays using the GetRows method.

The code in Listing 14.10 shows one example of loading reference data using these techniques. The ShowLookupData method of the clsConsultants class accepts ListBox and ComboBox controls as parameters and populates them with the list of skills and positions, respectively. It also accepts an optional argument to instruct the method whether to load the data from the database or simply use the variant arrays cached as private variables of the class. Keep in mind that this technique could also be used with the DE by creating a command.

Listing 14.10   Populating Reference Data in Controls Through the ShowLookupData Method

```
Option Explicit
Private varSkills As Variant
Private varPos As Variant

Public Sub ShowLookupData(lstSkills As ListBox, _
    cbPos As ComboBox, Optional ByVal flRefresh As Boolean = True)

Dim lrs As Recordset
Dim lcm As Command
Dim i As Integer

On Error GoTo ShowLookupErr
```

continues

Listing 14.10   continued

```
' If only loading, go straight to
' populating the controls
If Not flRefresh Then
    ' If both arrays are empty, this is the first
    ' time the proc has been called, so go ahead and
    ' load the data from the data source
    If Not IsEmpty(varPos) And Not IsEmpty(varSkills) Then
        GoTo LoadLookup
    End If
End If

' Connect if not already connected
If cnADO.State = adStateClosed Then
    ' Connect to the database
    cnADO.Open "server=" & mstrServer & ";" & DATABASE, mstrUID, mstrPWD
End If

' Create the Command
Set lcm = New Command
With lcm
    .CommandText = "GetLookupData"
    .CommandType = adCmdStoredProc
    .ActiveConnection = cnADO
End With

' Create a firehose cursor. This is the default
' because adUseServer is the default on the Connection
' object and no other options were specified.
Set lrs = lcm.Execute
If Not lrs.EOF Then
    ' First get the Skills
    varSkills = lrs.GetRows
End If

' Get the next recordset if available
Set lrs = lrs.NextRecordset

' Check whether there is another recordset
If Not lrs Is Nothing Then
    If Not lrs.EOF Then
        ' Get the positions
        varPos = lrs.GetRows
    End If
End If

' Deallocate resources
Set lrs = Nothing
```

```
Set lcm = Nothing

LoadLookup:

' Load the variant arrays into the controls

    lstSkills.Clear
    If Not IsEmpty(varSkills) Then
        For i = 0 To UBound(varSkills, 2)
            lstSkills.AddItem varSkills(1, i)
            lstSkills.ItemData(i) = CLng(varSkills(0, i))
        Next
    End If

    cbPos.Clear
    If Not IsEmpty(varPos) Then
        For i = 0 To UBound(varPos, 2)
            cbPos.AddItem varPos(1, i)
            cbPos.ItemData(i) = CLng(varPos(0, i))
        Next
    End If

Exit Sub
ShowLookupErr:
    Err.Raise vbObjectError + 810, "ShowLookupData", Err.Description

    ' Deallocate resources
    Set lrs = Nothing
    Set lcm = Nothing

End Sub
```

The source stored procedure, GetLookupData, contains two SELECT statements and returns multiple Recordset objects through the Command object.

NOTE

If you want to create multiple resultsets using SQL, instead of a stored procedure, you can populate the CommandText property with a string such as "SELECT * FROM Skills;SELECT * FROM Positions".

Note that the class method uses the NextRecordset method of the Recordset object to query the next resultset and that the Recordset object variable will be set to Nothing if no more resultsets are pending.

After the recordsets are retrieved, a call to GetRows loads the data in a multidimensional variant array. The arrays are then traversed using the UBound function to load the data into the controls.

Although this technique is good for a form-based application, it would have to be modified for use in a distributed system. If the ShowLookupData method was contained in a component running in Microsoft Transaction Server (MTS), you could not, for example, pass ListBox and ComboBox controls to the method. Even if you could, this would be poor design because it would incur immense overhead as roundtrips are made on the network with each call to AddItem. Additionally, components running in MTS may not want to cache data in private variables because this adds state to the component (a concept discussed in Chapter 16, "Building ActiveX Components").

> **NOTE**
>
> The method in Listing 14.10 uses a line label, LoadLookup, and a Goto statement to separate the code that loads the controls from the code that performs the database work. I know that some of you cringe to see this technique employed ("Real languages don't use Gotos"). However, as long as they are not overused, Gotos can increase the maintainability and efficiency of your code. Normally, I would use Gotos only when the code segment in question does not have to return when completed (which would incur multiple redirections) and when the code segment is also called in the normal flow of execution. For more information see Chapter 3, "Control of Flow Language."

Loading the MS FlexGrid Control

Just as you can easily load reference data using the GetRows method of the Recordset object, you can also populate the MS FlexGrid control with read-only data using the GetString method. The FlexGrid control is popular because of its flexibility (surprise!), being capable of displaying images and merging data at the row, column, or cell level.

The basic technique, shown in Listing 14.11, is to create a Recordset (in this case, by using a DE object) and use its properties and Fields collection to configure the grid by populating its Rows and Cols properties. First, iterate through the Fields collection, extracting column header information and placing it in the header row of the grid using the TextMatrix method. In addition, you can use the DefinedSize property of the Field object to set the ColumnWidth based on the width of a typical string in the current ScaleMode. Next, create the region you are going to populate by setting the RowSel and ColSel properties. Finally, call the GetString method to return all the data (or optionally *n* number of rows specified as an argument to the method) in a delimited string. By assigning the string to the Clip property of the control, the data is loaded.

Listing 14.11   Populating the MS FlexGrid Control with Read-Only Data

```
Dim rs As Recordset
Dim i As Integer

' Invoke the Data Environment command and
' populate the Recordset object
objDE.GetProjects
```

```
Set rs = objDE.rsGetProjects

' Clear the existing control
flxProjects.Clear

' Set up the header row
flxProjects.Rows = rs.RecordCount
flxProjects.Cols = rs.Fields.Count
For i = 0 To rs.Fields.Count - 1
    flxProjects.TextMatrix(0, i) = rs.Fields(i).Name
    flxProjects.ColWidth(i) = Me.TextWidth( _
        String(rs.Fields(i).DefinedSize, "M")) * 0.5
Next

' Create a region to paste the data into
With flxProjects
    .Row = 1
    .Col = 0
    .RowSel = rs.RecordCount - 1
    .ColSel = rs.Fields.Count - 1
End With

' Paste the data
flxProjects.Clip = rs.GetString

' Reset the cursor
flxProjects.Row = 0
flxProjects.Col = 0

' Deallocate the Recordset
Set rs = Nothing
```

NOTE

The MS `FlexGrid` is good for read-only data but does not, by default, support editing. To edit data directly in a grid, you can use any of the following methods. Use the `DataGrid` control shipped with VB 6 to bind an updateable ADO `Recordset` to the grid (less coding, but allows less control). Use a technique by which you programmatically place "invisible" editable controls over cells in the `FlexGrid` to simulate editing (much more code, but the ultimate in control). Use an unbound `DBGrid` control (available before version 6) to allow editing, and intercept the grid events to update the data source manually.

Working with Binary Large Objects (BLOBs)

Many data sources support the use of BLOBs to handle complex data types, such as the IMAGE data type in SQL Server or the LONG RAW data type in Oracle. In many instances, although handling data such as images might be more efficiently done through external files, sometimes requirements dictate that this information must be stored in the data source and will have to be manipulated.

ADO supports the handling of small amounts of binary data as it does with other types of data. For example, when retrieving a TEXT column from SQL Server that allows 2GB of text, the entire value can be read using the syntax

```
strData = rs("memo").Value
```

if the amount of data is small. However, with larger amounts of data, you should use the GetChunk and AppendChunk methods of the ADO Field and Parameter objects, which allows your code to read and write the data in smaller pieces to avoid using all the available memory. You can determine programmatically whether a field can be manipulated using these methods by checking the Attributes property of the Field object for a value of adFldLong.

For an example of how to use these methods, examine the code in Listing 14.12, which implements the SaveLikeness and GetLikeness methods in the clsConsultants class. These methods allow the application to save and retrieve images of consultants into the ConsImages table in SQL Server. This table simply contains the ID of the consultant, along with an IMAGE column to hold the picture.

Listing 14.12   The LoadLikeness and GetLikeness Methods of the clsConsultants Class Module, Used to Store and Retrieve Images in the Database

```
Public Function SaveLikeness(ByVal pID As Long, _
    ByVal pFile As String) As Boolean


Dim cm As Command
Dim intFileNum As Integer
Dim lngSize As Long
Dim intChunks As Integer
Dim intRemainder As Integer
Dim arData() As Byte
Dim i As Integer
Dim lngAffected As Long



On Error GoTo LoadLikeErr

' First open the file
intFileNum = FreeFile
Open pFile For Binary Access Read As intFileNum

' Create the command
Set cm = New Command
With cm
    .CommandText = "SaveImage"
    .CommandType = adCmdStoredProc
End With
```

```
' Determine the file size and number of loops to perform
lngSize = FileLen(pFile)
intChunks = lngSize \ 8192
intRemainder = lngSize Mod 8192

' Append the parameters
cm.Parameters.Append cm.CreateParameter("@id", adInteger, _
    adParamInput, 4, pID)
cm.Parameters.Append cm.CreateParameter("@likeness", _
    adVarBinary, adParamInput, 2147483647)
cm.Parameters(1).Attributes = 64

' Pass the image data in chunks
ReDim arData(lngSize)
For i = 1 To intChunks
    Get intFileNum, , arData()
    cm.Parameters("@likeness").AppendChunk arData()
Next

' Pick up the last portion of the image
ReDim arData(intRemainder)
Get intFileNum, , arData()
cm.Parameters("@likeness").AppendChunk arData()


' Connect if not already connected
If cnADO.State = adStateClosed Then
    ' Connect to the database
    cnADO.Open "server=" & mstrServer & ";" & DATABASE, mstrUID, mstrPWD
End If

' Set the activeconnection
Set cm.ActiveConnection = cnADO

' Execute the stored procedure
cm.Execute lngAffected, , adExecuteNoRecords

If lngAffected = 1 Then
    SaveLikeness = True
Else
    SaveLikeness = False
End If

' Close and deallocate
Close intFileNum
Set cm = Nothing
```

continues

Listing 14.12   continued

```
Exit Function
LoadLikeErr:
    ' Raise an error and deallocate
    Err.Raise vbObjectError + 1024, "GetConsultants", Err.Description

    SaveLikeness = False

    Close intFileNum
    Set cm = Nothing

End Function

Public Function GetLikeness(ByVal pID As Long) As String

Dim rs As Recordset
Dim cm As Command
Dim intFileNum As Integer
Dim lngSize As Long
Dim intChunks As Integer
Dim intRemainder As Integer
Dim arData() As Byte
Dim i As Integer
Dim lngAffected As Long
Dim strTempFile As String


On Error GoTo LoadLikeErr

' Open the temporary file
intFileNum = FreeFile
strTempFile = WinGetTempFileAndPath("con")
Open strTempFile For Binary Access Write As intFileNum

' Create the command
Set cm = New Command
With cm
    .CommandText = "GetImage"
    .CommandType = adCmdStoredProc
End With

' Append the parameter
cm.Parameters.Append cm.CreateParameter("@id", adInteger, _
    adParamInput, 4, pID)

' Connect if not already connected
If cnADO.State = adStateClosed Then
    ' Connect to the database
```

```
        cnADO.Open "server=" & mstrServer & ";" & DATABASE, mstrUID, mstrPWD
End If


' Set the activeconnection
Set cm.ActiveConnection = cnADO

' Execute the stored procedure
Set rs = New Recordset
rs.Open cm, , adOpenStatic, adLockReadOnly

' Find out how to chop up the image
lngSize = rs.Fields("likeness").ActualSize
intChunks = lngSize \ 8192
intRemainder = lngSize Mod 8192

' Pass the image data in chunks to the temporary file
ReDim arData(8192)
For i = 1 To intChunks
    arData() = rs("likeness").GetChunk(8192)
    Put intFileNum, , arData()
Next

' Pick up the last portion of the image
ReDim arData(intRemainder)
arData() = rs("likeness").GetChunk(intRemainder)
Put intFileNum, , arData()

GetLikeness = strTempFile

' Close and deallocate
Close intFileNum
Set cm = Nothing

Exit Function
LoadLikeErr:
    ' Raise an error and deallocate
    Err.Raise vbObjectError + 1025, "GetConsultants", Err.Description

    GetLikeness = ""

    Close intFileNum
    Set cm = Nothing

End Function
```

SaveLikeness takes an image filename as a parameter and loads this file into the database using the SaveImage stored procedure. This illustrates using the AppendChunk method of the Parameter object to populate the parameter passed to the stored procedure. You will notice that the size of the file is used to find out how many 8KB blocks of data are in the file. AppendChuck is called for each 8KB block as the file is read into a byte array using the Get statement. The final Get reads the remainder of the file (because the size of the file is unlikely to be evenly divisible by 8KB) and places it in the Parameter object. The stored procedure is then executed to insert the image into the database.

TIP

Obviously, the more data you read and write, the fewer loops will have to be executed. In this example, I've used 8,192 bytes, which is conservative. You should adjust this setting, depending on the size of the binary data you expect to work with.

The GetLikeness method uses the same basic algorithm as SaveLikeness but uses the GetChuck method of the Field object to read the data into a temporary file using the Put statement. Note that the WinGetTempFileAndPath function discussed in Chapter 13, "Using Win32 API Techniques," is used to create a temporary file to save the data. The method then returns a string with the name of the temporary file that can be used with the LoadPicture function to load the file into an image or picture control.

The following code snippet contains sample code to save and load an image into an image control named Image1:

```
Dim objCon As clsConsultants
Dim strTempFile As String
Dim lngID As Long

lngID = 4

Set objCon = New clsConsultants

' If the image is saved, read it back
If objCon.LoadLikeness(lngID, "d:\jbrandt.bmp") = True Then
    strTempFile = objCon.GetLikeness(lngID)
    If Len(strTempFile) > 0 Then
        ' Load the image into the control
        Image1.Picture = LoadPicture(strTempFile)
    End If
End If
```

Implementing Asynchronous Processing

Beginning with version 2.0, ADO includes support for asynchronous operations. This, coupled with events raised by the Connection and Recordset objects, makes implementing asynchronous connections, command execution, and fetching of resultsets straightforward. The example given in this section implements asynchronous retrieval for the list of consultants in the clsConsultants class module.

ADO is a multithreaded component that allows it to open up new threads on the operating system to perform background operations and then post the results to event handlers in the application. In this way, ADO performs in much the same way as the multithreaded file search class module discussed in Chapter 13, "Using Win32 API Techniques."

Issues to Consider

You have to address a couple issues when considering asynchronous operations. The first, and certainly most important, is the need. As previously mentioned, although it's relatively simple from a programming standpoint to add asynchronous features, it introduces a set of debugging and timing issues and increases the dependencies in your code. As a rule, I would consider using asynchronous operations only when a command against a data source will run more than four or five seconds and the user could be freed up to do another operation. This is a key point because even if you stop ADO from blocking the main thread of your application while a data modification or query completes, the user must be in a position to do useful work. For example, an application that requires the user to pick from a list of customers or accounts before performing any work is a poor candidate for implementing an asynchronous fetch of the customer list.

The second issue involves the technique to use when implementing asynchronous operations. Although not recommended, you can test the State property of the Recordset or Connection objects in a loop while executing the DoEvents statement. For example, to test whether a Recordset is still fetching records, you could execute this code:

```
Do While (rs.State AND adStateFetching)
    DoEvents
Loop
```

However, as those with some VB experience know, executing a tight loop with DoEvents does not exactly free up the user to perform other work. A cleaner and more flexible approach is to use the events exposed by the Connection and Recordset objects. Therefore, the example employs this technique.

Handling ADO Events

As mentioned before, ADO supports two types of events: those associated with the Connection or Recordset objects. To use events, you simply declare the objects, using the WithEvents keyword in a form, UserControl, or Class module. In the case of the clsConsultants class, a form-level Recordset variable is declared so that asynchronous events can be passed back to the user interface.

```
Public WithEvents mrsConAsync As Recordset
```

NOTE

If you're using a DE, you can add event handlers to the project by double-clicking on a command or connection in the Data Environment designer. Keep in mind that you can use ADO events without implementing asynchronous operations, but asynchronous operations provide the most compelling reason to use most applications.

The `Recordset` object contains 11 events, whereas the `Connection` object contains 9. These events can be broken down into four categories based on the prefix of the event name: *Will* events, *Complete* events, *Informational* events (`Connection` object only), and *Fetch* events (`Recordset` object only). Chapter 20, "ADO Reference," includes a complete description of each event, so for the purposes of this example, you will focus on the *Fetch* events of the `Recordset` object.

The `FetchProgress` and `FetchComplete` events are fired during and after the rows in a `Recordset` are populated. `FetchProgress` can be used to update a progress meter that provides a visual cue to the user. `FetchComplete` signals that the `Recordset` has been fully populated. Each event passes in a reference to the `Recordset` object in question—as well as, in the case of `FetchProgress`, the current number of records fetched, the maximum number to fetch, and a status indicator that can be used to suppress future `FetchProgress` events. `FetchComplete` also returns error information.

One technique for handling these types of events while maintaining some separation between user interface code and code that deals with data, is to abstract the ADO code and events in a class module. As many examples in this chapter illustrate, the `clsConsultants` class has been used to encapsulate the bulk of the ADO code that deals with consultants. To keep this paradigm in place, the class can implement two events declared with the `Event` keyword that simply raise the *Fetch* events back to the user interface.

```
Event rsConAsyncFetchComplete()
Event rsConAsyncFetchProgress(ByVal Progress As Long, MaxProgress As Long)

Private Sub mrsConAsync_FetchComplete(ByVal pError As ADODB.Error, _
        adStatus As ADODB.EventStatusEnum, _
        ByVal pRecordset As ADODB.Recordset)
    RaiseEvent rsConAsyncFetchComplete
End Sub

Private Sub mrsConAsync_FetchProgress(ByVal Progress As Long, _
        ByVal MaxProgress As Long, adStatus As ADODB.EventStatusEnum, _
        ByVal pRecordset As ADODB.Recordset)
    RaiseEvent rsConAsyncFetchProgress(Progress, MaxProgress)
End Sub
```

Although the code shown here is simple, it allows `clsConsultants` to be independent of the user interface code and therefore to be reused in other applications.

The form-level variable that references `clsConsultants` must then be declared using the `WithEvents` keyword so that it will be notified both during the fetch and when it completes. The method `GetConsultantsAsync` is called from a private procedure to start the asynchronous retrieval.

```
Private WithEvents objCon As clsConsultants

Private Sub FetchConsultants()
    ' Invoke the asynchronous method and wait for the events
    objCon.GetConsultantsAsync
End Sub

Private Sub objCon_rsConAsyncFetchComplete()
    ShowConsultants objCon.mrsConAsync
End Sub

Private Sub objCon_rsConAsyncFetchProgress(ByVal Progress As Long, _
    MaxProgress As Long)
On Error Resume Next
    pbFetch.Value = pbFetch.Value + 7
End Sub
```

In this case, the event that fires repeatedly during the fetch increments a progress bar on the form while the complete event accesses a public property of the class module referencing the `Recordset` and passes it to a form-level procedure that displays the results.

TIP

Although you can see that the `Progress` and `MaxProgress` values are being passed back by the `FetchProgress` event, the arguments always seem to return 0 and 1, respectively, until the `Recordset` is fully populated. To work around this, the `pbFetch` progress bar is simply incremented by a set value.

Executing an Asynchronous Fetch

After the requisite events are set up in the class module and in the form, the resultset can be opened asynchronously. To do this, you use the `Execute` method of the `Command` or `Connection` objects, or the `Open` and `Requery` methods of the `Recordset` object. In each case, a constant, or constants, must be passed to the method. Table 14.7 presents the available options.

Table 14.7   The ADO ExecuteOptionEnum Constants Used to Perform Asynchronous Operations

Constant	Description
adAsyncExecute	Instructs ADO to execute the command asynchronously. In other words, this determines whether control is returned to your application immediately after the Execute or Open or only when the data source has completed execution. For commands performing data modifications, this must be specified for the command to execute asynchronously. Can be cancelled using the Cancel method of the Connection or Recordset objects.
adAsyncFetch	Instructs ADO to fetch all rows (after the initial number defined in the Initial Fetch Size property of the Recordset) asynchronously when using a client-side cursor. If a request is made for a row not yet fetched by the background thread, ADO blocks the main thread while it is being fetched. This can be used with adAsyncExecute. Can be cancelled using the Cancel method of the Connection or Recordset objects.
adAsyncFetchNonBlocking	Same as adAsyncFetch, but if the requested row has not yet been fetched, the main thread of the application is not blocked, and the Recordset is repositioned at the last available row. Can be cancelled using the Cancel method of the Connection or Recordset objects.

NOTE

ADO always sets the Initial Fetch Size property of the Recordset object to 50. Thus, your program's main thread will be blocked, and you will not get back control until the first 50 records have been retrieved. Do not confuse this with the CacheSize property, which indicates how many rows to pull from the provider each time more rows are needed.

In the clsConsultants class, as previously discussed, the new method GetConsultantsAsync creates the Recordset object with a client-side static and read-only cursor using a Command object. It then executes the statement and fetches its results asynchronously by passing the constants as the final arguments to the Open method.

```
mrsConAsync.Open mcmCon, , , , adAsyncExecute Or adAsyncFetchNonBlocking
```

Listing 14.13 gives the complete asynchronous example, containing the code in clsConsultants that supports the asynchronous execution and retrieval.

Listing 14.13   Key Segments of the `clsConsultants` *Class Module Used to Implement an Asynchronous Execution and Retrieval Through the GetConsultantsAsync Method*

```
Option Explicit

Event rsConAsyncFetchComplete()
Event rsConAsyncFetchProgress(ByVal Progress As Long, MaxProgress As Long)

Private Const DATABASE = "Database=ConTracker"
Public WithEvents mrsConAsync As Recordset

Public Sub GetConsultantsAsync()

On Error GoTo GetConAsyncErr

' Create the recordset and set its properties if it does not exist
    If mrsConAsync Is Nothing Then
        Set mrsConAsync = New Recordset
        With mrsConAsync
            .CursorLocation = adUseClient
            .CursorType = adOpenStatic
            .LockType = adLockReadOnly
            ' Pull records from the provider in blocks of 50
            .CacheSize = 50
            ' Initially fetch 1 row before returning control
            ' to the main thread
            .Properties("Initial Fetch Size") = 1
        End With
    Else
        mrsConAsync.Close
    End If

' Connect if not already connected
If cnADO.State = adStateClosed Then
    ' Connect to the database
    cnADO.Open "server=" & mstrServer & ";" & DATABASE, mstrUID, mstrPWD
End If

' Set the ActiveConnection and fetch the records asynchronously
mcmCon.ActiveConnection = cnADO
mrsConAsync.Open mcmCon, , , , adAsyncExecute Or adAsyncFetch

Exit Sub
GetConAsyncErr:
    ' Raise an error and deallocate
    Err.Raise vbObjectError + 820, "GetConsultantsAsync", Err.Description
    Set mrsConAsync = Nothing
```

continues

Listing 14.13 continued

```
End Sub

Private Sub mrsConAsync_FetchComplete(ByVal pError As ADODB.Error, _
        adStatus As ADODB.EventStatusEnum, _
        ByVal pRecordset As ADODB.Recordset)
    ' Raise the fetch complete back to the UI
    RaiseEvent rsConAsyncFetchComplete
End Sub

Private Sub mrsConAsync_FetchProgress(ByVal Progress As Long, _
        ByVal MaxProgress As Long, adStatus As ADODB.EventStatusEnum, _
        ByVal pRecordset As ADODB.Recordset)
    ' Raise the progress back to the UI
    RaiseEvent rsConAsyncFetchProgress(Progress, MaxProgress)
End Sub
```

Using ADO in Distributed Applications

The preceding section deals with techniques that are useful when you are building form-based applications with the ADO code running on the client workstation. Even though the several variations of the clsConsultants class are logically separate from the user interface code, they are not intended to be physically separate (running on a different machine). In this section, you will modify the clsConsultants class in order to look at the issues surrounding the use of ADO from COM components running on remote servers in MTS. These issues include preserving connections, passing resultsets back to the client, batch updating, and persisting recordsets on the client.

Creating and Preserving Connections

In distributed applications that are meant to scale to hundreds or thousands of users, one of the most precious resources is database connections. Obviously, each client cannot create and hold on to a connection for the entire run of the application if you don't want the resources and available connections on the server to be depleted. For this reason, when using ADO in components or in IIS, you should create and release the connection inside each method of the component or ASP page. For example, a template for a method using ADO in a component running MTS would look like the following:

```
Public Function foo(ByVal pConnectString as String) As returnvalue

Dim cnADO as Connection

On Error Goto fooErr

Set cnADO = New Connection

' Set any special connection properties
cnADO.Open pConnectString
```

```
' Do database work on the connection

' Close and Deallocate
cnADO.Close
Set cnADO = Nothing

Exit Function
FooErr:
    Err.Raise ' back to the client
    Set cnADO = Nothing
End Function
```

Although this might seem inefficient, creating and destroying the Connection object in each method will allow ADO to take advantage of the connection and session pooling mechanisms of ODBC and OLE DB. Which type of pooling and the benefit it gives to the application depends on which provider is in use and the format of the connection string passed into the method.

For pooling to be maximally effective, the pConnectString argument passed to each method from all users should be identical. This is the case because methods will be able to use only pooled connections created with similar attributes in the connection string. This restriction ensures that an application is not allocated a connection that has an improper security context, is connected to the wrong server, or is in the wrong database context. Obviously, when an application passes connection strings with different login ids, the component could reuse connections created only by the same user, largely defeating the purpose of connection pooling in the first place.

WARNING

Some statements performed during a connection—such as using the SQL Server SET statements, using prepared commands, or setting the transaction isolation level—will have an effect on how the connection behaves for its entire lifetime. If the connection remains in a pool, other components will inherit its new settings. For this reason, you should avoid modifying the connection properties of connections you intend to pool.

To get the connection information into the method, some developers opt to pass the connection string as a parameter of the method, others hardcode the connection string into the components, and still others store it in the system Registry on the server computer using an ODBC DSN or an application-specific Registry entry. All these techniques have pros and cons (maintainability versus performance), but I've chosen to use the first method because it is more flexible and allows for maintainability, but does not incur the overhead of a Registry call for each method invoked by the client.

TIP

Remember that in previous examples, pieces of the `ConnectString` were stored as private variables of the class and populated through properties. The method used here is more efficient for MTS components because those private variables would cause MTS to have to maintain the state of the component and thereby not allow it to be released as quickly. This is critical for components that must release database resources as quickly as possible.

ODBC Connection Pooling

ODBC connection pooling is enabled by the ODBC Driver Manager in versions 3.0, 3.5, and higher, and is used when the ADO `Connection` object uses the MSDASQL provider that shipped with MDAC 2.0. In a nut shell, ODBC will create up to $n + 1$ pools, where n is the number of processors in the server, for each process (application) on the server that connects using ODBC. As I hinted in the previous section, the pools for each process contain all the connections that have been initiated from the process. When the process initiates a new connection, the ODBC Driver Manager locks and traverses the pools, looking for connections that were created with the same attributes. If one is found, it is assigned from the pool, and the pool is unlocked.

TIP

Make sure that you explicitly use the `Close` method of the `Connection` object to release connections back to the pool. Simply setting the `Connection` object to `Nothing` does not have the same effect.

ODBC connection pooling works only with 32-bit drivers that are thread safe and (under ODBC 3.5) have the string value `CPTimeout` in the Registry under HKEY_LOCAL_MACHINE\Software\ODBC\ODBCINST.INI*driver*. The `CPTimeout` is used to configure how long a connection remains in the pool before it is destroyed. The default value is 60 seconds but can be changed so that connections remain in the pool for different periods. Under ODBC 3.0, connection pooling cannot be disabled or configured, and consequently the timeout value is hard-coded to 60 seconds.

If you begin to encounter errors (which could indicate that the driver is not thread safe), you can disable connection pooling on a per-driver basis in ODBC 3.5 by removing the `CPTimeout` value in the Registry key. Other than setting `CPTimeout`, you have no way to configure how many connections remain in the pool or to preallocate connections before they are initiated by a process.

The ODBC Driver Manager also uses a retry wait time of 120 seconds that can be changed in the ODBC applet in the Control Panel. Basically, this setting is used to tell ODBC to wait for 120 seconds before attempting to reconnect, if it determines that a database server is unavailable.

As implied at the beginning of this section, ODBC connection pooling operates only when MSDASQL is used with the OLE DB 2.0 release. As of MDAC version 2.1, MSDASQL uses the OLE DB session pooling mechanism discussed next.

OLE DB Session Pooling

OLE DB session pooling was introduced in OLE DB 2.0 and is used with native OLE DB providers or when using MSDASQL under OLE DB 2.1. In many respects, OLE DB session pooling is the same as ODBC connection pooling. Both create pools of database connections for each process on the server and use a 60-second timeout value (in OLE DB this value is not adjustable). However, OLE DB takes this a step further by also creating separate pools for each distinct set of connection attributes used by the process. This creates less contention during the process of locking and finding connections to assign. In addition, an index is maintained on the pools in each process and makes finding the correct pool more efficient (rather than having to traverse each pool).

OLE DB also handles the issue of unresponsive data sources differently in that it requeries the data source at intervals of 5, 10, and 50 seconds before giving up and destroying the connection.

Enabling and Disabling

To enable session pooling, in the Registry, you must add a DWORD value of OLEDB_SER-VICES to the HKEY_CLASSES_ROOT\CLSID*provider* key, in which *provider* is the COM class identifier for the data provider, such as SQLOLEDB. By setting this value to 0xffffffff, all OLE DB services will be enabled, one of which is session pooling. Session pooling can be disabled by setting this value to 0xfffffffe. You can also enable or disable session pooling on a per-connection basis by adding OLE DB SERVICES = -1; to enable or OLE DB SERVICES = -2; to disable pooling in the connect string.

Creating a Pool

One of the important points to keep in mind about session pooling is that OLE DB will not begin pooling connections for a process until it has more than one connection open simultaneously. In other words, code such as this

```
Dim cn1 as Connection
Dim cn2 as Connection

Set cn1 = New Connection
cn1.Open "Provider=SQLOLEDB;server=myserver;database=pubs;uid=sa"
' Do some work
cn1.Close

Set cn2 = New Connection
cn2.Open "Provider=SQLOLEDB;server=myserver;database=pubs;uid=sa"
```

will create and maintain two connections to SQL Server, even though the first connection was closed before the second was opened. You might think that the first connection would be added to the pool and immediately reused by cn2. In fact, cn1 will be used to initialize the pool when Close is invoked, and cn2 will initiate a new connection. Consequently, if a third Connection object were instantiated and opened within 60 seconds, the original connection would be reused because there is now an inactive connection in the pool.

However, if the code were altered slightly,

```
Dim cn1 as Connection
Dim cn2 as Connection

Set cn1 = New Connection
cn1.Open "Provider=SQLOLEDB;server=myserver;database=pubs;uid=sa"
' Do some work
cn1.Close
Set cn1 = Nothing

Set cn2 = New Connection
cn2.Open "Provider=SQLOLEDB;server=myserver;database=pubs;uid=sa"
```

no pool would be created because cn1 was set to Nothing, rather than simply closed before cn2 was opened. The determining factor here is that the process did not keep a reference to an ADO Connection object alive. After the process drops all references, the connection pools are destroyed unless the ADO code is running within MTS or IIS, where the pool is always maintained. This is why the template method design for MTS, shown previously, can set the ADO Connection object to Nothing before completion and still continue to use connections from the pool on subsequent calls.

Passing Resultsets to the Client

In a distributed application, only two techniques are commonly used to pass resultsets from components running in MTS to client applications. In this section, you will look at brief examples of implementing both variant arrays and disconnected recordsets.

Using Variant Arrays

Multidimensional variant arrays have traditionally been used to pass resultsets from server components to client applications. The array is created using the GetRows method of the Recordset object discussed in the section on handling reference data.

Before VB 6.0, the array was passed back as an argument to the method because VB could not return arrays from functions. However, with VB 6.0 this has changed, and methods can simply return the array. Listing 14.14 shows the code required to implement the GetConsultants method in a component running in MTS.

Listing 14.14   The GetConsultants Method in an MTS Component That Returns a Variant Array

```
Public Function GetConsultants(ByVal pConnectString As String) As Variant

Dim cnADO As Connection
Dim cmADO As Command
```

```
Dim rsADO As Recordset

On Error GoTo GetConErr

Set cnADO = New Connection

' Set any special connection properties
cnADO.Open pConnectString

' Create the command object to call the stored procedure
Set cmADO = New Command
With cmADO
    .CommandText = "GetConsultants"
    .CommandType = adCmdStoredProc
    .ActiveConnection = cnADO
End With

' Default is a firehose cursor
Set rsADO = cmADO.Execute

' Retrieve all rows into the array
GetConsultants = rsADO.GetRows(adGetRowsRest)

' Close and Deallocate
Set rsADO = Nothing
Set cmADO = Nothing

cnADO.Close
Set cnADO = Nothing

Exit Function
GetConErr:
    Err.Raise vbObjectError + 900, "GetConsultants", Err.Description
    Set rsADO = Nothing
    Set cmADO = Nothing
    Set cnADO = Nothing

End Function
```

The main advantage to this approach is that the client machine does not have to have ADO loaded, nor does it require a cursor library to manipulate the resultset.

This method has the drawback of only being able to provide read-only data to the client and does not contain any metadata, such as the column names, sizes, and data types. Although you could write code in the component to traverse the Fields collection of the Recordset object and pass the data back in a second variant array, using disconnected recordsets is much simpler.

Using Disconnected Recordsets

ADO 2.0 introduced the concept of disconnected recordsets. This feature allows server components to pass copies of resultsets across process or machine boundaries without maintaining a persistent connection to the data source.

The key to implementing this technique is to create the Recordset using a client-side static cursor. After the Recordset has been created, you can disassociate it from the connection by setting its ActiveConnection property to Nothing. The Recordset can then be freely scrolled and perhaps modified (see the next section) without maintaining a reference to the connection or even the MTS component that created the resultset.

The code in Listing 14.15 implements a second version of the GetConsultants method that uses this technique to pass back a read-only Recordset to the client.

Listing 14.15   The GetConsultants Method in an MTS Component That Returns a Disassociated Recordset

```
Public Function GetConsultants(ByVal pConnectString As String) As Recordset

Dim cnADO As Connection
Dim cmADO As Command
Dim rsADO As Recordset

On Error GoTo GetConErr

Set cnADO = New Connection

' Set any special connection properties
cnADO.CursorLocation = adUseClient
cnADO.Open pConnectString

' Create the command object to call the stored procedure
Set cmADO = New Command
With cmADO
    .CommandText = "GetConsultants"
    .CommandType = adCmdStoredProc
    .ActiveConnection = cnADO
End With

' Create and open the recordset, static and read-only
Set rsADO = New Recordset

rsADO.CacheSize = 50
rsADO.Open cmADO, , adOpenStatic, adLockReadOnly

' Pass it back to the client
Set GetConsultants = rsADO
```

```
' Disassociate the recordset
Set rsADO.ActiveConnection = Nothing

' Close and Deallocate
Set rsADO = Nothing
Set cmADO = Nothing

cnADO.Close
Set cnADO = Nothing

Exit Function
GetConErr:
    Err.Raise vbObjectError + 900, "GetConsultants", Err.Description
    Set rsADO = Nothing
    Set cmADO = Nothing
    Set cnADO = Nothing
    Set GetConsultants = Nothing

End Function
```

On the client machine, you can use either the standard ADO Recordset object to retrieve the resultset or the lightweight ADOR Recordset. This smaller implementation of ADO contains only the Recordset object and is useful when thin client machines will be dealing only with resultsets created from MTS components. Here is the code to call the preceding method using ADOR:

```
Dim objCon As MTSConTracker.MTSConsultants
Dim rs As ADOR.Recordset

Set objCon = New MTSConsultants

Set rs = objCon.GetConsultants(CONNECT_STRING)

Set objCon = Nothing
```

Implementing Batch Updating

One of the primary advantages of using disconnected ADO recordsets is that they can be updated. Although in many instances it is better practice to use a stored procedure to perform the updates, using the batch update capabilities of ADO is flexible and simple to use. It is particularly useful when your application has to allow the user to peruse and update multiple rows offline in laptop or browser-based applications.

To implement batch updating through MTS components, you must implement two methods in the component: one that sends the updateable recordset to the client and one that receives the recordset and updates the data source. The code in Listing 14.13 can serve as the method to return the recordset if the LockType property of the Recordset object is changed to adLockBatchOptimistic before the Recordset is opened. The second method then receives the modified recordset, reconnects it to a valid

Connection object, and calls the UpdateBatch method to make the changes on the data source. Listing 14.16 contains the code to implement the SaveConsultants method.

Listing 14.16   The SaveConsultants Method in an MTS Component That Performs the Batch Update for a Disassociated Recordset

```
Public Function SaveConsultants(ByVal pConnectString, _
    pCon As Recordset, varStatus As Variant, pMessage As String) As Boolean

Dim cnADO As Connection
Dim lngRows As Long
Dim i As Integer

On Error GoTo SaveConErr

Set cnADO = New Connection
cnADO.CursorLocation = adUseClient

' Return the status
SaveConsultants = True

' Set any special connection properties
cnADO.Open pConnectString

' Create the command object to call the stored procedure
Set pCon.ActiveConnection = cnADO

' Set the batch size based on the number of records
' that were modified. This is so one round trip can be
' made to the data source.
pCon.Filter = adFilterPendingRecords
lngRows = pCon.RecordCount
pCon.Properties("Batch Size") = lngRows
pCon.Filter = adFilterNone

' Update the records that have changed
pCon.UpdateBatch adAffectAll

' Resync only the conflicting records
On Error GoTo SaveConflictErr
pCon.Filter = adFilterConflictingRecords
If pCon.RecordCount > 0 Then
    pCon.Resync adAffectGroup, adResyncUnderlyingValues
End If

' Take off the filter
pCon.Filter = adFilterNone

' Disconnect the recordset
pCon.ActiveConnection = Nothing
```

```
' Close and Deallocate
cnADO.Close
Set cnADO = Nothing

Exit Function
SaveConErr:

    ' Set the error message to return
    pMessage = Err.Description

    ' Populate the array of rows with their statuses
    pCon.Filter = adFilterAffectedRecords
    ReDim varStatus(pCon.RecordCount)
    Do While Not pCon.EOF
        ' Each row that was not updated should be added to the array
        If (pCon.Status <> adRecUnmodified) And _
                (pCon.Status <> adRecOK) Then
            varStatus(i) = pCon(0).Value & ": " & pCon.Status
            i = i + 1
        End If
        pCon.MoveNext
    Loop
    If i > 0 Then
        ReDim Preserve varStatus(i - 1)
    End If

    ' Add the count to the return message
    pMessage = pMessage & vbCrLf & CStr(i) & " records were not updated."

    ' Return false because errors occurred
    SaveConsultants = False
    Resume Next

Exit Function
SaveConflictErr:
    ' Return false because errors occurred
    pMessage = pMessage & vbCrLf & Err.Description & _
        ": Recordset was not resynced"
    Resume Next

End Function
```

One of the points to note in Listing 14.16 is that the UpdateBatch method can send multiple updated rows to the server in a single statement. By default, the Batch Size property of the Recordset object is set to 15. You will notice that the code uses a filter of the pending records (adFilterPendingRecords) to determine how many rows were updated and then resets the Batch Size property to this value. This instructs ADO to send all the modified rows to the server in a single statement.

NOTE

Depending on the data source, this might not be feasible if the number of modified rows causes the statement length of the data source to be exceeded. Another
approach would be to code an `If...Then` statement that sets the Batch Size to
either a maximum value or the number of modified rows.

When one or more of the rows being updated fails, a trappable error occurs, and the
remainder of the rows will be saved to the data source. The code following the
`SaveConErr` line label resets the filter to show only those rows affected by the batch
update (which should normally be the same set as the pending records discussed earlier). The rows can then be traversed to save their primary keys and status values in a
variant array. Rows that were not saved because of some error will have their `Status`
property set to a value other than `adRecUnmodified` or `adRecOK`. This can be useful
information to the client program that indicates why each row was rejected. The original error message is then saved in a string variable that will be returned to the caller.

Of course, in an application that performs batch updates, the primary reason updates
should fail is conflicts. Conflicts generally take the form of rows that were updated by
another user or that were deleted. ADO makes it simple for the `SaveConsultants`
method by using a filter (`adFilterConflictingRecords`) to find those rows that failed
the update because of conflicts. The conflicting rows are then resynchronized with the
data source, using the `Resync` method. The constant `adResyncUnderlyingValues`
instructs ADO to repopulate only the `UnderlyingValue` property of each row with the
current value in the data source. In this way, the client application will be able to determine the new values that caused the conflict.

Note that the recordset is passed by reference so that the client application receives the
resynchronized values from the data source, as well as all the status information.

Persisting Resultsets on the Client

One of the most interesting features added in ADO 2.0 is the capability to persist resultsets. This opens up myriad possibilities for applications to work more easily with occasionally connected users. A typical example would be an application that a salesman
uses on a laptop computer to track consultants and projects. In this scenario, the salesman would download project data while in the office and be able to manipulate the
data, perhaps adding projects and doing forecasting, while out visiting clients during
the day. When the salesman comes back to the office, the application can read in the
changed data and update the database.

To implement persistence, you can use the `Save` method of the `Recordset` object to
save an open recordset to a file. The method takes two arguments, the filename to use,
and a constant representing the format to write the data to. ADO 2.0 allows the recordset to be saved using only the proprietary ADTG (Advanced Data Tablegram) format
(`adPersistADTG`), whereas ADO 2.1 supports both ADTG and XML (`adPersistXML`).
Obviously, XML is the more versatile of the two because it will allow other

applications to use the data. However, ADTG is a more compact format. To open a saved recordset, you can use the Open method of the Recordset object, passing it the constant adCmdFile as the last argument.

NOTE

The first time you call the **Save** method, you must pass it a filename. On subsequent calls within the same run of the application, you should omit the filename, or else a trappable error will occur. This implies that both the recordset and the file remain open until the **Close** method of the recordset is called. After the recordset is closed, the file is also closed.

The code in Listing 14.17 implements SaveLocal and LoadLocal methods of the clsConsultants class discussed previously. Keep in mind that this code will run on the client computer and is populating and saving the mrsCon private variable with the data.

Listing 14.17   The SaveLocal and LoadLocal Methods of the Client-Side clsConsultants Class to Save and Load the Recordset

```
Private mrsCon As Recordset

Public Function SaveLocal(ByVal pFile As String) As Boolean

Dim objFileSys As New FileSystemObject

On Error GoTo SaveLocalErr

Set objFileSys = New FileSystemObject

' Check whether file exists and if so, delete it
If objFileSys.FileExists(pFile) Then
    objFileSys.DeleteFile pFile, True
End If

' Save to a local file
mrsCon.Save pFile, adPersistADTG

SaveLocal = True

Exit Function
SaveLocalErr:
    Err.Raise vbObjectError + 901, "SaveLocal", Err.Description
    SaveLocal = False

End Function

Public Function LoadLocal(ByVal pFile As String, _
    pCon As Recordset) As Boolean
```

continues

Listing 14.17   continued

```
Dim objFileSys As New FileSystemObject

On Error GoTo LoadLocalErr

Set objFileSys = New FileSystemObject

' Check to make sure that recordset is opened
If mrsCon Is Nothing Then
    Set mrsCon = New Recordset
    With mrsCon
        .CursorLocation = adUseClient
        .CursorType = adOpenStatic
        .LockType = adLockOptimistic
        .CacheSize = 25
    End With
End If

On Error GoTo 0
' Check to make sure that file exists
If Not objFileSys.FileExists(pFile) Then
    Err.Raise vbObjectError + 902, "LoadLocal", "File does not exist"
    LoadLocal = False
    Exit Function
End If

On Error GoTo LoadLocalErr

' Load the recordset from a file
mrsCon.Open pFile, , , , adCmdFile
' Return a local reference
Set pCon = mrsCon

' Return success
LoadLocal = True

Exit Function
LoadLocalErr:
    Err.Raise vbObjectError + 902, "LoadLocal", Err.Description
    LoadLocal = False

End Function
```

Note that both methods use the `FileSystemObject` (which is further discussed in Chapter 18, "Adding Professional Features") to check for the existence of the file before it is read from or deleted.

Designing an Application Using Persistence

As with many new features, persisting resultsets is an attractive technology, but it should be used with care in applications designed to take advantage of it.

When considering an application that works in either an online or offline mode (such as the sample sales application discussed at the beginning of this section), you must make numerous design decisions. For example, the flowchart in Figure 14.8 highlights the decisions that must be made during the run of an application that supports an offline mode.

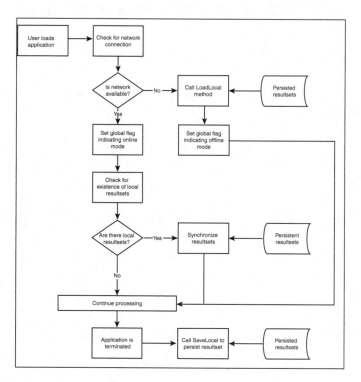

Figure 14.8

A flowchart that shows the processing of an application that requires both offline and online modes.

In addition, you have other considerations. For instance, when the application is working in offline mode, it should not attempt to connect to the database to retrieve result-sets. Therefore, when calling methods such as GetConsultants, shown in Listing 14.2, the Refresh argument must be set to False so that the recordset is read from the private cached variable rather than populated from the database. In the same vein, when the recordset has to be saved, the code must redirect to the SaveLocal method rather than attempt to call a stored procedure to make the update or the Update method of the recordset.

Summary

ADO provides a wealth of new features and opportunities for VB developers to create professional applications. Techniques such as calling stored procedures with different combinations of arguments and return values, implementing asynchronous processing, and using disassociated and persistent recordsets will all assist in building the next generation of corporate applications.

The goal of this chapter is to highlight these techniques and discuss some key considerations (such as using cursors efficiently and connection pooling) when you use ADO for corporate development. Now, all you have to do is start coding.

CHAPTER 15

Using Object-Oriented Techniques

Starting with version 4.0, Visual Basic began the transformation from a primarily procedural and event-driven programming language toward a component-based and object-oriented tool. By adding support for class modules and the creation of ActiveX (COM) DLLs and EXEs, VB now provides the infrastructure for using techniques that are more sophisticated than the simple CBF (code behind the form).

This chapter explores the relationship between object-oriented programming (OOP) and VB and where it makes sense to leverage these features of the language. After a brief refresher on the concepts of OOP and how they're addressed in VB, I'll get practical and show techniques that take advantage of the OOP features of VB to create both form-based and distributed applications.

NOTE

As you're probably aware, VB derives its object-oriented features from the Component Object Model (COM). Although this chapter focuses mainly on how to use object-oriented techniques from within VB itself, seeing the broader picture requires a proper understanding of COM. For those who want to brush up on the fundamentals, you should read Chapter 23, "A COM Primer for VB Developers," in conjunction with this chapter.

Object-Oriented Fundamentals

At its core, object-oriented programming can be thought of as the task of packaging together the behavior of an entity (implemented as methods and events) with its identity and state information (implemented through properties). This combination is what is termed an *object*. The benefit of using objects is you can more easily model the business of a company by allowing programs to work simultaneously with both the processes of an object and its attributes. In systems and development tools that do not provide object orientation, the identity and state of information are manipulated apart from the procedures that work with the data. This decoupling makes for software with more dependencies, leading to designs that are difficult to debug, maintain, and extend.

On a more academic level, object-oriented systems support generally has three core characteristics: encapsulation, polymorphism, and inheritance.

Encapsulation

The first core concept of OOP is *encapsulation*. Basically, this means that an object can hide its internal data structures from consumers of the object. Therefore, all the object's internal data is manipulated through methods of the object rather than through direct references.

As you will see, VB supports encapsulation by allowing both form and class modules to use private scope when declaring variables used internal to the module so as not to allow direct access from the outside. Further, both types of modules can contain user-defined property procedures, public methods and events (its public interface) that are used to manipulate the internal data.

The primary benefits of encapsulation are maintainability and reusability. Code that takes advantage of encapsulation is more maintainable because consumers of the code are forced to work with the object through its public interface. With a fully encapsulated class module in VB, for example, code outside the module cannot directly change a variable declared inside the class. By shutting off this direct access, fewer bugs are introduced because consumers of the class cannot inadvertently change the state of an object.

Abstracting the internal data of the object from consumers also leads to greater reusability. This follows because encapsulation leads to fewer dependencies between the consumer and the object and fewer dependencies are a prerequisite for creating reusable software. In fact, if forms and class modules are fully encapsulated in VB (as they can be), they will have no dependencies on other forms and classes in the application. This is, of course, not true of the consumer of the object because it will be dependent on the interface of the object.

Polymorphism

The second characteristic of object-oriented systems is *polymorphism*. This concept can be defined as the ability to write code that treats objects as if they were the same when, in fact, they are different. In other words, polymorphism allows you to write code that is generic across a set of objects that provide the same public interface. Underneath the covers, each object may implement the methods of the interface differently and may support additional interfaces as well. However, as far as the consumer is concerned, each object looks the same and can be treated as such.

The benefits of polymorphism revolve around the central fact that consumers of objects do not have to be aware of how the object performs its work, only that it does so through a specific interface. This makes writing code that uses objects simpler by allowing the code to treat the object as if it were a black box, which leads to increased maintainability. Along the same lines, polymorphism allows you to write less code because each individual object does not have to be dealt with separately. Finally, polymorphism lends itself to writing code that can be reused because it will not be specific to a particular object but will instead rely on its interface.

This concept is fundamental for developing component-based software that allows objects to be plugged in where they are needed. By relying on different objects implementing the same interface, software can be designed to depend on the interface of an object instead of the implementation. For example, ActiveX controls such as those used in VB, use the polymorphic characteristics of COM to provide a consistent interface to all development environments (technically termed *containers*) that use them. In this way, each container does not have to know the particulars of each control in order to allow it to be placed on a form and manipulated by developers and the code they write. As you can see, polymorphism is a powerful concept.

VB provides polymorphism on two levels. First, intrinsic classes and objects such as Me, Form, Object, Control, TextBox, and ListBox provide access to the interfaces of instances of forms, objects, and controls in the application. By using these generic objects rather than referencing particular instances, you can write code that is more general and flexible. For example, assume that a form contains a Save button, cmdSave, that should be enabled only after all the TextBox controls on the form have been filled in. Without the type of polymorphism just described, you would have to write code that checks each individual instance of the TextBox control on the form before enabling the Save button. However, by using the Controls collection of the Form object, you can simply loop through all the controls on the form as keys are pressed. Further, you can inspect the type of each control at runtime using the TypeOf statement to determine whether it is a TextBox. If so, you can exit the procedure rather than let it run through to enable the Save button.

```
Private Sub Form_KeyPress(KeyAscii As Integer)
Dim objControl As Control

' Loop through all controls on the form
For Each objControl In Me.Controls
    If TypeOf objControl Is TextBox Then
        If Len(objControl.Text) = 0 Then
            Exit Sub
        End If
    End If
Next objControl

cmdSave.Enabled = True

End Sub
```

The key point about this code snippet is that it does not explicitly reference any instance of a form or control in the application. This obviously lends itself to be reused in multiple forms and projects.

The second form of polymorphism that VB supports involves user-defined interfaces implemented in class modules. Using this form of polymorphism, developers can create their own interfaces and implement them in class modules using the Implements keyword. This technique (which is discussed in more detail later) allows developers to specify the interface of the object apart from its implementation. Clients that use software created in this way can take full advantage of polymorphism by treating all objects that implement the same interface in a like manner.

Inheritance

The final OOP concept to be discussed is *inheritance*. Inheritance allows objects to share their interfaces and/or implementation in a hierarchical fashion. For example, Vendor and Supplier objects may be derived or inherited from a more generic Company object. All three objects share a basic interface that includes properties such as Name, Address, and City. The Vendor descendant object, however, may also include a property that determines whether it is a preferred vendor. Inheritance allows objects to become more specific further down the hierarchy by adding additional methods and properties. In a nutshell, inheritance allows objects to reuse features of other objects to which they are naturally related. The primary benefit of inheritance is reuse.

Obviously, inheritance and polymorphism are closely related, and, in fact, inheritance is what makes polymorphism possible in object-oriented systems. It is always the case that objects in an inheritance relationship can be treated polymorphically. For example, if the Vendor object is inherited from the Company object, any consumer designed to work with Company objects will also work with Vendor objects.

VB does support the inheritance of interfaces between objects but does not support the inheritance of the implementation. In other words, if you write code in a class module named clsCompany, VB cannot automatically reuse it in the clsVendor class. In this respect, VB follows the COM specification and will allow the clsVendor class to inherit the interface of clsCompany (by using the Implements keyword), but not its implementation. In this case clsVendor will have to reimplement the methods on its own.

Although VB developers cannot benefit directly from the code reuse of implementation inheritance, it is possible to reuse code by using designs that take advantage of the concepts of *containment* and *delegation*. Basically, this means that a class accessible by a consumer will *contain* a private instance of a second class and *delegate* its services to the consumer through its own interface. In the case of clsVendor, rather than reimplement all the methods in clsCompany, clsVendor would create a private instance of clsCompany and call its methods directly, passing the results to the consumer through its own public interface. Once again, *containment* and *delegation* are familiar terms (along with aggregation) to COM programmers.

> Implementation inheritance is a powerful feature for code reuse, and VB developers have been requesting it for years. Unfortunately, if not tightly controlled, it can lead to designs that are fragile and difficult to maintain.

Using OOP in Visual Basic

Using the object-oriented features of VB is not difficult, but it does require a certain level of dedication and a different mindset. Developers who have internalized OOP are always thinking about how a feature or specific functionality in an application can be encapsulated and made reusable. This is manifested in the attitude that each form, standard, or class module in the application should be selfish about what it reveals to the rest of the application. This kind of thinking leads developers to be more disciplined about how modules in an application communicate, leading to the creation of well-defined interfaces.

That being said, there is obviously a trade-off between employing OOP techniques blindly to the nth degree versus using them appropriately. The former method is a recipe for code that is bloated and more complex than need be, whereas the latter fosters maintainable and reusable code that performs well.

In this section, you will look at specific techniques that use the OOP features of VB in form-based applications, multitiered applications, and the implementation of user-defined interfaces.

Form-Based OOP Techniques

With the introduction of class modules, VB developers started to become accustomed to thinking in terms of objects. What many developers might not have realized is that VB forms have also taken on the OOP characteristics of class modules and fully support encapsulation through property procedures, public methods, and events. In fact, you can think of and work with forms simply as classes that contain a user interface.

NOTE

> Under the covers, the `Form` object—like the class module—is actually a COM object.

For example, consider the simple case in which an application requires the user to provide a login id and password to create a connection to a data source using ADO. Because this is such a common function, it is a good candidate for reuse. The code in Listing 15.1 shows the complete code for a login form that contains `TextBox` controls to accept the login id and password and is fully encapsulated. Listing 15.2 contains sample code used to call the login form from the main form of an application.

Listing 15.1   The frmLogin Form Illustrates Using the Encapsulation Techniques Available to Form Modules

```
Option Explicit

' Internal private data
Private mcnConnection As Connection
Private mstrProvider As String
Private mstrConnectString As String
Private mstrLoginID As String
Private mlngIsolationLevel As IsolationLevelEnum

' Events that are raised at completion
Event ConnectionSuccess(ByVal pConnection As Connection)
Event ConnectionFailure()
Event ConnectionCanceled()

Public Property Get Connection() As Connection
    ' Allow consumers to retrieve the connection object
    Set Connection = mcnConnection
End Property

Public Property Get Provider() As String
    Provider = mstrProvider
End Property

Public Property Let Provider(ByVal vNewValue As String)
    ' Set the OLE DB provider
    If Len(vNewValue) = 0 Then
        Err.Raise vbObjectError + 1001, Me.Caption, "Provider required"
    Else
        mstrProvider = vNewValue
    End If
End Property

Public Property Get ConnectString() As String
    ConnectString = mstrConnectString
End Property

Public Property Let ConnectString(ByVal vNewValue As String)
    ' Set the connect string
    If Len(vNewValue) = 0 Then
        Err.Raise vbObjectError + 1002, Me.Caption, _
            "Connect string required"
    Else
        mstrConnectString = vNewValue
    End If
End Property

Public Property Get LoginID() As String
```

```
        LoginID = mstrLoginID
End Property

Public Property Let LoginID(ByVal vNewValue As String)
    ' Check to make sure the login id is supplied
    If Len(vNewValue) = 0 Then
        Err.Raise vbObjectError + 1000, Me.Caption, "Login ID required"
    Else
        mstrLoginID = vNewValue
        txtUserName.Text = mstrLoginID
    End If
End Property

Public Property Get IsolationLevel() As IsolationLevelEnum
    IsolationLevel = mlngIsolationLevel
End Property

Public Property Let IsolationLevel(ByVal vNewValue As IsolationLevelEnum)
    mlngIsolationLevel = vNewValue
End Property

Private Sub cmdCancel_Click()

    ' Unload the form
    Unload Me

End Sub

Private Sub cmdOK_Click()

    ' Call the private procedure to attempt to log in
    Call Login

End Sub

Private Sub Form_Activate()

    ' When the form is activated, set the focus appropriately
    If Len(mstrLoginID) = 0 Then
        txtUserName.SetFocus
    Else
        txtPassword.SetFocus
    End If

End Sub

Private Sub Form_Unload(Cancel As Integer)
```

continues

Listing 15.1   continued

```
    ' If the form unloads without a connection,
    ' raise the appropriate failure event back to the caller

    If Not mcnConnection Is Nothing Then
        If mcnConnection.State = adStateClosed Then
            RaiseEvent ConnectionFailure
        End If
    Else
        RaiseEvent ConnectionCanceled
    End If

    ' Destroy the connection object
    Set mcnConnection = Nothing

End Sub

Private Sub Login()

On Error GoTo LoginErr

' Create a new connection and populate it
If mcnConnection Is Nothing Then
    Set mcnConnection = New Connection
End If

With mcnConnection
    .Provider = mstrProvider
    .ConnectionString = mstrConnectString
    .ConnectionTimeout = 10
    .IsolationLevel = mlngIsolationLevel
    .Properties("Prompt") = adPromptNever
End With

' Attempt to open the connection
mcnConnection.Open , mstrLoginID, _
    txtPassword.Text

' If success, raise event to calling code
RaiseEvent ConnectionSuccess(mcnConnection)
Unload Me

Exit Sub
LoginErr:
    ' Raise an error back to the caller
    MsgBox "An error occurred: " & Err.Description, _
        vbApplicationModal + vbExclamation, Me.Caption
```

```
' Set focus back to txtPassword
txtPassword.SetFocus
txtPassword.SelStart = 0
txtPassword.SelLength = Len(txtPassword.Text)

End Sub
```

One key feature of the code in Listing 15.1 is that the internal data of `frmLogin` is accessible only through property procedures. This allows the `ConnectString`, `LoginID`, and `Provider` property procedures to check to make sure that valid values are being passed in. In addition, the implementation of the `Login` procedure is declared as `Private` so as not to allow consumers access to the code that actually performs the login.

Finally, you will notice that the form declares and raises three events with the `Event` and `RaiseEvent` keywords, respectively. The events are raised before the login form is closed to notify the consumer of the state of the connection. In particular, the `ConnectionSuccess` event passes back a copy of the ADO `Connection` object that was successfully connected to the data source. This technique of allowing forms to raise events can be used in numerous cases to provide notification as events occur on the form. For example, a modal dialog that modifies data can raise an event back to the main form in an application so that it may refresh its display.

NOTE

In the case of `frmLogin`, the valid `Connection` object can be returned to the consumer either through the `ConnectionSuccess` event or the `Connection` property. The property was added because standard modules cannot declare a form using the `WithEvents` keyword. This makes the form more flexible.

Listing 15.2   Calling frmLogin from the Main Form of an Application
```
Option Explicit
' Declare the form using the WithEvents
' keyword so that connection status can be returned
Private WithEvents pfrmLogin As frmLogin

Private Sub Form_Load()

' Initialization code goes here

' Show the form
Me.Show

' Create and initialize the login form
Set pfrmLogin = New frmLogin
With pfrmLogin
```

continues

Listing 15.2   continued

```
        .Provider = "SQLOLEDB"
        ' This value would likely be read from the Registry
        ' and reconstructed here
        .ConnectString = "server=ssosa;database=contracker"
        .IsolationLevel = adXactReadCommitted
        .Caption = "Consultant Tracker Login"
        ' This value would also be read from the Registry
        .LoginID = "sa"
        .Show vbModal
End With

' Destroy it when finished
Set pfrmLogin = Nothing

End Sub


Private Sub pfrmLogin_ConnectionCanceled()

    MsgBox "Connection cancelled"

End Sub


Private Sub pfrmLogin_ConnectionFailure()

    MsgBox "Connection failed"

End Sub


Private Sub pfrmLogin_ConnectionSuccess(ByVal pConnection As _
        ADODB.Connection)

    ' A valid connection object is returned
    MsgBox "Connection successful"

    ' Would likely save the connection in a global
    ' or form level variable
    Set gcnConnection = pConnection

End Sub
```

The technique shown for using `frmLogin` in Listing 15.2 relies on declaring the reference variable for the form using the `WithEvents` keyword. In this way, the main form can catch the three events raised by the form. The `Load` event of the main form also uses the technique of calling its own `Show` method after the form is initialized so that the form will be displayed. It then instantiates and shows the login form, which allows the login form to be shown on top of the main form.

You might notice that, contrary to the statement previously made, frmLogin is not completely encapsulated. This is certainly true because VB always adds controls on a form to its public interface. This is unfortunate because it allows consumers unfettered access to all the controls. To make this example fully encapsulated, you would have to implement the login form in its own ActiveX DLL or ActiveX control project.

As mentioned previously, form-based OOP techniques such as these are best suited to forms that you anticipate will be reusable across projects. These types of forms are generally termed *auxiliary forms* and include login, progress indicators, About dialogs, and perhaps even some forms that are business specific.

TIP

Writing code that is reusable does not in itself provide the benefits of reusability. The logistical step of actually publishing and making available the code is where the leverage for an organization and even an individual is gained.

Microsoft has been working on this problem for some time and has been refining its Microsoft Repository technology to address these issues. Simply put, the *Repository* is a set of COM interfaces and a storage engine that allow programmers to define information models and persist those models in a Jet or SQL Server database. Microsoft has used this framework to create an information model (the Microsoft Development Objects Model, or MDO) for publishing information of interest to VB programmers.

VB 6 ships with the Visual Component Manager (VCM), which is a graphical utility that can be used to publish to, and extend, the MDO. After invoking the VCM from the View menu, you can open either a local Jet database (the default) or create a SQL Server database. You will notice that the MDO folder hierarchy contains an entry for Visual Basic/Templates/Forms. By right-clicking on the folder, you can publish a new component to the Repository. Figure 15.1 shows the VCM running in a dockable window in VB 6 with the published frmLogin form. To use a published component in a project, you can simply right-click on it and select Add to Project.

Application Partitioning

Perhaps the biggest shift in development paradigms in the last several years has been the shift towards multitiered applications. The key concept behind this shift is that code that implements the user interface, the business logic, and the data access should be logically separated (shown in Figure 15.2). By separating each of these tiers, you will be able to develop applications that are more maintainable, reusable, and extensible because each tier (also referred to as *layers* or *services*) can be abstracted from the other two. For example, VB developers are keenly aware of the cost of maintaining applications that were developed using Data Access Objects (DAO) and now have to be updated to use ADO. If those applications had been logically partitioned, the transition would have been easier.

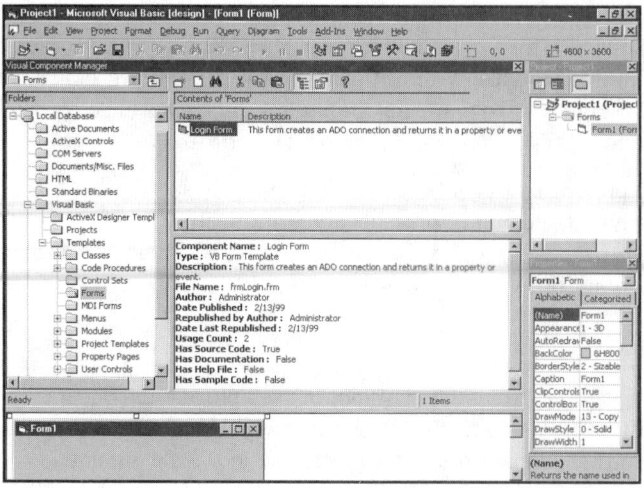

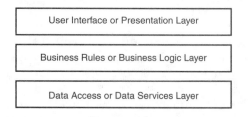

Figure 15.1

The Visual Component Manager running in VB 6 allows developers to publish reusable components.

```
┌─────────────────────────────────────────────────┐
│        User Interface or Presentation Layer       │
└─────────────────────────────────────────────────┘

┌─────────────────────────────────────────────────┐
│      Business Rules or Business Logic Layer       │
└─────────────────────────────────────────────────┘

┌─────────────────────────────────────────────────┐
│       Data Access or Data Services Layer          │
└─────────────────────────────────────────────────┘
```

Figure 15.2

The logical separation of user interface, business logic, and data services.

In addition, logical partitioning lends itself to physical partitioning, in which components that perform the business logic or data access can be running on separate servers and can, for example, take advantage of a new class of middleware products such as Microsoft Transaction Server (MTS). This physical separation is the basis for distributed applications that are scalable. Chapter 16, "Building ActiveX Components," takes a look at some considerations when using VB with MTS.

WARNING

Taking the time and effort to fully extract the user interface from business and data access logic is most effective in team and larger development scenarios where there is a likelihood that business logic and data access code can be reused across projects. This is because the design and implementation of a partitioned application is more costly. In small projects with a limited future, this type of development is often more costly in both the short and long run. Unfortunately, many VB developers do not consider this and end up applying these concepts where they are not warranted.

VB, with its basis in COM, naturally supports partitioning by allowing you to develop encapsulated forms and class modules that allow access only through their public interfaces.

The Object Model Approach

Since VB 4.0 was released, several techniques have become popular for partitioning applications. Perhaps the most familiar (and, to a degree, most natural with tools provided with VB) is the technique of creating an application-specific object model using class modules. With this approach, each business object is created as a class module that exposes methods and properties on the object. Instances of the objects are then managed using the intrinsic `Collection` object. Using this approach, for example, each customer referenced in the application is accessed through a `Customer` object, and all customers would be managed through a `Customers` collection. To obtain a list of all the customers, the user interface code would use the following type of loop:

```
Dim objCustomer as Customer
Dim objCustomers as Customers

For Each objCustomer in objCustomers
    Debug.print objCustomer.Name
    Debug.print objCustomer.Address
Next
```

In addition, if each customer placed orders, the orders would be modeled as a collection of `Order` objects referenced as a property of the `Customer` object.

```
Dim objOrder as Order

For Each objOrder in objCustomer.Orders
    Debug.Print objOrder.Amount
Next
```

Although this method makes for a purely object-oriented solution by cleanly abstracting the user interface from the underlying storage and manipulation of the data, it has drawbacks. Specifically, it requires a significant amount of code and usually merges the business logic with the data access code in monolithic components that are not, if needed, easily separated. If not done carefully, it can also lead to bloated solutions that consume significant resources on the client computer.

Using the Lightweight Business Object Model

To use the OOP features of VB efficiently, you must keep in mind the goal of using the features in the first place. The main goals are to create applications that are first and foremost, maintainable, second, extensible, and third, reusable. These three goals are listed in the order in which a developer must deal with them. Maintainability speaks to the issue of fixing defects, extensibility addresses future enhancements and the capability of the application to support future workloads, and reusability allows future applications to take advantage of what's been written.

To those ends, I advocate using a variant of the three-tier model, the Lightweight Business Object Model (LBOM). In this technique, an application is partitioned into four separate tiers, as depicted in Figure 15.3. This architecture separates the business logic required for the user interface; the data access code required to insert, update, and delete the data; and the business logic that implements more sophisticated business processes. Table 15.1 highlights each tier and its responsibilities.

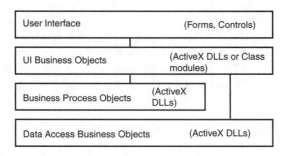

Figure 15.3

The tiers of the LBOM.

Table 15.1   The Tiers of the LBOM, as Depicted in Figure 15.3

Tier	Description
User Interface (UI)	Responsible for presenting the graphical interface to the user and in a pure VB application consists of forms, ActiveX controls, and modules that are involved only in the presentation of the data.
UI Business Objects (UBO)	Models each business object as a class module and provides properties and methods for the object. Responsible for single- and cross-attribute validation, as well as caching some data for quick client-side access. This object is lightweight because one instance of the object provides access to all "objects"

Tier	Description
	by populating properties as each object is accessed (just in time). Some methods and properties return disassociated read-only ADO `Recordset` objects for child data instead of collections of objects. The components that house these objects are normally installed on each client machine.
Business Process Objects (BPO)	Class modules that implement methods that perform business processes involving multiple business objects. The components that house these objects can be installed on each client or installed in MTS.
Data Access Business Objects (DABO)	Class modules that implement methods to perform all the data manipulation for the object. Some methods may return disassociated read-only ADO `Recordset` objects. The components that house these objects may be installed on each client or installed in MTS.

As noted in Figure 15.3, all communication from the user interface flows through the UBOs so that the UI does not communicate directly with the BPOs or DABOs. The UBOs then communicate directly with the DABOs or through the BPOs (say that 10 times fast).

Building a UBO

As an example, consider the implementation of an application that requires the manipulation of project data for a consulting company. To provide an object-oriented interface to the data, a class module (`clsProject`) is developed as the UBO. This object contains methods and properties shown in Table 15.2.

Table 15.2 Methods and Properties of the clsProject UBO

Member	Description
	Properties
`Assignments`	ADO `Recordset`. Property that returns a resultset containing all the consultants, their rates, and start and end dates assigned to the project. Calls the `GetAssignments` method of the DABO for projects.
`IsDirty`	`Boolean`. Property that determines whether the current object requires saving. Standard in all UBOs.
`Revenue`	`Currency`. Property that returns the amount of revenue projected for the project. Calls the `GetRevenue` method of the DABO.

continues

Table 15.2   Continued

Member	Description
EndDate	`Date`. Property that specifies the ending date for the project.
StartDate	`Date`. Property that specifies the starting date for the project.
Phone	`String`. Property that specifies the phone number of the client contact.
Contact	`String`. Property that specifies the contact name at the client company.
Company	`String`. Property that specifies the client company.
Description	`String`. Property that specifies the description of the project.
Code	`String`. Property that returns the engagement code for the project.
ConnectString	`String`. Property that specifies the connection string to use when connecting to the data source through the DABO. Standard in all UBOs.
ReadFromCache	`Boolean`. Property that determines whether data should be read from local storage or retrieved from the DABO. Standard in all UBOs.

Methods	
Remove	`Boolean`. Method that deletes the current project. Calls the `Remove` method of the DABO.
Save	`Boolean`. Method that saves the current project. Calls the `Add` or `Update` method of the DABO.
RemoveConsultant	`Boolean`. Method that takes a given consultant off the project. Calls the `RemoveConsultant` method of the DABO.
GetProject	`Boolean`. Method that, given an engagement code, makes the project current. Calls the `GetProject` method of the DABO.
AssignConsultant	`Boolean`. Method that assigns the given consultant to the project. Calls the `AssignConsultant` method of the DABO.
List	ADO `Recordset`. Method that returns a resultset of all the current projects. Calls the `List` method of the DABO.
NewProject	Method that resets all the internal data and flushes cached properties so that a new project can be created.

One of the keys to the LBOM approach and what makes it lightweight is the `GetProject` method. This method calls the project's DABO to return a single-row resultset populated with the given project. The fields of the resultset are then mapped into the properties of `clsProject` without requiring a new instance of the object. Using this approach, an expensive collection of project objects is not required while still giving the UI an object-oriented interface. In addition, the `List` method is used to provide a read-only ADO `Recordset` that allows the UI to retrieve a current list of projects without the expense of creating a collection of objects. Listing 15.3 gives the complete code for the `clsProject` class module.

Listing 15.3   The Code for the clsProject UBO

```
Option Explicit

'local variable(s) to hold property value(s)
Private mstrCode As String 'local copy
Private mstrDescription As String 'local copy
Private mstrCompany As String 'local copy
Private mstrContact As String 'local copy
Private mstrPhone As String 'local copy
Private mdtStartDate As Date 'local copy
Private mdtEndDate As Date 'local copy
Private mcurRevenue As Currency 'local copy
Private mflIsDirty As Boolean 'local copy
Private mrsAssignments As Recordset 'local copy
Private mrsProjects As Recordset 'local copy
Private mstrConnect As String 'local copy
Private mflCache As Boolean 'local copy


' Reference to data access business object
Private mobjProjectsData As clsProjectsData

' Error values
Enum ProjectErr
    E_NO_CURRENT_PROJECT = vbObjectError + 1050
    E_ASSIGNMENTS = vbObjectError + 1051
    E_REVENUE = vbObjectError + 1052
    E_DATE_ERROR = vbObjectError + 1053
    E_PHONE_FORMAT = vbObjectError + 1054
    E_COMPANY_TOO_LONG = vbObjectError + 1055
    E_CONTACT_TOO_LONG = vbObjectError + 1056
    E_DESC_TOO_LONG = vbObjectError + 1057
    E_REMOVE_FAILED = vbObjectError + 1058
    E_SAVE_FAILED = vbObjectError + 1059
    E_ASSIGN_DATES = vbObjectError + 1060
    E_ASSIGN_CON = vbObjectError + 1061
    E_PROJECT_LIST = vbObjectError + 1062
    E_DATA_CLASS = vbObjectError + 1063
    E_REQUIRED_FIELDS = vbObjectError + 1064
End Enum


' Error string
Private Const E_CURRENT_PROJECT_STR = "No project is current"
Private Const E_DATE_ERROR_STR = "Start and end dates are incompatible"
Private Const E_PHONE_FORMAT_STR = "Bad phone number format"
Private Const E_COMPANY_TOO_LONG_STR = "Company is too long"
Private Const E_CONTACT_TOO_LONG_STR = "Contact is too long"
Private Const E_DESC_TOO_LONG_STR = "Description  is too long"
```

continues

Listing 15.3   continued

```
Private Const E_ASSIGN_DATES_STR = _
    "Consultant dates conflict with project dates"
Private Const E_REQUIRED_FIELDS_STR = _
    "Not all required fields are filled in"


Public Property Get Assignments() As Recordset


On Error GoTo AssignErr


    ' Check to see if a project is current
    If Len(mstrCode) = 0 Then
        Set Assignments = Nothing
        Exit Property
    End If


    ' If cache is not specified or if no recordset exists then
    ' get it from the database, else use what's in the cache
    If mflCache = False Then
        If Not mrsAssignments Is Nothing Then
            mrsAssignments.Close
        End If
        Set mrsAssignments = mobjProjectsData.GetAssignments( _
            mstrConnect, mstrCode)
    Else
        mrsAssignments.MoveFirst
    End If

    Set Assignments = mrsAssignments

Exit Property
AssignErr:
    Err.Raise E_ASSIGNMENTS, "Assignment", Err.Description
    Set Assignments = Nothing

End Property

Public Property Get IsDirty() As Boolean
    IsDirty = mflIsDirty
End Property

Public Property Get Revenue() As Currency

On Error GoTo RevErr

    ' If cache is not set or the revenue has not been read yet
    ' get it from the database
    If mflCache = False Or mcurRevenue = -1 Then
```

```
            ' Get it from the database
            mcurRevenue = mobjProjectsData.GetRevenue(mstrConnect, mstrCode)
        End If


    Revenue = mcurRevenue
Exit Property
RevErr:
    Err.Raise E_REVENUE, "Revenue", Err.Description


End Property

Public Property Let EndDate(ByVal vData As Date)

    ' If start date has been set
    If mdtStartDate <> 0 Then
        ' Make sure the start date is before the end date
        If vData < mdtStartDate Then
            Err.Raise E_DATE_ERROR, "EndDate", E_DATE_ERROR_STR
            Exit Property
        End If
    End If

    ' Has been edited
    mflIsDirty = True
    mdtEndDate = vData

End Property

Public Property Get EndDate() As Date
    EndDate = mdtEndDate
End Property

Public Property Let StartDate(ByVal vData As Date)

    ' If end date has not been set
    If mdtEndDate <> 0 Then
        ' Make sure the start date is before the end date
        If vData > mdtEndDate Then
            Err.Raise E_DATE_ERROR, "StartDate", E_DATE_ERROR_STR
            Exit Property
        End If
    End If

    ' Has been edited
    mflIsDirty = True
    mdtStartDate = vData
```

continues

Listing 15.3   continued

```
End Property

Public Property Get StartDate() As Date
    StartDate = mdtStartDate
End Property

Public Property Let Phone(ByVal vData As String)

    ' Make sure the phone is numeric
    If Len(vData) < 10 Or Not IsNumeric(vData) Then
        Err.Raise E_PHONE_FORMAT, "Phone", E_PHONE_FORMAT_STR
    Else
        ' Has been edited
        mflIsDirty = True
        mstrPhone = vData
    End If

End Property

Public Property Get Phone() As String
    Phone = mstrPhone
End Property

Public Property Let Contact(ByVal vData As String)

    ' Make sure the length is valid
    If Len(vData) > 75 Then
        Err.Raise E_CONTACT_TOO_LONG, "Contact", E_CONTACT_TOO_LONG_STR
    Else
        ' Has been edited
        mflIsDirty = True
        mstrContact = vData
    End If
End Property

Public Property Get Contact() As String
    Contact = mstrContact
End Property

Public Property Let Company(ByVal vData As String)

    ' Make sure the length is valid
    If Len(vData) > 50 Then
        Err.Raise E_COMPANY_TOO_LONG, "Company", E_COMPANY_TOO_LONG_STR
    Else
        ' Has been edited
        mflIsDirty = True
```

```
            mstrCompany = vData
        End If

End Property

Public Property Get Company() As String
    Company = mstrCompany
End Property

Public Property Let Description(ByVal vData As String)

    ' Make sure the length is valid
    If Len(vData) > 100 Then
        Err.Raise E_DESC_TOO_LONG, "Description", E_DESC_TOO_LONG_STR
    Else
        ' Has been edited
        mflIsDirty = True
        mstrDescription = vData
    End If

End Property

Public Property Get Description() As String
    Description = mstrDescription
End Property

Public Property Get Code() As String
    Code = mstrCode
End Property

Public Property Get ConnectString() As String
    ConnectString = mstrConnect
End Property

Public Property Let ConnectString(ByVal vData As String)
    mstrConnect = vData
End Property

Public Property Get ReadFromCache() As Boolean
    ReadFromCache = mflCache
End Property

Public Property Let ReadFromCache(ByVal vData As Boolean)
    mflCache = vData
End Property

Public Function Remove() As Boolean
```

continues

Listing 15.3   continued

```
On Error GoTo RemoveErr
Dim flRet As Boolean

    ' If save was not called previously then just clear private data
    If Len(mstrCode) = 0 Then
        Remove = True
    Else
        ' Remove project from the database
        flRet = mobjProjectsData.Remove(mstrConnect, mstrCode)
        Remove = flRet
    End If

    ' Reset private variables
    ClearPrivateData

Exit Function
RemoveErr:
    Err.Raise E_REMOVE_FAILED, "Remove", Err.Description
    Remove = False

End Function


Public Function Save() As Boolean

On Error GoTo SaveErr

    ' If not dirty then just return
    If Not mflIsDirty Then
        Save = False
        Exit Function
    End If

    ' Check all required properties
    If (Len(mstrCompany) > 0) And (Len(mstrDescription) > 0) And _
        (mdtStartDate <> 0) And (mdtEndDate <> 0) And _
        (Len(mstrContact) > 0) And (Len(mstrPhone) > 0) Then

        ' Check to see if a save or update is required
        If Len(mstrCode) > 0 Then
            ' Update the database
            Save = mobjProjectsData.Update(mstrConnect, mstrDescription, _
                mstrCompany, mstrContact, mstrPhone, _
                mdtStartDate, mdtEndDate)
        Else
            ' Save to the database
            mstrCode = mobjProjectsData.Add(mstrConnect, mstrDescription, _
                mstrCompany, mstrContact, mstrPhone, _
```

```
                    mdtStartDate, mdtEndDate)
                ' Check to see if a project code was returned
                If Len(mstrCode) > 0 Then Save = True
            End If
        Else
            ' Required fields not filled in
            Err.Raise E_REQUIRED_FIELDS, "Save", E_REQUIRED_FIELDS_STR
            Save = False
            Exit Function
        End If


    If Save = True Then mflIsDirty = False


    Exit Function
    SaveErr:
        Err.Raise E_SAVE_FAILED, "Save", Err.Description


    End Function


    Public Function RemoveConsultant(ByVal pConID As Long) As Boolean


    Dim flRet As Boolean


        ' Check to see if a project is current
        If Len(mstrCode) = 0 Then
            On Error GoTo 0
            Err.Raise ProjectErr.E_NO_CURRENT_PROJECT, "RemoveConsultant", _
                E_CURRENT_PROJECT_STR
            RemoveConsultant = False
            Exit Function
        End If


    On Error GoTo RemoveConErr


        ' Remove the consultant from the database
        flRet = mobjProjectsData.RemoveConsultant(mstrConnect, _
            mstrCode, pConID)
        RemoveConsultant = flRet


    Exit Function
    RemoveConErr:
        Err.Raise E_REMOVE_CON, "RemoveConsultant", Err.Description
        RemoveConsultant = False


    End Function


    Public Function GetProject(ByVal pcode As String) As Boolean
```

continues

Listing 15.3   continued

```
Dim rs As Recordset

On Error GoTo GetProjErr

    ' Reset private variables
    ClearPrivateData

    Set rs = mobjProjectsData.GetProject(mstrConnect, pcode)
    If rs.EOF And rs.BOF Then
        GetProject = False
    Else
        ' Populate properties from the recordset
        mstrCode = rs.Fields("Code")
        mstrDescription = rs.Fields("Description")
        mstrCompany = rs.Fields("Company")
        mstrContact = rs.Fields("Contact") & vbNullString
        mstrPhone = rs.Fields("Phone") & vbNullString
        mdtStartDate = rs.Fields("StartDate")
        mdtEndDate = rs.Fields("EndDate")
        Set rs = Nothing
        GetProject = True
    End If

Exit Function
GetProjErr:
    Err.Raise E_NO_CURRENT_PROJECT, "GetProject", Err.Description
    ClearPrivateData
    GetProject = False

End Function

Public Function AssignConsultant(ByVal pConID As Long, _
    ByVal pRate As Currency, ByVal pStart As Date, _
    ByVal pEnd As Date) As Boolean

    ' Check to see if a project is current
    If Len(mstrCode) = 0 Then
        On Error GoTo 0
        Err.Raise ProjectErr.E_NO_CURRENT_PROJECT, "RemoveConsultant", _
            E_CURRENT_PROJECT_STR
        RemoveConsultant = False
        Exit Function
    End If

On Error GoTo AssignErr

    ' Make sure dates of assignment are not conflicting
```

```
        If (pStart >= pEnd) And (pStart >= mdtStartDate) _
            And (pEnd <= mdtEndDate) Then
            AssignConsultant = mobjProjectsData.AssignConsultant(mstrConnect, _
                mstrCode, pConID, pRate, pStart, pEnd)
        Else
            On Error GoTo 0
            Err.Raise E_ASSIGN_DATES, "AssignConsultant", E_ASSIGN_DATES_STR
            AssignConsultant = False
            Exit Function
        End If

Exit Function
AssignErr:
    Err.Raise E_ASSIGN_CON, "Assign Consultant", Err.Description
    AssignConsultant = False

End Function

Public Function List() As Recordset

On Error GoTo ListErr

    ' Check whether it should be retrieved from cache first
    If mflCache = False Then
        ' Retrieve all projects from the database
        If Not mrsProjects Is Nothing Then
            mrsProjects.Close
        End If
        Set mrsProjects = mobjProjectsData.List(mstrConnect)
    Else
        ' Return what is in the cache
        mrsProjects.MoveFirst
    End If

    Set List = mrsProjects

Exit Function
ListErr:
    Err.Raise E_PROJECT_LIST, "List", Err.Description
    Set List = Nothing

End Function

Public Sub NewProject()

    ' Reset internal data
    ClearPrivateData
```

continues

Listing 15.3   continued

```
End Sub

Private Sub Class_Initialize()

On Error GoTo InitErr

    ' Create data class
    Set mobjProjectsData = New clsProjectsData

    ' Indicates revenue has not been retrieved
    mcurRevenue = -1

Exit Sub
InitErr:
    Err.Raise E_DATA_CLASS, "Initialize", "Data class not created"

End Sub

Private Sub Class_Terminate()

    ' Destroy data class
    Set mobjProjectsData = Nothing

End Sub

Private Sub ClearPrivateData()

    ' Reset all private data
    mstrCode = vbNullString
    mstrDescription = vbNullString
    mstrCompany = vbNullString
    mstrContact = vbNullString
    mstrPhone = vbNullString
    mdtStartDate = 0
    mdtEndDate = 0
    mcurRevenue = -1
    mflIsDirty = False
    Set mrsAssignments = Nothing

End Sub
```

You will notice that much of the code in Listing 15.3 is concerned with validation. One of the primary tasks of the UBO is to validate data as it is entered. Other responsibilities include caching frequently used data in private variables such as the list of assignments, project list, and projected revenue, in addition to calling methods of the DABO.

In particular, you will notice that each Property Let procedure first checks the argument passed into it and subsequently raises a custom error defined in an enumerated type if the data is not valid. The procedures then set the mflIsDirty flag to True to indicate that the data is in need of saving. In each method, you will notice that the work of manipulating the underlying database is actually performed by the DABO while the UBO simply passes along the requests. In methods such as Save, the UBO actually makes the decision as to which method of the DABO will be invoked. Many of the procedures also check the mflCache variable to determine whether data should actually be read from module-level variables rather than from the database. In this way, the UBO acts as a buffer that can reduce round trips to the database server when unnecessary. In addition, the private procedure ClearPrivateData is invoked by methods such as GetProject and NewProject to reset all the module-level variables.

Building a DABO

The role of the DABO is to provide the data access interface to the object. Normally, this consists of ADO code to perform the inserts, updates, and deletes in the underlying data source. As mentioned in Table 15.1, the DABO can be installed on the client machine or in a distributed environment in MTS. To make the component ready for MTS, you might consider making the object stateless so that it can be more efficiently used in MTS in the event that it is involved in distributed transactions (which is discussed in Chapter 16). Typically, these types of operations would be initiated from the Business Process Object layer.

Because of space limitations—and because the subject of using ADO in distributed applications is covered in Chapter 14, "Using ADO for Data Access"—I won't reproduce the entire DABO here. The code in Listing 15.4 shows a small portion of the clsProjectsData DABO, highlighting the Add method that inserts a new project in the database and returns the assigned engagement code.

Listing 15.4   The Add Method of the clsProjectsData DABO

```
Public Function Add(ByVal pConnect As String, ByVal pDesc As String, _
    ByVal pCompany As String, ByVal pContact As String, _
    ByVal pPhone As String, ByVal pStart As Date, _
    ByVal pEnd As Date) As String

Dim cn As Connection
Dim cm As Command

On Error GoTo AddErr

' Create the command
Set cm = New Command
With cm
    .CommandText = "AddProject"
    .CommandType = adCmdStoredProc
End With
```

continues

Listing 15.4   continued

```
' Create the parameters
cm.Parameters.Append cm.CreateParameter("@description", adVarChar, _
    adParamInput, Len(pDesc), pDesc)
cm.Parameters.Append cm.CreateParameter("@company", adVarChar, _
    adParamInput, Len(pCompany), pCompany)
cm.Parameters.Append cm.CreateParameter("@contact", adVarChar, _
    adParamInput, Len(pContact), pContact)
cm.Parameters.Append cm.CreateParameter("@phone", adVarChar, _
    adParamInput, Len(pPhone), pPhone)
cm.Parameters.Append cm.CreateParameter("@startdate", adDate, _
    adParamInput, 4, pStart)
cm.Parameters.Append cm.CreateParameter("@enddate", adDate, _
    adParamInput, 4, pEnd)

' Establish connection
Set cn = New Connection
cn.ConnectionString = pConnect
cn.Open

' Execute the command
Set cm.ActiveConnection = cn
cm.Execute , , adExecuteNoRecords

' Get the new project code
Add = cm.Parameters("@code")

' Close and deallocate
cm.Close
Set cm = Nothing
Set cn = Nothing
Exit Function
AddErr:
    Err.Raise vbObjectError + 2000, "Project:Add", Err.Description
    Set cm = Nothing
    Set cn = Nothing

End Function
```

Using the UBO from the User Interface

As an example of using this model in an application, consider the form used to add a new project, shown in Figure 15.4. After filling in the fields for the project, the user clicks the OK button to save the project. The OK button calls a private procedure on the form to create a new project using the NewProject method. It then populates its properties and calls the Save method. If the save is successful, the engagement code returned from the DABO is displayed to the user, and the form closed.

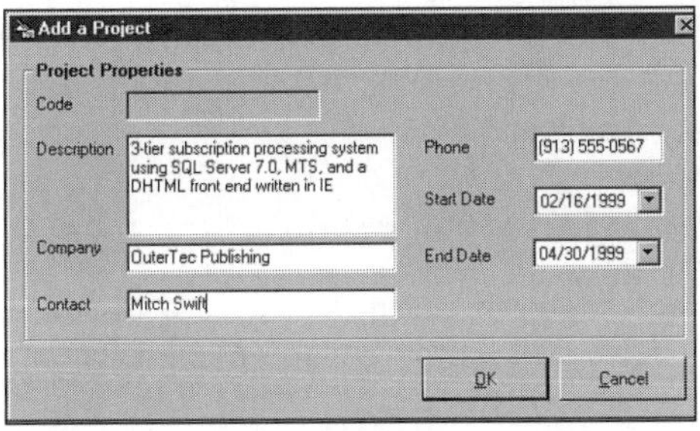

Figure 15.4

The Add a Project dialog box that uses the clsProject UBO.

Listing 15.5 shows the code for the OK button and the private `AddProject` procedure.

Listing 15.5   Code Behind the Add a Project Dialog (Shown in Figure 15.4)

```
' Event that is raised back to the parent form
Event ProjectAdded(ByVal pCode As String)

Private Sub cmdOK_Click()

    ' Call the private procedure to add the project
    If AddProject = True Then
        Unload Me
    End If

End Sub

Private Function AddProject() As Boolean

On Error GoTo AddProjErr

' Initialize the UBO object to accept a new project
' Note: objProject may be a global- or form-level
' variable declared as clsProject elsewhere in the application
objProject.NewProject

' Populate the project properties
With objProject
    .Company = txtCompany.Text
    .Description = txtDesc.Text
    .Contact = txtContact.Text
    .Phone = mskPhone.ClipText
    .StartDate = dtRange(0).Value
    .EndDate = dtRange(1).Value
End With
```

continues

Listing 15.5   continued

```
' Save the project
If objProject.Save = True Then
    ' Update the display
    txtCode.Text = objProject.Code
    ' Notify the user
    MsgBox "The project has been added with a code of " & _
        objProject.Code,          vbInformation, Me.Caption
    AddProject = True

    ' Raise an event back to the parent form
    ' so that it can refresh its display
    RaiseEvent ProjectAdded(objProject.Code)
Else
    MsgBox "The project was not added.", vbExclamation, Me.Caption
    AddProject = False
End If

Exit Function
AddProjErr:
    MsgBox "An error occurred: " & Err.Description, _
        vbExclamation, Me.Caption
    AddProject = False

End Function
```

Notice that in Listing 15.5 the event `ProjectAdded` is exposed by the form and is used to notify the parent form that a project was successfully added by the UBO with the new project code. In this way, the parent form is able to update its display accordingly and allows the Add a Project dialog to be more encapsulated. As noted in the listing, the UBO would typically be declared as a global variable that is accessible from the entire application.

Advantages of the LBOM

In summary, the technique presented here for creating an LBOM has the following advantages:

- Provides an object-oriented interface to the UI that increases the maintainability and reusability of the objects. For example, the UBOs can be reused in other COM-enabled environments, such as Microsoft Office or Active Server Pages.
- Puts the essential validation functions close to the UI so that extra round trips to the server are not required.
- Caches frequently used resultsets and properties to minimize round trips to the server.
- Allows data access code (DABOs) to be abstracted from the UI and run on the client or in MTS to take advantage of distributed transactions (initiated by BPOs) and connection pooling.

User-Defined Interfaces

As you might know, when a VB class module is compiled into an ActiveX DLL (COM component), a COM class id (CLSID) and an interface id (IID) are created. In COM, the class—identified by the CLSID and a ProgID (the human readable form)—represents the executable code for a specific interface identified by the IID. Unfortunately, when you allow VB to couple the interface of an object with its implementation (referred to as class-based referencing), it becomes difficult to separate the two and to design software that takes full advantage of the polymorphic features of VB.

> ## WARNING
>
> The drawback to using user-defined interfaces is that they cannot be accessed from clients who use Automation such as Active Server Pages (ASP). If your COM components must be accessed both by VB and ASP clients, you must use class-based references.

In this section, you will look at creating user-defined interfaces to implement Company and Vendor UBOs that can be used polymorphically.

Creating a User-Defined Interface

Fortunately, you can create interfaces separately from their implementation (referred to as *user-defined interfaces*). The technique used to do this is as follows:

1. Create a class module in an empty ActiveX DLL project.
2. Preface the name of the class module with an I (the convention for an interface). For example, ICompany.
3. Create the methods, properties, and event declarations that define the object, including all parameter and return values. This class is referred to as an *abstract class*.
4. Do not implement any code within the procedures.
5. Check the Remote Server Files check box on the Project Properties dialog box (Component tab).
6. Compile the project.

The end result will be a .TLB file that contains the type library for the interface just created. Listing 15.6 contains a sample class module for creating an interface for a UBO named ICompany.

> ## NOTE
>
> Although you can create the type library by using the Interface Definition Language (IDL) and a special compiler, using this method is simpler for the VB developer.

Listing 15.6   A Class Module Used to Create a Simplified ICompany User-Defined Interface

```
Option Explicit
' Interface definition for
' a company

Public Property Get Name() As String
End Property

Public Property Let Name(ByVal vNewValue As String)
End Property

Public Property Get CoCode() As String
End Property

Public Function Remove() As Boolean
End Function

Public Function Save() As Boolean
End Function

Public Function GetCompany(ByVal pCode As String) As Variant
End Function

Public Function Add() As Boolean
End Function

Public Property Get IsDirty() As Boolean
End Property

Public Property Get ReadFromCache() As Boolean
End Property

Public Property Let ReadFromCache(ByVal vNewValue As Boolean)
End Property
```

Keep in mind that after an interface has been created, it forms a binding contract between the clients that use the interface and the code that implements it. For this discussion, if you wanted to create an interface to work with vendors, you would create a separate interface named IVendor in the same fashion as the preceding example. Although much of the interface would likely be the same, IVendor would, for example, include additional members, such as a property named Preferred that indicates the preferred status of the vendor.

Implementing User-Defined Interfaces

As mentioned previously, VB supports the concept of interface inheritance to allow concrete classes to implement the interfaces defined in type libraries. After the interfaces ICompany and IVendor have been defined, you can reference their type libraries and begin to create concrete classes using their interfaces.

For example, to create the `clsVendor` UBO, you would use the `Implements` keyword in a class module to implement both the `ICompany` and `IVendor` interfaces. This would allow the `clsVendor` object to be called using a reference to either interface. This can be a powerful concept because user interface code can now be written to support either type of object. Listing 15.7 shows a skeleton implementation of `clsVendor` without the details filled in. Note that the comments in the procedures indicate where the work is done.

Listing 15.7 The clsVendor Object Implements Both the ICompany and IVendor Interfaces So That It Can Be Used Polymorphically

```
Option Explicit

Implements ICompany
Implements IVendor

'**************** Used when accessing object as ICompany ****************

Private Function ICompany_Add() As Boolean
    ' Call to IVendor's implementation
End Function

Private Property Get ICompany_CoCode() As String
    ' Call to IVendor's implementation
End Property

Private Function ICompany_GetCompany(ByVal pCode As String) As Variant
    ' Call to IVendor's implementation
End Function

Private Property Get ICompany_IsDirty() As Boolean
    ' Call to IVendor's implementation
End Property

Private Property Let ICompany_Name(ByVal VNewValue As String)
    ' Call to IVendor's implementation
End Property

Private Property Get ICompany_Name() As String
    ' Call to IVendor's implementation
End Property

Private Property Let ICompany_ReadFromCache(ByVal VNewValue As Boolean)
    ' Call to IVendor's implementation
End Property

Private Property Get ICompany_ReadFromCache() As Boolean
    ' Call to IVendor's implementation
End Property
```

continues

Listing 15.7   continued

```
Private Function ICompany_Remove() As Boolean
    ' Call to IVendor's implementation
End Function

Private Function ICompany_Save() As Boolean
    ' Call to IVendor's implementation
End Function

'***************** Used when accessing object as IVendor ******************

Private Function IVendor_Add() As Boolean
    ' Code to implement
End Function

Private Property Get IVendor_CoCode() As String
    ' Code to implement
End Property

Private Function IVendor_GetCompany(ByVal pCode As String) As Variant
    ' Code to implement
End Function

Private Property Get IVendor_IsDirty() As Boolean
    ' Code to implement
End Property

Private Property Let IVendor_Name(ByVal VNewValue As String)
    ' Code to implement
End Property

Private Property Get IVendor_Name() As String
    ' Code to implement
End Property

Private Property Let IVendor_Preferred(ByVal VNewValue As Boolean)
    ' Note that this is the new member
    ' Code to implement
End Property

Private Property Get IVendor_Preferred() As Boolean
    ' Code to implement
End Property

Private Property Let IVendor_ReadFromCache(ByVal VNewValue As Boolean)
    ' Code to implement
End Property
```

```
Private Property Get IVendor_ReadFromCache() As Boolean
    ' Code to implement
End Property

Private Function IVendor_Remove() As Boolean
    ' Code to implement
End Function

Private Function IVendor_Save() As Boolean
    ' Code to implement
End Function
```

In Listing 15.7, notice that even though the class implements both the IVendor and ICompany interfaces, you will want to structure the code so that only once do you have to write the code that does the actual work. As a result, in the members of ICompany you can redirect to the appropriate member of IVendor and return its result through ICompany. For example, the GetCompany method of ICompany could be implemented as follows:

```
Private Function ICompany_GetCompany(ByVal pCode As String) As Variant
    ' Call to IVendor's implementation
    ICompany_GetCompany = IVendor_GetCompany(pCode)
End Function
```

Leveraging User-Defined Interfaces

Of course, going to this extra work would be fruitless if it didn't buy you something in the end. The end result is that you can write less code by writing code that works on any object that implements the same interface.

For example, consider the task of adding new companies to the database. Each type of company (vendor, supplier, and so on) might require a different user interface for the user to define the company (because they support different properties). However, if all the objects, such as clsVendor, implement the ICompany interface, you can write one procedure that performs the save for all types of companies. The following code snippet shows a procedure that accepts a reference to an object supporting the ICompany interface. It then inspects the IsDirty property to determine whether a save is warranted and calls the Save method.

```
Private Sub AddCompany(ByVal pCompany As ICompany)

  ' Test whether the object needs saving
  If pCompany.IsDirty Then
      ' Save the object and display the new company code
      If pCompany.Save Then
          MsgBox "Company added with code " & pCompany.CoCode
      End If
  End If

End Sub
```

NOTE

You might be thinking, "Why not declare `pCompany` as `Object`? This would allow me to write the same code without dealing with user-defined interfaces at all." The answer is that if you declare `pCompany` as `Object`, you are forcing VB to use late binding. Late binding always uses the less efficient `IDispatch` interface instead of direct vtable binding. In addition, you do not gain the benefits of type checking and IntelliSense provided by the VB IDE.

On a related note, using interfaces such as `ICompany` allows you to take advantage of vtable binding when using the `CreateObject` function. In fact, the ProgID does not even have to be known at compile time for vtable binding to work. This allows you to create plug-compatible software that is flexible, as well as efficient.

Another technique you can use with user-defined interfaces is to test for the existence of an interface at runtime using the `TypeOf` keyword. The following code snippet shows this technique for dealing with a pCompany variable declared using the `ICompany` interface that supports the `IVendor` interface. In this case, the `Preferred` property will be set if the interface is supported.

```
' Test whether the object supports the IVendor
' interface
If TypeOf pCompany Is IVendor Then
    ' If so, cast a reference to an IVendor object
    ' and set the preferred property
    Dim objVendor As IVendor
    Set objVendor = pCompany
    objVendor.Preferred = chkPreferred.Value
End If
```

Summary

This chapter discusses several facets of using VB to develop object-oriented applications. At its core, OOP includes encapsulation, polymorphism, and inheritance. VB supports each of these concepts in varying degrees and can be used to create object-oriented applications using the Lightweight Business Object Model (LBOM) introduced in this chapter. Further, VB allows for the creation of user-defined interfaces to allow you to take full advantage of interface inheritance. This enables you to write code that is both efficient and flexible.

CHAPTER 16

Building ActiveX Components

In the preceding chapter, I focused on the object-oriented features of VB that allow developers to create maintainable and reusable software. In this chapter, I'll go beyond the language features and explore how VB exploits these features to allow developers to build component-based software.

Component-based development differs from pure object-oriented development in that it is concerned with not only encapsulation and code reuse, but specifically binary reuse. With VB's reliance on COM (which specifies just such a binary standard), it has become the premier tool for building components that can be reused in a variety of tools and languages.

The two major types of components VB supports are ActiveX control components and ActiveX code components. This chapter first explains how VB supports building ActiveX controls and then focuses on the implementation details of ActiveX code components and how they can be leveraged in the Microsoft Transaction Server (MTS) and COM+ environments.

Building ActiveX Control Components

Since version 5.0, VB has supported the creation of ActiveX controls. These components, packaged in OCX files, fully encapsulate their functionality behind standard COM interfaces implemented by development environments and tools that act as containers. At this time, the most popular containers for controls written in VB are Internet Explorer (MSIE) and Microsoft Office applications. VB itself, of course, both supports the creation of the controls and acts as a container for controls.

Using the UserControl Object

When you create an ActiveX control, the user interface (UI) of the control is created using the `UserControl` object. In fact, each ActiveX control project can contain multiple `UserControl` objects that, when compiled, will be housed in the same OCX file. Although multiple controls can be packaged in the same file, each acts independently when placed in a container. Using this technique, you can distribute multiple related controls, making installation and distribution simpler. Microsoft uses this technique for distributing the `ListView`, `TreeView`, `Toolbar`, `StatusBar`, and other common Windows controls.

The `UserControl` object acts as the canvas on which the visible elements of the control will reside. In many ways, the `UserControl` is analogous to the `Form` object but supports additional methods, properties, and events specific to interacting with containers. The key members of the `UserControl` object can be seen in Table 16.1.

Table 16.1   Key Properties, Methods, and Events of the UserControl Object

Member	Description
Properties	
AccessKeys, CanGetFocus, ForwardFocus	Enable a control to receive the focus (`CanGetFocus`), using a specific key or set of keys (`AccessKeys`), and to optionally forward the focus (`ForwardFocus`) from the control to the next control in the tab order of the form.
Ambient and AmbientChanged	A property and an event that return the set of ambient properties in an `AmbientProperties` object at runtime and raises notifications when ambient properties are changed. These properties provide hints about how the control should display itself. Properties include `UserMode`, `BackColor`, `Font`, and `TextAlign`, among others. Containers may implement additional ambient properties not shown in the Object Browser when viewing `AmbientProperties`.
BackStyle	Specifies whether the background style of the control is 0=Transparent, 1=Opaque, or 2=Invisible.
ClipBehavior	Specifies whether the output of graphics methods such as `Line` will appear anywhere within the control (0=None) or only within the region defined using `MaskRegion`.

Member	Description
`ControlContainer` and `ContainedControls`	Determines whether the control can act as a container for other controls and a collection of the controls that are placed on the control, respectively. Only the developer can add and remove controls to the `ContainedControls` collection.
`ContainerHWnd`	Long. Returns the window handle of the container.
`DataMembers`	Returns the collection of `DataMember` objects for a control that acts as a data source (`DataSourceBehavior=vbDataSource`).
`DefaultCancel`	Boolean. Specifies whether the control can be set as the Default or Cancel control on the container.
`EditAtDesignTime`	Boolean. Specifies whether the control can be activated by the developer at design time using the Edit context menu. When activated, the control will run normally in the container, although raised events will be ignored.
`EventsFrozen`	Boolean. Returns `True` when the container is ignoring events raised from controls.
`Extender`	Returns the `Extender` object, which contains properties that are tracked by the control. Examples of extender properties include `Name`, `Visible`, `Default`, `Cancel`, `Parent`, `Top`, `Width`, and `Left`. Not all containers support all properties, so error handling must be used when accessing these properties.
`HitBehavior` and `HitTest`	`HitBehavior` specifies which `HitResult` values will be returned by the `HitTest` event fired for windowless controls (0=None, 1=UseRegion, 2=UsePaint). The `HitTest` event fires as the user moves the mouse over a windowless control and allows you to determine whether the control will receive mouse events by changing the `HitResult` argument passed into the event.
`Hyperlink`	Returns a `Hyperlink` object that allows a hyperlink-aware container such as MSIE to navigate to a URL.
`MaskColor` and `MaskPicture`	Specify the color (`MaskColor`) that determines the transparent region of the bitmap (`MaskPicture`) assigned to the control. Available when the `BackStyle` property is set to 0 (Transparent).
`Parent`	Returns a reference to the container in which the control is placed. Used with the `TypeOf` statement to determine which type of container is being used.
`ParentControls`	Returns a collection of the other controls in a container.

continues

Table 16.1 continued

Member	Description
ParentControlsType	Specifies whether the collection returned by ParentControls includes the Extender object (1=vbExtender, 2=vbNoExtender). By default, the Extender object is included but may result in runtime errors when accessed in some containers. Can be used in conjunction with Parent at runtime, depending on the container.
PropertyPages	A String array that specifies the property pages associated with the control.
Windowless	Boolean. Specifies whether the control will be assigned its own window's handle (hWnd). Resource consumption is lessened with windowless controls, although restrictions apply to what the control's interface can contain and how the control is redrawn.

Methods

AsyncRead and CancelAsyncRead	Initiate and cancel the asynchronous downloading of data from a file or URL by the control. Can specify the destination, type of data, property to load, and options for determining how the read is performed. Chapter 12, "Using TreeView and ListView Controls," contains an example using AsyncRead.
CanPropertyChange	Boolean. Given a property name, returns whether the property bound to a data source can change. Used in controls that act as data sources.
PropertyChanged	Notifies the container that the given property has changed.

Events

AccessKeyPressed	Fires when one of the access keys specified by AccessKeys has been pressed or when the Enter or Esc keys are pressed if the control's Default or Cancel properties are set to True.
AsyncReadComplete and AsyncReadProgress	Fire after and during an asynchronous read. Both events pass in an object of type AsyncProp that encapsulates information about the data being downloaded (BytesRead, BytesMax, Target, and so on).
EnterFocus and ExitFocus	Fire as the control first receives focus and as it loses focus. These do not fire as focus moves between constituent controls.

Member	Description
GetDataMember	Fires when a data consumer requests a data member from a control that acts as a data source (`DataSourceBehavior=vbDataSource`).
GotFocus and LostFocus	Fire as the control gets and loses focus, if the control does not contain any constituent controls.
Initialize	Fires when the control is placed on a container in design mode and when the control is created at runtime.
InitProperties	Fires when the control is first placed on a container in design mode and is used to set default properties in the control.
ReadProperties	Fires when the control is created at runtime by the container or a container with an instance of the control is opened at design time. It is used to read properties from persistent storage and set their values.
Resize	Fires when the control is placed on a container and when the control is created at runtime. It is used to adjust the size of the constituent controls if needed.
Show and Hide	Fire when the control's `Visible` property is set to `True` or `False`, respectively.
Terminate	Fires when the container destroys the control instance.
WriteProperties	Fires when the control instance is destroyed by the container and is used to save properties to persistent storage.

Creating the UI for a Control

Normally, the UI of the control is made up of a combination of intrinsic VB controls (`TextBox`, `ListBox`, and so on) and Microsoft or third-party ActiveX controls. These controls are termed *constituent* controls because they constitute the interface of the control. The preprogrammed interaction of these controls is what gives ActiveX controls their usefulness.

NOTE

Using any of the intrinsic or ActiveX controls shipped with VB (except the `DBGrid` control) is permissible. However, using a third-party control or the preceding exempted control as a constituent control requires that all the licensing requirements for the third-party control be met before distribution. Microsoft also states that if you use its controls as constituent controls, you must add "significant and primary" functionality. In other words, you cannot simply repackage the `TreeView` control and sell it as your own.

As an example, consider an ActiveX control that is used to display product inventory and reorder levels from a database and periodically update its display. Because this type of functionality might have to be embedded in applications written using different development environments, it is a good candidate for reuse.

To create the UI, you can simply place constituent controls on the `UserControl` object and set their properties. Figure 16.1 shows the `InvChart` `UserControl` that contains instances of the `MSChart` and `Timer` controls. In this case, because the entire UI of the control should be covered with the chart, the `Resize` event of the `UserControl` can be coded to automatically resize the constituent control.

```
Private Sub UserControl_Resize()

' Automatically resize the chart
With chProducts
    .Top = 1
    .Left = 1
    .Width = UserControl.Width
    .Height = UserControl.Height
End With

End Sub
```

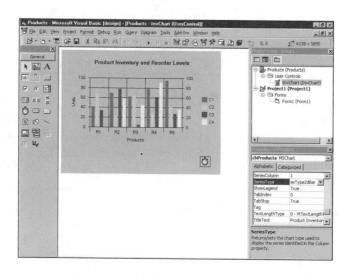

Figure 16.1

The UI for an ActiveX control that displays product inventory and reorder levels.

In addition, when developing the UI, you must consider the ambient properties of the container. For example, for the control to respond to changes in container properties such as the background color and font, you can write code in the `AmbientChanged` event to respond to these changes. In this case, the control can change its background color and title font to match those of the container.

```
Private Sub UserControl_AmbientChanged(PropertyName As String)

' Change the display properties in response to
' ambient property changes
Select Case PropertyName
    Case "BackColor"
        UserControl.BackColor = Ambient.BackColor
    Case "Font"
        Set chProducts.Title.Font = Ambient.Font
End Select

End Sub
```

Creating Methods, Properties, and Events

After the visible UI for the control has been created, the programmatic interface must be defined. By default, the control will contain only the ambient and extender properties of the container. User-defined properties, methods, and events can be created manually using public function, `Sub`, or property procedures or using the ActiveX Control Interface Wizard add-in.

Using the ActiveX Control Interface Wizard

Using the add-in is a good way to jump-start the creation of the public interface for the control. After loading the add-in from the Add-Ins menu, you can invoke it either to map members of constituent controls to members of the control or to create new members that will be implemented with custom code. After selecting from a list of common members and specifying new members, you are presented with the dialog that creates the mappings, shown in Figure 16.2. In this case, only the `TitleText` property of the `MSChart` control will be mapped to the `TitleText` property of the public interface. The wizard also gives you the opportunity to specify the read and write options for the properties at both design time and runtime, along with return values, arguments for methods and events, and comments for each member.

You will notice that after the wizard has completed, property procedures will have been created for each property, public procedures for each method, and `Event` declarations for each event. The wizard will also create private variables to store the values and defaults for each property.

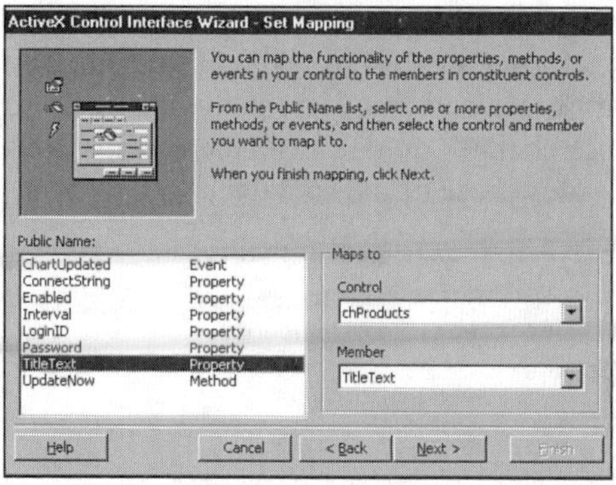

Figure 16.2

The Set Mapping dialog allows you to map public members of the control to constituent controls.

NOTE

You will probably want to modify some of the default values because the wizard uses the string "0" for properties defined as String.

The key events to focus on are the ReadProperties and WriteProperties events. These events are fired as the container loads and destroys instances of the control. Both events are passed a PropertyBag object that exposes ReadProperty and WriteProperty methods. The code within the events simply uses these methods to communicate with the container. Because the actual implementation used to persist and read properties differs from container to container, your control can simply delegate to the container, using WriteProperty to store the properties and ReadProperty to bring them back. For the InvChart control, the WriteProperties event is

```
Private Sub UserControl_WriteProperties(PropBag As PropertyBag)

    ' Tell the container to persist properties
    Call PropBag.WriteProperty("Enabled", UserControl.Enabled, _
        m_def_Enabled)
    Call PropBag.WriteProperty("Interval", m_Interval, m_def_Interval)
    Call PropBag.WriteProperty("TitleText", chProducts.TitleText, _
        "Product Inventory and Reorder Levels")
    Call PropBag.WriteProperty("ConnectString", m_ConnectString, _
        m_def_ConnectString)
    Call PropBag.WriteProperty("LoginID", m_LoginID, m_def_LoginID)

End Sub
```

A second use of the Ambient object can be seen in the Let property procedure for the Password property. In this case, the property was marked as read-only at design time. As a result, the wizard inserted code in the procedure that checks the UserMode property to determine whether the control is running in design or run mode. Keep in mind that code in an ActiveX control begins executing when the developer places an instance of the control on a container. If design mode is detected, error 387 is raised to notify the user that the property is read-only. Note that the PropertyChanged method is called to notify the container that the property has changed.

```
Public Property Let Password(ByVal New_Password As String)

    ' If in design mode, the property is read-only
    If Ambient.UserMode = False Then
        Err.Raise 387
        Exit Property
    End If

    m_Password = New_Password
    PropertyChanged "Password"
End Property
```

Mapping to Extender Properties

As explained in Table 16.1, the Extender object provides access to properties that the container provides to enable a developer to more easily work with the control. Each container implements different Extender properties, but common properties include Name, Visible, Enabled, and properties that specify the placement and size of the control.

Most controls have to implement an Enabled property so that the developer can enable and disable the control through code. To expose this property correctly, you have to communicate with the container's Enabled property. Unlike other Extender properties, which are referenced using the syntax

```
Extender.property
```

this is done by creating a user-defined property and calling the Enabled property of the UserControl.

```
Public Property Get Enabled() As Boolean
    Enabled = UserControl.Enabled
End Property
```

In addition, you must set the procedure ID attribute to Enabled in the Procedure Attributes dialog box. Doing so connects the Extender object's Enabled property (provided by the container) to the user-defined Enabled property.

In the case of the InvChart control, the Let property procedure for the Enabled property is more complex because it also uses the Ambient object's UserMode property to determine whether the constituent Timer control is enabled. By disabling the timer, its events will not fire while the container is in design mode. The Timer control's Enabled property must also be set to False when the control is authored, to ensure that it does not begin firing events until it is enabled by the ReadProperties event at runtime.

```
Public Property Let Enabled(ByVal New_Enabled As Boolean)
    UserControl.Enabled = New_Enabled


    ' Keep the timer off until runtime
    If Ambient.UserMode = True Then
        Timer1.Enabled = New_Enabled
    Else
        Timer1.Enabled = False
    End If


    PropertyChanged "Enabled"
End Property
```

Implementing the InvChart Control

The work of the InvChart is relatively simple, and Listing 16.1 contains the code for the entire control. The heart of the functionality lies in the PopulateChart private procedure. This procedure uses the ConnectString, LoginID, and Password properties of the control to create an ADO Connection object that connects to the data source. It then calls the GetProductsInventory stored procedure that returns a resultset from the Products table containing the ProductName, UnitsInStock, and ReorderLevel columns. The client-side ADO Recordset can then be bound directly to the MSChart control using the Datasource property. The MSChart control will automatically look for the X-Axis labels in the first column, followed by the series data in subsequent columns. Likewise, the titles for the series shown in the legend are also pulled from the column titles.

TIP

> An easy way to debug an ActiveX control project is to add a standard EXE project to the project group and place an instance of the control on the form. That way, you can use breakpoints to fully debug the control before compilation. Be aware that if the control appears hatched on the form, this means that the code in the control is in error or the UserControl designer is open.

Listing 16.1   The Complete Code for the InvChart ActiveX Control
```
Option Explicit

'Default Property Values:
Const m_def_Enabled = True
Const m_def_Password = ""
```

```
Const m_def_Interval = 0
Const m_def_ConnectString = ""
Const m_def_LoginID = ""
Const MAX_TIMEOUT = 120

'Property Variables:
Private m_Password As String
Private m_Interval As Long
Private m_ConnectString As String
Private m_LoginID As String

' Private data
Private mcnConn As Connection

'Event Declarations:
Event ChartUpdated()

Private Sub Timer1_Timer()

    ' Populate the chart each time the timer fires
    Call PopulateChart

End Sub

Private Sub UserControl_AmbientChanged(PropertyName As String)

' Change the display properties in response to
' ambient property changes
Select Case PropertyName
    Case "BackColor"
        UserControl.BackColor = Ambient.BackColor
    Case "Font"
        Set chProducts.Title.Font = Ambient.Font
End Select

End Sub

Private Sub UserControl_Resize()

' Automatically resize the chart
With chProducts
    .Top = 1
    .Left = 1
    .Width = UserControl.Width
    .Height = UserControl.Height
End With

End Sub
```

continues

Listing 16.1   continued

```
Private Sub UserControl_WriteProperties(PropBag As PropertyBag)

    ' Tell the container to persist properties
    Call PropBag.WriteProperty("Enabled", UserControl.Enabled, _
        m_def_Enabled)
    Call PropBag.WriteProperty("Interval", m_Interval, m_def_Interval)
    Call PropBag.WriteProperty("TitleText", chProducts.TitleText, _
        "Product Inventory and Reorder Levels")
    Call PropBag.WriteProperty("ConnectString", m_ConnectString, _
        m_def_ConnectString)
    Call PropBag.WriteProperty("LoginID", m_LoginID, m_def_LoginID)

End Sub

Public Property Get Enabled() As Boolean
    Enabled = UserControl.Enabled
End Property

Public Property Let Enabled(ByVal New_Enabled As Boolean)
    UserControl.Enabled = New_Enabled

    ' Keep the timer off until runtime
    If Ambient.UserMode = True Then
        Timer1.Enabled = New_Enabled
    Else
        Timer1.Enabled = False
    End If

    PropertyChanged "Enabled"
End Property

Public Property Get Interval() As Long
    Interval = m_Interval
End Property

Public Property Let Interval(ByVal New_Interval As Long)
    m_Interval = New_Interval
    ' The interval is in seconds, not milliseconds
    Timer1.Interval = m_Interval * 1000
    PropertyChanged "Interval"
End Property

Public Property Get TitleText() As String
    TitleText = chProducts.TitleText
End Property
```

```
Public Property Let TitleText(ByVal New_TitleText As String)
    chProducts.TitleText() = New_TitleText
    PropertyChanged "TitleText"
End Property

Public Property Get ConnectString() As String
    ConnectString = m_ConnectString
End Property

Public Property Let ConnectString(ByVal New_ConnectString As String)
    m_ConnectString = New_ConnectString
    PropertyChanged "ConnectString"
End Property

Public Property Get LoginID() As String
    LoginID = m_LoginID
End Property

Public Property Let LoginID(ByVal New_LoginID As String)
    m_LoginID = New_LoginID
    PropertyChanged "LoginID"
End Property

'Initialize Properties for User Control
Private Sub UserControl_InitProperties()
    UserControl.Enabled = m_def_Enabled
    m_Interval = m_def_Interval
    m_ConnectString = m_def_ConnectString
    m_LoginID = m_def_LoginID
    m_Password = m_def_Password
End Sub

'Load property values from storage
Private Sub UserControl_ReadProperties(PropBag As PropertyBag)

    UserControl.Enabled = PropBag.ReadProperty("Enabled", m_def_Enabled)
    ' Turn the constituent timer on if in run mode and enabled is True
    If UserControl.Enabled And Ambient.UserMode = True Then
        Timer1.Enabled = True
    End If

    m_Interval = PropBag.ReadProperty("Interval", m_def_Interval)
    chProducts.TitleText = PropBag.ReadProperty("TitleText", _
        "Product Inventory and Reorder Levels")
    m_ConnectString = PropBag.ReadProperty("ConnectString", _
        m_def_ConnectString)
    m_LoginID = PropBag.ReadProperty("LoginID", m_def_LoginID)

End Sub
```

continues

Listing 16.1   continued

```
Public Property Get Password() As String
    Password = m_Password
End Property

Public Property Let Password(ByVal New_Password As String)

    ' If in design mode, the property is read-only
    If Ambient.UserMode = False Then
        Err.Raise 387
        Exit Property
    End If

    m_Password = New_Password
    PropertyChanged "Password"
End Property

Private Sub PopulateChart()
' Used to get the data from the database
' using ADO

Dim rs As Recordset

On Error GoTo GetDataErr

' Create the connection object
If mcnConn Is Nothing Then
    Set mcnConn = New Connection
End If

' Open the connection
If mcnConn.State = adStateClosed Then
    mcnConn.Open m_ConnectString, m_LoginID, m_Password
End If

' Create the Recordset
Set rs = New Recordset
rs.CursorLocation = adUseClient
rs.Open "GetProductsInventory", mcnConn, adOpenForwardOnly, _
    adLockReadOnly, adCmdStoredProc

' Populate the chart
' Note that the first column should be the x-axis
' labels and the second and third columns, the series
Set chProducts.DataSource = rs

' Close the connection if the interval is more than
' the max timeout or if UpdateNow was called
```

```
If m_Interval > MAX_TIMEOUT Or m_Interval = 0 Then
    mcnConn.Close
End If

rs.Close
Set rs = Nothing

    ' Raise the notification back to the container
    RaiseEvent ChartUpdated

Exit Sub
GetDataErr:
    Err.Raise vbObjectError + 301, "PopulateChart", Err.Description

End Sub

Public Sub UpdateNow()

    ' Populate the chart now
    Call PopulateChart

End Sub
```

You will notice that the PopulateChart procedure also closes the connection to the data source in the event that the Interval property is set to 0 (indicating the UpdateNow method must have been called) or if the MAX_TIMEOUT value has been exceeded. By default, this value is set to 120 seconds. In this way, the control can conserve database connections. Finally, the ChartUpdated event is fired back to the container so that it is notified as the chart is updated.

NOTE

Obviously, this type of control could be enhanced to support finer control of the properties or to expose some of the many events exposed by the MSChart control. For example, an interesting exercise would be to create an event that would be raised when the user clicks on a series to bring back the actual UnitsInStock and ReorderLevel values for a particular product.

The following sample code populates the properties of the control and calls its UpdateNow method. Figure 16.3 shows the populated control on a form.

```
With InvChart1
    .ConnectString = "provider=sqloledb;server=ssosa;database=northwind"
    .LoginID = mstrLoginID
    .Password = mstrPassword
    .Interval = 60 'seconds
    .TitleText = "Product Inventory"
    .UpdateNow
End With
```

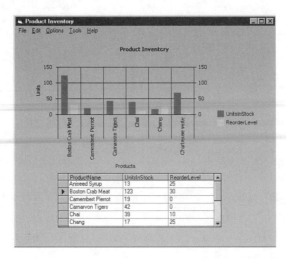

Figure 16.3

The InvChart control running in a form. The DataGrid control shows the actual numbers plotted in the graph.

Creating Property Pages

Although not required, property pages are a convenient way to organize properties exposed by your control. Using this technique, developers will have an easier time setting those properties at design time. For example, you can provide a property page that uses a custom UI to set the background color or font properties of your control, rather than force the developer using your control to type these values into the property window. Property pages also allow you to group related properties together.

In addition, all the property pages you create are available from a single tabbed dialog that the developer can access by simply right-clicking on your control in the development environment. Keep in mind that property pages are also desirable because not all containers that will house your control will allow developers to set the properties easily, as VB does.

To implement property pages, you must add one or more `PropertyPage` objects to the ActiveX control project. The resulting borderless form represents one of the tabs in the tabbed properties dialog box. For the `InvChart` control, you could create two property pages: one that can be used to set `LoginID`, `ConnectString`, and `TitleText` and the other that sets the `Enabled` and `Interval` properties. Figure 16.4 presents both property pages, and the complete code for the Data property page discussed next appears in Listing 16.2.

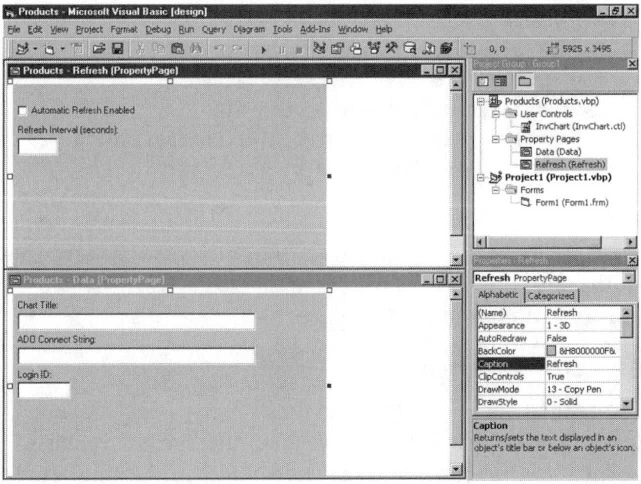

Figure 16.4

The property pages for the InvChart ActiveX control.

Listing 16.2   The Code for the Data Property Page

```
Option Explicit
' Data property page

Private Sub txtLoginID_Change()
    ' Notify the PropertyPage that a property has changed
    Changed = True
End Sub


Private Sub txtConnectString_Change()
    ' Notify the PropertyPage that a property has changed
    Changed = True
End Sub


Private Sub txtTitleText_Change()
    ' Notify the PropertyPage that a property has changed
    Changed = True
End Sub

Private Sub PropertyPage_ApplyChanges()
    ' Write the changed values back to the properties of the control
    SelectedControls(0).LoginID = txtLoginID.Text
    SelectedControls(0).ConnectString = txtConnectString.Text
    SelectedControls(0).TitleText = txtTitleText.Text
End Sub
```

continues

Listing 16.2   continued
```
Private Sub PropertyPage_SelectionChanged()
    ' Populate the UI elements with property values
    txtLoginID.Text = SelectedControls(0).LoginID
    txtConnectString.Text = SelectedControls(0).ConnectString
    txtTitleText.Text = SelectedControls(0).TitleText
End Sub
```

The PropertyPage objects contain two key events, SelectionChanged and ApplyChanges, that are called as the page is initialized and when the user clicks the OK or Apply buttons or switches to another page.

Coding SelectionChanged

The SelectionChanged event is fired when the property page is opened; it should contain code that populates the UI of the page with the current values of the properties from the control. In the case of the Data page in Listing 16.2, the code in SelectionChanged would populate the three Textbox controls in the property page with the values of the properties.

The SelectedControls collection is a special object available to the property page that contains all the instances of the control that are currently selected by the developer. In other words, a developer could put several instances of the InvChart control on a form and then select all of them before invoking the properties dialog. By referencing item 0 in the collection, the properties for only the first selected control will be retrieved. To determine whether multiple instances of a control have been selected, you can check the Count property of the SelectedControls collection.

Coding ApplyChanges

The second event to consider is the ApplyChanges event. This event is fired when the developer clicks OK or Apply or when another property page has been selected. This event is where you place code to persist any changed values back to the properties of the control. In most cases, the code will be the inverse of that in the SelectionChanged event.

However, as with the SelectionChanged event, the code shown in Listing 16.2 handles only the first instance of the control selected in the container. To handle multiple selected instances, you can loop through each item in the SelectedControls collection and set the properties.

```
For Each objControl in SelectedControls
    objControl.LoginID = txtLoginID.Text
    objControl.ConnectString = txtConnectString.Text
    objControl.TitleText = txtTitleText.Text
Next
```

The controls on the property page must also make sure that the page itself is notified when the developer modifies one of the properties. To do this, the Change event of controls on the page is used to set the Changed property of the PropertyPage object to True. This must be done so that the Apply button will be enabled and the ApplyChanges event will fire.

Connecting the PropertyPage

The final step is to connect the property page to the control. You do this by clicking on the PropertyPages property of the control in the properties window. The resulting Connect Property Pages dialog, shown in Figure 16.5, populates the string array with the checked property pages. Note that in addition to user-defined property pages, standard property pages are available for setting a font, color, picture, and data format. Any property defined with these standard types will automatically invoke the corresponding standard property page from the VB properties window. By making selections in this dialog, a property page will be added to the properties dialog, containing a list of all the properties that correspond to the checked standard type. Figure 16.6 shows the property pages as they are invoked by a developer using the control.

TIP

Also, you can invoke a Property Page Wizard Add-In from the Add-Ins menu or from the Add PropertyPage dialog that results from right-clicking on the project and selecting Add, Property Page.

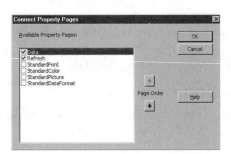

Figure 16.5

The Connect Property Pages dialog box.

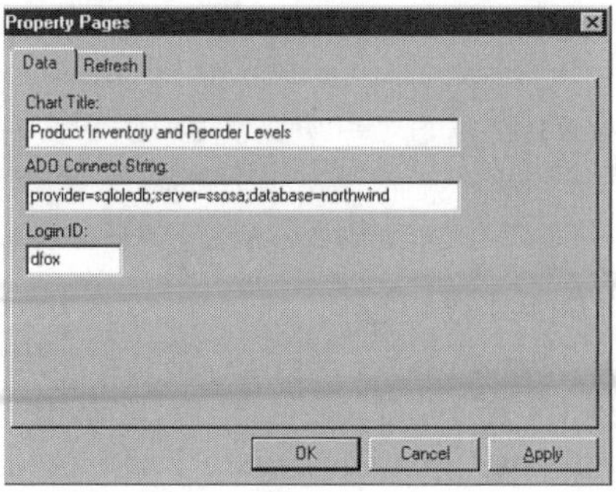

Figure 16.6

Property Pages as invoked by a developer.

Building ActiveX Code Components

The second type of component that VB can create is referred to as an *ActiveX code component* or simply a *COM component* and is created using the ActiveX DLL project template. Analogous to ActiveX control components, each project can contain multiple code components that are then compiled into a single DLL. The components are developed using VB class modules that, when compiled and instantiated, become COM objects (I'll refer to them as simply *objects*). ActiveX code components are useful for encapsulating functionality that does not require a UI and reusing it in any environment that supports COM.

In this section, I'll present several topics you should consider when developing code components (some of which also apply to control components), including compilation options, compatibility, and notification mechanisms and followed by a discussion of using code components developed in VB with MTS.

Using Compilation Options

When an ActiveX DLL is compiled, there are several considerations that have to be made. Specifically, these include choosing a threading model, picking a base address, unattended execution, and compatibility.

The Threading Model

As shown in Figure 16.7, the General tab of the Project Properties dialog contains threading model options that determine how the components will behave when loaded in the client process. These options differ, depending on the type of project, and are discussed in Table 16.2.

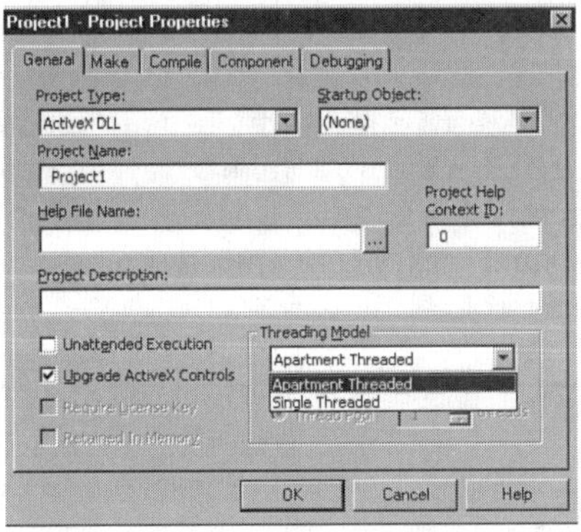

Figure 16.7

The Project Properties dialog for an ActiveX DLL project.

Table 16.2 Threading Model Options

Option	Description
Apartment Threaded	Available since service pack 2 of VB 5.0 and allows an STA to be created for each thread in the client process that creates an object.
Single Threaded	Available in ActiveX control and code components and ensures that all objects created from the component are contained in one single-threaded apartment (STA) in the client process.
Thread per Object	Discussed in Chapter 13, "Using Win32 API Techniques," and used in ActiveX EXE projects to allow each object to run in its own STA. Although it (and the next option) is useful for server processes that have to service multiple clients, the disadvantage of this technique is that there is no control on the number of threads created by the process.
Thread Pool	Discussed briefly in Chapter 13 and used in ActiveX EXE projects to create a pool of STAs that a client process can access using a round robin algorithm. The advantage to using this technique is control of the total number of threads created by the process, although the round robin algorithm cannot ensure that all objects created by a client will execute on the same thread. This can be a problem when the objects manipulate global data.

Single-Threaded Components

As mentioned in Chapter 13, an *apartment* is simply an execution context in which COM objects reside. An STA uses a message queue to serialize all method and property calls on objects that reside in the STA. In this way, no two objects in the same STA can be executing concurrently. For example, when creating a DLL that includes three components (A, B, and C) and uses Single Threaded as its threading model, the application conceptually appears as in Figure 16.8.

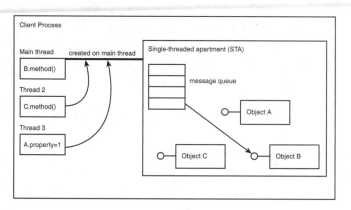

Figure 16.8

An application that uses a single-threaded component.

Notice that even single-threaded DLLs use an apartment. The difference is that they use one and only one apartment that is created on the main thread of the application.

The key consideration when using single-threaded components is how they behave when used with clients that are multithreaded. As the figure indicates, if the client application supports multiple threads, each thread that calls one of the objects will have to wait until the STA has processed all other requests on the queue. Further, when the second thread enters the STA, the process of transferring the call across threads (called *cross-thread marshaling*) adds more overhead to the call. Keep in mind that using single-threaded components in VB applications is not usually a problem because by default VB supports the creation of only single-threaded applications.

NOTE

> Sometimes you will be forced to use a single-threaded component in an ActiveX control component if a constituent control does not support multiple threads. This is the case with the MSChart control. In addition, you cannot use single-threaded components in MSIE 4.0 or later; they must be compiled as apartment-threaded.

Apartment-Threaded Components

Since service pack 2 of version 5.0, VB has been able to create multithreaded components by selecting Apartment Threaded in the Project Properties dialog. Although these
components also use STAs, the process can create an STA for each thread that creates
objects from the component, as depicted in Figure 16.9.

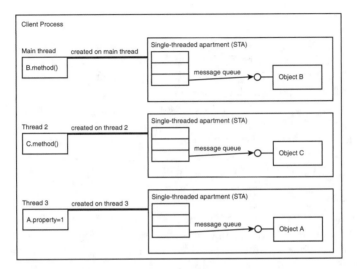

Figure 16.9

An application that uses a multithreaded (apartment-threaded) component.

When multithreaded components are used, they provide greater concurrency (because
each thread is swapped in and out of the CPU very rapidly) and do not incur the overhead of cross-thread marshaling. In environments such as MTS, this is especially
important, so components designed to run in MTS should always use apartment threading. However, unlike single-threaded components, a developer must consider the issues
of global variables and reentrancy.

- *Thread Local Storage*   To protect VB developers from issues of contention for
  shared data, the designers of VB chose to place a copy of all module and global
  data in thread local storage (TLS) for each STA created in a process. In other
  words, each apartment receives its own copy of all the module-level and global
  variables (declared as public in a standard module). This ensures that data in
  each apartment is isolated, but makes it difficult for objects created in separate
  STAs to share data. As a result, when components are designed to use apartment model threading, you should not assume that all objects will share module and global data when used in a multithreaded client application.

TIP

If a `Sub Main()` procedure exists in the component, it also will be called each time a new STA is created.

* *Reentrancy* The second issue to consider with apartment model threading is *reentrancy*. Reentrancy refers to the scenario in which an STA is processing a call to a method and while that method is executing, it yields control of the processor. As a result, the STA will look to its queue to process the next method or property call. The next call is free to then reenter any methods or properties of the object. Problems can occur if the second call modifies any of the data in TLS. When the first call returns, it will encounter changed variables that may or may not cause it to act unexpectedly.

  VB developers must consider reentrancy in designs that yield control of the processor by using `DoEvents`, showing a form, using a notification mechanism (discussed next), or communicating with other threads or processes.

Unattended Execution

In addition to the threading model, the General tab also includes an option for Unattended Execution. When this option is checked, all dialog and message boxes produced by the component will be suppressed. Obviously, this option is unavailable for ActiveX controls but is recommended for components running on remote servers (as in the case of MTS) to ensure that the component does not inadvertently wait for user interaction in the case of an error. With this option checked, all dialog boxes will be logged in the Windows NT Event Viewer.

When this option is checked, the Retained in Memory option is available, which instructs VB to keep the DLL loaded in the client process until the process terminates. This has the trade-off of potentially using more memory but allowing faster access to the component by the process because it is not swapped to disk.

Base Address

On the Compile tab of the Project Properties dialog exists the DLL Base Address option. This option is used to determine at which address the DLL is loaded. By default, VB attempts to load each DLL at the address &H11000000. However, if another DLL is already loaded at that location, the operating system will have to "rebase" or relocate the DLL to another physical memory location. Besides the overhead of accomplishing this, the operating system will not be able to reuse the physical memory if the DLL is subsequently loaded by a second process. This leads to both greater memory requirements and slower load times.

DLLs created with VB can be loaded in any 64K segment in the range from &H11000000 to &H80000000. This allows 28,416 locations to be used. As a result, it is a good idea to develop a scheme to assign a unique base address to each DLL created. Although you can never be completely sure that a DLL will not be rebased (for which you should be glad because that would imply a lot of work for developers), you can reduce the amount of rebasing by simply choosing a random value in the available range. Listing 16.3 presents a function to create a random base address.

Listing 16.3   A Function to Generate a Random DLL Base Address

```
Option Explicit
' Hex &H11000000
Const START_ADDRESS = 285212672
Const INCREMENT = 65536
Const NUM_ADDRESSES = 28416

Public Function RandomBase() As String

Dim lngSegment As Long
Dim lngBaseAddress As Long

' Initialize the random-number generator
' If no argument is passed, it will seed it with
' a timer value
Randomize

' Generate the segment number
lngSegment = Int((NUM_ADDRESSES - 1 + 0) * Rnd + 0)

' Generate the address in decimal
lngBaseAddress = (lngSegment * INCREMENT) + START_ADDRESS

' Convert to hex
RandomBase = "&H" & Hex$(lngBaseAddress)

End Function
```

As you'll notice, the code in Listing 16.3 uses the intrinsic Randomize and Rnd functions to generate a random number that represents one of the 28,416 segment locations. The base address is then calculated by multiplying the random location by the size of a segment (65,536) and adding it to the starting address. The hex equivalent of the calculated address is then returned by the function using the Hex$ function.

NOTE

A more complete discussion and a utility for tracking the base addresses of DLLs can be found in the article "Maximizing DLL Performance" by L.J. Johnson in the January 1999 issue of the *Visual Basic Programmer's Journal*.

Version Compatibility

The final compilation consideration for ActiveX components are the Version Compatibility options found on the Components tab of the Project Properties dialog box. Basically, the options found here are used to instruct the VB compiler how to handle the GUIDs associated with components contained in the project. The three options are No Compatibility, Project Compatibility, and Binary Compatibility.

No Compatibility

Using this option instructs the VB compiler to generate new type library information and GUIDs (CLSIDs and IIDs) each time the component is compiled. Existing clients that are compiled against previous versions of the component will not be able to use this component. This option should be used when you want to make a clean break with older versions of the component. You should also consider changing both the project name and filename to avoid overwriting the existing component and creating a second component that uses the same ProgID.

Project Compatibility

This option ensures that the type library information is maintained but generates new CLSIDs and IIDs for the component. This option is useful during the development of the first version of a component and makes sure that VB unregisters the preceding version before the new one is compiled, thereby keeping the system Registry free from clutter. By keeping the type library information the same, existing test projects will still be able to reference it. Do not use this option to release the component if you want to maintain compatibility with previous versions. When you select this option, the file box below it is enabled so that you can provide a path to the file containing the type library of the preceding version.

Binary Compatibility

This option keeps intact all CLSIDs and IIDs, as well as the type library, but will warn you if it detects that the definitions (signatures) of the existing members of one or more classes or UserControl objects have changed. This means that changes to the name of a member or its return data type and to its arguments or their data types or order, as well as adding optional arguments, all qualify as changes in signature. In VB 6, you may ignore the warning and reuse the GUIDs, but it may break existing clients because they'll be expecting a different calling syntax.

If you are not using user-defined interfaces as discussed in Chapter 15, "Using Object-Oriented Techniques," this option can also be used to extend existing classes with new members. The rules of COM do not allow definitions of members in the interface to be changed, nor do they allow new members to be added (termed *interface immutability*). However, VB provides a mechanism to get around this and does allow you to add new members to a class and compile it using (logically) the same GUIDs. In this way, existing clients can use the new implementation but will be aware of only the previous members of the interface. Like Project Compatibility, this option requires that you specify the path to the preceding version of the component.

Behind the scenes, VB actually creates a second IID (thereby adhering to the rules of COM under the covers) and includes some special code in the new component that can provide clients with a reference to either the old or new interface. Additionally, the new component contains registration code that adds a special registry entry (called *Forward*) in the key for the old IID, allowing old clients to find the new IID. This technique is known as *IID forwarding* and is provided to make it simple for VB developers to extend existing components that do not use user-defined interfaces.

However, if you follow the strict COM approach, you would only use binary compatibility in concrete classes that did not alter or add to the public interface of the component.

NOTE

If you create abstract interfaces such as IVendor, discussed in Chapter 15, you would not use any of these options because those interfaces would never be regenerated. In other words, after the initial type library for IVendor was created, you would not attempt to alter it. The only recourse for making changes would be to create a second interface, IVendor2, and then implement the new interface in the clsVendor concrete class. When recompiling clsVendor, binary compatibility could be used if existing clients were already compiled against its CLSID.

Implementing Notification

Many times, the communication, rather than be directed only from the client to the component, might have to be initiated by the component.

For example, as implied in the discussion on threading, when a thread in a client application calls a method in a component, that thread is blocked until the method completes. However, usually, if a long-running process is anticipated, a better design would be to allow the component to release the thread and simply notify the client when the processing completes.

NOTE

The approach you can use to implement this particular technique is shown in Chapter 13 in the discussion on multithreading.

A second scenario occurs when client applications simply want to register with a component and receive notifications, for example, when a component may notify clients when data changes in a data source.

Components created in VB can use two techniques to raise notifications to clients. In this section, I'll discuss the use of events and callbacks.

Using Events

Events are the simpler and less flexible of the two notification mechanisms. As seen in earlier examples, form and class modules in VB can define events using the Event keyword and raise those events to clients using the RaiseEvent function.

As an example, consider the code in Listings 16.4 (containing the clsProjects class) and 16.5 (containing a standard module added to the project). This example builds on the clsProjects UI Business Object developed in Chapter 15. In this scenario, the clsProjects object has an additional property, NotifyAdditions, which when set to True instructs the object to check the clsProjectsData class to see whether any projects have been added to the data source, based on the time the last check was made. If new projects are detected, the clsProjects object raises the event ProjectsAdded back to the client.

Listing 16.4   Additions to the clsProjects Class Shown in Chapter 15 to Support Asynchronous Notifications of Data Additions

```
Option Explicit

' Event to raise when project is added
Event ProjectsAdded()

Private mNotify As Boolean
Private mTimeChecked As Date ' last time data was checked
Private objProjectsData As clsProjectsData

Public Property Get NotifyAdditions() As Boolean
    ' Property used to determine whether project
    ' additions should be checked for
    NotifyAdditions = mNotify
End Property

Public Property Let NotifyAdditions(ByVal vNewValue As Boolean)

    mNotify = vNewValue

    ' If notifications are turned on, then enabled
    ' them
    If mNotify = True Then
        ' Stop and then start the timer using procedures
        ' in the standard module
        StopNotify
        StartNotify Me
    Else
        ' Stop the timer
        StopNotify
    End If

End Property
```

```
Public Function CheckNew() As Boolean

Dim flNew As Boolean

    ' Call a method in the data access business object
    ' that checks for new projects based on the
    ' last time it was checked
    flNew = objProjectsData.CheckNew(mTimeChecked)
    If flNew = True Then
        ' Raise the event because at least one project
        ' was added
        RaiseEvent ProjectsAdded
    End If

    ' Set the last time it was checked
    mTimeChecked = Now

End Function

Private Sub Class_Terminate()

    ' Stop the timer. If you don't, the component will keep
    ' receiving notifications after it's destroyed, which can get ugly.
    StopNotify

End Sub
```

Listing 16.5   The Standard Module Added to the Project in Which clsProject Resides to Support Asynchronous Notification

```
Option Explicit

Public Declare Function SetTimer Lib "user32" _
    (ByVal hWnd As Long, ByVal nIDEvent As Long, _
    ByVal uElapse As Long, ByVal lpTimerFunc As Long) As Long

Public Declare Function KillTimer Lib "user32" _
    (ByVal hWnd As Long, ByVal nIDEvent As Long) As Long

Private mlngTimerID As Long
Private objProject As clsProject
Private objProjectData As clsProjectsData

Public Sub StartNotify(pProject As clsProject)
    ' Start the timer at 2-minute intervals
    Set objProject = pProject
    mlngTimerID = SetTimer(0, 0, 120000, AddressOf TimerCallback)
End Sub
```

continues

Listing 16.5   continued
```
Public Sub StopNotify()
    ' Stop the timer
    KillTimer 0, mlngTimerID
End Sub


Public Sub TimerCallback(ByVal hWnd As Long, ByVal uMsg As Long, _
    ByVal idEvent As Long, ByVal dwTime As Long)


    ' Check for new additions
    objProject.CheckNew

End Sub
```

The technique used here to implement the check for additions uses the `SetTimer` Win32 API function. The property procedures for `NotfiyAdditions` call the `StartNotify` and `StopNotify` procedures in the standard module that start and stop the timer. In particular, `StartNotify` sets up the timer with a 2-minute callback into the `TimerCallback` procedure. `TimerCallBack` then uses the reference variable passed into `StartNotify` to call the `CheckNew` method of the `clsProject` object. This method communicates with the Data Access Business Object and raises the event as appropriate.

The client application then simply needs to declare the object using the `WithEvents` keyword and write code to handle the event as follows:

```
Private WithEvents objProject As clsProject
Private rsProject As Recordset

Private Sub Form_Load()
    Set objProject = New clsProject
    objProject.NotifyAdditions = True
End Sub

Private Sub objProject_ProjectAdded()
    ' Refresh the list of projects
    Set rsProjects = objProject.List
End Sub
```

Using events is relatively simple but does embody some drawbacks that make it a little inflexible. For starters, events are implemented behind the scenes using the `IDispatch` interface. This means that all notifications using events are not vtable bound but use the less efficient `Invoke` method of `IDispatch`. Although this is not a significant limitation when the component is running on a remote server, it is inefficient for in-process components.

Secondly, events cannot be declared in user-defined interfaces in VB. In other words, you cannot create the ICompany interface shown in Chapter 15 with events. This limits the creation of events to concrete classes and excludes the designs that use events from using user-defined interfaces. Finally, events are simply broadcast to all connected clients, which means that the component is unable to intelligently decide which clients should receive notifications and which should not and in which order they should be sent. These limitations can be addressed, however, by using callbacks.

Using Callbacks

To avoid the limitations imposed when using events, you can use the second technique, known as *callbacks*. Not to be confused with Win32 API callbacks discussed in Chapter 13, COM callbacks allow the client application to pass an object reference to the component that implements a well-known interface. The component can then call a method on the object to notify the client when activity occurs. Although this technique is more complicated, it supports user-defined interfaces and takes advantage of vtable binding.

As an example, the functionality from the preceding section on events is duplicated here to highlight the differences in the two notification mechanisms. The first step is to create an interface to handle the notification. For this simple example, a user-defined interface, IProjectNotify, could be created with a single method declaration.

```
Public Sub ProjectAdded()
End Sub
```

This well-known interface can then be referenced and used by the component, clsProject, to call back in to the client, as in Listing 16.6 (changes from Listing 16.4 are highlighted). Notice that the NotifyAdditions method accepts an argument of type IProjectNotify that is cached in a private variable. The ProjectAdded method of the objProjNotify object is then called each time new projects are discovered.

Listing 16.6   The clsProject Class Module with Changes Made to Support a Callback

```
Option Explicit

Private mTimeChecked As Date ' last time data was checked
Private objProjectsData As clsProjectsData
Private objProjNotify As IProjectNotify

Public Sub NotifyAdditions(ByVal pProjNotify As IProjectNotify)

    ' Set the private notification object to the specific client
    Set objProjNotify = pProjNotify
    ' Start the timer
    StartNotify Me

End Sub
```

continues

Listing 16.6   continued

```
Public Sub StopNotifyAdditions()
    ' Destroy the private notification object and stop the timer
    Set objProjNotify = Nothing
    StopNotify
End Sub


Public Function CheckNew() As Boolean

Dim flNew As Boolean

    ' Call a method in the data access business object
    ' that checks for new projects based on the
    ' last time it was checked
    flNew = objProjectsData.CheckNew(mTimeChecked)
    If flNew = True Then
        ' Call back the client using the notification interface
        objProjNotify.ProjectAdded
    End If

    ' Set the last time it was checked
    mTimeChecked = Now

End Function

Private Sub Class_Initialize()

    ' Create the instance of clsProjectsData
    Set objProjectsData = New clsProjectsData

End Sub

Private Sub Class_Terminate()

    ' Stop the timer. If you don't, the component will keep
    ' receiving notifications after it's destroyed, which can get ugly.
    StopNotify

End Sub
```

To pass an object of type IProjectNotify, the client application must contain a class module or form that implements this interface. In this case, the form can implement IProjectNotify and write a handler for its ProjectAdded method. Remember, in VB, form modules are also COM objects under the covers. The object that implements the callback interface is then passed to the component in the NotifyAdditions method. Notice that the Unload event of the form also calls the StopNotifyAdditions method to release the reference inside the component.

```
Private rsProject As Recordset
Private objProject As clsProject
Implements IProjectNotify

Private Sub Form_Load()
    Set objProject = New clsProject

    ' Send in the object to be called back in to
    objProject.NotifyAdditions Me
End Sub

Private Sub Form_Unload(Cancel As Integer)
    objProject.StopNotifyAdditions
End Sub

Private Sub IProjectNotify_ProjectAdded()
    ' Notification from the component

    ' Refresh the list of projects
    Set rsProject = objProject.List
End Sub
```

As you can see, this technique is more complex but certainly more flexible, especially for designs in which an out-of-process server (ActiveX EXE) allows multiple clients to connect to the same instance of an object (called *singletons* and created by setting the Instancing property of the class module to MultiUse and setting the thread pool size to 1). In these cases, it is often necessary to prioritize and customize the callbacks. Although the code in Listing 16.6 handles only one connection at a time, it could be enhanced to provide these services by storing a collection of IProjectNotify objects.

Using ActiveX Code Components in MTS

With the release of Microsoft Transaction Server 2.0, Microsoft has fused the concepts of an Object Request Broker (ORB) with a transaction monitor (TP-monitor) in a single product. In short, MTS allows a developer to create components that contain data access and business logic and run them in the middle tier (ORB). In addition, these components can create distributed transactions to modify data in different data sources while maintaining transactional consistency (TP-monitor).

To the VB developer, MTS provides a runtime environment for ActiveX code components. This produces several benefits:

- The components can run in a dedicated server process (thereby taking the load off the client).
- You can centralize business logic so that it can be easily updated.
- You can allow both thin and fat client applications access to the components.
- You can allow components to update multiple data sources consistently within a single transaction.

However, to take full advantage of these features, you have to understand the MTS environment and how code components can be modified to exploit MTS.

Understanding the MTS Environment

The runtime environment for code components implemented by MTS introduces some new terminology and a new architecture for running components. You should become familiar with these. The core concepts revolve around packages, context wrappers, activities, and transactions.

Packages

For starters, MTS defines packages on the server in which components run. A *package* is simply a process (MTX.EXE) that can contain one or more components from which it can create objects when it is running. When a component is placed in a package using the MTS Explorer (by specifying its DLL or its Registry entry if already registered on the server), the Registry on the MTS server is modified so that all activation requests for the component are redirected to MTX.EXE with the appropriate package identifier.

TIP

Placing components in separate packages gives you the benefits of process isolation and a security boundary between components. However, if components in separate packages have to communicate, the speed of cross-process calls is several orders of magnitude slower than for calls within the same package. Therefore, components that require access to one another should normally be placed in the same package.

By default, the package begins execution when the first object (component instance) is requested and remains active until 3 minutes after all objects have been destroyed. You can override this by instructing MTS to always keep the package running by changing the package properties. The remainder of the discussion focuses mostly on what happens inside a package.

Context Wrappers

MTS uses a technique known as *interception* when client applications (referred to as *base clients*) activate a component running in MTS using the `CreateObject` function or `New` keyword. By intercepting all communication between the base client and the component, MTS can insert a context wrapper between the base client and the object. This context wrapper (itself an object) is used to trick the base client into thinking that it has a reference to the actual object. In reality, of course, the client only has a reference to the context wrapper, which passes along all method calls on the object.

By using this technique, MTS can activate and deactivate objects within a package on demand, called *Just in Time Activation* (JIT), without the knowledge of the base client. This ensures that objects running in MTS can release database resources such as locks and connections as quickly as possible, which is critical in online transaction processing (OLTP) environments. Figure 16.10 shows the architecture of MTS packages and context wrappers.

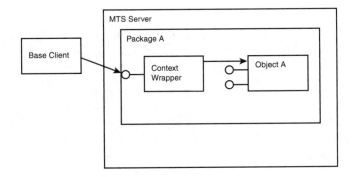

Figure 16.10

The basic MTS architecture of packages and context wrappers.

Activities

All the work done by MTS on behalf of a base client is contained within activities. Basically, an *activity* is a logical thread of execution for a base client that is created each time a client creates an object that resides in MTS. All subsequent objects created by the *root* (defined as the first object created in the activity) and its children also reside in the same activity. Using the concept of activities, MTS ensures that only one object in the activity is executing concurrently on behalf of the base client and that all objects in the activity are isolated from objects in other activities. This makes the programming model for MTS simple for developers who don't have to worry about issues such as synchronization and the physical threads that are running the components. Activities are also the containers for distributed transactions. In other words, transactions do not cross activities.

Internally, MTS implements activities as STAs. STAs are a good match for activities because, as discussed previously, STAs contain only a single thread, so only one object can be executing within the apartment at a time. Actually, MTS 2.0 works from a pool of 100 STAs per package, which are created and handed out as activities are constructed. When the pool is exhausted, MTS starts to multiplex activities into STAs. For this reason, and because activities logically span multiple packages (when an object creates a second object in a different package), activities are said to be a *logical thread of execution*. Figure 16.11 shows the expanded MTS architecture including activities.

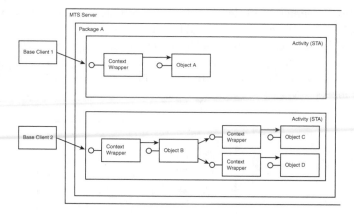

Figure 16.11

The MTS architecture depicting an MTS server running one package with two base clients and two activities.

Of course, to take advantage of the thread pool managed by MTS, code components written in VB have to use the apartment-threading model discussed previously. If the component is marked as single threaded, MTS will be forced to create all objects contained in the code component in a single STA. This can severely limit concurrency because all client requests will be processed by the thread in a single STA.

Transactions

In MTS, a *transaction* is a logical unit of work that executes within a single activity. Each component that you create can be marked with an attribute either at design time in VB 6 or in the MTS Explorer that indicates to what level objects created from the component participate in transactions. By marking a component as Requires a New Transaction or Requires a Transaction, MTS will enlist with the Microsoft Distributed Transaction Coordinator (MSDTC) to ensure that the work performed by its objects can be coordinated with work performed by other objects created in the activity. Although the details of the algorithm used are beyond the scope of this book, the MSDTC service uses a two-phase commit protocol to ensure that all the data sources affected by the activity either commit or roll back their changes together.

If the component is set to Supports Transactions, MTS will enlist the MSDTC only if the object is created in an activity for which a transaction is already present. Obviously, setting Does Not Support Transactions never enlists the MSDTC. Generally, components that run in MTS use the Requires a Transaction or Supports Transactions. However, Requires a New Transaction can be useful when the component is used for logging or audit trails and thus should be isolated from commits or rollbacks happening on other transactions within the activity.

Programming MTS

Although it is possible to simply place components you have already compiled in packages in MTS, doing so will not take advantage of MTS features such as JIT and will not allow you to perform distributed transactions. Fortunately, code components written in VB can be modified to be MTS aware by referencing the Microsoft Transaction Server Type Library and interacting with the ObjectContext object and the ObjectControl interface. As mentioned previously, in VB 6 you can optionally set the MTSTransaction mode property of class module in the project to set the level of transaction support.

Getting the ObjectContext

The primary means code components use to communicate with MTS is through the ObjectContext object. This object provides ambient properties that allow the object to discover attributes about the context wrapper, including security and the state of any distributed transactions in which the object may be participating. In addition, the ObjectContext is used to create objects in the same activity and instruct MTS when the object has finished its work and can be deactivated. After the type library has been included, a reference to the ObjectContext can be retrieved by calling GetObjectContext inside methods of the object.

```
Dim objCtx as ObjectContext
Set objCtx = GetObjectContext
```

This technique can be used without a call to CreateObject or New because the object that exposes GetObjectContext (AppServer) is a global multiuse object and is thus always available. After the context is retrieved, the methods (and properties) can be called as shown in Table 16.3.

TIP

The other global method that AppServer exposes is SafeRef. You can use this method in designs that rely on the callback technique shown in the section "Using Callbacks" in this chapter. SafeRef accepts the Me object as a parameter to pass the reference of an object that implements a callback interface. It is used so that the MTS interception scheme remains intact by passing a reference to the context wrapper instead of a direct reference to the object.

Table 16.3 *The ObjectContext Methods and Properties*

Member	Description
	Methods
CreateInstance	Is passed a ProgID and instructs MTS to create the object in the same activity (STA) as the current object. This method must be used in order to ensure that the new object will participate in any distributed transactions (provided the component's transaction property is marked as Requires or as Supports). This method should not be used for creating objects that do not reside in MTS. In other words, do not use it for creating ADO objects.
DisableCommit	Tells MTS that it should not commit the work done by this object. It does not, however, tell MTS to deactivate the object. Useful when subsequent calls to the object may cause it to be able to commit its changes.
EnableCommit	Tells MTS that it should commit the work done by this object but does not tell MTS to deactivate the object.
SetAbort	Tells MTS that the work done by this object should be rolled back and the object deactivated. Has the subsequent effect of causing a distributed transaction to be rolled back and its resources to be released.
SetComplete	Tells MTS that the work done by this object can be committed and the object deactivated. If all objects participating in a transaction call SetComplete or EnableCommit, the transaction will be committed.
	Properties
IsCallerInRole	Boolean. When given a role, returns whether the direct caller of the object is in the given role. Can be used to check security programmatically.
IsInTransaction	Boolean. Returns True when the object is running in the context of a distributed transaction.
IsSecurityEnabled	Boolean. Returns True when authorization checking is enabled for the component in the MTS Explorer.
Security	Returns a reference to a SecurityProperty object containing the methods GetDirectCallerName, GetDirectCreatorName, GetOriginalCallerName, and GetOriginalCreatorName. These can be used to find the name of the user that immediately created (Direct) the object and the name of the user who initiated the sequence of calls (Original) that resulted in the object being created. In MTS 2.0, the caller and creator will always be the same username.

Implementing ObjectControl

The other way that components can communicate with MTS is through the `ObjectControl` interface. Any class module that implements this interface (using the `Implements` keyword) will include the methods shown in Table 16.4 and can be notified by MTS during the object's lifetime.

Table 16.4 The Methods of the ObjectControl Interface

Member	Description
`Activate`	Called when MTS activates the component before the first method call is made. Can be used to initialize data used by the object.
`CanBePooled`	`Boolean`. Called by MTS upon deactivation to determine whether the object can be added to a pool to be reused. By returning `False`, you indicate that the component cannot be reused and should be discarded. In MTS 2.0, object pooling is not enabled, so this option has no effect. It is recommended that you set this method to `False` because the effects of object pooling in future versions of MTS (COM+) may cause your components to break. Initially, anyway, components created in VB will probably not be able to be pooled in COM+ because they won't run in the newer thread-neutral apartments (NTAs).
`Deactivate`	Called when MTS deactivates the component. Can be used to deallocate any data used by the object.

Stateless Components

Much has been written about creating *stateless components* (components that call `SetComplete` or `SetAbort` in each method) for use in MTS, and indeed they do have their place. However, MTS is perfectly happy also working with stateful components. The key factor in determining whether to make your components stateless is whether deactivating them would cause database resources to be released sooner. The primary resource in this case is database locks. If your methods do not call `SetComplete` or `SetAbort`, the locks acquired during a transaction are held until the base client releases the reference to the object. Obviously, in OLTP environments, you want to minimize the amount of time that locks are held.

Keep in mind that costs are associated with creating stateless components. Typically, methods that are stateless require more parameters, which consume network bandwidth and memory. In addition, the resources used to activate and deactivate the object outweigh the nominal amount of memory (usually no more than a few hundred bytes) consumed by the object.

A Code Example

To highlight the changes that must be made in order to support the MTS features of JIT and transactional processing, consider the code in Listing 16.7. This example shows the Add method of the clsProjectsData class, discussed in Chapter 15, designed to run in MTS. In this scenario, a project cannot be added to the database unless the company information also exists in the database. Likewise, the company information should not be added unless the project can be added to the database.

Listing 16.7   The Add Method of the clsProjectsData Class Designed to Run in MTS (MTS-Specific Code Is Highlighted)

```
Public Function Add(ByVal pConnect As String, ByVal pDesc As String, _
    ByVal pCompany As String, ByVal pContact As String, _
    ByVal pPhone As String, ByVal pStart As Date, _
    ByVal pEnd As Date) As String


Dim cn As Connection
Dim cm As Command
Dim lngCompanyID As Long
Dim ctx As ObjectContext
Dim objCompany As MTSContracker.clsCompanyData


On Error GoTo AddErr


' Get a reference to the context of the object
Set ctx = GetObjectContext


' Make sure that we're running in a transaction
If Not ctx.IsInTransaction Then
    Err.Raise vbObjectError + 2001, "clsProjectData:Add", _
        "No transaction present. Set the attributes of the package."
    ctx.SetAbort
    Exit Function
End If


' Make sure that the user has the security to perform this
' operation
If (Not ctx.IsSecurityEnabled) Or (Not ctx.IsCallerInRole("Sales")) Then
    Err.Raise vbObjectError + 2002, "clsProjectData:Add", _
        "Security violation. Invalid role or security not enabled."
    ctx.SetAbort
    Exit Function
End If


' Create an instance of the company object,
' and retrieve and insert the company and
' and contact (if they don't exist) in the
' database. Return the new company id
```

```
' Make sure that the instance is created in the same activity
Set objCompany = ctx.CreateInstance("MTSContracker.clsCompanyData")
lngCompanyID = objCompany.Add(pCompany)

' Create the command
Set cm = New Command
With cm
    .CommandText = "AddProject"
    .CommandType = adCmdStoredProc
End With

' Create the parameters
cm.Parameters.Append cm.CreateParameter("@description", adVarChar, _
    adParamInput, Len(pDesc), pDesc)
cm.Parameters.Append cm.CreateParameter("@company", adInteger, _
    adParamInput, 4, lngCompanyID)
cm.Parameters.Append cm.CreateParameter("@contact", adVarChar, _
    adParamInput, Len(pContact), pContact)
cm.Parameters.Append cm.CreateParameter("@phone", adVarChar, _
    adParamInput, Len(pPhone), pPhone)
cm.Parameters.Append cm.CreateParameter("@startdate", adDate, _
    adParamInput, 4, pStart)
cm.Parameters.Append cm.CreateParameter("@enddate", adDate, _
    adParamInput, 4, pEnd)
cm.Parameters.Append cm.CreateParameter("@user", adChar, _
    adParamInput, 25, ctx.Security.GetOriginalCallerName)

' Establish connection
Set cn = New Connection
cn.ConnectionString = pConnect
cn.Open

' Execute the command
Set cm.ActiveConnection = cn
cm.Execute , , adExecuteNoRecords

' Get the new project code
Add = cm.Parameters("@code")

' Close and deallocate
cm.Close
Set cm = Nothing
Set cn = Nothing

' Instruct MTS to commit the work and deactivate the object
ctx.SetComplete
```

continues

Listing 16.7   continued

```
Exit Function
AddErr:
    Err.Raise vbObjectError + 2000, "clsProjectData:Add", Err.Description
    Set cm = Nothing
    Set cn = Nothing

    ' Instruct MTS to roll back the work and deactivate the object
    ctx.SetAbort
End Function
```

You will notice that the method first checks whether the object has been loaded in a transaction, using the `IsInTransaction` method. If no transaction exists, an error is raised to the client, and the `SetAbort` method is called to deactivate the component. This implies that the transaction attribute of the component must be set to Requires or Requires New. The method then checks the user's security role using `IsCallerInRole` and whether authorization checking is enabled (done through the MTS Explorer) to make sure that the user is a member of the Sales role.

If the security and transaction attributes are in place, the method creates an instance of the `clsCompanyData` component in the same activity as `clsProjectsData`, using the `CreateInstance` method. This ensures that any work done by `clsCompanyData` can be committed or rolled back with changes made by `clsProjectsData`. The `Add` method of the company object is then called to add the company to the database or simply retrieve its existing ID. The company ID, stored in `lngCompanyID`, is then used as a parameter to the stored procedure that inserts the new project. Note also that the final parameter to the stored procedure uses the `Security` object's `GetOriginalCallerName` to store the user account of the salesperson who inserted the project.

If all the processing goes smoothly, the `SetComplete` method is called to signal MTS to commit the changes and deactivate object. However, the error handler includes a call to `SetAbort` so that MTS will release all resources and deactivate the component.

TIP

It's good practice to make sure that the root object (in this case, `clsProjects-Data`) always calls `SetAbort` if any child objects do (`clsCompanyData`). One way to do this is to make sure that all your methods raise errors back to their callers in the event a modification does not succeed. Each method can then call `SetAbort` in its error handler.

Summary

In this chapter, I've discussed many of the details involved in the creation of both ActiveX control and ActiveX code components. Obviously, VB has come a long way from a tool that can create only Windows applications. As VB matures, it will likely become even more useful for developing the components that make up an enterprise architecture.

CHAPTER 17

Building Web Applications

Beginning with version 6, Visual Basic includes two new types of applications that enable VB developers to leverage their knowledge of the language and development environment to build Web-based applications. These types of applications are known as IIS applications and DHTML applications. The fundamental difference between the two is that IIS applications run on the Web server, specifically Internet Information Server (IIS), whereas DHTML applications execute their code within MSIE. As a result, IIS applications enable you to build browser-independent applications, whereas DHTML applications enable you to take advantage of all the great features of dynamic HTML implemented in MSIE.

Because this is a new topic to many developers, this chapter takes the approach of introducing both types of applications and discussing their architecture and constituent parts, as well as the sequence of processing that occurs. This is done in the context of a sample Web application that maintains consulting projects and assignments for a consulting company.

IIS Applications

At its core, an *IIS application* is simply an ActiveX code component, called a `WebClass` at design time, that is registered and instantiated on the Web server at runtime. The `WebClass` is analogous to the class modules discussed in previous chapters and can support the creation of user-defined methods, properties, and events. To give you the big picture, I'll first discuss the runtime architecture of an IIS application and the sequence of events.

Runtime Architecture

When compiled, the `WebClass` component contains methods and properties that are invoked by a second component installed on the Web server, known as the *Web Class Manager* (WCM). The WCM is the component directly created in the ASP page requested by the browser. With each invocation of the WebClass, the WCM passes in references to the built-in Active Server Pages (ASP) objects, shown in Table 17.1. These objects, familiar to VBScript developers who use Visual InterDev, encapsulate the information being passed from the browser to the Web server, and vice versa. Internal to the WebClass, these ASP objects can be used to manipulate the flow of information between the browser and the Web server.

NOTE

Although space prohibits an in-depth discussion of ASP, you can get the basics from the MSDN article "An ASP You Can Grasp: The ABCs of Active Server Pages." Much of the discussion in this chapter assumes a basic familiarity with ASP and HTML.

Table 17.1   ASP Objects

Object	Description
Application	A global object that can store data for all users accessing the Web site. Also supports events that fire the first time any user enters the Web site and when the Web server shuts down.
Request	Encapsulates information sent from the browser to the Web server. Includes properties, such as QueryString, Form, and ServerVariables, that expose collections of data in name-value pairs sent from the browser.
Response	Represents information sent from the Web server to the browser. Includes methods such as Write and Redirect to send text to the browser and cause the browser to request a specific URL, respectively.
Server	An object that contains methods such as CreateObject to create ActiveX components on the Web server, as well as format data (HTMLEncode, URLEncode, URLPathEncode).
Session	Represents the current user. For each user accessing the Web site, Session objects can store data that is retrieved via a cookie sent to the browser and represented by the SessionID property. Also supports events that fire each time a user enters and leaves the Web site.

Figure 17.1 presents a diagram of this process.

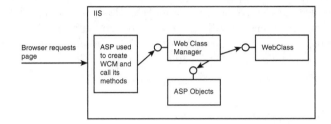

Figure 17.1

The runtime architecture of an IIS application.

As might be expected, the WCM is saved in the ASP Application object so that it does not have to be re-created with each call to a WebClass. However, by default the WebClass itself is created and destroyed with each request, to reduce overhead on the Web server. This default can be changed by setting the StateManagement property of the WebClass to wcRetainInstance at design time. Changing the property has the effect of saving the instance of the WebClass in a Session object so that subsequent calls to the WebClass by the same user will not require the creation of the component.

Although saving the instance of the WebClass in a Session object allows state information to be saved in variables within the WebClass, it is less scalable because all requests from a specific client must use the same Web server, and ASP must ensure that the same thread is used to process subsequent requests by the client. This may not be appropriate for large-scale installations where a single session may involve requests to multiple Web servers due to the use of load-balancing clusters.

NOTE

> In general, both IIS and DHTML Applications are useful for rapid development and deployment but are not particularly efficient or scalable. This makes them better suited for us in intranet applications rather than public Web sites.

The examples in this chapter do not retain state, so the WebClass StateManagement property is set to wcNoState.

TIP

> If you do set the StateManagement property to wcNoState, you can destroy the instance of the WebClass programmatically, using the ReleaseInstance method of the class. Note that the instance of the WebClass is terminated after the procedure in which it is called completes.

For a user to request an IIS application, you must create an ASP page to instantiate the WCM and call the WebClass. When you compile an IIS application or run it in the IDE using the F5 key, VB creates an ASP page with the name provided in the NameInURL property set at design time. For example, Listing 17.1 shows the page generated to start an application, ConTrackerWeb, that includes a WebClass named wcConTracker.

Listing 17.1   The ASP Page Generated by VB to Invoke an IIS Application

```
<%
Server.ScriptTimeout=600
Response.Buffer=True
Response.Expires=0

If (VarType(Application("~WC~WebClassManager")) = 0) Then
    Application.Lock
    If (VarType(Application("~WC~WebClassManager")) = 0) Then
        Set Application("~WC~WebClassManager") = _
            Server.CreateObject("WebClassRuntime.WebClassManager")
    End If
    Application.UnLock
End If

Application("~WC~WebClassManager").ProcessNoStateWebClass _
        "ConTrackerWeb.wcConTracker", _
        Server, _
        Application, _
        Session, _
        Request, _
        Response
%>
```

Event Processing

Each WebClass includes the events, shown in Table 17.2, that are fired when the component is created and as requests are processed. For WebClasses that do not retain state, the order in which these events occur the first time the component is invoked is the following:

```
Initialize
BeginRequest
Start
EndRequest
Terminate
```

Keep in mind that the Initialize and Terminate events will fire only once if the WebClass is not destroyed after each request. In addition, the Start event fires only in the event that no specific request is made (usually the first request). A typical use for the Start event is to begin the execution of the application using a defined WebItem, discussed next.

Table 17.2   WebClass Events

Event	Description
BeginRequest	Fired each time an element on an HTML page sends a request to the WebClass.
EndRequest	Fired when the WebClass has finished processing the request from the browser and has returned a response.
Initialize	Occurs when the WebClass is first created. Always occurs first but may not occur with each request if the StateManagement property is set to wcRetainInstance.
Start	Usually fired when the first BeginRequest event occurs in the WebClass unless the first request is for a specific event in a WebItem.
Terminate	Occurs when the WebClass is destroyed. Will occur after each request in the event that the StateManagement property is set to wcNoState.

Using WebItems

Conceptually, you can think of the WebClass as a container that handles all the communication between the Web server and the IIS application. Inside the WebClass, however, the HTML generated and sent to the browser—as well as the handling of events such as hyperlink clicks and form submittals—is done through one or more WebItem objects.

WebItem objects come in two flavors: HTML Template WebItems and Custom WebItems. The difference between these types is that Template WebItems are imported using the WebClass Designer from an HTML or ASP file created outside VB. VB then parses the page and displays a list of tags that are candidates for user interaction in the browser. You can see a typical example in Figure 17.2, where the WebClass Designer is shown with three HTML Template WebItems. Custom WebItems are simply programmatic resources where any HTML sent to the browser is generated through code (such as Response.Write).

Each WebItem also contains standard methods, properties, and events shown in Table 17.3.

Table 17.3   The WebItem Properties, Method, and Events

Member	Description
Properties	
ReScanReplacements	Boolean. Determines whether replacement text will be recursively scanned until no tokens prefixed with TagPrefix remain.

continues

Table 17.3 continued

Member	Description
TagPrefix	`String.` Determines the prefix of tags designated to be replaced in the HTML template.

Method

WriteTemplate	Processes an HTML template associated with the `WebItem`.

Events

ProcessTag	Fired when tags containing the `TagPrefix` are found in the HTML template. The replacement HTML is passed back as an argument passed into the event procedure. The event is fired once for each tag found.
Respond	Fired when an event is processed for a `WebItem` that is not directly connected. Also occurs when a `WebItem` is navigated to, using `NextItem`.
UserEvent	Fired in response to a request made using an event declared dynamically.

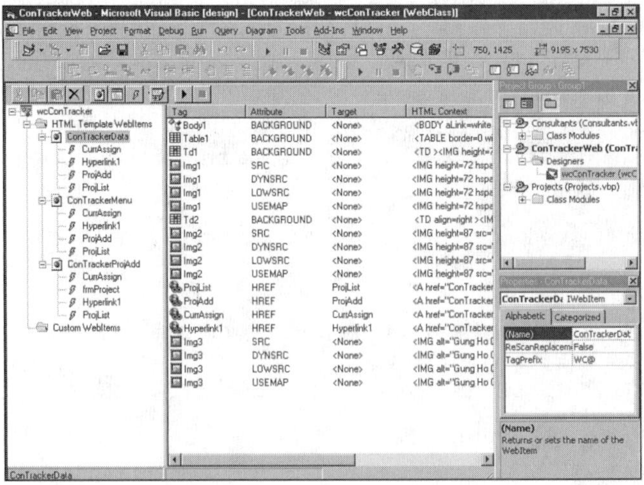

Figure 17.2

The WebClass designer showing HTML Template WebItems in the tree control in the left pane.

As mentioned previously, to begin using a WebItem, the Start event of the WebClass uses the WriteTemplate method of the WebItem to process the template and send it to the browser. For example, a WebClass in an application that displays consulting project and assignment information might contain the following code:

```
Private Sub WebClass_Start()

    ' Send the first template to the browser
    ConTrackerMenu.WriteTemplate

End Sub
```

in which ConTrackerMenu is a WebItem associated with an HTML template. Figure 17.3 shows the resulting page in the browser.

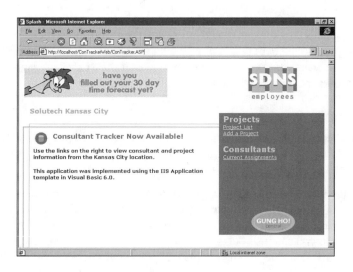

Figure 17.3

The browser after the ConTrackerMenu WebItem is invoked using WriteTemplate.

Connecting Events

The interaction between users and an IIS application occurs through events associated with tags in an HTML template. Associating or connecting events is typically done by double-clicking on the tag in the WebClass Designer to insert an event procedure that is invoked when the event is fired. As you can see in the example in Figure 17.2, events have been connected to four tags, as denoted by the name of the event in the Target column on the right and the events listed under the WebItem on the left.

For each connected event, VB automatically writes a query string into the HTML template as it is sent to the browser. This string identifies the WebItem and event that is to be processed when the user activates it. For example, in Figure 17.3, the Project List hyperlink is connected to an event named `ProjList`. In the `ConTrackerMenu` WebItem, the following code is used to initiate the display of the list of projects using the `WriteTemplate` method of the `ConTrackerData` WebItem:

```
Private Sub ConTrackerMenu_ProjList()

    ' Set the state information to view the project list
    strDataView = "PrjLst"
    ' Write out the template to the browser
    ConTrackerData.WriteTemplate

End Sub
```

TIP

The `strDataView` private variable is populated with a string that indicates the data to be displayed by the `ConTrackerData` WebItem. You can employ this technique when you use the WebItem to display different types of data. Keep in mind that all WebClass variables are reset with each request if the `StateManagement` property is set to `wcNoState`, as in this example.

Replacement Processing

When `WriteTemplate` is invoked for a WebItem, the WebClass pulls in the HTML template and processes it before sending the resulting HTML to the browser. The key process that takes place during this time is *replacement processing*.

Of course, the idea behind having an HTML template is so that your WebItem does not have to generate all the HTML dynamically. However, you will likely want certain sections of the page to be created on-the-fly from data in a database, for example. To accomplish this, you can insert tags that contain the `TagPrefix` property discussed earlier in the HTML template. As the template is processed, these tags are replaced as the `ProcessTag` event is fired with dynamically generated HTML from the WebClass.

As an example, consider the page shown in Figure 17.4. This page was designed in Visual InterDev (VB does not contain an HTML editor) to act as the template for the `ConTrackerData` WebItem. Note the `<WC@DataTable>` tag in the middle of the page.

When `ProcessTag` is fired for the WebItem, you can write code that uses a `Select Case` statement to differentiate between tags and then use the `TagContents` argument to pass back the HTML string that will serve as the replacement.

```
Private Sub ConTrackerData_ProcessTag(ByVal TagName As String, _
    TagContents As String, SendTags As Boolean)

    ' Determine the tag name and go get the data
    Select Case TagName
        Case "WC@DataTable"
            TagContents = ShowData(strDataView)
```

```
        Case Else
            ' Should never get here because only one tag in the page
            TagContents = "Could not determine the contents of the tag"
    End Select

End Sub
```

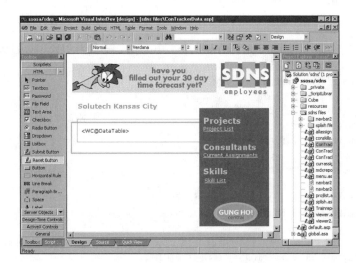

Figure 17.4

An HTML template page with a tag that will be replaced at runtime.

Note that a private function procedure ShowData has been created to determine which data the template should display, given the strDataView variable discussed earlier, and to pass back the contents to the new HTML. In this particular example, ShowData is used to handle three data views: the project list, all consultants currently assigned to a project, and a list of consultants assigned to a particular project. As a result, the ShowData procedure itself uses a Select Case statement to call the appropriate private procedure.

NOTE

Code for the entire WebClass can be seen in Listing 17.4 later in the chapter.

The heart of this technique, however, is formulating the HTML that is sent back to the browser. In this example, the ShowData procedure calls a function procedure, ShowProjList, shown in Listing 17.2, that uses the clsProject UI Business Object discussed in Chapter 15, "Using Object-Oriented Techniques." This object contains a List method that returns a disconnected ADO Recordset populated with all the projects in the database. You will notice that ShowProjList simply creates an HTML

<TABLE> tag that includes the data from the resultset. This string is returned from the function procedure and is passed back to the ProcessTag event to replace the TagContents.

NOTE

To use the UI Business Object, the WebClass project must also include a reference to the LBOM component and ADO, which are both required by the UBO.

Listing 17.2   The ShowProjList Function Procedure Is Used to Build the HTML That Replaces the <WC@DataTable> Tag

```
Private Function ShowProjList() As String

Dim objProject As Projects.clsProject
Dim rsData As Recordset
Dim strContents As String

On Error GoTo ShowProjErr

    ' Instantiate the UI Business object
    Set objProject = New Projects.clsProject

    ' Pass in the connect string (could also be defined in global.asa)
    objProject.ConnectString = CONNECT_STRING

    ' Get the recordset and check for existing projects
    Set rsData = objProject.List
    If rsData.EOF And rsData.BOF Then
        ShowProjList = "There are no projects in the database."
        Set objProject = Nothing
        Exit Function
    End If

    strContents = "<strong>Project List</strong><HR>"

    ' Create the header
    strContents = strContents & "<TABLE BORDER=1><TR>"
    strContents = strContents & "<TD><strong>Description</strong></TD>"
    strContents = strContents & "<TD><strong>Company</strong></TD>"
    strContents = strContents & "<TD><strong>Contact</strong></TD>"
    strContents = strContents & "<TD><strong>Start Date</strong></TD>"
    strContents = strContents & "<TD><strong>End Date</strong></TD>"
    strContents = strContents & "</TR>"

    ' Loop through the resultset
    Do While Not rsData.EOF
        ' Create the body
        strContents = strContents & "<TR>"
```

```
        strContents = strContents & "<TD><A HREF=""" & _
            URLFor(ConTrackerData, "Assign" & rsData("Code")) & """>" & _
                rsData("Description") & "</A></TD>"
        strContents = strContents & "<TD>" & rsData("Company") & "</TD>"
        strContents = strContents & "<TD>" & rsData("Contact") & "</TD>"
        strContents = strContents & "<TD>" & Format(rsData("StartDate"), _
            "mm/dd/yyyy") & "</TD>"
        strContents = strContents & "<TD>" & Format(rsData("EndDate"), _
            "mm/dd/yyyy") & "</TD>"
        strContents = strContents & "</TR>"

        rsData.MoveNext
    Loop

    ' Clean up
    Set rsData = Nothing
    Set objProject = Nothing

    ' Finish the table and return the results
    strContents = strContents & "</TABLE>"
    ShowProjList = strContents

Exit Function
ShowProjErr:
    ShowProjList = "An error occurred  processing the Project List: " _
        & Err.Description
    ' Clean up
    Set rsData = Nothing
    Set objProject = Nothing

End Function
```

The resulting page in the browser, showing the list of projects, can be seen in Figure 17.5.

Dynamic Events

You will notice in Figure 17.5 that each project description itself is a hyperlink that displays all the consultants assigned to the project. Unlike the ProjList event discussed previously, hyperlinks created in dynamically generated HTML cannot be connected to events at design time. As a result, you can create dynamic events to handle these types of cases.

A dynamic event is processed by the UserEvent event of the WebItem and is created using the URLFor method of the WebItem. For example, the code in ShowProjList in Listing 17.2 uses URLFor to construct an anchor tag for the description of the project.

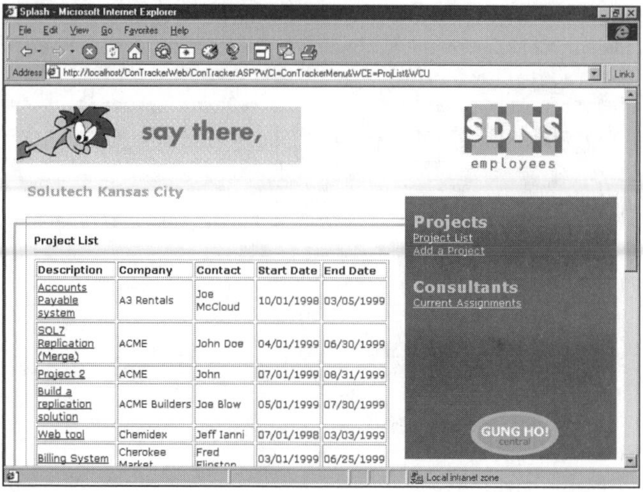

Figure 17.5

The fully populate ConTrackerData template showing a list of projects.

```
strContents = strContents & "<TD><A HREF=""" & _
    URLFor(ConTrackerData, "Assign" & rsData("Code")) & """>" & _
        rsData("Description") & "</A></TD>"
```

At runtime, this creates the following hyperlink:

```
<A HREF="ConTracker.ASP?WCI=ConTrackerData&WCE=Assign10817">
```

Notice that the method takes arguments to specify the `WebItem` that will respond to the event and the event name. In this case, you're embedding the project code in the event name so that the `ShowData` procedure can parse the event name to extract the code and pass it to a private function procedure, `ShowAssignments`, that retrieves the assigned consultants. Figure 17.6 shows the resulting page, listing the consultants assigned to project 10817.

Form Submission

In most instances, data is sent to the Web server from a `<FORM>` tag in the page. Users of the page populate HTML elements (typically defined with `<INPUT>` tags) such as textboxes, check boxes, and radio buttons and select lists within the form and submit it to the Web server via a submit button.

In a `WebClass`, handling the submission of forms is accomplished by connecting the `<FORM>` tag to an event handler using the WebClass Designer. As an example, consider the form shown in Figure 17.7 to gather data required to add a new project to the database. This page is created using a `WebItem` defined as an HTML template named `ConTrackerProjAdd`. Inside the template, the form `frmProject` has been connected to an event named `frmProject`. As a result, when the user submits the form using the Submit button, the contents of all the elements in the form are packaged and sent to the Web server, and the `frmProject` event is fired within the `WebItem`.

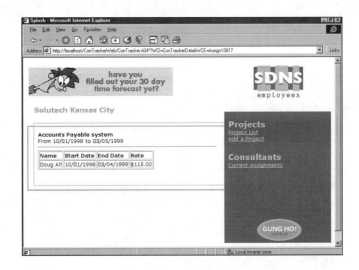

Figure 17.6

The list of consultants assigned to a project generated through a dynamic event.

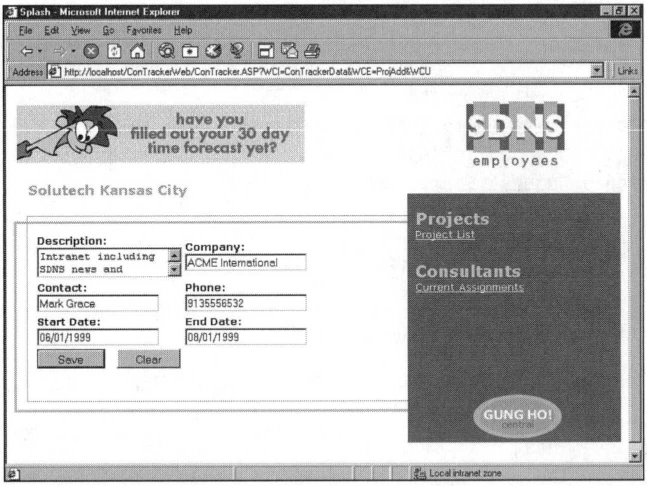

Figure 17.7

A <FORM> tag can also be connected to an event for processing by the WebClass.

To process the elements sent with the form, the event procedure can use the ASP Request object to read the values from the Forms collection corresponding to elements within the form. This information can then be inserted into the database using the clsProject UBOs discussed in Chapter 15. Listing 17.3 presents the code for the frmProject event handler.

NOTE

This is a good example of where to consider using the LBOM approach because it not only separates the UI from data validation and business logic but also increases productivity. In this case, you want the same data validation and business rules to apply to data entered over the Web and through a VB interface. Using the LBOM saves you from having to rewrite the data validation logic in both interfaces and keeps it consistent.

Listing 17.3   The Event Handler for the Form Submission

```
Private Sub ConTrackerProjAdd_frmProject()

Dim objProject As Projects.clsProject

' Fired when the user submits the add form

On Error GoTo AddProjErr

' Instantiate a UI Business object
Set objProject = New Projects.clsProject

With objProject
    .NewProject  ' create a new project
    ' Set the properties (note that validation is done inside
    ' the object, as shown in Chapter 15)
    .Description = Request.Form("txtDesc")
    .Company = Request.Form("txtCompany")
    .Phone = Request.Form("txtPhone")
    .StartDate = Request.Form("txtStart")
    .EndDate = Request.Form("txtEnd")
    .Contact = Request.Form("txtContact")
End With

' Save the new project
If objProject.Save Then
    strDataView = "The project was saved and assigned code " & _
        objProject.Code & "."
End If

' Clean up
Set objProject = Nothing
```

```
' Navigate back to the page
ConTrackerData.WriteTemplate

Exit Sub
AddProjErr:
    ' Send the error message back to the template
    strDataView = "An error occurred while saving the project: " _
        & Err.Description
    Set objProject = Nothing
    ConTrackerData.WriteTemplate

End Sub
```

Note that the strDataView private variable is used here as well to contain a success or error message sent back to the user via the ConTrackerData WebItem.

A Code Example

Because IIS applications are new to many developers, I've included the code for the entire WebClass in Listing 17.4.

NOTE

Keep in mind that this discussion is not exhaustive and that other techniques can be employed. For example, a typical requirement is to store state information between requests to the WebClass. This can be accomplished using the ASP Session object or the URLData method of the WebItem in the event the WebClass is destroyed with each request.

Listing 17.4 The Code for the wcConTracker WebClass

```
Option Explicit
Option Compare Text

Private Const CONNECT_STRING = "provider=sqloledb;Server=ssosa;" & _
    Database=Contracker;uid=sa;pwd=;"
Private strDataView As String


Private Sub ConTrackerData_CurrAssign()

    ' Set the state information to view the current assignments
    strDataView = "CurAsn"
    ' Write out the template to the browser
    ConTrackerData.WriteTemplate

End Sub

Private Sub ConTrackerData_Hyperlink1()
```

continues

Listing 17.4   continued

```
      ' Go home using the ServerVariables collection to determine
      ' the server name dynamically.
      Response.Redirect "http://" & _
          Request.ServerVariables("SERVER_NAME") & "/sdns"

End Sub

Private Sub ConTrackerData_ProcessTag(ByVal TagName As String, _
          TagContents As String, SendTags As Boolean)

' Fired when WriteTemplate is called

    ' Determine the tag name and go get the data
    Select Case TagName
        Case "WC@DataTable"
            TagContents = ShowData(strDataView)
        Case Else
            ' Should never get here because only one tag in the page
            TagContents = "Could not determine the contents of the tag"
    End Select

End Sub

Private Sub ConTrackerData_ProjAdd()

    ' Show the project add page
    ConTrackerProjAdd.WriteTemplate

End Sub

Private Sub ConTrackerData_ProjList()

    ' Set the state information to view the project list
    strDataView = "PrjLst'"
    ' Write out the template to the browser
    ConTrackerData.WriteTemplate

End Sub

Private Sub ConTrackerData_UserEvent(ByVal EventName As String)

    ' Called when a user clicks on a project to display the assignments
    strDataView = EventName
    ConTrackerData.WriteTemplate

End Sub
```

```
Private Sub ConTrackerMenu_CurrAssign()

    ' Set the state information to view the current assignments
    strDataView = "CurAsn"
    ' Write out the template to the browser
    ConTrackerData.WriteTemplate

End Sub

Private Sub ConTrackerMenu_Hyperlink1()

    ' Go home using the ServerVariables collection to determine
    ' the server name dynamically.
    Response.Redirect "http://" & _
        Request.ServerVariables("SERVER_NAME") & "/sdns"

End Sub

Private Sub ConTrackerMenu_ProjAdd()
    ' Show the project add page
    ConTrackerProjAdd.WriteTemplate
End Sub

Private Sub ConTrackerMenu_ProjList()

    ' Set the state information to view the project list
    strDataView = "PrjLst"
    ' Write out the template to the browser
    ConTrackerData.WriteTemplate

End Sub

Private Sub ConTrackerProjAdd_CurrAssign()

    ' Set the state information to view the current assignments
    strDataView = "CurAsn"
    ' Write out the template to the browser
    ConTrackerData.WriteTemplate

End Sub

Private Sub ConTrackerProjAdd_frmProject()

Dim objProject As Projects.clsProject

' Fired when the user submits the add project form
```

continues

Listing 17.4   continued

```
On Error GoTo AddProjErr

' Instantiate a UI Business object
Set objProject = New Projects.clsProject

With objProject
    .NewProject   ' Create a new project
    ' Set the properties (note that validation is done inside
    ' the object, as shown in Chapter 15)
    .Description = Request.Form("txtDesc")
    .Company = Request.Form("txtCompany")
    .Phone = Request.Form("txtPhone")
    .StartDate = Request.Form("txtStart")
    .EndDate = Request.Form("txtEnd")
    .Contact = Request.Form("txtContact")
End With

' Save the new project
If objProject.Save Then
    strDataView = "The project was saved and assigned code " _
        & objProject.Code & "."
End If

' Clean up
Set objProject = Nothing

' Navigate back to the page
ConTrackerData.WriteTemplate

Exit Sub
AddProjErr:
    ' Send the error message back to the template
    strDataView = "An error occurred while saving the project: " _
        & Err.Description
    Set objProject = Nothing
    ConTrackerData.WriteTemplate

End Sub

Private Sub ConTrackerProjAdd_Hyperlink1()
    ' Go home using the ServerVariables collection to determine
    ' the server name dynamically.
    Response.Redirect "http://" & _
        Request.ServerVariables("SERVER_NAME") & "/sdns"
End Sub
```

```
Private Sub ConTrackerProjAdd_ProjList()

    ' Set the state information to view the project list
    strDataView = "PrjLst"
    ' Write out the template to the browser
    ConTrackerData.WriteTemplate

End Sub

Private Sub WebClass_Start()

    ' Send the first template to the browser
    ConTrackerMenu.WriteTemplate

End Sub

Private Function ShowData(ByVal pView As String) As String

Dim strContents As String

On Error GoTo ShowDataErr

' Go to the private function that builds the table or displays the message
Select Case Mid(pView, 1, 6)
    Case "PrjLst"
        strContents = ShowProjList
    Case "CurAsn"
        strContents = ShowCurrAssign
    Case "Assign"
        ' Here we must parse the view to find the project code
        strContents = ShowAssignments(Mid(pView, 7))
    Case Else
        ' A message, could be an error or success
        strContents = pView
End Select

ShowData = strContents

Exit Function
ShowDataErr:
    ShowData = "An error occurred while processing the results: " _
        & Err.Description

End Function

Private Function ShowProjList() As String

Dim objProject As Projects.clsProject
```

continues

Listing 17.4   continued

```
Dim rsData As Recordset
Dim strContents As String

On Error GoTo ShowProjErr

    ' Instantiate the UI Business object
    Set objProject = New Projects.clsProject

    ' Pass in the connect string (could also be defined in global.asa)
    objProject.ConnectString = CONNECT_STRING

    ' Get the recordset and check for existing projects
    Set rsData = objProject.List
    If rsData.EOF And rsData.BOF Then
        ShowProjList = "There are no projects in the database."
        Set objProject = Nothing
        Exit Function
    End If

    strContents = "<strong>Project List</strong><HR>"

    ' Create the header
    strContents = strContents & "<TABLE BORDER=1><TR>"
    strContents = strContents & "<TD><strong>Description</strong></TD>"
    strContents = strContents & "<TD><strong>Company</strong></TD>"
    strContents = strContents & "<TD><strong>Contact</strong></TD>"
    strContents = strContents & "<TD><strong>Start Date</strong></TD>"
    strContents = strContents & "<TD><strong>End Date</strong></TD>"
    strContents = strContents & "</TR>"

    ' Loop through the resultset
    Do While Not rsData.EOF
        ' Create the body
        strContents = strContents & "<TR>"
        strContents = strContents & "<TD><A HREF=""" & _
            URLFor(ConTrackerData, "Assign" & rsData("Code")) & """>" _
                & rsData("Description") & "</A></TD>"
        strContents = strContents & "<TD>" & rsData("Company") & "</TD>"
        strContents = strContents & "<TD>" & rsData("Contact") & "</TD>"
        strContents = strContents & "<TD>" & Format(rsData("StartDate"), _
            "mm/dd/yyyy") & "</TD>"
        strContents = strContents & "<TD>" & Format(rsData("EndDate"), _
            "mm/dd/yyyy") & "</TD>"
        strContents = strContents & "</TR>"

        rsData.MoveNext
    Loop
```

```
    ' Clean up
    Set rsData = Nothing
    Set objProject = Nothing

    ' Finish the table and return the results
    strContents = strContents & "</TABLE>"
    ShowProjList = strContents

Exit Function
ShowProjErr:
    ShowProjList = "An error occurred while processing the Project List: " _
        & Err.Description
    ' Clean up
    Set rsData = Nothing
    Set objProject = Nothing

End Function

Private Function ShowAssignments(ByVal pCode As String) As String

Dim objProject As Projects.clsProject
Dim rsData As Recordset
Dim strContents As String

On Error GoTo ShowAssignErr

    ' Instantiate the UI Business object
    Set objProject = New Projects.clsProject

    ' Pass in the connect string (could also be defined in global.asa)
    objProject.ConnectString = CONNECT_STRING

    ' Get the current project
    If Not objProject.GetProject(pCode) Then
        ShowAssignments = "Could not retrieve project. No data displayed"
        Set objProject = Nothing
        Exit Function
    End If

    ' Get the assignments and check if there are consultants
    Set rsData = objProject.Assignments
    If rsData.EOF And rsData.BOF Then
        ShowAssignments = "No consultants are assigned to this project."
        Set objProject = Nothing
        Exit Function
    End If
```

continues

Listing 17.4   continued

```
   ' Display project information
   strContents = "<strong>" & objProject.Description & "</strong><BR>"
   strContents = strContents & "From " & _
      Format(objProject.StartDate, "mm/dd/yyyy") _
      & " to " & Format(objProject.EndDate, "mm/dd/yyyy") & "<HR>"

   ' Create the header
   strContents = strContents & "<TABLE BORDER=1><TR>"
   strContents = strContents & "<TD><strong>Name</strong></TD>"
   strContents = strContents & "<TD><strong>Start Date</strong></TD>"
   strContents = strContents & "<TD><strong>End Date</strong></TD>"
   strContents = strContents & "<TD><strong>Rate</strong></TD>"
   strContents = strContents & "</TR>"

   ' Loop through the resultset
   Do While Not rsData.EOF
      ' Create the body
      strContents = strContents & "<TR>"
      strContents = strContents & "<TD>" & rsData("Name") & "</TD>"
      strContents = strContents & "<TD>" & Format(rsData("StartDate"), _
         "mm/dd/yyyy") & "</TD>"
      strContents = strContents & "<TD>" & Format(rsData("EndDate"), _
         "mm/dd/yyyy") & "</TD>"
      strContents = strContents & "<TD>" & Format(rsData("Rate"), _
         "currency") & "</TD>"
      strContents = strContents & "</TR>"

      rsData.MoveNext
   Loop

   ' Clean up
   Set rsData = Nothing
   Set objProject = Nothing

   ' Finish the table and return the results
   strContents = strContents & "</TABLE>"
   ShowAssignments = strContents

Exit Function
ShowAssignErr:
   ShowAssignments = "An error occurred processing the Project List: " _
      & Err.Description
   ' Clean up
   Set rsData = Nothing
   Set objProject = Nothing
```

```
End Function


Private Function ShowCurrAssign() As String

Dim objCon As Consultants.clsConsultant
Dim rsData As Recordset
Dim strContents As String

On Error GoTo ShowCurrErr

    ' Instantiate the UI Business object for consultants
    ' This is analogous to the clsProject business object
    Set objCon = New Consultants.clsConsultant

    ' Pass in the connect string (could also be defined in global.asa)
    objCon.ConnectString = CONNECT_STRING

    ' Get the recordset containing all current assignments
    ' and check for current assignments
    Set rsData = objCon.GetAssignments
    If rsData.EOF And rsData.BOF Then
        ShowCurrAssign = "There are no assignments in the database."
        Set objCon = Nothing
        Exit Function
    End If

    strContents = "<strong>Current Assignments</strong><HR>"

    ' Create the header
    strContents = strContents & "<TABLE BORDER=1><TR>"
    strContents = strContents & "<TD><strong>Name</strong></TD>"
    strContents = strContents & "<TD><strong>Project</strong></TD>"
    strContents = strContents & "<TD><strong>Start Date</strong></TD>"
    strContents = strContents & "<TD><strong>End Date</strong></TD>"
    strContents = strContents & "<TD><strong>Rate</strong></TD>"
    strContents = strContents & "</TR>"

    ' Loop through the resultset
    Do While Not rsData.EOF
        ' Create the body
        strContents = strContents & "<TR>"
        strContents = strContents & "<TD>" & rsData("Name") & "</TD>"
        strContents = strContents & "<TD>" & rsData("Description") _
            & "</TD>"
        strContents = strContents & "<TD>" & _
            Format(rsData("StartDate"), "mm/dd/yyyy") & "</TD>"
        strContents = strContents & "<TD>" & _
```

continues

Listing 17.4   continued

```
            Format(rsData("EndDate"), "mm/dd/yyyy") & "</TD>"
        strContents = strContents & "<TD>" & _
            Format(rsData("Rate"), "currency") & "</TD>"
        strContents = strContents & "</TR>"

        rsData.MoveNext
    Loop

    ' Clean up
    Set rsData = Nothing
    Set objCon = Nothing

    ' Finish the table and return the results
    strContents = strContents & "</TABLE>"
    ShowCurrAssign = strContents

Exit Function
ShowCurrErr:
    ShowCurrAssign = "An error occurred processing the Assignment List: " _
        & Err.Description
    ' Clean up
    Set rsData = Nothing
    Set objCon = Nothing

End Function
```

DHTML Applications

The second type of Web-based application that can be created in VB 6 is a DHTML application. When this project template is employed, you can write code in the VB IDE to create and manipulate elements on Web pages referenced by the project using the Document Object Model (DOM). This allows a VB developer to use his or her familiar tools and programming model while working in an environment that is fundamentally different from traditional form-based applications.

NOTE

> The DOM is simply an object model exposed by Internet Explorer when a Web page is downloaded and parsed by the browser. Using this object model, developers can programmatically manipulate elements (tags) on the page.

The primary benefit of building DHTML applications is that the compiled code component is downloaded and executed within MSIE. This allows local processing of user actions and events, which in turn creates a more responsive interface. In addition, the code is compiled for better performance and allows the code you write to be invisible to the user. This can be especially beneficial for security reasons and intellectual property rights. Also, as you will see, DHTML applications can be downloaded and can manipulate data without having to make subsequent round trips to the server, as an IIS application.

NOTE

The main downside to this architecture, of course, is that it is available only for MSIE 4.01 service pack 1 or higher. Although this makes it a great solution for intranet applications in which the browser can be mandated, it does not extend well onto the Internet where you're likely to encounter other browsers. In addition, this approach requires that a component be downloaded and installed by the browser.

Runtime Architecture

Like IIS applications, the end result of a DHTML application is one or more ActiveX code components housed in a DLL. This DLL includes a reference to the Microsoft HTML Object Library (mshtml.dll) that exposes all the methods, properties, and events of the DOM to the DHTML project. This relationship enables the components created in a DHTML project to interact with the elements on the page, using the DOM.

Internally, a DHTML project is made up of one or more DHTMLPage objects (a special type of class module that, when compiled, becomes an ActiveX code component). Each DHTMLPage object represents a Web page and is loaded by MSIE when the page is requested. At compile time, the pages themselves are written to a location specified in the BuildFile property of each DHTMLPage object. Figure 17.8 depicts this architecture.

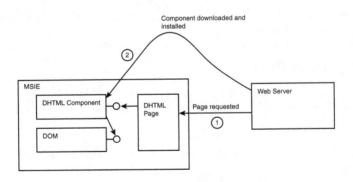

Figure 17.8

The runtime architecture of a DHTML application: (1) The page is requested by the browser, and (2) the component is downloaded and installed.

The following code snippet shows a simple DHTML page generated when compiling a DHTML application. Note that the <OBJECT> tag is used to instruct MSIE to download and instantiate the component.

```
<HTML>
<HEAD>
<META NAME="GENERATOR" Content="Microsoft Visual Studio 6.0">
<META content="text/html" http-equiv=Content-Type>
<TITLE></TITLE>
</HEAD>
<BODY>
<!-METADATA TYPE="MsHtmlPageDesigner" startspan->
  <object id="DHTMLPage2"
      classid="clsid:0EBA559F-E89F-11D2-A0B5-006008EB5F25"
      width=0 height=0>
  </object>
<!-METADATA TYPE="MsHtmlPageDesigner" endspan->

<P>This is a sample DHTML page.
Normally there would be  many other tags here.</P>

</BODY>
</HTML>
```

A second key point you should note about this code is that there are no client-side script tags. All script that would normally be embedded in <SCRIPT> tags is encapsulated in, and executed from, the component.

NOTE

When distributing a DHTML application, the CODEBASE attribute of the <OBJECT> tag is used to specify the location of the distributable .cab file that houses the DLL, as discussed in Chapter 10, "Compiling and Distributing," in the section on the Internet Component Download.

Event Processing

Each DHTMLPage object includes four events and two objects, shown in Table 17.4, that are used to determine when the page is loaded and to programmatically manipulate elements on the page.

Table 17.4   Properties and Events of the DHTMLPage Object

Member	Description
Properties	
BaseWindow	Returns the topmost object in the DOM. This object is used to manipulate the browser window.
DHTMLEvent	Returns an event object representing the most recent event that occurred on the page. This is often used to programmatically determine from where the event originated.

Member	Description
Document	Returns the `Document` object in the DOM that refers to the current page. This object is used to programmatically manipulate elements of the page.
	Events
Initialize	Fired when the `DHTMLPage` object is loaded by MSIE. When this event is fired, elements on the page may not yet be available.
Load	Fires as the page is loaded by the browser. Depending on how the `AsyncLoad` property is set, the event may fire after all elements of the page are loaded (`False`) or immediately after the first element is loaded (`True`).
Terminate	Fired when MSIE unloads the component. Used for cleanup.
UnLoad	Fired when the user navigates away from the current page or when the browser is closed.

As described in Table 17.4, each `DHTMLPage` object includes `BaseWindow` and `Document` objects. In particular, the `BaseWindow` object exposes onload, onbeforeunload, and onunload events that are fired when the page is loaded and unloaded. In a typical scenario, the event sequence is the following:

```
Initialize
Load
onload
onbeforeunload
onunload
unload
Terminate
```

The primary difference between the onload event of the `BaseWindow` object and the Load event of the `DHTMLPage` object is that the onload event does not fire until the elements on the page have been drawn by the browser, whereas the Load event of the `DHTMLPage` object fires after the elements are loaded but before they are rendered.

The DHTML Page Designer

To create the interface for a DHTML application, you can use the DHTML Page Designer. In many respects, this designer is similar to the WebClass Designer discussed earlier in the chapter. It contains a tree on the left, where each element of the page is represented hierarchically as it fits in the DOM. The right side of the designer, however, contains a graphical depiction of the page and actually serves as a basic editor. For the remainder of this chapter, I will discuss a DHTML project that contains one `DHTMLPage` object, ConTracker, that is used to display projects, consultants, and skills in much the same way as the form-based application discussed in Chapter 12 and shown in Figure 12.1. The DHTML Page Designer with the ConTracker DHTMLObject loaded is shown in Figure 17.9.

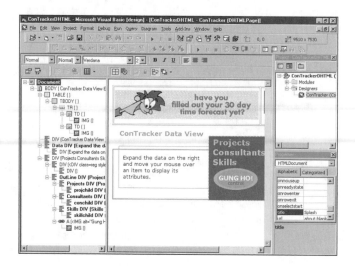

Figure 17.9

The DHTML Page Designer with the ConTracker page loaded.

Importing Pages

As noted earlier, when compiled, an HTML file is generated for each `DHTMLPage` object in the project. The `DHTMLPage` object contains `BuildFile` and `SourceFile` properties that are used to determine where the file will be generated and whether the source of the file is external to the project. By pointing the `SourceFile` property to an HTML page, the page is imported into the DHTML Page Designer and parsed hierarchically.

TIP

> Setting the `SourceFile` can be done through the properties window or by using the Properties toolbar icon in the DHTML Page Designer.

It is often advantageous to import a file because the editor provided by the VB IDE is not full featured and does not allow you to view the HTML that will be generated before running the project. In addition, importing a file allows it to be edited outside VB and reparsed at any time. In the example in Figure 17.9, the page was designed in Visual InterDev and imported into the project. After it's imported, you can also add elements to the page using the toolbars in the designer window and typing directly into the pane on the right.

Using DHTML

After you design the visual elements of the page, you can programmatically manipulate them by writing code in the code window, using the DOM. Figure 17.10 shows the available objects and their hierarchy.

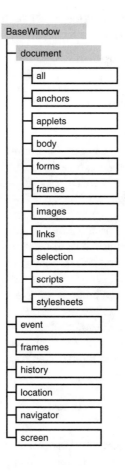

Figure 17.10

The DHTML object model exposed in a DHTML application.

TIP

Using the `All` collection of the `Document` object, you can manipulate every element on the page.

In addition, each element on the page assigned an ID attribute can be manipulated directly, using a number of standard methods, properties, and events. Table 17.5 presents several of the important properties and methods.

Table 17.5   Important Properties and Methods of an Element in a DHTML Page

Member	Description
	Properties
children	Returns a collection of all the elements nested inside this element.
className	Returns the name of the class associated with the element. Classes can be linked using cascading style sheets (CSS) to provide a consistent look and feel across pages.
dataFld	Specifies which field in the data source specified by dataSrc is to display in the tag.
dataSrc	Can be set to an ActiveX control that provides a recordset to display in the page.
ID	Specifies the ID of the element. Elements that have IDs can be more easily programmed.
innerHTML	Specifies the HTML (including all tag references) inside the tag. Can be used to replace the contents of the element.
innerText	Specifies the text inside a tag, excluding all tag references. Can be used to replace the contents of the element.
outerHTML	Specifies the HTML (including all tag references) within and including the tag. Can be used to replace the element entirely.
outerText	Specifies the text of the tag and can be used to replace the entire tag with text.
	Methods
insertAdjacentHTML	Inserts the provided HTML string into the given location specified as the first argument. Valid positions include BeforeBegin, BeforeEnd, AfterBegin, and AfterEnd.
insertAdjacentText	Inserts the provided text string into the given location specified as the first argument. Valid positions include BeforeBegin, BeforeEnd, AfterBegin, and AfterEnd.
parentElement	Returns a reference to the element within which the current element is nested.
style	Returns a style object used to manipulate attributes such as the color and position of the element.
tagName	Returns the type of tag for the element. For example, <DIV>, <INPUT>, <BODY>, and so on.
title	Specifies the ToolTip text to display as the user moves the cursor over the element.

When an ID is assigned, the object appears in the code window so that its events can be handled and it can be programmed in the same way that controls are referenced in a form-based application. For example, to manipulate a <DIV> tag on the page, you can assign an ID to it, such as Projects (because it will contain the list of projects), and set its `Title` property to display a ToolTip window when the user hovers the cursor over the tag.

```
Projects.Title = "Displays the list of projects in the database"
```

The key to using DHTML is to assign ID attributes to all tags on the page you want to manipulate dynamically. In the remainder of this section, I'll discuss the two primary ways these tags are used, through events and dynamic modification.

Event Handling

Perhaps the most powerful way to use DHTML is through events. Although the events fired by elements on DHTML pages differ from those in a form-based application, the VB IDE handles them identically, and many of them should be familiar. For example, Table 17.6 shows several of the events that are fired tags and their VB counterparts.

Table 17.6 Several Standard DHTML Events and Their VB Counterparts

DHTML Event	VB Event
onchange	Change
onclick, ondblclick	Click and DblClick
ondragstart	DragDrop and DragOver
onfocus, onblur	GetFocus and LostFocus
onkeydown, onkeyup	KeyDown and KeyUp
onkeypress	KeyPress
onmousemove	MouseMove
onmouseover	(No equivalent event)
onmouseout	(No equivalent event)
onmouseup, onmousedown	MouseUp and MouseDown
onselectstart, onselect	SelChange

As you will notice, the DHTML events begin with on and do not pass in arguments indicating the cursor coordinates, shift state of the keyboard, or the key that was pressed.

A typical way to use events appears in the following code snippet. Here, a <DIV> tag with an ID of Consultants exists that implements a simple tree display. When the user clicks on the contents of the tag, the following event procedure fires, and a private procedure is called to expand or collapse the tree:

```
Private Function Consultants_onclick() As Boolean

    ' Expand or collapse tree
    ExpandCollapseTree
```

```
' Cancel the bubbling
DHTMLEvent.cancelBubble = True

End Function
```

The interesting aspect of this code is the `cancelBubble` property of the `DHTMLEvent` object. Unlike traditional VB, in DHTML, multiple tags can handle the same event (analogous to setting the `KeyPreview` property to `True` on a form but much more extensive). In this case, because the Consultants `<DIV>` is nested inside a `<DIV>` tag named `OutlineDIV` that is embedded in a second `<DIV>` tag that exists in the `Document`, the event would bubble up through the hierarchy and be fired on all four levels. This bubbling effect can be prevented by setting the `cancelBubble` property to `True`.

The other feature of DHTML revealed by this code is that information about the event currently firing can be discovered, using the `DHTMLEvent` object. This object exposes properties such as `srcElement`, `keyCode`, and x and y that specify the ID of the element for which the event was fired, which key was pressed, and the coordinates of the mouse, respectively. You can think of the `DHTMLEvent` object as providing all the information normally found in the arguments to traditional VB events.

TIP

The `DHTMLEvent` object is a shortcut for using the syntax `BaseWindow.event`.

A typical use of the `srcElement` property is to discover for which element the event was fired and then change its properties. For example, the following code changes the text color of the source element to yellow:

```
DHTMLEvent.srcElement.Style.Color = vbWhite
```

Dynamically Modifying Elements

After events are captured for elements on the page, the elements can be manipulated using dynamic styles, dynamic content, and dynamic positioning. Basically, these terms are ways of describing setting properties and calling methods to change the appearance, representation, or position of the tag. To give you an example of how to use these, you will look at two specific scenarios in the page shown in Figure 17.9.

Dynamic Styles

The typical technique used to manipulate the style of an element is to set the properties associated with the element's `Style` object. Consider the example of the `<DIV>` tags on the right side of the page shown in the development environment in Figure 17.9. These `<DIV>` tags are nested to form a tree structure that can be expanded and collapsed by the user:

```
<DIV ID=OutLineDIV>
    <DIV ID=Projects>Projects
        <DIV ID=projchild>
```

```
...
      </DIV>
   </DIV>
   <DIV ID=Consultants>Consultants
      <DIV ID=conchild>
...
      </DIV>
   </DIV>
   <DIV ID=Skills>Skills
      <DIV ID=conchild>
...
      </DIV>
   </DIV>
</DIV>
```

To visually expand and collapse the tree, the tags nested within the Projects, Consultants, and Skills tags are toggled visible and invisible when the user clicks on the tag using the Style object. To perform this manipulation, a private procedure can be written to change the style of the child <DIV> tags when the user clicks the parent tag. This procedure, ExpandCollapseTree, is shown in Listing 17.5.

Listing 17.5   The ExpandCollapseTree Procedure Used to Dynamically Change the Style of a Tag

```
Private Sub ExpandCollapseTree()

Dim objElement As Object
Dim objChildDiv As Object

' Get a reference to the element for which the event was fired
Set objElement = DHTMLEvent.srcElement

' Get a reference to the child div
Set objChildDiv = objElement.children(0)

' If the child div is populated, toggle the display
If objChildDiv.children.length > 0 Then
    If objChildDiv.Style.display = "none" Then
        objChildDiv.Style.display = vbNullString
    Else
        objChildDiv.Style.display = "none"
    End If
End If

End Sub
```

Note that because this procedure is used to expand and collapse three <DIV> tags, the srcElement property of the DHTMLEvent object is used to get a reference to the tag for which the event was raised. This reference is then used to get a reference to the child <DIV> using the children collection (such as projchild, conchild, or skillchild).

The length property of the collection can then be used to determine how many tags are nested within the current tag. In this case, if there are nested tags, the display property of the Style object is toggled. By setting the display property to "none", the tag and all its children are not only made invisible, but their space within the page is also reclaimed. Conversely, setting the property to an empty string reverts the tag back to its original display. The resulting page showing the tree on the right can be seen in Figure 17.11.

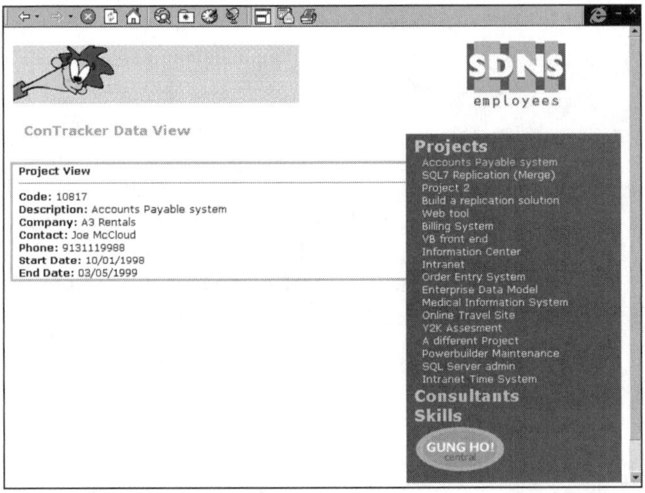

Figure 17.11

The populated page showing the set of nested <DIV> tags populated with data.

Dynamic Content

A second technique used to manipulate elements on the page is to dynamically alter their content. Essentially, this means using one of the four properties (innerHTML, outerHTML, innerText, and outerText) or two methods (insertAdjacentHTML and insertAdjacentText) described in Table 17.5. For example, consider the task of displaying the information about a specific project in a <DIV> tag on the left side of the page, as shown in Figure 17.11. This tag is populated dynamically as the user moves the mouse over a project contained in the tree on the right.

A simple technique for populating the tag is to build an HTML string and use the innerHTML property of the tag to replace the contents of the tag with an HTML string. The DisplayProject procedure in Listing 17.6 uses an ADO Recordset to build the HTML string by navigating to the appropriate record and using the Fields collection of the ADO Recordset. The resulting string is used to set the innerHTML property of the <DIV> tag with the ID of Data.

Listing 17.6   The DisplayProjects Procedure Replaces the HTML of a <DIV> Tag with Project Information

```
Private Sub DisplayProject(ByVal pPos As Long)

Dim strHTML As String

On Error Resume Next

    ' Navigate to the record
    rsProj.AbsolutePosition = pPos

    ' Build the HTML
    strHTML = "<strong>Project View</strong>"
    strHTML = strHTML & "<HR>"

    strHTML = strHTML & "<strong>Code:</strong> " & _
        rsProj.Fields("Code") & "<BR>"
    strHTML = strHTML & "<strong>Description:</strong> " & _
        rsProj.Fields("Description") & "<BR>"
    strHTML = strHTML & "<strong>Company:</strong> " & _
        rsProj.Fields("Company") & "<BR>"
    strHTML = strHTML & "<strong>Contact:</strong> " & _
        rsProj.Fields("Contact") & "<BR>"
    strHTML = strHTML & "<strong>Phone:</strong> " & _
        rsProj.Fields("Phone") & "<BR>"
    strHTML = strHTML & "<strong>Start Date:</strong> " & _
        Format(rsProj.Fields("StartDate"), _
            "mm/dd/yyyy") & "<BR>"
    strHTML = strHTML & "<strong>End Date:</strong> " & _
        Format(rsProj.Fields("EndDate"), _
            "mm/dd/yyyy") & "<BR>"

    ' Replace the inner html of the data div
    Data.innerHTML = strHTML

End Sub
```

Retrieving Data in DHTML Applications

One of the key features of DHTML applications is the ability to download and work with resultsets within the browser, as opposed to having to make multiple round trips to the Web server. One of the technologies Microsoft makes available to do this is Remote Data Services (RDS). RDS is a component of MDAC 2.0 and higher that allows an ADO Recordset to be created on a Web server, disconnected from its data source, and transmitted via HTTP to the browser. This architecture requires both client and server components to be installed and works only with MSIE and IIS. The components of this architecture can be seen in Figure 17.12.

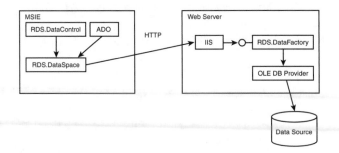

Figure 17.12

Retrieving data using RDS.

Using the RDS DataControl

On the client are several options for building the ADO Recordset. Perhaps the simplest of those options is to use the RDS DataControl installed with MSIE 4 and higher. This ActiveX control contains properties such as Connect, Server, and SQL that specify the connection string, URL of the server on which to create the resultset, and SQL string to send to the server, respectively. In addition, it contains a Refresh method used to send the SQL to the server and return the resultset.

TIP

Typically, the RDS DataControl is embedded in Web pages directly using an <OBJECT> tag. The RDS DataControl also acts as a data source object (DSO). It can be bound to HTML elements such as the <TABLE> and <DIV> tags using the dataSrc and dataFld attributes in much the same way that intrinsic VB controls can bind to DAO, RDO, and ADO data controls.

Using the RDS DataSpace

A second option on the client is to use the RDS DataSpace ActiveX code component also installed with MSIE. The DataSpace component is used indirectly by the RDS DataControl because the DataSpace component acts as the proxy for COM invocation and method calls to the Web server using HTTP (on the Web, server recordsets are created using a generic COM component called the RDS DataFactory). However, you can also use the DataSpace directly to instantiate a custom ActiveX code component (such as those discussed in Chapter 15) on the Web server and call its methods to return ADO recordsets. The DataSpace contains the method CreateObject to instantiate the component on the Web server. Once instantiated, methods and properties can be called in the normal fashion.

```
Dim rdsDS as New RDS.Dataspace
Dim objProjects as Object
Dim rsProj as Recordset
```

```
Set objProject = rdsDS.CreateObject("Projects.clsProjects", _
    "http://ssosa")
Set rsProj = objProject.List
```

(**NOTE**

For more information on the requirements for instantiating custom ActiveX code components on the Web server, see the technical article "Remote Data Service in MDAC 2.0" in MSDN.

Using the MS Remote Provider

The third option, and the one used in the example in Listing 17.7, is to invoke the RDS DataSpace object using ADO.

(**NOTE**

Using the RDS DataSpace object from within ADO requires that the MDAC components be installed on the client computer. This can be done using the Internet Component Download feature of MSIE, discussed in Chapter 10.

To use this technique, you must set the Provider property of the Connection object to MS Remote. This setting instructs ADO to look at the Remote Server and Remote Provider properties that contain the URL of the Web server on which to create the resultset and the OLE DB provider to use on that server, respectively. After the connection is established, you can create an ADO Recordset using the techniques discussed in Chapter 14, "Using ADO for Data Access." In the following example, the properties are simply passed in the connection string to the Open method of the Connection object, and a Recordset containing the project information is created by executing a stored procedure on the Web server:

```
Dim cnCon As New ADODB.Connection

Set rsProj = New ADODB.Recordset
cnCon.Open "Provider=MS Remote;Remote Server=http://ssosa;" & _
    "Remote Provider=SQLOLEDB;database=contracker;", "sa", ""

Set rsProj.ActiveConnection = cnCon
rsProj.Source = "exec GetProjects"
rsProj.Open
```

After the Recordset has been created, you can traverse it and use properties such as innerHTML to dynamically place the data into the page. Figure 17.11 shows the resulting data.

NOTE

Note that in the preceding example, the login ID and password are provided to log in to the database server. By using a DHTML application, this information is compiled into the component rather than be visible inside the page when the user invokes the View, Source menu.

A Code Example

Listing 17.7 contains the code for the entire DHTMLPage object discussed in this section.

Listing 17.7   The Code for the DHTMLPage Object

```
Option Explicit

' Recordsets used to persist project and consultant data
' in the Web page
Private rsProj As ADODB.Recordset
Private rsCon As ADODB.Recordset

Private Sub InsertChild(ByVal pParentID As String, _
    ByVal pName As String, ByVal pPos As Long)

Dim strHTML As String
Dim objTemp As Object

' Build the div tag to place inside the child
' Note that the position of the record is embedded in the ID
strHTML = "<DIV ID=" & Mid(pParentID, 1, 1) & CStr(pPos) & ">" & _
    "  " & pName & "</DIV>"

' Get a reference to the parent div tag
Set objTemp = Document.All.Item(pParentID)

' Place the new tag inside the child
objTemp.children(0).insertAdjacentHTML "BeforeEnd", strHTML

End Sub

Private Function Consultants_onclick() As Boolean

    ' Expand or collapse tree
    ExpandCollapseTree

    ' Cancel the bubbling
    DHTMLEvent.cancelBubble = True

End Function

Private Sub DHTMLPage_Load()
```

```
    ' Get and display the projects
    InsertProjects

    ' Get and display the consultants
    InsertConsultants

End Sub

Private Sub ExpandCollapseTree()

Dim objElement As Object
Dim objChildDiv As Object

' Get a reference to the element for which the event was fired
Set objElement = DHTMLEvent.srcElement

' Get a reference to the child div
Set objChildDiv = objElement.children(0)

' If the child div is populated, toggle the display
If objChildDiv.children.length > 0 Then
    If objChildDiv.Style.display = "none" Then
        objChildDiv.Style.display = vbNullString
    Else
        objChildDiv.Style.display = "none"
    End If
End If

End Sub

Private Sub projchild_onmouseout()

    ' unhighlight the item
    DHTMLEvent.srcElement.Style.Color = vbWhite

    ' Cancel the bubbling
    DHTMLEvent.cancelBubble = True

End Sub

Private Sub projchild_onmouseover()

    ' Highlight the item
    DHTMLEvent.srcElement.Style.Color = vbYellow

    ' Display the project information
    DisplayProject CLng(Mid(BaseWindow.event.srcElement.id, 2))
```

continues

Listing 17.7   continued

```vb
    ' Cancel the bubbling
    DHTMLEvent.cancelBubble = True

End Sub

Private Function Projects_onclick() As Boolean

    ' Expand or collapse tree
    ExpandCollapseTree

    ' Cancel the bubbling
    DHTMLEvent.cancelBubble = True

End Function

Private Sub InsertProjects()

Dim cnCon As New ADODB.Connection
Dim strText As String

On Error GoTo InsProjErr

Set rsProj = New ADODB.Recordset

' Open a connection using the remote data provider
' This is a part of Remote Data Services
cnCon.Open "Provider=MS Remote;Remote Server=http://ssosa;" & _
    "Remote Provider=SQLOLEDB;database=contracker;", "sa", ""

' Execute the stored procedure
Set rsProj.ActiveConnection = cnCon
rsProj.Source = "exec GetProjects"
rsProj.Open

Do While Not rsProj.EOF
    ' Insert each child and pass it the absolute position so
    ' that it can be found again
    InsertChild "Projects", rsProj.Fields("Description"), _
        rsProj.AbsolutePosition
    rsProj.MoveNext
Loop

' Clean up
Set cnCon = Nothing

Exit Sub
InsProjErr:
```

```vb
        MsgBox "An error occurred: " & Err.Description, _
            vbCritical, Document.Title
        ' Clean up
        Set cnCon = Nothing

End Sub

Private Sub DisplayProject(ByVal pPos As Long)

Dim strHTML As String

On Error Resume Next

    ' Navigate to the record
    rsProj.AbsolutePosition = pPos

    ' Build the HTML
    strHTML = "<strong>Project View</strong>"
    strHTML = strHTML & "<HR>"

    strHTML = strHTML & "<strong>Code:</strong> " & _
        rsProj.Fields("Code") & "<BR>"
    strHTML = strHTML & "<strong>Description:</strong> " & _
        rsProj.Fields("Description") & "<BR>"
    strHTML = strHTML & "<strong>Company:</strong> " & _
        rsProj.Fields("Company") & "<BR>"
    strHTML = strHTML & "<strong>Contact:</strong> " & _
        rsProj.Fields("Contact") & "<BR>"
    strHTML = strHTML & "<strong>Phone:</strong> " & _
        rsProj.Fields("Phone") & "<BR>"
    strHTML = strHTML & "<strong>Start Date:</strong> " & _
        Format(rsProj.Fields("StartDate"), "mm/dd/yyyy") & "<BR>"
    strHTML = strHTML & "<strong>End Date:</strong> " & _
        Format(rsProj.Fields("EndDate"), "mm/dd/yyyy") & "<BR>"

    ' Replace the inner html of the data div
    Data.innerHTML = strHTML

End Sub

Private Sub InsertConsultants()

Dim cnCon As New ADODB.Connection
Dim strText As String

On Error GoTo InsConErr

Set rsCon = New ADODB.Recordset
```

continues

Listing 17.7   continued

```
' Open a connection using the remote data provider
' This is a part of Remote Data Services
cnCon.Open "Provider=MS Remote;Remote Server=http://ssosa;" & _
         "Remote Provider=SQLOLEDB;database=contracker;", "sa", ""

' Execute the stored procedure
Set rsCon.ActiveConnection = cnCon
rsCon.Source = "exec GetConsultants"
rsCon.Open

Do While Not rsCon.EOF
    ' Insert each child and pass it the absolute position so
    ' that it can be found again
    InsertChild "Consultants", rsCon.Fields("FName") & " " & _
        rsCon.Fields("LName"), rsCon.AbsolutePosition
    rsCon.MoveNext
Loop

' Clean up
Set cnCon = Nothing

Exit Sub
InsConErr:
    MsgBox "An error occurred: " & Err.Description, _
        vbCritical, Document.Title
    ' Clean up
    Set cnCon = Nothing

End Sub
```

Summary

In this chapter, you've looked at the two new project types supported in VB 6 that allow developers to create Web-based applications. These can be especially powerful for developers familiar with VB because they can leverage their existing knowledge and expertise with the IDE.

CHAPTER 18

Adding Professional Features

This chapter takes a look at various techniques commonly used by the corporate developers, including

- Working with the file system
- Manipulating the Registry
- Printing using the `Printer` object
- Sending and receiving email

Each of these topics deserves broader coverage than space permits. However, I've included the basics here because each can play an important role in building applications that are professional and useful.

In this chapter, you will first explore how to manipulate the file system and read and write text files using the `FileSystemObject`. Corporate developers often use techniques like those discussed in this chapter to add features such as auditing and text import of data. Next, you will dig down into the system Registry, using both the intrinsic VB functions and the Win32 API to create and retrieve data that your applications need to persist between sessions. In the section on printing, I'll cover the basic methods and properties of the `Printer` object and show an often used technique for providing native print preview capabilities in your application when that application must create complex output. Finally, you will explore using the Collaborative Data Objects (CDO) to add messaging functionality to your applications and discuss some scenarios in which using this technology is appropriate in corporate applications.

Although this is not by any means an exhaustive list of complementary techniques, this chapter is designed to provide a reminder of how to perform these basic tasks and of common scenarios for their use.

Using the FileSystem Object

Obtaining information about the file system and files has always been a tedious business for VB developers. This hasn't been a significant limitation for most corporate developers for two primary reasons. First, most corporate applications get their data from relational databases instead of files and as a result deal with files only peripherally to support tasks such as auditing, data import, and temporary persistence. Secondly, VB has always included, first, VBX and later, ActiveX controls that represent drives, directories, and files. However, dealing with the combination of intrinsic functions and controls sometimes proved awkward.

With the release of VB 6, much of this has changed, thanks to the addition of the `FileSystemObject`. This object is not intrinsic to the VB runtime, as are the previous file functions such as `FileLen`, `FileDateTime`, and `FileAttr`. The `FileSystemObject` is included in the Microsoft Scripting Runtime component in SCRRUN.DLL. A rudimentary version of this object (version 2.0 of the Scripting Runtime) has been available to VBScript developers developing ASP pages and can be downloaded from Microsoft's scripting site (`http://msdn.microsoft.com/scripting/`) and shipped with the Windows Scripting Host. The new version that ships with VB 6 is version 4.

The `FileSystemObject` contains collections of `Drives`, `Folders`, and `Files` that are arranged hierarchically, as shown in Figure 18.1. One of the nice features of the model, however, is that it is not strictly hierarchical in that the root object contains a series of methods prefixed with `Get` to obtain references to the underlying objects if their full path is known. In this way, you can easily create a reference to a folder or file with a single statement. Table 18.1 presents the important methods.

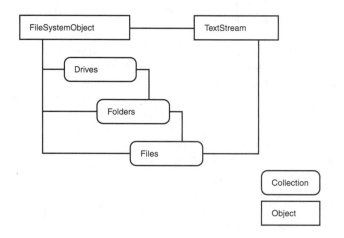

Figure 18.1

The object model of the FileSystemObject.

Table 18.1   Important Methods of the FileSystemObject

Method	Description
BuildPath	`String`. Returns a new path, given a path and a name to append to it. It correctly appends the new information given, using the correct separator, and does not check for the existence of either argument.
CopyFile and CopyFolder	Take arguments for source and destination, as well as an optional argument to overwrite files or folders if they already exist. These methods will raise trappable errors if arguments are not valid, and they do not return a result. Can reference network files using the UNC name.
CreateFolder	Returns a `Folder` object. Takes a relative or absolute path to create a folder. Will generate a trappable error if it fails because of permissions or invalid paths.
CreateTextFile	Returns a `TextStream` object that can be used to read and write to the file. Can optionally overwrite an existing file and create Unicode or ASCII files.
DeleteFile and DeleteFolder	Take the file path and a flag to force deletion in the event the file or folder is marked as read-only. Will generate a trappable error if the path is invalid. Can delete multiple files or folders.
DriveExists, FileExists, and FolderExists	`Boolean`. Determine whether the given file specification exists.
Drives	`Drives`. Returns a collection of `Drive` objects available to the local machine. Includes local and mapped drives.
GetAbsolutePathName	`String`. Returns the unambiguous path (a complete path that includes the drive), given a path specification. The path specification can contain wildcards or partial paths.
GetBaseName	`String`. Returns the name of a folder, file, or drive without any extension or path.
GetFile, GetDrive, and GetFolder	Return a File object, Drive object, or Folder object, respectively, given a file or path specification.
GetDriveName, GetFileName, GetParentFolderName, and GetExtensionName	`String`. Parse the given path, and specification and return the appropriate part of the specification. These do not verify the existence of the path and are akin to string manipulation functions. Return zero-length string if no match can be found.
GetSpecialFolder	`Folder`. Given a constant, returns a reference to the system folder. 0 = WindowsFolder, 1 = SystemFolder, 2 = `Temporary Folder`.

continues

Table 18.1   continued

Method	Description
GetTempName	String. Returns a randomly generated temporary file-name that can be used to store temporary data. Does not create the file.
MoveFile and MoveFolder	Take arguments for source and destination, as well as an optional argument to overwrite files or folders if they already exist. These methods will raise trappable errors if arguments are not valid, and they do not return a result. Can reference network files using the UNC name.
OpenTextFile	TextStream. Opens or creates a file, given the argument's filename, mode (1 = ForReading, 2 = ForWriting, 8 = ForAppending), an optional flag specifying whether to create the file if it does not exist, and format. The format can be −2 = TriStateUseDefault, −1 = TristateTrue (Unicode), 0 = TristateFalse (ASCII).

Opening and Writing Files

The FileSystemObject can be used to create, read, and write to sequential text files in either Unicode or ASCII format. After a file is referenced using either the OpenTextFile or CreateTextFile methods referenced in Table 18.1, a TextStream is created to refer to the open file. This object contains the properties and methods for reading or writing to the file, shown in Table 18.2.

Table 18.2   Important Properties and Methods of the TextStream Object

Member	Description
Properties	
AtEndOfLine and AtEndOfStream	Boolean. Specify whether the pointer is at the end of the current line of file.
Column	Long. Returns the column number position of the current pointer in the file.
Line	Long. Returns the line number position of the current pointer in the file.
Methods	
Close	Closes an open TextStream object.
Read, ReadLine, and ReadAll	String. Return either the next *n* characters as specified in the argument, the entire line excluding the newline character, or the entire file, respectively.
Skip and SkipLine	Skip the next *n* characters as specified in the argument or the entire next line, respectively.

Member	Description
`Write` and `WriteLine`	Given a string, `Write` writes the string to the file, and WriteLine appends a newline character.
`WriteBlankLines`	Given a `Long` value, creates blank lines in the file by appending newline characters.

You will find typical examples of writing to and reading from text files using the `FileSystemObject` in Listings 18.1 and 18.2. Listing 18.1 shows how an application can write an event log to a text file as events occur in the application. This allows the developer to inspect the audit file in the case of error reports or to analyze the usage of the application. The code to write to the event log can be encapsulated in a procedure, `LogEvent`, that uses the `OpenTextFile` method and the `TextStream` object to writeuser, timing, and even event-specific data to the log.

Listing 18.1   Opening and Writing to a Text File to Log Event Information for Your Application

```
Option Explicit
Private objFileSystem As New FileSystemObject

Public Sub LogEvent(ByVal strLogFile As String, _
    ByVal strEventName As String, ByVal strEventText As String, _
    ByVal strEventData as String, ByVal strUserName As String)

Dim objText As TextStream
Dim strLogString As String

On Error GoTo LogEventErr

' Open the existing file or create a new
' file if not present
Set objText = objFileSystem.OpenTextFile(strLogFile, _
    ForAppending, True, TristateFalse)

' Create and format a tab-delimited entry in the log
strLogString = CStr(Format(Date, "mm/dd/yyyy")) & " " & _
    CStr(Format(Time, "hh:mm:ss")) & vbTab & strEventName & _
    vbTab & strEventText & vbTab & strUserName & vbTab & strEventData

' Write the event to a new line
objText.WriteLine strLogString

' Close the file
objText.Close
Set objText = Nothing

Exit Sub
LogEventErr:
```

continues

```
' Raise an error back to the calling program
Err.Raise vbObjectError+6000, "LogEvent", _
    Err.Description & ". Event was not logged."

End Sub
```

Listing 18.2 shows a common usage for reading from a comma-delimited text file using a procedure named `LoadTreeArray` and loading an array of UDTs with the results. This is excerpted from an example shown in Chapter 12, "Using TreeView and ListView Controls." Note that the `ParseTreeData` private procedure takes the comma-delimited string and returns the next data item in the string. This procedure is the functional equivalent of using the `Split` function included in VB 6. I've included the older method here for those developers who might need a more flexible solution or who are working with older versions of VB.

TIP

The `LogEvent` method, as well as the properties `LogMode` and `LogPath` of the `App` object, can also be used to log messages to a file. Its strength is its versatility because it can overwrite the file each time the application starts and optionally log on to the Windows NT Event Viewer if your application is running on Windows NT.

Listing 18.2   Reading a Comma-Delimited Text File Using the
FileSystemObject—the Results Are Loaded into an Array of UDTs

```
Option Explicit
Private objFileSystem As New FileSystemObject

Private TreeItems() As TreeData

' Type declaration for tracking
Private Type TreeData
    Caption As String
    Key As String
    Parent As String
    URL As String
    Frame As String
    Folder As Boolean
    NodeIndex As Long
End Type


Public Sub LoadTreeArray(ByVal pstrFileName As String)

Dim objText As TextStream
Dim strData As String
Dim i As Integer


' Check to see whether the file exists
If Not objFileSystem.FileExists(pstrFileName) Then
```

```
        Err.Raise vbObjectError+6001, "LoadTree", "File does not exist"
        Exit Sub
    End If

    ' Open the text file for reading
    Set objText = objFileSystem.OpenTextFile(pstrFileName, _
        ForReading, False, TristateFalse)

    ' Clear the array
    Erase TreeItems

    'Load the array of structures
    Do While Not objText.AtEndOfStream
        On Error GoTo ReDimErr
        ReDim Preserve TreeItems(UBound(TreeItems) + 1)

        On Error GoTo LoadArrayErr
        i = UBound(TreeItems)
        strData = objText.ReadLine

        With TreeItems(i)
          .Caption = ParseTreeData(strData)
          .Key = ParseTreeData(strData)
          .Parent = ParseTreeData(strData)
          .URL = ParseTreeData(strData)
          .Frame = ParseTreeData(strData)
          .Folder = ParseTreeData(strData)
        End With
    Loop

    objText.Close
    Set objText = Nothing

    Exit Sub
    ReDimErr:
        ReDim TreeItems(0)
        Resume Next
        Exit Sub

    LoadArrayErr:
        Err.Raise vbObjectError+6002, "LoadTreeArray", Err.Description

End Sub

Private Function ParseTreeData(pstrData As String)

' This function chops off the next value and returns
' it through the function
```

continues

```
Dim strWorking As String

' If there is no delimiter, assume that the rest of the string is it
If InStr(1, pstrData, ",") = 0 Then
    strWorking = pstrData
    pstrData = vbNullString
Else
    strWorking = Mid(pstrData, 1, InStr(1, pstrData, ",") - 1)
    pstrData = Mid(pstrData, InStr(1, pstrData, ",") + 1)
End If

ParseTreeData = strWorking

End Function
```

Displaying Folders and Files

In addition to working with text files directly, the `FileSystemObject` provides collections of `File` and `Folder` objects that allow you to traverse and inspect files in the file system. These collections are populated with all the local and mapped drives on the local computer. The properties and methods for the `File` and `Folder` objects themselves are quite similar and are listed in Table 18.3.

Table 18.3   Important Properties and Methods of the File and Folder Objects

Member	Description
Properties	
Attributes	FileAttribute. Bit mask that specifies the attributes that are set on a file or folder. Most common bits set are 1 = ReadOnly, 2 = Hidden, 4 = System, 64 = Alias, 128 = Compressed. If multiple attributes are set, use the And keyword to extract.
DateCreated, DataLastAccessed, and DateLastModified	Date. Return the date and time the file or folder was created, last accessed, or modified, respectively.
Drive	String. Returns the drive letter on which the file or folder resides.
Name	String. Returns the name of the file or folder.
ParentFolder	Folder. Returns a reference to the Folder object in which the file or folder resides.
Path	String. Returns the full path of the file or folder, including drive letter or network path.
ShortName	String. Returns the DOS 8.3 name of the file or folder.
ShortPath	String. Returns the DOS 8.3 full path of the file or folder, including the drive letter or network path.

Size	`Variant`. Returns the size of the file in bytes. For folders, returns the size of the data contained in the folder in bytes.
Type	`String`. Returns the registered Windows type description (also displayed in the Windows Explorer). If no type is registered, `File` is returned.

Methods

Copy	Takes a destination path and flag to specify whether to overwrite the file or folder if it exists. Will raise a trappable error if the file or folder cannot be copied.
Delete	Deletes the file or folder and takes an optional argument to force the deletion if the file or folder is read-only. Will raise a trappable error if the method fails (for example, a permissions violation).
Move	Takes a destination argument and moves the file or folder (a `copy` and then `delete`). Cannot use wildcards in the destination but can use a relative path.
OpenAsTextStream	`TextStream`. Valid only for the `File` object. Returns a `TextStream` object to allow reading and writing the file. Takes arguments for specifying the I/O mode (reading, writing, appending) and the format (Unicode, ASCII, system default).
Files	`Files`. Returns the collection of files in the specified folder.
IsRootFolder	`Boolean`. Valid only for the `Folder` object and returns `True` if the folder is the root of a drive.
SubFolders	`Folders`. Valid only for the `Folder` object and returns a collection of folders that are contained in the given folder.
CreateTextFile	`TextStream`. Valid only for the `Folder` object. Creates a new file in the folder and optionally overwrites the file if it exists. Takes arguments to specify the name and format of the file.

Using the `Files` and `Folders` collections of the `FileSystemObject` is a relatively simple operation. After you determine the path at which to start, your code can navigate through the directory structure using the `For...Each` syntax with the `SubFolders` and `Files` collections of the `Folder` and `File` objects, respectively. A typical use of these collections is to display files and folders in a `ListView` control, which can be seen in Listing 18.3. Figure 18.2 shows the resulting window.

Listing 18.3   The DisplayPath Procedure That Traverses a Given Path and Loads a ListView Control

```
Option Explicit
Private objFileSystem As FileSystemObject
```

continues

```
Private Sub DisplayPath(ByVal strPath As String)
Dim objFolder As Folder
Dim objSubFolder As Folder
Dim objFile As File
Dim objItem As ListItem

' Check for the existence of the path
If Not objFileSystem.FolderExists(strPath) Then
    Err.Raise vbObjectError+6003, "DisplayPath", _
        "Path " & strPath & " does not exist."
    Exit Sub
End If

' Set a reference to the folder
Set objFolder = objFileSystem.GetFolder(strPath)

' Traverse the folders and load them in the ListView control
For Each objSubFolder In objFolder.SubFolders
    Set objItem = lvFileObjects.ListItems.Add(, , _
        objSubFolder.Name, "closed", "closed")
    objItem.SubItems(1) = Format(objSubFolder.Size, "#,###")
    objItem.SubItems(2) = objSubFolder.Type
    objItem.SubItems(3) = objSubFolder.ShortName
    ' Folders without a created date are set to 1/1/80
    If objSubFolder.DateCreated <> "1/1/80" Then
        objItem.SubItems(4) = objSubFolder.DateCreated
    End If
    objItem.SubItems(5) = objSubFolder.DateLastModified
    objItem.SubItems(6) = objSubFolder.DateLastAccessed
Next

' Traverse the files and load them in the ListView control
For Each objFile In objFolder.Files
    Set objItem = lvFileObjects.ListItems.Add(, , _
        objFile.Name, "leaf", "leaf")
    objItem.SubItems(1) = Format(objFile.Size, "#,###")
    objItem.SubItems(2) = objFile.Type
    objItem.SubItems(3) = objFile.ShortName
    ' Files without a created date are set to 1/1/80
    If objFile.DateCreated <> "1/1/80" Then
        objItem.SubItems(4) = objFile.DateCreated
    End If
    objItem.SubItems(5) = objFile.DateLastModified
    objItem.SubItems(6) = objFile.DateLastAccessed
Next

End Sub
```

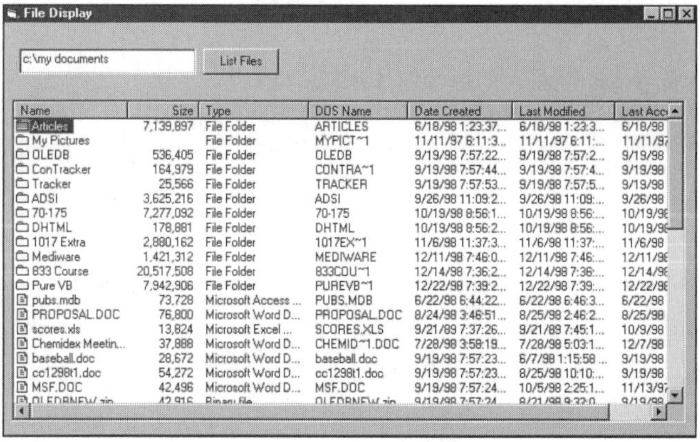

Figure 18.2

The resulting ListView control from Listing 18.3, displaying the files and folders of a given path.

Searching for Files

Although the `FileSystemObject` can be used to display files and folders, its real power is evident when your applications need to implement file manipulation functions absent a user interface. One example of this is implementing a file search method in a class module that can be used in multiple projects.

The class module in Listing 18.4 implements a public method named `FindFile` that takes as arguments the prefix of the filename to find and the path at which to start the search. The method returns a collection of `File` objects that match the search string. Internally, `FindFile` validates the starting path using the `FolderExists` method, obtains a reference to the folder, and passes the `Folder` object to a private procedure named `SearchFolder`. `SearchFolder` then traverses each subfolder, calling itself recursively. It then traverses the `Files` collection in the folder and adds them to the collection if a match is found.

Listing 18.4   The Class Module Used to Implement a Recursive Search for Files Matching a Given Specification

```
Option Explicit
Private objFileSystem As New FileSystemObject
Private objFilesFound As New Collection

Public Function FindFile(ByVal strFileName As String, _
    ByVal strStartPath As String) As Collection

Dim objFolder As Folder
Dim objSubFolder As Folder
Dim objFile As File
```

continues

```
Dim objItem As ListItem

' Check for the existence of the starting path
If Not objFileSystem.FolderExists(strStartPath) Then
    Err.Raise vbObjectError+6004, "FindFile", _
        "Start path does not exist"
    Set FindFile = Nothing
    Exit Function
End If

' Get a reference to the starting folder
Set objFolder = objFileSystem.GetFolder(strStartPath)

' Search the folders recursively
SearchFolder objFolder, strFileName

' Return the collection of file objects
Set FindFile = objFilesFound

End Function

Private Sub SearchFolder(ByVal objFolder As Folder, _
    ByVal strFileName As String)

Dim objSubFolder As Folder
Dim objFile As File

On Error GoTo SearchFolder

' Traverse the subfolder in the given folder
For Each objSubFolder In objFolder.SubFolders
    ' Call this procedure recursively
    SearchFolder objSubFolder, strFileName
Next

' Traverse the files in the folder and look for matches
For Each objFile In objFolder.Files
    If Mid(objFile.Name, 1, Len(strFileName)) = strFileName Then
        ' Match! Add it to the collection
        objFilesFound.Add objFile
    End If
Next
Exit Sub
SearchFolder:
    ' Raise an error back to the calling program
    Err.Raise vbObjectError+6005, "SearchFolder", Err.Description

End Sub
```

The following code uses this class module and calls it:

```
Dim clsFileFunctions As New FileFunctions
Dim objFiles As New Collection
Dim objFile As File

'Search for the file specification
Set objFiles = clsFileFunctions.FindFile(txtPath.Text, "c:\")

' Add the results to a list box
For Each objFile In objFiles
    lstFiles.AddItem objFile.Path
Next
```

Querying Drives

The final object supplied by the `FileSystemObject` is the `Drive` object. This object contains no methods and only properties that provide information about the local or network drives, such as the available free space and file system. Table 18.4 presents the properties.

Table 18.4 Important Properties of the Drive Object

Property	Description
AvailableSpace	`Variant`. Returns the number of unused bytes on the drive.
DriveLetter	`String`. The drive letter used for the drive on the local machine.
DriveType	`DriveType`. Returns the type of drive (0 = Unknown, 1 = Removable, 2 = Fixed, 3 = Remote, 4 = CDROM, 5 = RAM Disk). Drives on other machines always appear as Remote even though they may in fact be Fixed, for example.
FileSystem	`String`. The file system of the drive, typically FAT, NTFS, or CDFS.
FreeSpace	`Variant`. Returns the number of unused bytes on the disk.
IsReady	`Boolean`. Specifies whether the drive is ready for reading. Applies primarily to CDROM and Removable drives.
Path	`String`. The drive name followed by a colon.
RootFolder	`Folder`. Returns a reference to the `Folder` object at the root of the drive. Can be used to traverse the drive.
ShareName	`String`. If it's a network drive, the UNC name (\\computer-name\share).
TotalSize	`Variant`. The total number of bytes on the drive.

The primary use of the `Drive` object is to check for available space on the drive before attempting to save data. For example, the code in Listing 18.5 shows the function `IsThereRoom`, which, when passed in a drive letter and the amount of space needed, returns a `Boolean` value and optionally how many bytes are free on the drive.

Listing 18.5   The IsThereRoom Function, Which Calculates Available Space on a Given Drive

```
Public Function IsThereRoom(ByVal strDrive As String, _
    ByVal varFileSize As Variant, _
    Optional varBytesFree As Variant) As Boolean

Dim objDrive As Drive

Dim lvarbytes As Variant
On Error GoTo IsThereRoomErr

' Obtain a reference to the Drive object
Set objDrive = objFileSystem.GetDrive(strDrive)

' Check to make sure drive is ready
If Not objDrive.IsReady Then
    Err.Raise vbObjectError+6006, "IsThereRoom", _
        "Drive is not ready. Place media in drive."
    IsThereRoom = False
    Exit Function
End If

' Return how many bytes are free on the drive
lvarbytes = objDrive.AvailableSpace

' Only return the value if it has been supplied
If Not IsMissing(varBytesFree) Then
    varBytesFree = lvarbytes
End If

' Check to see whether enough space is there
If varFileSize < lvarbytes Then
    IsThereRoom = True
Else
    IsThereRoom = False
End If

Exit Function
IsThereRoomErr:
    ' Raise an error back to the client
    Err.Raise vbObjectError+6006, "IsThereRoom", Err.Description
    IsThereRoom = False

End Function
```

Storing Settings in the Registry

To be good Windows citizens, most Visual Basic applications store some information persistently between sessions. In this way, the application can reconstruct the environment the user was working with and the state of any user interface elements that were manipulated.

Before Windows 9x and Windows NT, this information was stored in text-based INI files that could be manipulated using the Win32 API functions `GetProfileString`, `WriteProfileString`, `GetPrivateProfileString`, `WritePrivateProfileString`, and so on. Although some applications might still require this method (for example, when the user needs to be able to easily modify the information), most can now use the Windows Registry to centralize the storage of user settings.

Simply put, the *Registry* is a systemwide hierarchical database made up of keys and values. Each key can contain subkeys and/or values. *Values* are the actual data, which consists of a value name and value data that can be stored as either a text string, binary string, or long integer. Table 18.5 shows the top-level keys.

Table 18.5   High-Level Keys in the Registry

Key	Description
HKEY_CLASSES_ROOT	Stores file associations and COM globally unique identifiers (GUIs) that the COM Library uses to find and invoke components. This is an alias of HKEY_LOCAL_MACHINE\ Software\Classes.
HKEY_CURRENT_CONFIG	Stores the current hardware profile in use by the computer. This is an alias to HKEY_LOCAL_MACHINE\ SYSTEM\CurrentControlSet\Hardware Profiles\Current.
HKEY_CURRENT_USER	Stores all the user-specific information for the user currently logged on to the system. This is an alias for HKEY_USERS_user_. This is where VB programs should store user-specific information.
HKEY_DYN_DATA	A temporary key that exists in RAM and is used to configure plug and play devices.
HKEY_LOCAL_MACHINE	Stores all the information about the local machine, both hardware and software.
HKEY_USERS	Stores keys for each defined user on the system that stores user-specific information.

NOTE

In Windows NT, you can also store data in expandable string and multistring formats. Windows NT also allows data up to 1MB in size, whereas Windows 9x allows only 64KB in each data value.

Using Intrinsic Registry Functions

As noted in Table 18.5, VB applications should store user-specific settings in the HKEY_CURRENT_USER key. To make this simple, VB provides four Registry manipulation functions (shown in Table 18.6) to read, write, and delete settings from keys in HKEY_CURRENT_USER. To guard against security problems and potential corruption of

the Registry, these functions have been hard-wired to manipulate only the HKEY_CUR-
RENT_USER\Software\VB and VBA Program Settings key.

The provided Registry functions also use the terminology of INI files instead of the
Registry because they were developed to use both 16-bit INI files and the Registry in
VB 4.0. Specifically, the appname argument used in the functions in Table 18.6 refers
to the key directly underneath the VB and VBA Program Settings key, *section* refers to
the subkey underneath appname and can include multiple keys in the hierarchy separated by a \, and *key* refers to the value to be stored.

Table 18.6   Registry Manipulation Functions

Function	Description
DeleteSetting	Deletes keys or values from the Registry. Can delete all the settings for the application.
GetAllSettings	Retrieves all the values from a key, given the appname and section. It returns the results in a two-dimensional variant array of strings.
GetSetting	Retrieves a value from the Registry, given the appname, sec- tion, and key, and optionally a default value if the value does not exist. If no default is specified, it returns an empty string.

The most common usage of the Registry is to store user-specific settings including
information such as form placement and size, username, and a reference to the data the
user has recently worked with. To make this process easier, I developed two procedures, SaveStandardSettings and LoadStandardSettings (shown in Listing 18.6).
These take as arguments a variant that holds a two-dimensional array of name-value
pairs to store in the Registry and an optional argument to reference a Form object to
store its position and size. Sample code to use the functions in the Load and Unload
events of a form appears in Listing 18.7, with the results in the Registry shown in
Figure 18.3.

Listing 18.6   Functions to Read and Write Standard Settings to the Registry

```
Public Sub SaveStandardSettings(varData As Variant, _
    Optional objForm As Form)

Dim i As Integer

On Error GoTo SaveErr

' Loop through array and save values using
' SaveSetting
For i = 0 To UBound(varData, 1)
    SaveSetting App.ProductName, "Settings", CStr(varData(i, 0)), _
```

```
        CStr(varData(i, 1))
Next


' Check to make sure the form is passed
If Not IsMissing(objForm) Then
    ' Save the standard form settings
    SaveSetting App.ProductName, "Position", "Left", objForm.Left
    SaveSetting App.ProductName, "Position", "Top", objForm.Top
    SaveSetting App.ProductName, "Position", "Width", objForm.Width
    SaveSetting App.ProductName, "Position", "Height", objForm.Height
End If


Exit Sub
SaveErr:
    ' Raise an error back to the caller
    Err.Raise vbObjectError+7000, "SaveStandardSettings", Err.Description


End Sub


Public Sub LoadStandardSettings(varData As Variant, _
    Optional objForm As Form)
Dim i As Integer


On Error GoTo LoadErr


' Load the entire key into the array
varData = GetAllSettings(App.ProductName, "Settings")


' Check to make sure that the form is passed
If Not IsMissing(objForm) Then
    ' Load and set the standard form settings
    objForm.Left = GetSetting(App.ProductName, "Position", "Left",
objForm.Left)
    objForm.Top = GetSetting(App.ProductName, "Position", "Top", objForm.Top)
    objForm.Width = GetSetting(App.ProductName, "Position", "Width",
objForm.Width)
    objForm.Height = GetSetting(App.ProductName, "Position", "Height",
objForm.Height)
End If


Exit Sub
LoadErr:
    ' Raise an error back to the caller
    Err.Raise vbObjectError+7001, "LoadStandardSettings", Err.Description


End Sub
```

TIP

The procedures in Listing 18.6 use the `App.ProductName` value as the key to save the data. This value is usually more readable and unique than `App.EXEName` but must be set on the Project Properties dialog box in the Make tab under Version Information. If this value is not set, a trappable error will occur.

Listing 18.7   The Code to Call the SaveStandardSettings and LoadStandardSettings Procedures

```
Option Explicit
Private varRegData As Variant


Private Sub Form_Load()

' Load the settings from the Registry
' to resize and place the form
LoadStandardSettings varRegData, Me

End Sub
Private Sub Form_Unload(Cancel As Integer)

' Sample code to load the variant array with
' data to save in the Registry
varRegData(0, 0) = "File1"
varRegData(0, 1) = "c:\hello.txt"
varRegData(1, 0) = "File2"
varRegData(1, 1) = "c:\hello1.txt"
varRegData(2, 0) = "File3"
varRegData(2, 1) = "c:\hello2.txt"
varRegData(3, 0) = "File4"
varRegData(3, 1) = "c:\hello3.txt"

varRegData(4, 0) = "User"
varRegData(4, 1) = "dfox"

' Save the data
SaveStandardSettings varRegData, Me

End Sub
```

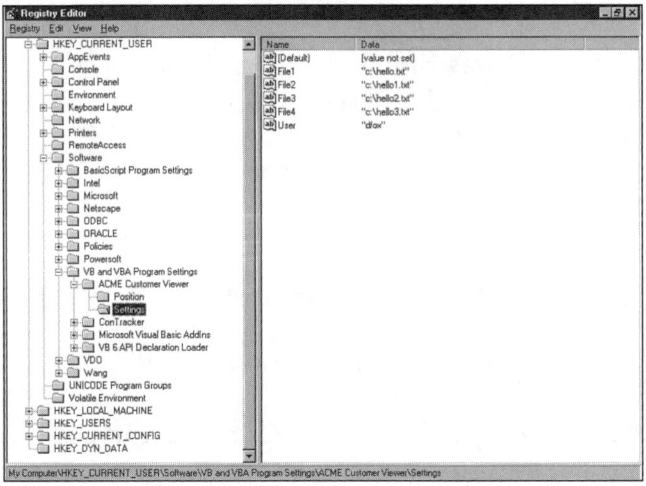

Figure 18.3

The Registry viewed with Regedit.exe, showing the Registry values saved by the code in Listing 18.7.

Using the Win32 API Registry Functions

Although the intrinsic VB functions for manipulating the Registry are sufficient for most applications, they are somewhat limited in their functionality. For example, the functions discussed previously can manipulate only the key HKEY_CURRENT_USER\Software\VB and VBA Program Settings. This limitation is especially frustrating because settings cannot then be shared between users on the same system. In addition, the functions cannot assign or read the default value that can be assigned to each key and can work only with text strings.

As a result of these and other limitations, you will sometimes have to use the Win32 API functions that were designed to manipulate the Registry.

WARNING

Keep in mind that because the Registry is used to store configuration information for all aspects of the system, using the API functions improperly can have serious consequences. Make sure that you back up the Registry on your development system before working with these functions.

The functions most frequently used are those listed in Table 18.7. A typical example of using these functions can be seen in Listing 18.8, in which they are used with the procedures SaveMachineSettings and LoadMachineSettings to store and retrieve information that is necessary for all users of the application—such as a central server's IP address and database platform.

Table 18.7   Win32 API Registry Manipulation Functions

Function	Description
RegCloseKey	Given a handle to an open key, the function closes it.
RegCreateKeyEx	Creates the specified key and returns a handle to it in the parameter `phkResult`. If the key already exists, it simply returns the handle of the key.
RegDeleteKey	Given the handle to a subkey, it deletes it. Under Windows 9x, it deletes all descendants, but under Windows NT, the subkey cannot have descendants.
RegQueryValueEx	Retrieves the data type and value for a specified value name, given an open key handle.
RegSetValueEx	Sets the data type and value for a specified value name, given an open key handle.

Listing 18.8   The Code to Use the Win32 API Functions to Manipulate the Registry

```
Option Explicit

Public Declare Function RegCreateKeyEx Lib "advapi32.dll" _
    Alias "RegCreateKeyExA" (ByVal hKey As Long, _
    ByVal lpSubKey As String, ByVal Reserved As Long, _
    ByVal lpClass As String, ByVal dwOptions As Long, _
    ByVal samDesired As Long, _
    lpSecurityAttributes As SECURITY_ATTRIBUTES, _
    phkResult As Long, lpdwDisposition As Long) As Long

Public Declare Function RegOpenKeyEx Lib "advapi32.dll" _
    Alias "RegOpenKeyExA" (ByVal hKey As Long, _
    ByVal lpSubKey As String, ByVal ulOptions As Long, _
    ByVal samDesired As Long, phkResult As Long) As Long

Public Declare Function RegCloseKey Lib "advapi32.dll" _
    (ByVal hKey As Long) As Long

' This declaration has been modified to accept VB strings
Public Declare Function RegSetValueExStr Lib "advapi32.dll" _
    Alias "RegSetValueExA" (ByVal hKey As Long, _
    ByVal lpValueName As String, ByVal Reserved As Long, _
    ByVal dwType As Long, ByVal lpData As String, _
    ByVal cbData As Long) As Long

' This declaration has been modified to accept VB strings
Public Declare Function RegQueryValueExStr Lib "advapi32.dll" _
    Alias "RegQueryValueExA" (ByVal hKey As Long, _
    ByVal lpValueName As String, ByVal lpReserved As Long, _
    lpType As Long, ByVal lpData As String, lpcbData As Long) As Long
```

```
Public Declare Function RegDeleteKey Lib "advapi32.dll" _
    Alias "RegDeleteKeyA" (ByVal hKey As Long, _
    ByVal lpSubKey As String) As Long

Public Const HKEY_LOCAL_MACHINE = &H80000002

Public Const STANDARD_RIGHTS_ALL = &H1F0000
Public Const READ_CONTROL = &H20000
Public Const STANDARD_RIGHTS_READ = (READ_CONTROL)
Public Const REG_SZ = 1
Public Const ERROR_SUCCESS = 0&
Public Const KEY_QUERY_VALUE = &H1
Public Const KEY_SET_VALUE = &H2
Public Const KEY_CREATE_LINK = &H20
Public Const KEY_CREATE_SUB_KEY = &H4
Public Const KEY_ENUMERATE_SUB_KEYS = &H8
Public Const KEY_NOTIFY = &H10
Public Const SYNCHRONIZE = &H100000
Public Const REG_OPTION_NON_VOLATILE = 0
Public Const KEY_ALL_ACCESS = ((STANDARD_RIGHTS_ALL Or _
    KEY_QUERY_VALUE Or KEY_SET_VALUE Or KEY_CREATE_SUB_KEY Or _
    KEY_ENUMERATE_SUB_KEYS Or KEY_NOTIFY Or KEY_CREATE_LINK) And _
    (Not SYNCHRONIZE))
Public Const KEY_READ = ((STANDARD_RIGHTS_READ Or _
    KEY_QUERY_VALUE Or KEY_ENUMERATE_SUB_KEYS Or KEY_NOTIFY) _
    And (Not SYNCHRONIZE))

Public Type SECURITY_ATTRIBUTES
        nLength As Long
        lpSecurityDescriptor As Long
        bInheritHandle As Long
End Type


Public Sub SaveMachineSettings(ByVal strTCPAddress As String, _
    strDBPlatform As String)

Dim hKey As Long
Dim lngDisposition As Long
Dim lngRet As Long
Dim lngRet1 As Long
Dim lngRet2 As Long
Dim sec As SECURITY_ATTRIBUTES

' Open or create the Registry key
lngRet = RegCreateKeyEx(HKEY_LOCAL_MACHINE, "Software\" & _
    App.ProductName, 0, vbNull, REG_OPTION_NON_VOLATILE, _
```

continues

```
        KEY_ALL_ACCESS, sec, hKey, lngDisposition)

' Save the values
If lngRet = ERROR_SUCCESS Then
    lngRet1 = RegSetValueExStr(hKey, "ServerAddress", 0, _
        REG_SZ, strTCPAddress, Len(strTCPAddress) + 1)

    lngRet2 = RegSetValueExStr(hKey, "DBPlatform", 0, _
        REG_SZ, strDBPlatform, Len(strDBPlatform) + 1)

    If lngRet2 <> ERROR_SUCCESS Or lngRet1 <> ERROR_SUCCESS Then
        GoTo SaveErr
    End If

    ' Close the open key
    RegCloseKey hKey
Else
    GoTo SaveErr
End If


Exit Sub
SaveErr:
    ' Close the open key
    If hKey <> 0 Then
        RegCloseKey hKey
    End If
    Err.Raise vbObjectError + 8000, "SaveMachineSettings", _
        "Registry settings could not be saved."

End Sub

Public Sub LoadMachineSettings(strTCPAddress As String, _
    strDBPlatform As String)

Dim hKey As Long
Dim lngDisposition As Long
Dim lngRet As Long
Dim lngRet1 As Long
Dim lngRet2 As Long
Dim lngType As Long
Dim strValue As String
Dim lngLen As Long


' Open Registry key
lngRet = RegOpenKeyEx(HKEY_LOCAL_MACHINE, "Software\" & _
    App.ProductName, 0, KEY_READ, hKey)
```

```
' Read the values
If lngRet = ERROR_SUCCESS Then
    ' Create a buffer to store the value
    strValue = Space(255)
    lngLen = 255
    lngRet1 = RegQueryValueExStr(hKey, "ServerAddress", 0, _
        lngType, strValue, lngLen)
    strTCPAddress = Left(strValue, lngLen - 1)

    ' Create a buffer to store the value
    strValue = Space(255)
    lngLen = 255
    lngRet2 = RegQueryValueExStr(hKey, "DBPlatform", 0, _
        lngType, strValue, lngLen)
    strDBPlatform = Left(strValue, lngLen - 1)

    If lngRet2 <> ERROR_SUCCESS Or lngRet1 <> ERROR_SUCCESS Then
        GoTo LoadErr
    End If

    ' Close the open key
    RegCloseKey hKey
Else
    GoTo LoadErr
End If

Exit Sub
LoadErr:
    ' Close the open key
    If hKey <> 0 Then
        RegCloseKey hKey
    End If
    Err.Raise vbObjectError + 8001, "LoadMachineSettings", _
        "Registry settings could not be loaded."

End Sub
```

As you will note in Listing 18.8, the SaveMachineSettings procedure takes the two arguments, a TCP/IP address for the server and a database platform name, as arguments to the procedure. It then uses the RegCreateKeyEx API function to create or retrieve the registry key (named using the ProductName property of the App object) under the HKEY_LOCAL_MACHINE entry. Note that by placing the entries under this key rather than KEY_CURRENT_USER, all users will have access to the settings. The RegSetValueExStr is then used to create the two values under the newly created key. Finally the RegCloseKey function is used to close the registry key.

The `LoadMachineSettings` function works much the same way by using the `RegOpenKeyEx` function to open the registry key and the `RegQueryValueExStr` function to read the two values from the key. Note that as with many Win32 API functions, the `RegQueryValueExStr` function requires that a buffer be created and passed to the function to hold the returned value.

TIP

If you find that you commonly require access to the API Registry manipulation functions, a better approach might be to use one of the encapsulation techniques discussed in Chapter 13, "Using Win32 API Techniques." These techniques will make your code more readable and save development time in the long run.

Using the Printer Object

Most of the printing requirements for business applications written in VB (up to 90% in my experience) can be satisfied using third-party report writers such as Crystal Reports or the new Data Report Designer available in VB 6. However, occasionally the application requirements call for printing data that is not pulled directly from a database or must be formatted in ways that are not easy to do with banded report writers.

To address these issues, VB developers can use the intrinsic `Printers` collection and the `Printer` object and its graphics methods to control printers and send output to a print device. Although this technique is often tedious and time-consuming, it provides maximum control of the printed page. Table 18.8 contains the key properties and methods of the `Printer` object.

Table 18.8   Key Properties and Methods of the Printer Object

Member	Description
Properties	
ColorMode	Long. Specifies whether color printers print in color mode (1 = vbPRCMMonochrome, 2 = vbPRCColor).
CurrentX and CurrentY	Long. Specify the coordinates for the next output to the printer. Units are determined by the `ScaleMode` property.
Copies	Long. Specifies the number of copies to be printed.
DrawWidth	Long. Specifies the width of lines drawn using the graphics methods in pixels, with the default being 1 pixel.
DrawStyle	Long. Specifies the style of the lines drawn using the graphics methods. If `DrawWidth` is greater than 1, this property is ignored. Valid settings are (0 = vbSolid, 1 = vbDash, 2 = vbDot, 3 = vbDashDot, 4 = vbDashDotDot, 5 = vbInvisible, 6 = vbInsideSolid).
DriverName and DeviceName	String. Return the name of the driver and device currently targeted, respectively.

Member	Description
Duplex	Long. Specifies whether output is printed to both sides of a page (1 = vbPRDSimplex, 2 = vbPRDHorizontal, 3 = vbPRDVertical).
FillColor	Long. Specifies the RGB color value or VB constant to use when filling in shapes created with the graphics methods.
FillStyle	Long. Specifies the pattern used to fill in shapes created with the graphics methods. Most common settings are 0 = vbFSSolid and 1 = vbFSTransparent.
FontTransparent	Boolean. If True, allows background graphics to show behind text output to the printer.
Fonts, Font, of FontSize, FondBold, FontItalic, FontStrikeThru, FontUnderline, FontName,FontCount	Properties that enumerate, set, and change the properties the current font that will be used to display printed text.
hDC	Long. Returns a handle to the device context used by the operating system. Can be used in API calls to manipulate the output.
Orientation	Long. Specifies whether the page is printed in landscape or portrait (1 = vbPRORPortrait 2 = vbPRORLandscape).
Page	Long. Returns the current page number.
PaperSize	Long. Specifies one of 41 different page sizes that may be available for the print device. This property affects and is affected by the Width and Height properties.
Port	String. Returns the name of the port the document will print on, for example, LPT1.
PrintQuality	Long. Specifies the resolution to use (−1 = vbPRPQDraft, −2 = vbPRPQLow, −3 = vbPRPQMedium, −4 = vbPRPQHigh).
ScaleHeight and ScaleWidth	Long. Specify the horizontal and vertical coordinates to use for width and height when setting up a user-defined coordinate system. Changing these properties sets ScaleMode to user-defined.
ScaleLeft and ScaleTop	Long. Specify the horizontal and vertical coordinates to use for left and top when setting up a user-defined coordinate system. Changing these properties sets ScaleMode to user-defined.
ScaleMode	Long. Specifies the unit of measure to use. Most frequent settings are 0 = vbUser, 1 = vbTwips, 2 = vbPoints, 3 = vbPixels, 5 = vbInches.
TwipsPerPixelX and TwipsPerPixelY	Long. Return the number of twips per pixel given the current resolution both horizontally and vertically.

continues

Table 18.8 continued

Member	Description
TrackDefault	Boolean. Specifies whether the Printer object reflects a new default printer chosen from the Control Panel.
Zoom	Long. Specifies the percentage the printed output will be zoomed when printed.
Methods	
Circle	A graphics method that draws a circle, ellipse, or arc, given coordinates, a radius, color, and aspect ratio.
EndDoc	Sends output to the print device ending the print job.
KillDoc	Terminates the current print job.
Line	A graphics method that draws a line or rectangle, given coordinates, color, a flag indicating whether a rectangle should be drawn and whether the rectangle is to be filled.
NewPage	Finishes the current page and advances the printer to the next.
PaintPicture	A graphics method that draws the contents of a graphic file, given the Picture property of a Form or PictureBox and coordinates. Optionally supports clipping regions and bit-wise operations using width, height, coordinates, and opcode.
Pset	A graphics method that sets a single point, given the coordinates and a color.
Scale	Resets the coordinate system, given coordinates that define the upper-left and lower-right corners of the coordinate system.
ScaleX and ScaleY	Convert width and height, respectively, from one ScaleMode to another, given a source and destination ScaleMode.
TextHeight and TextWidth	Given a string, return the height and width of the text in the current ScaleMode.

An example of using the Printer object appears in Listing 18.9. This procedure, DisplayReports, takes as its main arguments objDest (defined simply as Object) and objPict, which is a PictureBox. The purpose of this procedure is to use the graphics methods to display a simple organizational chart for a department, using the PictureBox to display the company logo. Because the Form, PictureBox, and Printer objects all support many of the methods and properties in Table 18.8, the procedure can work on any of these polymorphically, using the object variable objDest. This technique enables you to build routines that provide both print preview and printing capability. In other words, to draw the output on a PictureBox control, you would use the following syntax:

```
DisplayReports PictureBox1, ...
```

To print it, you would use

```
DisplayReports Printer, ...
```

You will notice that the procedure also takes arguments that specify the users in a variant array, a department name, a manager, and the manager's title used in the report. This information can easily be queried from a database or business object.

Listing 18.9   The DisplayReports Procedure Provides Print Preview and Print Support for a Simple Organizational Chart

```
Public Sub DisplayReports(objDest As Object, objPict As PictureBox, _
    Optional varemps As Variant, Optional ByVal strDeptName As String, _
    Optional ByVal strManager As String, Optional ByVal strTitle As String)

Dim i As Long
Dim lngMargin As Long
Dim lngEndBox As Long
Dim lngManagerBoxWidth As Long
Dim lngBoxWidth As Long
Dim lngBoxHeight As Long
Dim lngBetweenBox As Long
Dim lngBoxOffset As Long


' Set the scale mode of the object
objDest.ScaleMode = vbTwips

' If printing to the printer, end the last document
' and create a header
If TypeOf objDest Is Printer Then
    objDest.EndDoc
    ' Write the header
    objDest.FontSize = 6
    objDest.Print "Printed " & Format(Date, "mm/dd/yyyy") & " " & Time
    objDest.FontSize = 8
Else
    ' Otherwise, clear the picture control
    ' Note: On a PictureBox, AutoRedraw must be True
    objDest.Cls
End If
```

continues

```
' Set the margins, widths, and heights
lngMargin = 100
lngBoxHeight = 750
lngBetweenBox = 250
lngBoxOffset = 250

' Create the header
' Add Logo
objDest.PaintPicture objPict.Picture, lngMargin, _
    objDest.CurrentY + 50, objPict.Width, objPict.Height

' Add Report Header
With objDest
    .CurrentX = lngMargin + objPict.Width + 50
    .CurrentY = .CurrentY + 50
    .FontBold = True
    objDest.Print ("Departmental View of Direct Reports")
    .CurrentX = lngMargin + objPict.Width + 50
    objDest.Print strDeptName
    .CurrentX = lngMargin
    .CurrentY = objPict.Height + 100
    objDest.Line Step(1, 1)-Step(.Width - (lngMargin * 2), 1), 0
    .FontBold = False
End With

'Create the box for the manager
objDest.CurrentX = lngMargin
lngManagerBoxWidth = objDest.TextWidth(strManager) + 750
objDest.Line Step(150, 150)-Step(lngManagerBoxWidth, lngBoxHeight), , B
lngEndBox = objDest.CurrentY

' Display the name and title
With objDest
    .CurrentY = .CurrentY - lngBoxHeight
    .CurrentX = 200 + lngMargin
    objDest.Print strManager
    .CurrentX = 200 + lngMargin
    objDest.Print strTitle
End With

' Create the vertical line to branch off of
objDest.Line (lngMargin + (lngManagerBoxWidth / 2), _
    lngEndBox)-Step(0, lngBoxHeight * (UBound(varemps, 1) + 1 - 0.5) + _
    (lngBoxOffset * (UBound(varemps, 1) + 1)))

' Loop through subordinates and create boxes for them
For i = 0 To UBound(varemps, 1)
```

```
    ' Create the horizontal line from the tree to the box
    objDest.Line ((lngMargin + (lngManagerBoxWidth / 2)), _
        lngEndBox + lngBetweenBox + (lngBoxHeight / 2))-((lngMargin + _
        (lngManagerBoxWidth / 2) + lngBoxOffset), _
        lngEndBox + lngBetweenBox + (lngBoxHeight / 2))

    ' Draw the box for the employee
    lngBoxWidth = objDest.TextWidth(varemps(i, 0)) + 750
    objDest.Line (lngMargin + (lngManagerBoxWidth / 2) + lngBoxOffset, _
        lngEndBox + lngBetweenBox)-Step(lngBoxWidth, lngBoxHeight), , B

    ' Track where the last box ended
    lngEndBox = objDest.CurrentY

    ' Place employee names and titles in the boxes
    With objDest
        .CurrentY = lngEndBox - lngBoxHeight
        .CurrentX = 50 + (lngMargin + _
        (lngManagerBoxWidth / 2)) + lngBoxOffset
        objDest.Print varemps(i, 0)
        .CurrentX = 50 + (lngMargin + _
        (lngManagerBoxWidth / 2)) + lngBoxOffset
        objDest.Print varemps(i, 1)
    End With

Next

' If printing, send it to the printer
If TypeOf objDest Is Printer Then
    objDest.EndDoc
End If

End Sub
```

Because this procedure can also be used for print preview, an application can use it to send the output to a `PictureBox` control that can then be displayed. Figure 18.4 shows the application that retrieves department information from a database when the department is selected in the `TreeView` control. The information is then passed to `DisplayReports`, along with the `PictureBox` control that displays the organizational chart. The Print toolbar button then invokes `DisplayReports` again, this time passing in a `Printer` object to send the output to the current print device.

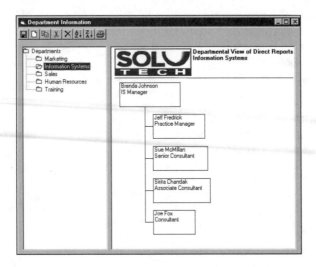

Figure 18.4

The application that calls DisplayReports to provide a print preview of the organizational chart.

Message-Enabling Your Application

In many ways, email systems are the backbone of modern organizations and are critical to the success of companies all over the world. Because email has become more prevalent, it's more important to develop applications that are integrated into this stream of information. These messaging-enabled applications should be able to perform functions such as logging on to multiple email providers, retrieving new messages, responding to messages, and moving messages appropriately.

Unfortunately, when developers understand the significance and functionality that message-enabled applications can provide, they have a tendency to go too far. This usually takes the form of duplicating functions that already exist in mail clients such as Outlook 98 or generating a spate of useless email that simply clutters up their users inbox. The judicious use of a powerful technology is always more important than using the technology simply because you can.

Collaborative Data Objects

In recent years, Microsoft has been steadily refining the way it packages its Messaging API (MAPI) for developers to use. Simply put, MAPI provides for messaging clients what ODBC provides for database clients, namely, API independence.

In its first incarnations, MAPI was accessible only through DLL-based API calls or two .VBX/.OCX controls that ship with VB. These methods, which are still available, were both limiting because coding to the DLLs meant that you had to write a significant amount of code, and using the ActiveX controls did not expose all the functionality that your application might require.

That being said, VB's capability to use COM objects has made the integration of messaging services straightforward. Most recently, Microsoft has released and refined a set of COM objects called the Collaborative Data Objects (CDO). This set of objects (formerly known as OLE Messaging and Active Messaging in previous versions) provide an object model (see Figure 18.5) and programmatic access to any MAPI provider.

NOTE

The current version of CDO is 1.2 and is not installed as a part of VB. To obtain the component, you have to install Outlook 98. Also, a CDO Rendering Library is available that allows you to develop server-side ASP applications that integrate with a MAPI provider. The Rendering Library renders the objects exposed by CDO as HTML.

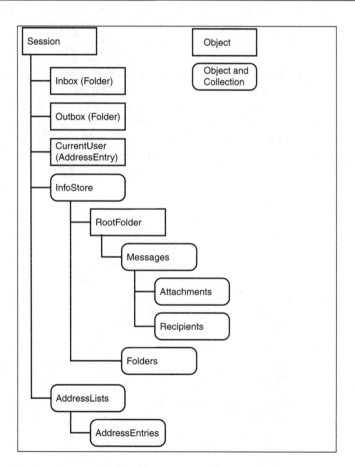

Figure 18.5

The CDO Object Model. Note that this should be used to message-enable client-based applications.

I won't list all the methods and properties of the various CDO objects because they are so numerous. You can find the complete reference online at Microsoft's MSDN Web site at msdn.microsoft.com/developer.

> **NOTE**
>
> I know that it's difficult, but don't confuse CDO with CDO NTS. The latter is a lightweight implementation of CDO for Windows NT Server that installs with IIS 4.0 and allows server-side applications such as ASP to send email through the SMTP service of Windows NT Server. It does not support any of the folder or calendar functionality of CDO.

Starting a Session

To work with the objects exposed by CDO, you must first set a reference to the Microsoft CDO 1.21 Library component and establish a session. A *session* represents a connection to a profile and is established using the Logon method of the Session object. An interesting aspect of this interaction (which is common throughout CDO) is that all the arguments to the Logon method are optional so that CDO will prompt the user for the information required if it is not passed in the method call. This allows maximum flexibility when designing applications. For example, in an application that is used interactively, you may allow the user to enter his or her profile name (or create one on-the-fly), username, and password. However, an application that processes messages in bulk (such as a Windows NT service that periodically checks for the existence of messages) may automatically log on, using settings stored in the system Registry as shown here:

```
Dim cdoMySession as Session
Set cdoMySession = New Session
cdoMySession.Logon strProfile, strPassword, False, False
```

In addition, you can specify whether CDO should use an existing session if one exists (specified by the last argument here) or create a new one. This "piggy backing" is useful when the user may already have his or her mail client running and the application can use the same profile and authentication. You will notice that the third argument in the call to Logon specifies whether CDO displays a dialog box in the event that more information is required to establish the session.

After the session has been established, you can traverse the object model and drill down into the objects provided. The folders themselves are contained in one of more InfoStore objects contained in the InfoStores collection of the Session object. Each InfoStore represents the folder hierarchy of a message store. A typical Outlook client may have access to InfoStore objects representing Personal Folders, Public Folders, and an Exchange Server mailbox. Each InfoStore contains a RootFolder object that contains the collection of Folder objects and may itself contain messages. These collections can be traversed to inspect messages in a particular folder, as in the following code to delete all the messages from the Sent Items folder that were sent before a particular day:

```
Dim cdoFolder As Folder
Dim cdoStore As InfoStore

For Each cdoStore In cdoMySession.InfoStores
   If cdoStore.Name = "Personal Folders" Then
      For Each cdoFolder In cdoStore.RootFolder.Folders
         If cdoFolder.Name = "Sent Items" Then
            For Each cdoMessage In cdoFolder.Messages
                If cdoMessage.TimeSent < #11/1/1998# Then
                    cdoMessage.Delete
                End If
            Next
         End If
      Next
   End If
Next
```

Creating Messages and Attachments

The primary activity of most messaging-enabled applications is to create and send messages. The simplest way to accomplish this is to add a message to the Messages collection of the exposed Outbox object. You can then set the message properties and create recipients before invoking the Send method.

```
Dim cdoMess as Message
Set cdoMess = cdoMySession.OutBox.Messages.Add
cdoMess.Subject = "Test"
cdoMess.Text = "Text of the message"
' Create Recipients

' Send the message
cdoMess.Send
```

The Message object exposes more than 25 properties that allow you to change characteristics of the message, such as its importance, encryption, digital signature, sensitivity, and attachments. The Attachments collection is particularly interesting because it allows you to attach and read attached files using the ReadFromFile and WriteToFile methods of the Attachment object. An example of attaching a file appears in Listing 18.10.

TIP

When you are working offline, the messages will be queued in the Outbox. After reconnecting, the application can force the sending of messages from the Outbox, using the DeliverNow method of the Session object.

Adding Recipients

Messages that are to be sent must be associated with a collection of Recipient objects. The provider must resolve each Recipient object so that the message may be sent. To add recipients to the message, you simply use the Add method of the Recipients collection.

```
Dim cdoRecip as Recipient
Set cdoRecip = cdoMess.Recipients.Add
```

You can then set the recipient properties such as Address and Type (To, Cc, or Bcc) before calling the Resolve method. When the recipient is resolved, CDO will by default display a dialog box to the user if the address cannot be resolved. By passing False to the Resolve method, a trappable error occurs, and you can then traverse the AmbiguousNames collection of AddressEntries that suggests addresses to use. In most applications, you will either allow the user to resolve the addresses using the supplied user interface or raise an error in the event the address is unresolvable. You may also resolve all the recipients for a message by invoking the Resolve method on the entire Recipients collection.

For applications that involve creating appointments or scheduling meetings, the GetFreeBusy method is particularly useful. This method returns a string that represents whether the recipient is busy, free, tentatively scheduled, or out of the office for each time slot passed into the method. This allows your application to determine whether an employee is already busy before scheduling another commitment.

The Recipients collection is also closely tied to the concept of AddressLists. The collection of AddressList objects expose the various address books available in the profile, such as the Global Address List, Personal Address Book, and Contacts. Each AddressList can be used to add, delete, and traverse entries in the address book. Most applications do not require access to these objects.

Reading New Mail

The other primary functionality for these types of applications is to receive new mail and parse messages to look for a particular type of message. In one application I wrote several years ago, a set of email surveys were sent to thousands of internal employees. A mailbox was set up to receive the responses and catalog them in a relational database. The application periodically checked for new mail, validated the subject line, and then parsed the message text before logging the responses in the database.

In CDO, to perform this technique, you simply traverse the Inbox object of the Session object for all messages where the Unread property is set to True. Messages will be automatically added to the Inbox as they are received. The following code snippet checks all messages in the Inbox and takes action if the subject line matches a constant specifying the subject to search for. It then moves the processed message to an archive folder.

```
For Each cdoMessage In cdoMySession.Inbox.Messages
    If cdoMessage.Unread = True Then
        If cdoMessage.Subject = SEARCH_SUBJECT Then
            ' Process the message
                cdoMessage.MoveTo strFolderId
        End If
    End If
Next
```

Note that the MoveTo method of the Message object requires a folder id to move to. This unique identifier is assigned by MAPI when the folder is first created and can be read using the FolderID property of the Folder object.

WARNING

Depending on the folder you are traversing, the members of the Messages collection may actually be messages, appointment items, group headers, or meeting items. As a result, you might want to declare the variable used in the For...Each loop to use a late bound reference (as Object) when traversing the collection.

Alternatively, to make the algorithm more efficient, you can use a MessageFilter object to automatically filter on various properties, including Unread.

```
Dim cdoMessages As Messages
Dim cdoFilter As MessageFilter

Set cdoMessages = cdoMySession.Inbox.Messages

' Set the filter to view only unread messages
Set cdoFilter = cdoMessages.Filter
cdoFilter.Unread = True

For Each cdoMessage In cdoMessages
    If cdoMessage.Subject = SEARCH_SUBJECT Then
        ' Process the message
        cdoMessage.MoveTo strFolderId
    End If
Next
```

The filter is automatically applied when the application iterates through the messages using either the For...Each syntax or the GetFirst and GetNext methods of the Messages collection. The filter can be taken off by simply setting the MessageFilter object to Nothing.

A Sample Application

To give you an example of what a typical messaging-enabled application might do, consider the application shown in Figure 18.6. This application allows a training coordinator for a company such as Solutech to create classes by assigning instructors to teach a course at a specific location and time. When you click Assign, the application updates a central database where the information is published on the company intranet. To ensure that the instructor is aware of the assignment, the user interface contains Notify and Attach Setup Guide check boxes. When checked, these boxes instruct the application to send a notification email to the instructor and optionally attach the setup guide for the course after the class has been created.

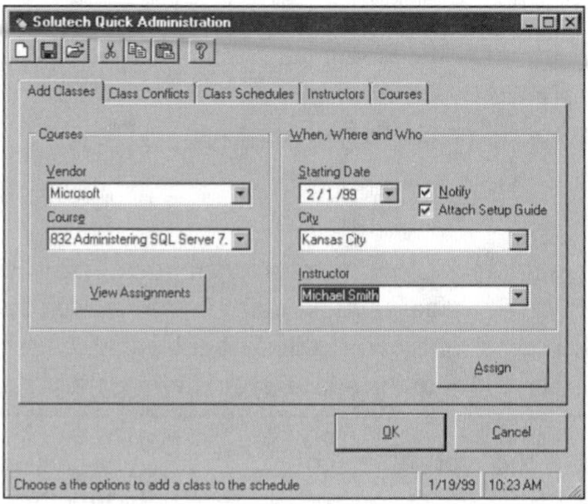

Figure 18.6

This application allows a training coordinator to schedule classes and optionally notify an instructor, via email, of the assignment.

The functionality to send the message has been abstracted in the `NotifyInstructor` procedure and appears in Listing 18.10.

Listing 18.10   The NotifyInstructor Procedure Sends an Email to the Instructor and Optionally Attaches the Setup Guide for the Course

```
Option Explicit
Private cdoSession As Session

Private Sub NotifyInstructor(ByVal strEmail As String, _
    ByVal strCourse As String, ByVal dtStart As Date, _
    ByVal strCity As String, Optional ByVal flSetup As Boolean, _
    Optional ByVal strSetupGuide As String)

Dim cdoMessage As Message
Dim cdoAttach As Attachment

On Error GoTo NotifyErr

' Piggy back on to existing session if there
' is one but log on if not
If cdoSession Is Nothing Then
```

```
      Set cdoSession = New Session
      cdoSession.Logon , , , False
End If

' Create the message
Set cdoMessage = cdoSession.Outbox.Messages.Add
cdoMessage.Subject = "Class Assignment: " & strCourse
cdoMessage.Text = "You have been assigned to teach " & _
      "the course " & strCourse & " on " & _
      Format(dtStart, "mm/dd/yyyy") & " in " & strCity & _
      ". If there is a problem with this assignment " & _
      "please contact the training coordinator."

' Add the Recipient and resolve it
cdoMessage.Recipients.Add strEmail
cdoMessage.Recipients.Resolve True 'show dialog if error
' High priority message
cdoMessage.Importance = ActMsgHigh

' Add the attachment if necessary
If flSetup Then
      Set cdoAttach = cdoMessage.Attachments.Add
      cdoAttach.Position = Len(cdoMessage.Text) + 1
      cdoAttach.ReadFromFile strSetupGuide
End If

' Send the message
cdoMessage.Send

' Deallocate
Set cdoMessage = Nothing

Exit Sub
NotifyErr:
      MsgBox "An error has occurred when attempting to " _
          & "notify the instructor. Error message is " & _
          Err.Description, vbExclamation, Me.Caption

      ' Deallocate
      Set cdoMessage = Nothing

End Sub
```

Note that because this application interacts with the user, NotifyInstructor attempts to piggy back onto an existing session. In both the logon and resolution of recipients, the application allows CDO to display its dialog boxes so that the user can provide the appropriate information. The email message in Outlook 98 appears in Figure 18.7.

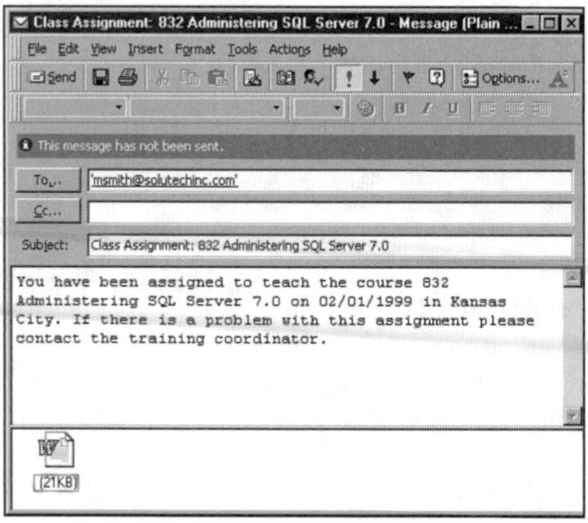

Figure 18.7

The email message generated by the code in Listing 18.10.

Summary

Each of the techniques presented in this chapter can be used to add useful functionality to corporate applications, making the applications more usable and professional. Keep in mind, however, that the overuse of features such as email can often make the application more difficult than necessary to develop and debug.

CHAPTER 19

Creating a Windows NT Service

In the corporate world, many VB applications run on Windows NT networks and communicate with the BackOffice suite of products. This results in the desire to take advantage of some of the features of Windows NT. Perhaps the most requested feature in this area is the capability to run a VB application as a Windows NT service.

Implementing a VB application as a service has several benefits, such as allowing it to run unattended and allowing it to be administered using the Services applet in the Control Panel or through the command line. Typically, applications that perform some background or batch process are good candidates for services. This chapter first discusses the anatomy of a Windows NT service and the various options that exist for creating one using VB. Then I'll drill down into the recommended approach for building a service and provide a sample application that implements a service written in VB.

Services Defined

Simply defined, a *service* is a process in the operating system that runs in the background and can be started, paused, stopped, and continued using the Services applet in the Control Panel or the command-line net command. A component of NT called the *service controller* loads, starts, unloads, and notifies these services as an administrator manipulates them.

> **NOTE**
>
> The service controller is also called the *service control manager* in much of the documentation. To avoid confusion with the COM Service Control Manager (SCM) discussed previously, I'll stick to the term *service controller* for this discussion.

Through the Services applet, administrators can also run the service in the context of a specific NT user account and can determine whether the service starts each time the server is booted, manually, or is disabled. Services typically run without a user interface and log error messages and events to the NT Event Viewer's Application Log. Examples of common services that run on NT are SQL Server, the DHCP service that assigns TCP/IP addresses, and the Server service that handles all incoming network requests for NT.

The capability to create processes on NT that run in the background and perform tasks becomes very useful for applications that must periodically perform work throughout the day. A typical example is a service that waits for files to be FTP'd to the server and then loads them into a relational database. Other examples include services that check the status of database tables and send email based on the results.

Which Method Should I Use?

Historically, there have been three methods for creating a Windows NT service using VB: using the SRVANY utility, the Win32 API functions, and the NTSRVOCX ActiveX control.

SRVANY

SRVANY is a command-line utility that first shipped with the Windows NT 3.51 Resource Kit to allow any application to run as a service. Although this technique works well in some instances (such as when you want the Performance Monitor to run as a service so that applications such as SQL Server can take advantage of its counters and notification mechanisms unattended), it is somewhat limited in that it does not provide the capability to pause and continue the service and does not provide logging to the Event Viewer.

Win32 API Functions

All the Win32 APIs for creating and managing a service can be called from VB. Table 19.1 lists those required to install, create, and manipulate the service.

Table 19.1 Win32 API Methods Located in advapi32.dll That Are Used to Manipulate a Service

Method	Description
CloseServiceHandle	Closes a service opened by OpenSCManager, OpenService, or CreateService.
CreateService	Creates the service and adds it to the service controller's database, opened with OpenSCManager. Used during the installation of a service.
DeleteService	Deletes a service from the service controller's database.
OpenSCManager	Connects to and opens the service controller's database. Used when adding or removing a service.
OpenService	Opens an existing service and is normally used when removing a service.
RegisterServiceCtrlHandler	Passes the address of a function to handle service control requests such as stop and start.
SetServiceStatus	Used to notify the service controller of the status of the service.
StartServiceCtrlDispatcher	Connects the application to the service controller and is called each time the service is started. It passes in the address of the function that performs the work of the service.

Although these APIs can be called, and there is even a knowledge base (KB) article that provides the framework (Q175948), Microsoft does not recommend using this approach. The KB article cited notes that because VB uses single-threaded apartments, "there is no way for Visual Basic to marshal multiple calls back into [an] application through AddressOf."

Because of this limitation, and the fact that the framework code provided is definitely unstable, I would recommend staying away from this approach.

NTSRVOCX

Before VB supported the AddressOf operator, using the Win32 API to create a service was not even an option to be considered. Because of the limitations of SRVANY and the need to create services, Mauricio Ordonez of Microsoft Consulting Services created an ActiveX control named NTSRVOCX, which wraps the API functions discussed previously that provide the necessary methods, properties, and events to create a Windows NT service.

Because NTSRVOCX requires less code, can be debugged from the VB development environment, and is more stable, I've used it here for the example that follows.

NOTE

The original KB article that discusses NTSRVOCX is Q170883. This article includes a link to the C++ source code but not the compiled OCX. Rather than compile the control yourself, you can download it from http:\\vb.duke.net\howto\ntsr-vocx.zip.

The NTSRVOCX ActiveX control is an invisible control that sits on a form in the VB application in the same fashion as the intrinsic Timer control. The control handles all the communication with the service controller through methods and properties and raises events when the administrator manipulates the service. The key properties, methods, and events of NTSRVOCX can be seen in Table 19.2.

Table 19.2 Properties, Methods, and Events of the NTSRVOCX Control

Member	Description
Properties	
Account and Password	Specify the NT user account to run the service when it is installed.
ControlsAccepted	Specifies which service control events the service responds to (for example, pause and continue).
Debug	Specifies whether the control attempts to communicate with the service controller. When set, the service can be debugged in the VB IDE.
DisplayName and ServiceName	Set the name of the service as it is displayed in the Services applet and the name used to control it from the command line, respectively.
Interactive	Determines whether the service can interact with the desktop. Can also be set from the Service applet.
StartMode	Specifies when the service is started (automatic, manual, or disabled).
Methods	
GetSetting, GetAllSettings, and DeleteSetting	Read and write to the HKEY_LOCAL_MACHINE\SYSTEM\CurrentControlSet\Services*servicename* Registry key. Used to store initialization information for the service.

Member	Description
Methods	
`Install` and `Uninstall`	Call the `OpenSCManager`, `CreateService`, `OpenService`, and `DeleteService` APIs to install and uninstall the service with the service controller.
`LogEvent`	Logs an event to the Event Viewer. Arguments include the event type, id, and the message itself.
`Running`	Returns whether the service is running.
`StartService` and `StopService`	Start and stop the service.
Events	
`Continue`, `Pause`, `Start`, and `Stop`	Fired by the control when the service is manipulated through the Services applet or the command line.
`Control`	Catch-all event that is fired any time the service is manipulated.

Creating a Service Using NTSRVOCX

As an example of creating a service using NTSRVOCX, I created a simple service named DataImport that periodically checks for the existence of files in a given directory using a timer. If files are found, the service processes them (passing them to a stub function in this example), moves them to a different directory, and logs the result. The service shows examples of installation, removal, and debugging the service, interacting with the Registry, and responding to service control events. You can use the code in Listing 19.1 (showing the form code) and Listing 19.2 (showing the standard module) as the basis for other services you need to create. The remainder of the chapter explicates the details of these code listings.

Listing 19.1   The Complete Code for the Form of the DataImport Service

```
Option Explicit

Private Sub Form_Load()

' The Load event is called each time the service is
' started or when it is run from the command line

Dim lstrTemp As String

On Error GoTo LoadErr

' Make sure that the form is invisible
Me.Visible = False
```

continues

Listing 19.1   continued

```
' Set up the service properties
NTService.DisplayName = "DataImport"
NTService.ServiceName = "DataImport"

Select Case Command
Case "/i"  ' Install the service with the service control manager
    If NTService.Install = True Then
        ' Set the default parameters (should be changed in the Registry)
        NTService.SaveSetting "Parameters", "Interval", 5
        NTService.SaveSetting "Parameters", "FileFromPath", App.Path
        NTService.SaveSetting "Parameters", "FileToPath", App.Path
    End If
Case "/u"  ' Uninstall the service
    NTService.Uninstall
Case "/d" ' Run in debug mode
    NTService.Debug = True
End Select

' If there is a command line, do not run the service
If Len(Command) > 0 Then
    Unload Me
    Exit Sub
End If

' Initialize internal data
lstrTemp = NTService.GetSetting("Parameters", "Interval", "")
glngInterval = CLng(lstrTemp) * 1000
gstrFileFromPath = NTService.GetSetting("Parameters", _
    "FileFromPath", "")
gstrFileToPath = NTService.GetSetting("Parameters", _
    "FileToPath", "")

' Enable pause and continue
NTService.ControlsAccepted = svcCtrlPauseContinue

' Now Start the Service
NTService.StartService

Exit Sub
LoadErr:
    ' Log the error
    NTService.LogEvent svcMessageError, svcEventError, _
        "[" & Err.Number & "] " & Err.Description

End Sub
```

```
Private Sub NTService_Continue(Success As Boolean)
On Error GoTo ContinueErr

    ' Reset the Timer to continue
    glngTimerId = SetTimer(0, 0, glngInterval, AddressOf TimerProc)
    If glngTimerId = 0 Then
        Success = False
        NTService.LogEvent svcMessageError, svcEventError, _
            "Timer could not be started."
    Else
        ' Must set to true or else an error will occur
        Success = True
        NTService.LogEvent svcMessageInfo, svcEventSuccess, _
            "Service Continued Successfully"
    End If

Exit Sub
ContinueErr:
    NTService.LogEvent svcMessageError, svcEventError, _
        "[" & Err.Number & "] " & Err.Description
End Sub

Private Sub NTService_Pause(Success As Boolean)
On Error GoTo PauseErr
    ' Kill the timer so that the service stops responding
    KillTimer 0, glngTimerId
    Success = True
    NTService.LogEvent svcMessageInfo, svcEventSuccess, _
        "Service Paused Successfully"
Exit Sub
PauseErr:
    NTService.LogEvent svcMessageError, svcEventError, _
        "[" & Err.Number & "] " & Err.Description
End Sub

Private Sub NTService_Start(Success As Boolean)
On Error GoTo StartErr

    ' Start the timer
    glngTimerId = SetTimer(0, 0, glngInterval, _
        AddressOf TimerProc)

    If glngTimerId = 0 Then
        Success = False
        NTService.LogEvent svcMessageError, svcEventError, _
            "Timer could not be started."
    Else
```

continues

Listing 19.1   continued

```
        ' Must set to true or else an error will occur
        Success = True
    End If

Exit Sub
StartErr:
    NTService.LogEvent svcMessageError, svcEventError, _
        "[" & Err.Number & "] " & Err.Description


End Sub

Private Sub NTService_Stop()
On Error GoTo StopErr

    ' Unload the form to stop the service
    Unload Me

Exit Sub
StopErr:
    NTService.LogEvent svcMessageError, svcEventError, _
        "[" & Err.Number & "] " & Err.Description
End Sub
```

Listing 19.2   The Complete Code for the Standard Module of the DataImport Service—A Standard Module Must Be Used Because a Callback Function, SetTimer, Is Used by the Service

```
Option Explicit

Public Declare Function SetTimer Lib "user32" (ByVal hwnd As Long, _
    ByVal nIDEvent As Long, ByVal uElapse As Long, _
    ByVal lpTimerFunc As Long) As Long

Public Declare Function KillTimer Lib "user32" _
    (ByVal hwnd As Long, ByVal nIDEvent As Long) As Long

Public glngTimerId As Long
Public glngInterval As Long
Public gstrFileFromPath As String
Public gstrFileToPath As String

Private objFileSys As FileSystemObject

Public Sub TimerProc(ByVal hwnd As Long, ByVal uMsg As Long, _
    ByVal idEvent As Long, ByVal dwTime As Long)
```

```
Dim llngFiles As Long

    ' Stop the timer while the service is processing so
    ' that it won't step on itself
    KillTimer 0, glngTimerId

    ' Do processing
    llngFiles = FindFiles

    ' Restart the timer
    glngTimerId = SetTimer(0, 0, glngInterval, _
        AddressOf TimerProc)

    ' Log the fact that processing occurred
    frmMain.NTService.LogEvent svcEventInformation, svcMessageInfo, _
        llngFiles & " files processed at " & Time

End Sub

Private Function FindFiles() As Long

Dim objStartFolder As Folder
Dim objFile As File
Dim llngFiles As Long

On Error GoTo FindFilesErr

' Look through the directory and collect the files
Set objFileSys = New FileSystemObject

' Reference the folders
Set objStartFolder = objFileSys.GetFolder(gstrFileFromPath)

For Each objFile In objStartFolder.Files
    If ProcessFile(objFile) Then
        objFile.Move gstrFileToPath & "\" & objFile.Name
        llngFiles = llngFiles + 1
    End If
Next

' Return the number of files processed
FindFiles = llngFiles

' Clean up
Set objFile = Nothing
Set objStartFolder = Nothing
Set objFileSys = Nothing
```

continues

Listing 19.1   continued

```
Exit Function
FindFilesErr:
    ' Log the error and clean up
    frmMain.NTService.LogEvent svcMessageError, svcEventError, _
        "[" & Err.Number & "] " & Err.Description

    FindFiles = llngFiles

    Set objFile = Nothing
    Set objStartFolder = Nothing
    Set objFileSys = Nothing

End Function

Private Function ProcessFile(pFile As File) As Boolean

' Stub function that would contain code to open the file,
' connect to the database, and load records in a loop.

    ' Success
    ProcessFile = True
End Function
```

Installation and Removal

After dropping an instance of NTSRVOCX on a form in a standard executable, you can write code in the Load event of the form to install and remove the service from the service controller. A good technique for doing this is to take advantage of the intrinsic Command function to read the values passed in from the command line. A Select Case statement can be used to install, uninstall, or set up debugging using the methods and properties of NTService, the instance of NTSRVOCX.

```
' Setup the service properties
NTService.DisplayName = "DataImport"
NTService.ServiceName = "DataImport"

Select Case Command
Case "/i"  ' Install the service with the service controller
    If NTService.Install = True Then
        ' Set the default parameters in the Registry
    End If
Case "/u"  ' Uninstall the service
    NTService.Uninstall
Case "/d"  ' Run in debug mode
    NTService.Debug = True
Case Else  ' Entered invalid command line
```

```
If Len(Command) > 0 Then
    MsgBox "Invalid command line", vbCritical, _
        NTService.DisplayName
End IfEnd Select
```

You can then install the service by typing DataImport /i at the command line. Note that the service name and display name should be set at either design time or runtime before the service is installed. The service will now be visible in the Services applet, shown in Figure 19.1.

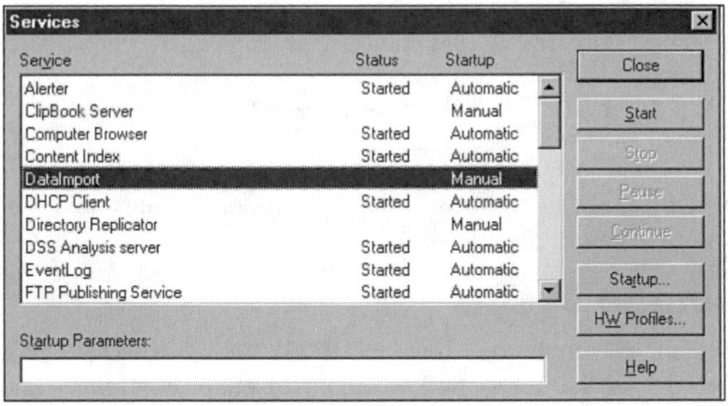

Figure 19.1

The DataImport service after being installed in the Services applet.

After the service is successfully installed or uninstalled, you should immediately unload the form if the command line was used.

```
If Len(Command) > 0 Then
    Unload Me
    Exit Sub
End If
```

TIP

> To debug the service in the IDE, you can set the command-line argument to \d in the Project Properties dialog box. You also have to comment out the unload code when debugging so that the application continues to run.

If the command line was not used, the service must have been started from the Services applet or the net start command. In this event, you should call the StartService method to start the service.

Interacting with the Registry

As the service is installed, a good practice is to create Registry keys using the SaveSetting method that the service will use to initialize data. The DataImport service creates subkeys in the Parameters key for the folder to check, the destination folder for processed files, and the interval in seconds at which to check for new files.

When the service is started, these same values are read using the GetSetting method and caching the values in global variables.

```
lstrTemp = NTService.GetSetting("Parameters", "Interval", "")
glngInterval = CLng(lstrTemp) * 1000
gstrFileFromPath = NTService.GetSetting("Parameters", _
    "FileFromPath", "")
gstrFileToPath = NTService.GetSetting("Parameters", _
    "FileToPath", "")
```

Note that GetSetting always returns strings, so numeric values must be converted, as in the case of the Interval parameter.

Responding to Events

After the StartService method is invoked, NTSRVOCX will fire service control events indicating when the service is stopped, started, paused, or continued. Each event, with the exception of Stop, passes in an argument that can be set to True if the event was successfully processed. In the case of the Start event, you must set the argument to True for the service to continue running.

In the DataImport service, the Start event is used to start the timer using the SetTimer API function. Each invocation of the timer initiates the process of checking for and processing files.

```
Private Sub NTService_Start(Success As Boolean)
On Error GoTo StartErr

    ' Start the timer
    glngTimerId = SetTimer(0, 0, glngInterval, _
        AddressOf TimerProc)

    If glngTimerId = 0 Then
        Success = False
        NTService.LogEvent svcMessageError, svcEventError, _
            "Timer could not be started."
    Else
        Success = True
    End If

Exit Sub
```

```
StartErr:
    NTService.LogEvent svcMessageError, svcEventError, _
        "[" & Err.Number & "] " & Err.Description
End Sub
```

Each event also uses the `LogEvent` method to log success and failure to the Event Viewer.

TIP

Because applications that use **NTSRVOCX** require a form, they cannot be set to unattended execution in the Project Properties dialog box. Because the service is meant to run unattended, however, you should not allow the application to pop up message boxes or visible forms (the main form's `Visible` property should be set to `False`). To keep this from happening, add an error handler to every procedure in the application, and log each error to the Event Viewer.

Checking for Files

The main function of DataImport is to check for the existence of files in a given directory and process them. The `FindFiles` function is called by `TimerProc` each time the timer fires and uses the `FileSystemObject` (discussed in Chapter 18, "Adding Professional Features"), to check for files and pass them off to the `ProcessFile` function. If the file is processed correctly, a counter is incremented and returned by `FindFiles`. `TimerProc` uses the count to log a message to the Event Viewer, indicating how many files were processed. The following is the code for `TimerProc`:

```
Dim llngFiles As Long

    ' Stop the timer while the service is processing so
    ' that it won't step on itself
    KillTimer 0, glngTimerId

    ' Do processing
    llngFiles = FindFiles

    ' Restart the timer
    glngTimerId = SetTimer(0, 0, glngInterval, _
        AddressOf TimerProc)

    ' Log the fact that processing occurred
    frmMain.NTService.LogEvent svcEventInformation, svcMessageInfo, _
        llngFiles & " files processed at " & Time
```

Notice that `TimerProc` always stops the timer while processing is occurring and restarts it after it is complete. This ensures that the service will not step on itself in an attempt to simultaneously call `FindFiles` in response to multiple timer events. The Event Viewer showing logged events appears in Figure 19.2.

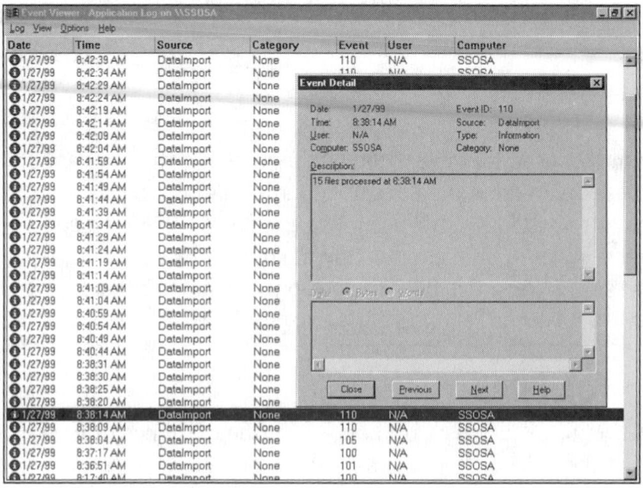

Figure 19.2

The NT Event Viewer showing logged events each time files are processed.

Summary

Creating a Windows NT service can be a powerful addition to a VB developer's toolbox, allowing you to create applications that run unattended and provide backend services. Keep in mind, however, that if you write a service that handles incoming requests from clients (not the simple polling service discussed in this chapter), your application acting as a service does not automatically mean it will be able to scale to hundreds or even tens of users. Only a well-thought-out design can ensure that type of scalability.

The final section of the book includes chapters designed for your reference as you build solutions in VB. This section includes chapters on ADO, functions, and constants, as well as a COM primer for VB developers and a survey of implementing sorting and searching algorithms in VB.

PART III

QUICK REFERENCE

The final section of the book is structured as a classic reference (Chapters 20, 21, and 22) and appendix section (Chapters 23 and 24); it is not intended to be read sequentially or even completely. The topics covered in these chapters include intrinsic functions and statements, constants, and the various algorithms used for sorting and searching multidimensional arrays; also included are a reference for the ADO objects referred to frequently throughout the book and a COM primer.

When selecting the level of detail to include in the descriptions of functions, methods, properties, and events found in Chapters 20–22, I attempted to provide enough information to make the purpose clear without simply regurgitating facts that can also be found in the online help. This section is intended to be a starting point for you, not an exhaustive reference.

The final chapters on COM and sorting and searching are meant to be read completely and are targeted at developers who need a basic understanding of COM and who want to implement one of the well-known sorting or searching algorithms.

CHAPTER 20

ADO Reference

As discussed in Chapter 14, "Using ADO for Data Access," ADO is the preferred data access mechanism for use with Visual Basic. This chapter provides the descriptions of all methods, properties, and events included in the ADO 2.1 object model. For additional information, see the "ActiveX Data Objects" topic included in the MSDN online help.

The Connection Object

The Connection object is used to open and maintain a connection to a data source using an OLE DB provider. Although not discussed in Chapter 14, you can use the Connection object to execute commands or stored procedures directly. For example, the code in Listing 20.1 shows a small example of creating a Command object and executing it as if it were a method of the Connection object. The key to this technique is to name the Command using its Name property.

Listing 20.1   Executing a Command as a Method

```
Dim objCn As New Connection
Dim objCm As New Command
Dim objRs As New Recordset

' Open a connection
objCn.Provider = "SQLOLEDB"
objCn.Open "database=contracker;server=ssosa;uid=sa"

' Create and name a Command object
With objCm
    .CommandText = "SELECT * FROM Projects"
    .CommandType = adCmdText
    .Name = "ListProj"
    .ActiveConnection = objCn
End With

' Open the command by referencing it as a method
objCn.ListProj objRs
```

Note that the actual invocation of the command accepts a `Recordset` object used to catch the resultset. If the command accepts parameters, however, you can pass the parameter values as arguments before the `Recordset` is specified. For example, if the command accepted two parameters, you could execute it using code such as the following:

```
objCn.ListProj "Microsoft", "Bill Gates", objRs
```

TIP

The other variant of this syntax is to use a stored procedure name as the method. In this case, you do not even have to define the `Command` object and can simply execute the procedure passing it any parameters. This technique also does not incur additional round trips to the data source to discover the names and data types of the parameters.

The properties, methods, and events for the `Connection` object appear in Tables 20.1, 20.2, and 20.3, respectively.

Table 20.1 The ADO Connection Object Properties

Property	Description
Attributes	Determines whether retaining commits and aborts are performed by setting the property to `adXactCommitRetaining` or `adXactAbortRetaining`. When the sum of the two options is used, the provider (if supported) will automatically start a new transaction when the `CommitTrans` or `RollbackTrans` methods are invoked.
CommandTimeout	Long. Determines how long in seconds to wait for a command to execute.
ConnectionString	String. Specifies the string to use to connect to the data source.
ConnectionTimeout	Long. Determines how long in seconds to wait for a valid connection to be opened.
CursorLocation	Determines the location of the cursor driver. Can be set to `adUseServer` to use a provider-supplied or server-side cursor or `adUseClient` to use a local cursor library (`adUseNone` and `adUseClientBatch` are supported for backward compatibility).
DefaultDatabase	String. Specifies the default database to use when the connection is established.
Errors	Errors. Returns a collection of `Error` objects.
IsolationLevel	Specifies the level of isolation used for the session. Can be set to one of 9 values. SQL Server defaults to using `adXactReadCommitted`.

Property	Description
Mode	Specifies the permission for modifying data. Can be set to one of 8 values, including `adModeRead`, `adModeWrite`, `adModeReadWrite`, `adModeShareDenyRead`, `adModeShareDenyWrite`, `adModeShareExclusive`, and `adModeShareDenyNone`.
Properties	`Properties`. Returns a collection of `Property` objects that allow provider-specific attributes to be set or interrogated for the `Connection`. Examples for SQL Server include Network Library and Integrated Security.
Provider	`String`. Specifies the OLE DB provider to use to connect to the data source. Defaults to MSDASQL to use the OLE DB provider for ODBC.
State	Returns the status of the `Connection` object and can return `adStateOpen` or `adStateClosed`.
Version	`String`. Returns the ADO version number.

Table 20.2   The ADO Connection Object Methods

Method	Description
BeginTrans, CommitTrans, and RollbackTrans	Instructs the provider to begin a new transaction, commit a transaction, or roll back a transaction, respectively. The return value of `BeginTrans` may indicate the nesting level of the transaction, depending on the provider. What occurs when `CommitTrans` and `RollbackTrans` are invoked is dependent on the setting of the `Attributes` property.
Cancel	Cancels the current `Execute` or `Open` method called asynchronously.
Close	Closes the connection to the data source, as well as any active `Recordset` object created from the `Connection`. Also sets the `ActiveConnection` object of `Command` objects that use the connection to `Nothing`. Does not deallocate the object.
Execute	Executes a query contained in a SQL statement, table name, stored procedure, or provider-specific text. Also takes arguments that return the number of records affected by the statement, and options that specify the format of the command text (`adCmdText`, `adCmdTable`, `adCmdStoredProc`, `adCmdUnknown`, or `adCmdTableDirect`) and whether the statement executes asynchronously (`adAsyncExecute` and `adAsyncFetch`).

continues

Table 20.2   continued

Method	Description
Open	Opens a connection to the data source, given the optional arguments connection string, user id, password, and connection method that determines whether the connection should be opened synchronously (`adConnectUnspecified`) or asynchronously (`adAsyncConnect`).
OpenSchema	Obtains database schema information from the provider, given a query type, criteria, and optionally a schema ID (GUID). The query type can be one of 31 constants, including `adSchemaTables` and `adSchemaViews`.

Table 20.3   The ADO Connection Object Events

Event	Description
BeginTransComplete, CommitTransComplete, RollbackTransComplete	Fired after the associated operation has finished executing. All three may pass back an `Error` object and status information (`adStatusOK` or `adStatusErrorsOccurred`), as well as a reference to the `Connection` object for which the operation completed. `BeginTransComplete` also passes back the transaction level.
ConnectComplete and Disconnect	Fired after a connection starts and after the connection ends, respectively. Both pass back status information (`adStatusOK` or `adStatusErrorsOccurred`) and a reference to the `Connection` object for which the operation completed. `ConnectComplete` may also pass back an `Error` object, depending on the status.
ExecuteComplete	Fired after a command has finished executing. Passes back the number of records affected, an optional `Error` object, the status (`adStatusOK` or `adStatusErrorsOccurred`), and references to the `Command` object (if any), `Recordset` (may be empty), and the `Connection` object.
InfoMessage	Fired whenever a warning occurs while a connection is being made. Passes back an optional `Error` object, status information (`adStatusOK`), and a reference to the `Connection` object for which the warning occurred. The `Error` object contains the warning.

Event	Description
WillConnect	Fired before a connection is initiated and passes in relevant information, including the connection string, user id, password, options, and a reference to the Connection object. Other arguments include the status (adStatusOK or adStatusCantDeny) that can be set to adStatusUnwantedEvent to prevent subsequent notifications or adStatusCancel to cause the connection request to be cancelled.
WillExecute	Fired just before a command executes on and passes in the source string, cursor type, lock type, and options. Also passes in the status (adStatusOK or adStatusCantDeny) that can be set to adStatusUnwantedEvent to prevent subsequent notifications or adStatusCancel to cause the operation to be cancelled. May also pass in references to the Command and Recordset, in addition to the Connection object.

The Recordset Object

The Recordset object is used to refer to results returned from a data source. Its properties, methods, and events are shown in Tables 20.4, 20.5, and 20.6, respectively.

Table 20.4   The ADO Recordset Properties

Property	Description
AbsolutePage	Long. Specifies on which page the current record resides. May also return one of the constants adPosUnknown, adPosBOF, or adPosEOF. Affected by the settings of PageSize.
AbsolutePosition	Long. Specifies the ordinal position of the current record. May also return one of the constants adPosUnknown, adPosBOF, or adPosEOF.
ActiveCommand	Command. Returns the Command object used to create the Recordset, if any.
ActiveConnection	Connection. Returns a string representing the Connection object associated with the Recordset but can be set to a Connection object. Setting this property to Nothing disassociates the Recordset from a Connection object.
BOF and EOF	Boolean. Indicate whether the Recordset pointer is at the beginning or end of the Recordset.

continues

Table 20.4   continued

Property	Description
Bookmark	Returns a `Variant` that uniquely identifies the current record or positions the `Recordset` to the record pointed to by the bookmark.
CacheSize	Long. Indicates the number of records the provider retrieves with each call to the data source and keeps in its local cache.
CursorLocation	Same as the `CursorLocation` property of the `Connection` object, although it applies to only this `Recordset`.
CursorType	Indicates the type of cursor used in the `Recordset`. Can be set to `adOpenForwardOnly`, `adOpenKeyset`, `adOpenDynamic`, or `adOpenStatic`.
DataMember	`String`. Specifies the name of the data member to retrieve from the object specified in the `DataSource` property.
DataSource	Specifies an object containing data to be placed in the `Recordset` object. Typically used to specify a Data Environment object that contains multiple data members, one of which is specified in the `DataMember` property.
EditMode	Returns the editing status of the current record and can be set to `adEditNone`, `adEditInProgress`, `adEditAdd`, or `adEditDelete`.
Fields	`Fields`. Returns a reference to a collection of `Field` objects contained in the `Recordset`.
Filter	`Variant`. Specifies a filter for the `Recordset` that can be a criteria string, array of bookmarks, or a filter constant (`adFilterNone`, `adFilterPendingRecords`, `adFilterAffectedRecords`, `adFilterFetchedRecords`, or `adFilterConflictingRecords`).
Index	`String`. Indicates the name of the current index and is used in conjunction with the `Seek` method. To determine whether the `Recordset` object supports indexes, use the `Supports` method with the `adIndex` constant.
LockType	Determines the type of locks placed on records during editing and may be `adLockReadOnly`, `adLockPessimistic`, `adLockOptimistic`, or `adLockBatchOptimistic`.
MarshalOptions	Specifies that records are to be sent (marshaled) back to the server and can be set to `adMarshalAll` or `adMarshalModifiedOnly`.

Property	Description
MaxRecords	Long. Specifies the maximum number of records to return to the Recordset. A value of 0 indicates no limit.
PageCount	Long. Indicates how many pages of data the Recordset contains. Is affected by the PageSize property.
PageSize	Long. Indicates how many records are in a single page. Default is 10.
Properties	Properties. Returns a collection of Property objects. Used to set or return provider-specific information.
RecordCount	Long. Indicates the number of records in the Recordset. If the RecordCount is –1, ADO cannot determine how many records are in the Recordset.
Sort	String. Specifies a comma-delimited list of field names to sort on. May also include ASC or DESC keywords to sort in ascending or descending order.
Source	Indicates the source for the data in the Recordset. Can be set to a Command object but may return a string.
State	Returns the current state of the Recordset (adStateOpen, adStateClosed, adStateConnecting, adStateExecuting, or adStateFetching). Can return multiple values, for example, adStateOpen and adStateExecuting.
Status	Returns the status of the current record when performing a batch update or other bulk operation (Resync, UpdateBatch, or CancelBatch). Can return one of 18 constants.
StayInSync	Boolean. In a hierarchical Recordset, determines whether the underlying child records change when the parent row changes.

Table 20.5   The ADO Recordset Methods

Method	Description
AddNew	Creates a new record for a Recordset that is updateable. Optionally supports arguments that can contain arrays of field names or ordinal positions and values.
Cancel	Cancels an asynchronous call to the Open method.
CancelBatch	Cancels a pending batch update and is optionally passed a constant indicating how many records the method will affect (adAffectCurrent, adAffectGroup, or adAffectAll).

continues

Table 20.5   continued

Method	Description
CancelUpdate	Cancels changes made to the current record or a new record before the Update method is called.
Clone	Creates a copy of the Recordset into a new Recordset object that can be set to read-only using the constant adLockReadOnly.
Close	Closes the Recordset and releases the data and any locks placed on the data. If a record is being edited, an error will occur.
CompareBookmarks	Given two bookmarks, the method returns a constant specifying their relative positions. Return values include adCompareLessThan, adCompareEqual, adCompareGreaterThan, adCompareNotEqual, or adCompareNotComparable.
Delete	Deletes the current record or group of records, depending on the optional argument specified (adAffectCurrent, adAffectGroup, adAffectAll, or adAffectAllChapters).
Find	Repositions the Recordset at a record, given search criteria, the offset from the current or starting position, the search direction (adSearchForward or adSearchBackward), and an optional bookmark indicating the position at which to start the search.
GetRows	Retrieves records into a multidimensional array. Includes arguments to specify the number of rows to retrieve (defaults to adGetRowsRest), the starting position to begin the retrieval (either a bookmark or one of the constants adBookmarkCurrent, adBookmarkFirst, or adBookmarkLast), and a Variant that specifies the names or original positions of the fields to return.
GetString	Variant. Returns the Recordset formatted as a string. Includes optional arguments that specify whether a custom string format (adClipString) will be used, the number of rows to convert, the column delimiter, the row delimiter, and the expression to be used for null values.
Move	Repositions the Recordset pointer, given the offset and a starting position (adBookmarkCurrent, adBookmarkFirst, or adBookmarkLast).

Method	Description
MoveFirst, MoveLast, MoveNext,	Repositions the `Recordset` to the first, last, next, or previous record. May generate a trappable error if the `Recordset` does not support backwards `MovePrevious` scrolling or if an attempt is made to move beyond the beginning or end of the `Recordset`.
NextRecordset	`Recordset`. Returns the next `Recordset` generated by a command. May generate a trappable error if an update is pending. If there are no more resultsets, the `Recordset` will be set to `Nothing`.
Open	Opens a cursor to populate the `Recordset`. Optional arguments include the source (a `Command` object or SQL statement to be executed against the data source), the `Connection` object or string containing the connection information to be used, the cursor type (see the `CursorType` property), lock type (see the `LockType` property), and options indicating the type of command implied by the source and asynchronous options (`adAsyncExecute`, `adAsyncFetch`, and `adAsynchFetchNonBlocking`).
Requery	Re-executes the query associated with the `Recordset`. Can optionally take an argument to specify the asynchronous options `adAsyncExecute`, `adAsyncFetch`, and `adAsynchFetchNonBlocking`. All other attributes of the cursor cannot be changed unless the `Recordset` is explicitly closed and reopened.
Resync	Refreshes data in the current `Recordset` with data from the data source. Can optionally accept arguments indicating how many records will be affected (`adAffectCurrent`, `adAffectGroup`, `adAffectAll`, or `adAffectChapter`) and whether the underlying data is overwritten and pending changes cancelled (`adResyncAllValues` or `adResyncUnderlyingValues`).
Save	Persists the `Recordset` to a file. Takes arguments that specify the filename and format (`adPersistADTG` or `adPersistXML`).
Seek	Searches the current index of a `Recordset` using a server-side cursor and repositions the pointer. Accepts a `Variant` that includes an array of field values to compare against and the type of comparison to perform (`adSeekAfterEQ`, `adSeekAfter`, `adSeekBefore`, `adSeekBeforeEQ`, `adSeekLastEQ`, or `adSeekFirstEQ`). Used in conjunction with the `Index` property. If the row is not found, the `Recordset` is positioned to the EOF.

continues

Table 20.5   continued

Method	Description
Supports	Boolean. Determines whether the Recordset supports the given functionality that may include adAddNew, adApproxPosition, adBoomark, adDelete, adHoldRecords, adMovePrevious, adResync, adUpdate, adUpdateBatch, adIndex, or adSeek.
Update	Saves changes made to the current record in the Recordset. Optionally supports arguments that can contain arrays of field names or ordinal positions and values.
UpdateBatch	Saves all pending batch updates made to the Recordset. The optional argument specifies which records to update (adAffectCurrent, adAffectGroup, adAffectAll, or adAffectChapters).

Table 20.6   The ADO Recordset Events

Event	Description
EndOfRecordset	Fired when an attempt is made to move past the end of the Recordset. Passes in a Boolean value that can be set to True if you append records to the Recordset in this event. Also provides status information (adStatusOK, adStatusErrorsOccurred, or adStatusCantDeny) and a reference to the Recordset object for which the operation completed. As with many of these events, by setting the status to adStatusUnwantedEvent, subsequent notifications will be suppressed.
FetchComplete	Fired after all records in an asynchronous operation have been retrieved. Passes back an Error object and status information (adStatusOK or adStatusErrorsOccurred), as well as a reference to the Recordset object for which the operation completed.
FetchProgress	Fired periodically during a long asynchronous operation. Passes in the number of records that have been fetched, the maximum number of records expected, status information, and a reference to the Recordset object for which the operation is executing.

WillChangeField and FieldChangeComplete	Fired just before and immediately after the value of one or more Field objects is changed. Passes in the number of fields, an array of variants that includes the Field objects, status information (adStatusOK, adStatusErrorsOccurred, or adStatusCantDeny), and a reference to the Recordset object to which the changes are being made. FieldChangeComplete also passes in an Error object.
WillMove and MoveComplete	Fired immediately before and after an operation changes the current position in the Recordset. Passes in the reason for the move (adRsnMoveFirst, adRsnMoveLast, adRsnMoveNext, adRsnMovePrevious, adRsnMove, or adRsnRequery), status information (adStatusOK, adStatusErrorsOccurred, or adStatusCantDeny), and a reference to the Recordset object that is being repositioned. MoveComplete also passes in an Error object.
WillChangeRecord and RecordChangeComplete	Fired just before and immediately after one or more rows in the Recordset are changed. Fires in response to Update, Delete, CancelUpdate, AddNew, UpdateBatch, or CancelBatch methods. Passes in the reason for the change (adRsnAddNew, adRsnDelete, adRsnUpdate, adRsnUndoUpdate, adRsnUndoAddNew, adRsnUndoDelete, or adRsnFirstChange), the number of rows changing, status information (adStatusOK, adStatusErrorsOccurred, or adStatusCantDeny), and a reference to the Recordset object that is being changed. RecordChangeComplete also passes in an Error object.
WillChangeRecordset and RecordsetChangeComplete	Fired just before and immediately after the Recordset is changed. Passes in the reason for the change (adRsnReQuery, adRsnReSynch, adRsnClose, adRsnOpen), status information (adStatusOK, adStatusErrorsOccurred, or adStatusCantDeny), and a reference to the Recordset object that is being changed. RecordsetChangeComplete also passes in an Error object.

The Command Object

The Command object is used to encapsulate the definition of a particular command that will be executed against a data source. The properties and methods for the object appear in Tables 20.7 and 20.8, respectively.

Table 20.7   The ADO Command Object Properties

Property	Description
ActiveConnection	Connection. Returns a string representing the Connection object associated with the Recordset but can be set to a Connection object. Setting this property to Nothing disassociates the Command from a Connection object.
CommandText	String. Contains the text of the command you want to execute against the data source. The property is interpreted based on the value of the CommandType property.
CommandTimeout	Long. Indicates how many seconds to wait for a command to execute before raising a trappable error.
CommandType	Specifies the type of command in the CommandText property to execute. Possibilities include adCmdText, adCmdTable, adCmdTableDirect, adCmdStoredProc, adCmdUnknown, or adCmdFile. Can be combined with adExecuteNoRecords if the command does not return a Recordset.
Name	String. Name used to refer to the Command object.
Parameters	Parameters. Returns a collection of Parameter objects that will be passed to the data source.
Prepared	Boolean. Specifies whether the provider should save a compiled version of the command for later use.
Properties	Properties. Returns a collection of Property objects used to specify provider-specific information.
State	Returns whether the Command is opened (adStateOpen) or closed (adStateClosed).

Table 20.8   The ADO Command Object Methods

Method	Description
Cancel	Cancels an asynchronous operation performed by the Execute method.
CreateParameter	Creates a new Parameter object but does not append it to the Parameters collection. It accepts the name, type (one of 38 constants of DataTypeEnum—see Table 20.11), direction (adParamUnknown, adParamInput, adParamOutput, adParamInputOutput, or adParamReturnValue), the maximum length of the parameter, and a Variant specifying the value of the Parameter object.

Method	Description
Execute	Executes the command specified in the CommandText property. It accepts optional arguments that return the number of records affected, a Variant array of parameters to be passed to the statement (output parameters do not work with this technique), and a constant indicating how the CommandText property should be interpreted (see the CommandType property).

The Parameter Object

The Parameter object is used to encapsulate the definition of a parameter passed to a data source using a Command object. The properties and methods for the object appear in Tables 20.9 and 20.10, respectively. In addition, the DataTypeEnum enumerated constants used by the Parameter object are shown in Table 20.11.

Table 20.9   The ADO Parameter Object Properties

Property	Description
Attributes	Specifies the characteristics of the Parameter object and can be set to adParamSigned (accepts signed values), adParamNullable (accepts Null values), and adParamLong (accepts long binary data).
Direction	Determines whether the parameter is an input (adParamInput), output (adParamOutput), both (adParamInputOutput), or a return value (adParamReturnValue) from a stored procedure.
Name	String. Specifies a name used to refer to the Parameter.
NumericScale	Byte. Specifies the number of decimal places to which numeric values will be resolved.
Precision	Byte. Specifies the maximum number of digits used to represent the numeric value.
Properties	Returns a collection of Property objects used to specify provider-specific information.
Size	Long. Specifies the maximum size in bytes or characters for values represented by the Parameter. This property must be set for variable-length parameters, such as those using the adVarChar data type.
Type	Specifies the data type of Parameter object. See Table 20.11 for the complete list.
Value	Variant. Specifies the value assigned to the parameter.

Table 20.10　**The ADO Parameter Object Methods**

Method	Description
AppendChunk	Appends data to a large text or binary `Parameter` object. Accepts a `Variant` containing the data to be appended. Can be used when the `Attributes` property of the `Parameter` object contains `adParamLong`. The first use of `AppendChunk` overwrites existing data for the parameter, whereas subsequent calls simply append data.

Table 20.11　**The ADO DataTypeEnum Enumerated Constants**

Constant	Description
adArray	When used with another constant (logical OR), it indicates that the data is actually an array.
adBigInt	An 8-byte signed `Integer`.
adBinary	A binary value.
adBoolean	A `Boolean` value.
adBSTR	A null-terminated Unicode character string.
adByRef	When used with another constant (logical OR), it indicates that the data is actually a pointer.
adChar	A `String` value.
adCurrency	An 8-byte value with 4 digits to the right of the decimal point.
adDate	A date value stored as a `Double`.
adDBDate	A date value in the form of *yyyymmdd*.
adDBTime	A time value in the form *hhmmss*.
adDBTimeStamp	A date-time value in the form *yyyymmddhhmmss*.
adDecimal	An exact numeric value with a fixed precision and scale.
adDouble	An 8-byte double-precision floating point value.
adEmpty	No value specified.
adError	A 32-bit error code.
adGUID	A globally unique identifier.
adIDispatch	A pointer to an `IDispatch` interface of a COM component.
adInteger	A 4-byte signed integer.
adUnknown	A pointer to an `IUnknown` interface of a COM component.
adLongVarBinary	A long binary value used by the `Parameter` object.
adLongVarChar	A long string value used by the `Parameter` object.
adLongVarWChar	A long null-terminated Unicode string value used by the `Parameter` object.

Constant	Description
adNumeric	An exact numeric value with a fixed precision and scale.
adSingle	A 4-byte single precision floating point value.
adSmallInt	A 2-byte signed Integer.
adTinyInt	A 1-byte signed Integer.
adUnsignedBigInt	An 8-byte unsigned Integer.
adUnsignedInt	A 4-byte unsigned Integer.
adUnsignedSmallInt	A 2-byte unsigned Integer.
adUnsignedTinyInt	A 1-byte unsigned Integer.
adUserDefined	A user-defined variable.
adVarBinary	A binary value used with the Parameter object.
adVarChar	A String value used with the Parameter object.
adVariant	A Variant.
adVector	When used with another constant, it indicates that the data is a vector that contains a count of elements and a pointer to the data.
adVarWChar	A null-terminated variable-length Unicode string used with the Parameter object.
adWChar	A null-terminated Unicode string used with the Parameter object.

The Field Object

The Field object represents one column of data returned by a data source and contained in a Recordset. The properties and methods for the object appear in Tables 20.12 and 20.13, respectively.

Table 20.12   The ADO Field Object Properties

Property	Description
ActualSize	Long. Returns the actual length of the Value of the Field for the current record. May return adUnknown if the size cannot be determined.
Attributes	A read-only value that returns the characteristics of the Field. May be set to one or more of the following: adFldMayDefer (retrieved only when explicitly requested), adFldUpdateable, adFldUnknownUpdateable, adFldFixed (contains fixed-length data), adFldIsNullable, adFldMayBeNull, adFldLong (can use AppendChunk and GetChunk), adFldRowID, adFldRowVersion (Field contains a time or data stamp), or adFldCacheDeferred (Field value is cached).

continues

Table 20.12   continued

Property	Description
DataFormat	Specifies the standard data format object (StdDataFormat) to be applied to the Field as it is retrieved from the data source. Useful when using bound controls.
DefinedSize	Long. Returns the size of the Field as defined for the Recordset and not dependent on the current record.
Name	String. Returns the name of the Field from the data source.
NumericScale	Byte. Specifies the number of decimal places to which numeric values will be resolved.
OriginalValue	Variant. Returns the value of the Field before any changes were made.
Precision	Byte. Specifies the maximum number of digits used to represent the numeric value.
Properties	Properties. Returns a collection of Property objects that contain provider-specific information.
Type	Returns the data type of the Field. Can be one of the types shown in Table 20.11.
UnderlyingValue	Variant. Returns the current Field's value from the data source. It is used with the OriginalValue property to resolve conflicts when performing batch updates.
Value	Variant. Specifies the value of the Field in the current record.

Table 20.13   The ADO Field Object Methods

Method	Description
AppendChunk	Appends data to a large text or binary Field object. Accepts a Variant containing the data to be appended. Can be used when the Attributes property of the Field object contains adFldLong. The first use of AppendChunk overwrites existing data for the field, whereas subsequent calls simply append data.
GetChunk	Returns all or a portion of the long data in the Field. Accepts an argument that specifies the number of bytes (or characters, in the case of Unicode data) to retrieve.

The Error Object

The Error object represents one error returned from the data source through the provider. Each command executed against the provider may return one or more errors that are placed in the Errors collection of the Connection object. In addition, the first error also populates the intrinsic Visual Basic Err object. The properties for the object appear in Table 20.14.

Table 20.14   The ADO Error Object Properties

Property	Description
Description	String. A description of the error returned by the provider.
HelpContext and HelpFile	Specifies the help topic and file associated with the Error object. These properties can be used to display context-sensitive help when a specific error occurs.
NativeError	Long. Returns the provider-specific error code returned from the data source.
Number	Long. Returns a number that uniquely identifies the error.
Source	String. Specifies the name of the object, method, or application that originally caused the error.
SQLState	String. Returns a five-character string that follows the ANSI SQL standard.

The Property Object

The Property object represents a dynamic attribute of an ADO object implemented by the provider. This flexibility allows different providers to implement their own set of functionality outside the built-in properties provided by ADO. ADO objects, with the exception of the Error object, contain a collection of Property objects. In many cases, the Property objects for a particular instance of a Recordset or Connection, for example, will mimic some of the built-in properties while also defining new properties not accessible through the built-in object model.

Some properties in the Properties collection are read-only, and others can be modified. Also, as with built-in properties, what you can change the properties to may be restricted by the way in which the object was created or the values of dependent properties.

TIP

To determine whether a property is updateable, you can interrogate the Attributes property for the constant adPropWrite, as explained in Table 20.15.

Access to these dynamic properties is provided only through the `Properties` collection. For example, to discover whether other users' inserts are visible in an open `Recordset` created with the SQL Server provider, you could use the following code:

```
Dim flVisible as Boolean

flVisible = objRs.Properties("Others' Inserts Visible").Value
```

The property can also be referenced by its ordinal position in the collection.

NOTE

To discover the meanings of the properties, you will have to consult the documentation for the specific provider you're using. For SQLOLEDB, the OLE DB provider for SQL Server, the documentation is in the Microsoft Data Access SDK under Microsoft OLE DB/OLE DB Providers/SQL Server Provider.

To get a quick look at the dynamic properties and their values supported by any particular object, you can use code such as the following:

```
Dim objCn As New Connection
Dim objRs As Recordset
Dim objProp As Property

' Open a connection
objCn.Provider = "SQLOLEDB"
objCn.Open "database=contracker;server=ssosa;uid=sa"

' Create a Recordset
Set objRs = objCn.Execute("SELECT * FROM Projects")

' Loop through the collection of properties
' using the properties of the object to display it
For Each objProp In objRs.Properties
    Debug.Print objProp.Name & " = " & objProp.Value & _
        " Data Type: " & objProp.Type
Next
```

Note that although the `Property` object supports a `Type` property to display the data type, this code will display only the number associated with the type. Unless you're very familiar with these constants, you will have to reference the `DataTypeEnum` set of enumerated constants (refer to Table 20.11) using the Object Browser.

The properties for the object appear in Table 20.15.

Table 20.15   The ADO Property Object Properties

Property	Description
Attributes	A read-only property that can be set to one or more of the following: `adPropNotSupported`, `adPropRequired`, `adPropOptional`, `adPropRead`, or `adPropWrite`.
Name	`String`. The name of the property. Note that the name can contain spaces, as well as single quotes.
Type	Returns the data type of the `Property`, as documented in Table 20.11.
Value	`Variant`. Specifies the current `Value` of the `Property`.

Summary

Because ADO is such an integral component in VB applications that access data, in this chapter we've looked at the seven objects of the ADO object model and listed their methods, properties, events, and uses.

CHAPTER 21

Visual Basic Function Reference

The Visual Basic language includes intrinsic functions and statements to do everything from date and time calculations to string manipulations. This chapter includes a section for each type of function or statement, grouped by the type of data the function or statement works with.

NOTE

The difference between a function and statement is that functions typically return values, whereas statements are used to change some system value.

Date and Time Manipulation

The functions and statements used to work with date and time values appear in Table 21.1.

Table 21.1   Date and Time Functions and Statements

Function or Statement	Description
Date	Variant. Both a function that returns the current system date and a statement that changes the system date.
Date$	String. Returns a string populated with the current system date.
DateAdd	Variant. Returns a date to which a specified interval (yyyy, q, m, y, d, w, ww, h, n, or s) has been added. Arguments include the interval, number of units to add, and a Variant representing the date to which the interval will be added.
DateDiff	Variant. Returns the number of specified intervals (same as in DateAdd) between two dates. Optional arguments include the first day of the week and the first day of the year.
DatePart	Variant. Returns the specified part of a date given the interval (as in DateAdd) and the date. Optional arguments include the first day of the week and the first day of the year.
DateSerial	Variant. Returns a date given Integers representing the year, month, and day.
DateValue	Variant. Returns a date given any expression that can represent a date.
Day	Variant. Returns a value between 1 and 31 representing the day of the given date.
FileDateTime	Variant. Returns the date and time a given file was created or last modified.
Hour	Variant. Returns a value between 0 and 23 representing the hour of the given date.
IsDate	Boolean. Returns True if the given expression can be interpreted as a date.
Minute	Variant. Returns a value between 0 and 59 representing the minute of the given date.
Month	Variant. Returns a value between 1 and 12 representing the month of the given date.
MonthName	String. Returns the name of the month or its abbreviation, given its numeric designation (1 through 12) and an argument indicating whether the abbreviation should be returned.

Function or Statement	Description
Second	Variant. Returns a value between 0 and 59 representing the second of the given date.
Time	Variant. Both a function and a statement that return and set the system time.
Time$	String. Returns a string containing the current system time.
Timer	Single. Returns the number of seconds elapsed since midnight.
TimeSerial	Variant. Returns a time value given Integers representing the hour, minute, and second.
TimeValue	Variant. Returns a time value given any expression that can represent a time value.
Weekday	Variant. Returns a number representing the day of the week (1–7) for the given date. The returned value is dependent on the first day of the week value passed as the second argument.
WeekdayName	String. Returns the name or abbreviation of the day of the week, given the numeric designation of the day (1–7), a Boolean value indicating whether abbreviations should be returned, and a constant to determine on which day the first day of the week falls.
Year	Variant. Returns a value representing the year for the given date.

Financial Functions

The functions and statements used to work with annuities, investments, and depreciation appear in Table 21.2. Many of these functions work with annuities that are based on periodic fixed payments and a fixed interest rate. A typical example of using these functions is to calculate the payment for a car loan using the Pmt function. The following code snippet calculates the total payment based on a five-year, 7% loan for a $20,000 car:

```
Dim dblRate As Double
Dim dblPeriods As Double
Dim dblPV As Double
Dim dblPayment As Double

dblRate = 0.07 / 12      ' Convert to monthly rate
dblPeriods = 5 * 12      ' 5-year loan
dblPV = 20000            ' Amount of the loan

dblPayment = Pmt(dblRate, dblPeriods, dblPV)
```

Table 21.2 *Financial Functions*

Function	Description
DDB	Double. Returns the depreciation of an asset for a specified period of time given the cost, value of the asset at the end of its useful life, length of the useful life of the asset, period for which the asset depreciation is calculated, and factor (optional) specifying the rate at which the balance declines.
FV	Double. Returns the future value of an annuity based on periodic, fixed payments and a fixed interest rate given the rate, the total number of payments, the amount of each payment, the present value (optional), and a value (optional) indicating when the payments are due (0 = end of period, 1 = beginning of period).
IPmt	Double. Returns the interest payment for a particular period of an annuity given the rate, the period number, the total number of payments, the present value, the future value (optional), and a value (optional) indicating when the payments are due (0 = end of period, 1 = beginning of period).
IRR	Double. Returns the internal rate of return for a series of periodic cash flows given an array of Doubles specifying the cash flow values and an optional argument indicating your estimation of the return (10% is the default).
MIRR	Double. Returns the modified rate of return for a series of periodic cash flows given an array of Doubles specifying the cash flow values, interest rate paid as the cost of financing, and interest rate received on gains from cash reinvestment.
NPer	Double. Returns the number of payments for an annuity based on periodic, fixed payments and fixed interest given the rate, the payment, the present value, the future value (optional), and a value (optional) indicating when the payments are due (0 = end of period, 1 = beginning of period).
NPV	Double. Returns the net present value of an investment based on a series of periodic cash flows and a discount rate, given the rate and an array of Doubles specifying the cash flow values.

Function	Description
Pmt	Double. Returns the payment for an annuity based on periodic, fixed payments and fixed interest given the rate, the total number of payments, the present value, the future value (optional), and a value (optional) indicating when the payments are due (0 = end of period, 1 = beginning of period).
PPmt	Double. Returns the principal payment for a given period for an annuity based on periodic, fixed payments and fixed interest. Accepts arguments for the rate, the payment period, the total number of payments, the present value, the future value (optional), and a value (optional) indicating when the payments are due (0 = end of period, 1 = beginning of period).
PV	Double. Returns the present value of an annuity based on periodic, fixed payments to be paid in the future and a fixed interest rate. Accepts arguments for the rate, the total number of payments, the payment, the future value (optional), and a value (optional) indicating when the payments are due (0 = end of period, 1 = beginning of period).
Rate	Double. Returns the interest rate per period for an annuity given the total number of payments, the payment, the present value, the future value (optional), a value (optional) indicating when the payments are due (0 = end of period, 1 = beginning of period), and an optional argument indicating your estimation of the return (10% is the default).
SLN	Double. Returns the straight-line depreciation of an asset given the initial cost, value of the asset at the end of its useful life, and length of the useful life of the asset.
SYD	Double. Returns the sum-of-years' digits depreciation for an asset given the initial cost, value of the asset at the end of its useful life, length of the useful life of the asset, and period for which the asset depreciation is calculated.

Formatting Functions

VB contains various functions used to format data for display purposes. A typical use for these functions is to format date and time values. For example, using the Format$ function, you can format the current date and time for display using a user-defined format string.

```
strNow = Format$(Now, "mmm dd, yyyy h:m AM/PM")
```

As a result, the strNow variable is populated with the value "Apr 11, 1999 3:17 PM".

The functions used to format data appear in Table 21.3, whereas the available named formats and the user-defined formatting characters are found in Tables 21.4 and 21.5, respectively.

Table 21.3 Formatting Functions

Function	Description
Format	Variant. Returns an expression formatted according to the given format expression. Optional arguments include constants to specify the first day of the week and the first day of the year. The format expression may be a named format or a user-defined expression. Named formats are shown in Table 21.4. User-defined expressions can be built from the individual characters shown in Table 21.5 and consist of different sections separated by semicolons. For string formats, you can have as many as two sections that are for all strings and those that evaluate to null or the empty string. For numeric data, four sections are available and apply to all data, negative values, zeros, and null values, respectively.
Format$	String. Same as Format, but it returns a String instead of a Variant and is faster.
FormatCurrency	String. Returns a String formatted as currency given the expression, the number of digits to the right of the decimal, whether to include a leading zero, whether to put negative values in parentheses, and whether numbers are grouped using the delimiter specified in the computer's regional settings. All arguments except the expression are optional and can each be set to one of three values indicating True, False, or whether to use the settings from the computer's regional settings.
FormatDateTime	String. Returns a String formatted as a date or time given the expression and an optional named format shown in Table 21.4.
FormatNumber	String. Returns a String formatted as a number given the expression, the number of digits to the right of the decimal, whether to include a leading zero, whether to put negative values in parentheses, and whether numbers are grouped using the delimiter specified in the computer's regional settings. All arguments except the expression are optional and can each be set to one of three values indicating True, False, or whether to use the computer's regional settings.

Function	Description
FormatPercent	String. Returns a String formatted as a percentage with a trailing % character given an expression. Accepts optional arguments, including the number of digits to the right of the decimal, whether to include a leading zero, whether to put negative values in parentheses, and whether numbers are grouped using the delimiter specified in the computer's regional settings. All arguments except the expression are optional and can each be set to one of three values indicating True, False, or whether to use the computer's regional settings.

Table 21.4   Valid Named Formats Used in Formatting Functions

Formatting Function	Description
General Date	Display date and times according to the system
Long Date	settings
Medium Date	
Short Date	
Long Time	
Medium Time	
Short Time	
General Number	A number with no thousands separator
Currency	A number with a thousands separator, currency symbol, and if appropriate, two decimal places to the right of the decimal point
Fixed	A number with at least two digits to the right and one digit to the left of the decimal point
Standard	A number with a thousands separator and at least one digit to the left and two digits to the right of the decimal point
Percent	A number multiplied by 100 with a percent sign to the right and two digits to the right of the decimal point
Scientific	A number using standard scientific notation
Yes/No	Displays No if the number is zero; otherwise, Yes
True/False	Displays False if the number is zero; otherwise, True
On/Off	Displays Off if the number is zero; otherwise, On

Table 21.5   User-Defined Formatting Characters

Formatting Character	Description
: and /	Time and date separators, respectively.
c	Displays a complete date.
d, dd, ddd, dddd, cdddd and dddddd	Options for displaying the day. Display the system short date and long date formats, respectively.
w and ww	Options for displaying the day of the week and the week of the year, respectively.
m, mm, mmm, mmmm	Options for displaying the month.
q	Displays the quarter number.
y, yy, yyyy	Options for displaying the year.
h and hh	Display the hour without and with leading zeros, respectively.
n and nn	Display the minute without and with leading zeros, respectively.
s and ss	Display the seconds without and with leading zeros, respectively.
ttttt	Displays a complete time.
AM/PM, am/pm, A/P, a/p, AMPM	Options for displaying time values using the 12-hour clock and the AM/PM designation.
0 and #	Digit placeholders that display a digit or either a zero (0) or nothing (#).
.	Decimal placeholder.
%	Percentage placeholder.
,	Thousands placeholder.
E-, E+, e-, e+	Options for displaying the number in scientific format.
\	Displays the character following the backslash in the formatted value. This is the same as putting double quotes around a single character.
("ABC")	Displays the string inside double quotes in the formatted value.
@ and &	Character placeholders that display the character or either a space (@) or nothing (&).
<, >	Force all characters to lowercase or uppercase, respectively.
!	Forces left-to-right fill of placeholders.

Interactive Functions

Visual Basic also includes functions and statements that interact with the user and the operating system that appears in Table 21.6.

Table 21.6   *Interactive Functions and Statements*

Function or Statement	Description
`Beep`	A statement used to sound a tone through the computer's speaker.
`DoEvents`	Yields control of the processor to other applications until the operating system has finished processing events in its queue and all keystrokes that have been queued have been processed. Used for a basic form of multitasking. More sophisticated methods involve using a timer or creating a multithreaded application as discussed in Chapter 15, "Using Object-Oriented Techniques."
`InputBox`	`String`. Displays a modal dialog box prompting the user for input. Returns the value the user enters or an empty string if the user presses Cancel. Accepts arguments that include the prompt, dialog title (optional), default response (optional), distance from the left edge of the screen in twips (optional), distance from the top of the screen in twips (optional), help file (optional), and help context id (optional) that can be used to display context-sensitive help.
`MsgBox`	`Integer`. Displays a message in a modal dialog box. Accepts arguments that include the message, buttons and icon to display (`vbOkOnly`, `vbOKCancel`, `vbAbortRetryIgnore`, `vbYesNoCancel`, `vbYesNo`, `vbRetryCancel`, `vbCritical`, `vbQuestion`, `vbExclamation`, or `vbInformation`), dialog title, help file, and help context id. The function returns the number of the button that was clicked by the user. Other options that can be set in the buttons argument include which button will be set to the default, the modality of the dialog, whether the help button is displayed, and how text is aligned.
`SendKeys`	A statement that sends one or more keystrokes to the active window as if typed at the keyboard. Accepts a string argument that includes the keystrokes and a `Boolean` argument that, when set to `False`, indicates that the statement executes asynchronously.

continues

Table 21.6   continued

Function or Statement	Description
Shell	`Variant`. Runs an executable program asynchronously and returns the program's task `ID` if successful. Returns `0` if unsuccessful. The optional second argument specifies the window style to use when the program runs (`vbHide`, `vbNormalFocus`, `vbMinimizedFocus`, `vbMaximizedFocus`, `vbNormalFocus`, or `vbMinimizedNoFocus`).

Math Functions

Visual Basic includes various functions and statements that are mathematical in nature and are used, for example, in geometric algorithms. These functions and statements appear in Table 21.7.

Table 21.7   Math Functions and Statements

Function or Statement	Description
Abs	Returns the absolute value of the number passed to it using the same data type as the given number.
Atn	`Double`. Returns the arctangent of the given number.
Cos	`Double`. Returns the cosine of an angle passed to it in radians.
Exp	`Double`. Returns the base of natural logarithms (approximately 2.718282) raised to a power.
Int and Fix	`Integer`. Return the integer portion of the given number, the difference being that `Int` returns the smaller integer value for negative numbers, whereas `Fix` returns the larger.
Log	`Double`. Returns the natural logarithm of a number.
Randomize	A statement that initializes the random number generator. If no argument is passed to the statement, the generator will be seeded with a value based on the system clock. Using the same number as the seed does not repeat the same sequence of random numbers. To repeat a sequence, call the `Rnd` function with a negative value before using `Randomize` with a numeric argument.

Function or Statement	Description
Rnd	`Single`. Returns a value less than 1 but greater than or equal to 0. If passed a negative number, the function returns the same number each time. If passed a positive number or no argument, the next random number in the sequence is generated. If passed a 0, the most recently generated random number is returned. A typical use for the `Rnd` function is to generate a random number in a given range. To do this, you can use the expression `Int((upperbound - lowerbound) + 1) * Rnd + lowerbound)`, in which upperbound and lowerbound are the highest and lowest numbers in the range.
Sgn	`Variant`. Returns the sign of the given number. If the number is greater than zero, the function returns 1; if zero, then 0; and if negative, then –1.
Sin	`Double`. Returns the sine of an angle specified in radians.
Sqr	`Double`. Returns the square root of the given number.
Tan	`Double`. Returns the tangent of an angle specified in radians.

String Manipulation

Visual Basic also includes various string manipulation functions and statements that can be used to do everything from compare strings, to search and replace within a string, to manipulate strings that can be used to convert. These functions and statements appear in Table 21.8.

Table 21.8   String Functions and Statements

Function or Statement	Description
Asc, AscB, and AscW	`Integer`. Returns the character code of the first letter in the given string. The **B** and W versions of this function return the first byte (`AscB`) or the first Unicode character (`AscW`) on systems where Unicode is supported.
Chr, ChrB, and ChrW	`Variant`. Returns a string containing the character associated with the given character code. This is the reverse of the `Asc` function. The **B** and W versions of this function return a single byte (`ChrB`) or a `String` containing the Unicode character (`ChrW`) on systems where Unicode is supported.

continues

Table 21.8   *continued*

Function or Statement	Description
Chr$, ChrB$, and ChrW$	String. Same as Chr but returns a String.
Filter	Filters a one-dimensional array of strings and returns a zero-based subset of that array based on arguments that include the filter criteria, a Boolean value indicating whether the filter criteria is included (True) or excluded (False), and an optional numeric value indicating the kind of comparison to perform (vbUseCompareOption, vbBinaryCompare, vbTextCompare, or vbDatabaseCompare).
Instr and InstrB	Variant. Returns the position of the first occurrence of one string within another given the starting position, the string being searched, the string expression sought, and an optional numeric value indicating the kind of comparison to perform (vbUseCompareOption, vbBinaryCompare, vbTextCompare, or vbDatabaseCompare). The B version returns the byte position instead of the character position.
InStrRev	Variant. Returns the position of the first occurrence of one string within another searching from the end of the string. Arguments include the string being searched, the string expression sought, the starting position, and an optional numeric value indicating the kind of comparison to perform (vbUseCompareOption, vbBinaryCompare, vbTextCompare, or vbDatabaseCompare). The B version returns the byte position instead of the character position.
Join	String. Returns a String created by joining multiple strings passed in as a one-dimensional array. Also, accepts an optional argument used to delimit the string with a space as the default. Reverse of the Split function.
LCase and UCase	Variant. Returns a Variant converted to lowercase or uppercase, respectively.
LCase$ and UCase$	String. Returns a String converted to lowercase or uppercase, respectively.
Left and LeftB	Variant. Returns a value containing the specified numbers of characters from the left side of the string, given the string and the number of characters. Using the B version, the length specifies the number of bytes to return.

Function or Statement	Description
Left$ and LeftB$	String. Same as Left and LeftB but returns a String instead of a Variant.
Len and LenB	Long. Returns the number of characters in a String. The B version returns the number of bytes required to store the data.
LTrim and RTrim	Variant. Returns a copy of the value without leading spaces (LTrim) or trailing spaces (RTrim).
LTrim$ and RTrim$	String. Same as LTrim and RTrim but returns a String instead of a Variant.
Mid and MidB	Variant. Returns a subset of a String given the String to search, the starting position, and optionally the number of characters to return. If omitted, the remainder of the string is returned. The B version returns a subset of the string based on the number of bytes passed in the second and third arguments.
Mid$ and MidB$	String. Same as Mid and MidB but returns a String instead of a Variant.
Replace	String. Returns a string in which a substring has been replaced by a given string a specified number of times. Arguments include the string in which to perform the replacement, the substring to be replaced, the string to insert, and optional arguments for the starting position, number of substitutions to perform, and a numeric value indicating the kind of comparison to perform (vbUseCompareOption, vbBinaryCompare, vbTextCompare, or vbDatabaseCompare).
Right and RightB	Variant. Returns a value containing the specified numbers of characters from the right side of the string, given the string and the number of characters. Using the B version, the length specifies the number of bytes to return.
Right$ and RightB$	String. Same as Right and RightB but returns a String instead of a Variant.
Space	Variant. Returns a Variant consisting of the given number of spaces.
Space$	String. Same as Space but returns a String instead of a Variant.

continues

Table 21.8   continued

Function or Statement	Description
Split	Returns a zero-based, one-dimensional array of strings created by splitting a given string based on the delimiter passed to the function. Optional arguments include the number of substrings to be returned and a numeric value indicating the kind of comparison to perform (vbUseCompareOption, vbBinaryCompare, vbTextCompare, or vbDatabaseCompare). Reverse of the Join function.
Str	Variant. Returns the String representation of a given number.
StrComp	Variant. Returns a value indicating the result of a comparison given the two strings to compare and an optional numeric value indicating the kind of comparison to perform (vbUseCompareOption, vbBinaryCompare, vbTextCompare, or vbDatabaseCompare). The value returned is –1 if the first string is less than the second, 0 if they are equal, 1 if the first string is greater than the second, and Null if either of the strings is Null.
StrConv	Variant. Returns a given string converted as specified in the second argument (vbUpperCase, vbLowerCase, vbProperCase, vbWide, vbNarrow, vbKatakana, vbHiragana, vbUnicode, or vbFromUnicode). Not all conversion constants are available for all locales. The locale ID can optionally be specified as the third argument.
String	Variant. Returns a string containing the given string repeated the number of times specified.
String$	String. Same as String but returns a String instead of a Variant.
StrReverse	String. Returns the given string in reverse order.
Trim	Variant. Returns a copy of the given value without leading or trailing spaces.
Trim$	String. Same as Trim but returns a String instead of a Variant.

Operators

Visual Basic supports several types of operators that you can use in expressions. In this section, I'll review the assignment, unary, string, arithmetic, logical, and comparison operators, in addition to their precedence.

The Assignment Operator

The assignment operator used in VB is the equal sign (=). It can be used to assign values to variables and properties and optionally can be prefixed with the Let statement, as follows:

```
Let x = 50
```

When assigning values to object variables, the Set keyword is required.

The Unary Operator

The only unary operator VB supports is AddressOf. This operator works on a procedure name and returns its memory address. It is often used when dealing with callback functions in the Win32 API, as discussed in Chapter 13, "Using Win32 API Techniques." A typical example is to pass the address of a public procedure used as the callback procedure for the Win32 API function SetTimer, as follows:

```
mlngTimerID = SetTimer(0, 0, 1, AddressOf TimerCallback)
```

The String Operators

Basically, VB supports only concatenation on strings using the & or + operators. For example, to concatenate two strings, you can use the syntax

```
strName = strFName & " " & strLName
```

Although performance tests indicate that using the + operator is faster, it is recommended you use the & because using the + operator can lead to confusion and errors when dealing with Variant data.

The Arithmetic Operators

Five arithmetic operators are used in VB, and these appear in Table 21.9.

Table 21.9 Arithmetic Operators

Operator	Description
+	Used to sum two numbers.
-	Used to subtract one number from another or indicate that a number is negative.
/	Used to divide two numbers and return a floating-point result.
\	Used to divide two numbers and returns an Integer result.
*	Used to multiply two numbers.
^	Used to raise a number to the power of an exponent, as in 10 ^ 2 = 100.
Mod	Used to find the modulus (remainder) of two numbers, for example, 3 Mod 2 = 1.

The Logical Operators

Visual Basic supports six logical operators that are also used as bitwise operators. A *bitwise* operator simply compares the bit positions of numbers and sets or clears the corresponding bit in the result. Bitwise operations are sometime required when working with the Win32 API or when dealing with events such as MouseDown. The operators and their descriptions appear in Table 21.10.

Table 21.10   Logical and Bitwise Operators

Operator	Description
And	Returns True when both expressions are True. Often used with the If statement, as in If intAge > 18 And strGender = "F" Then.... In a bitwise operation, the bit is set to 1 only if both bits are set to 1. For example, to test the Shift argument passed into the MouseDown event to determine whether the Alt key is pressed, you can execute the code Shift And vbAltMask. If the expression returns a 0, the Alt key was not pressed. This is because the binary value of vbAltMask is 100 (4), which will only return a positive value if the first bit in the Shift argument is also set to 1.
Eqv	Used to perform a logical equivalence on two expressions. In other words, if both expressions evaluate to True or False, the operator returns True. In a bitwise operation, two 0 bits or two 1 bits set the resulting bit to 1.
Imp	Used to perform logical implication (not often, however). If the expression to the left of the operator is False, the result is True. If the both expressions are True, the result is True. If the first expression is True and the second False, the result is False. In bitwise operations, both bits set to 0 or 1 evaluate to 1. If the first bit is set to 1 and the second to 0, the result is 0. If the first bit is set to 0 and the second to 1, the result is 1.
Not	Performs logical negation and is often used with functions that return Boolean values such as IsDate and IsNumeric. For example, If Not IsDate(strDate) Then.... In bitwise operations, it simply reverses the bit.
Or	Performs logical disjunction. In other words, if one of the two expressions evaluates to True, the result is True. For example, If intPos = pos1B Or intPos = posDH Then.... In bitwise operations, if one of the two bits is set to 1, the result is set to 1.
Xor	Performs logical exclusion, which is the opposite of Eqv. If one of the two expressions evaluates to True, the result is True. In all other cases, the result is False. In bitwise operations, if one of two bits is set to 1, the result is 1; in all other cases, it is 0.

The Comparison Operators

The final collection of operators Visual Basic supports are comparison operators. These operators can be used on different types of data and are shown in Table 21.11.

Table 21.11   Comparison Operators

Operator	Description
<	Less than operator that returns True if the first expression is less than the second expression.
>	Greater than operator that returns True if the first expression is greater than the second expression.
<=	Less than or equal operator that returns True if the first expression is less than or equal to the second expression.
>=	Greater than or equal operator that returns True if the first expression is greater than or equal to the second expression.
=	Returns True if the expressions are equal.
<>	Returns True if the expressions are not equal.
Is	Used to compare two object variables and returns True if they are the same. For example, If objCust1 Is objCust2 Then....
Like	Used to compare two strings where the second string is a regular expression. The expression can use the ? to represent any single character, the * to represent zero or more characters, the # to represent any single digit, and brackets ([ ]) to enclose a character list. A typical example might be to determine whether a last name is spelled as *Smith* or *Smythe* using the following code: Dim strName As String strName = "Smythe" If strName Like "Sm[iy]th*" Then ' do something here

Operator Precedence

Although it is recommended that you always use parentheses to ensure that your expressions are evaluated as you intended, Visual Basic must use a set of precedence rules to determine the order in which an expression that contains multiple operators will be parsed.

On the highest level, VB will follow the order arithmetic, concatenation, comparison, and finally, logical. However, within each set of operators, another set of rules is applied. For example, comparison operators are always evaluated from left to right, whereas arithmetic operators are evaluated in the order ^ (exponentiation), / (floating-point division) and * (multiplication) evaluated left to right, \ (integer division), and Mod (modulus), followed by + (addition) and – (subtraction) evaluated from left to right.

In addition, the logical operators follow the precedence Not, And, Or, Xor, Eqv, and Imp. The most common logical error VB developers make is not paying attention to these rules. For example, if I want to return True if a baseball player has 500 homeruns and either 1,000 runs batted in or a .300 batting average, my VB code might look like this:

```
If intHR >= 500 Or intRBI >= 1000 And dblAvg >= 0.3 Then
    ' good player
End If
```

Unfortunately, this would result in an error because And has a higher precedence than Or. In this case, the code inside the If statement would execute if the player has 500 homeruns or 1,000 RBI, in addition to a .300 average. To correct this problem, I would simply rewrite the statement to force VB to evaluate it differently.

```
If (intHR >= 500) Or (intRBI >= 1000 And dblAvg >= 0.3) Then
    ' good player
End If
```

Summary

In this chapter, you've looked at the various intrinsic statements and functions in Visual Basic that are used to perform date and time, financial, formatting, interactive, mathematical, and string calculations. In addition, this chapter discusses the operators that can be used in expressions and their precedence. In the next chapter, you will look at many of the constants that can be used with these statements and functions.

CHAPTER 22

Visual Basic Constants

Many of the methods, properties, functions, and statements used in Visual Basic take advantage of intrinsic constants. This chapter contains a reference of the important constants and indicates where they can be used. In VB, constants are defined in both the VBA and VB runtime components and exposed through enumerated types. These enumerated types are available through the code window's IntelliSense feature. You can also view the constants using the Object Browser.

Throughout this chapter, the name of the enumerated type is used to refer to the set of constants, and each constant with its equivalent numeric value is discussed.

Asynchronous Constants

The constants in this section are used when performing asynchronous operations in ActiveX controls and documents.

The `AsyncTypeConstants` are used to specify the type of data returned by the `Value` property of the `AsyncProperty` object.

```
vbAsyncTypePicture = 0
vbAsyncTypeFile = 1
vbAsyncTypeByteArray = 2
```

The `AsyncReadConstants` are used in the `AsyncRead` method of the `UserControl` and `UserDocument` objects to specify how the data is presented.

```
vbAsyncReadSynchronousDownload = 1
vbAsyncReadOfflineOperation = 8
vbAsyncReadForceUpdate = 16
vbAsyncReadResynchronize = 512
vbAsyncReadGetFromCacheIfNetFail = 524288
```

The AsyncStatusCodeConstants are used to specify the status of an asynchronous operation in the StatusCode property of the AsyncProperty object.

```
vbAsyncStatusCodeError = 0
vbAsyncStatusCodeFindingResource = 1
vbAsyncStatusCodeConnecting = 2
vbAsyncStatusCodeRedirecting = 3
vbAsyncStatusCodeBeginDownloadData = 4
vbAsyncStatusCodeDownloadingData = 5
vbAsyncStatusCodeEndDownloadData = 6
vbAsyncStatusCodeUsingCachedCopy = 10
vbAsyncStatusCodeSendingRequest = 11
vbAsyncStatusCodeMIMETypeAvailable = 13
vbAsyncStatusCodeCacheFileNameAvailable = 14
vbAsyncStatusCodeBeginSyncOperation = 15
vbAsyncStatusCodeEndSyncOperation = 16
```

Calling Procedures

One of the more interesting new features of VB 6 is the capability to call a procedure using a variable. This allows for the creation of dynamic code that can be more flexible. The CallByName function is used to implement this functionality and uses the VbCallType constants to specify the type of procedure being called.

```
VbMethod = 1      VbGet = 2
VbLet = 4         VbSet = 8
```

The Clipboard and DDE Constants

This section enumerates the constants used when performing Clipboard and DDE operations.

The ClipBoardConstants are used with methods of the Clipboard object including GetData, GetFormat, GetText, SetData, and SetText to specify the format of the data on the Clipboard.

```
vbCFLink = -16640    vbCFText = 1
vbCFBitmap = 2       vbCFMetafile = 3
vbCFDIB = 8          vbCFPalette = 9
vbCFEMetafile = 14   vbCFFiles = 15
vbCFRTF = -16639
```

The LinkErrorConstants are used in the LinkError event of controls and forms to specify the type of error that occurred during a DDE conversation.

```
vbWrongFormat = 1      vbDDESourceClosed = 6
vbTooManyLinks = 7     vbDataTransferFailed = 8
```

The `LinkModeConstants` are used to set the `LinkMode` property of the `Form` and `MDIForm`, as well as the `Label`, `PictureBox`, and `TextBox` controls. These constants are used to specify the type of link used in a DDE conversation.

```
vbLinkNone = 0          vbLinkSource = 1
vbLinkAutomatic = 1     vbLinkManual = 2
vbLinkNotify = 3
```

Color Constants

Constants that specify colors can be used to set various properties of controls and forms, such as `BackColor`, `ForeColor`, `Border`, and `FillColor`. The two sets of constants that can be used (in addition to values returned by the `RGB` function) are the `ColorConstants` and `SystemColorConstants`.

The `ColorConstants` are

```
vbBlack = 0          vbRed = 255
vbGreen = 65280      vbYellow = 65535
vbBlue = 16711680    vbMagenta = 16711935
vbCyan = 16776960    vbWhite = 16777215
```

The `SystemColorConstants` specify colors defined by the operating system and set in the Control Panel. These settings can be accessed at design time by choosing the System tab of the Properties dialog.

```
vbScrollBars = -2147483648           vbDesktop = -2147483647
vbActiveTitleBar = -2147483646       vbInactiveTitleBar = -2147483645
vbMenuBar = -2147483644              vbWindowBackground = -2147483643
vbWindowFrame = -2147483642          vbMenuText = -2147483641
vbWindowText = -2147483640           vbTitleBarText = -2147483639
vbActiveBorder = -2147483638         vbInactiveBorder = -2147483637
vbApplicationWorkspace = -2147483636 vbHighlight = -2147483635
vbHighlightText = -2147483634        vbButtonFace = -2147483633
vbButtonShadow = -2147483632         vbGrayText = -2147483631
vbButtonText = -2147483630           vbActiveTitleBarText = -2147483639
vb3DHighlight = -2147483628          vb3DFace = -2147483633
vb3DShadow = -2147483632             vb3DDKShadow = -2147483627
vb3DLight = -2147483626              vbInfoText = -2147483625
vbInactiveCaptionText = -2147483629  vbInfoBackground = -2147483624
vbInactiveTitleBarText = -2147483629
```

Comparison Constants

The `InStr` and `StrComp` functions use the `VbCompareMethod` constants to determine the way strings are compared.

```
vbBinaryCompare = 0
vbTextCompare = 1
vbDatabaseCompare = 2
```

Control Constants

The constants presented in this section are used with intrinsic controls and objects.

The `ScrollBarConstants` are used to set to the `ScrollBars` property of the `TextBox` control.

```
vbSBNone = 0        vbHorizontal = 1
vbVertical = 2      vbBoth = 3
```

The `PictureTypeConstants` are used with the `Picture` object's `Type` property to determine the graphic format of the image.

```
vbPicTypeNone = 0        vbPicTypeBitmap = 1
vbPicTypeMetafile = 2    vbPicTypeIcon = 3
vbPicTypeEMetafile = 4
```

The `ComboBoxConstants` are used with the `Style` property of the `ComboBox` control to determine how the control will behave.

```
vbComboDropdown = 0
vbComboSimple = 1
vbComboDropdownList = 2
```

The `MultiSelectConstants` are used with the `MultiSelect` property of the `FileListBox` and `ListBox` controls to determine whether multiple items can be selected in those controls.

```
vbMultiSelectNone = 0
vbMultiSelectSimple = 1
vbMultiSelectExtended = 2
```

The `ListBoxConstants` are used to set the `Style` property of the `ListBox` control to determine whether check boxes are displayed.

```
vbListBoxStandard = 0
vbListBoxCheckbox = 1
```

The `CheckBoxConstants` are used to set or return the `Value` property of the `CheckBox` control.

```
vbUnchecked = 0
vbChecked = 1
vbGrayed = 2
```

The `ButtonConstants` are used to set the `Style` property of the `CheckBox`, `CommandButton`, and `OptionButton` controls to determine whether the control displays as in versions of VB before 6 or whether it appears in a graphical style.

```
vbButtonStandard = 0
vbButtonGraphical = 1
```

The `AlignConstants` are used to set the `Align` property of controls such as `PictureBox` to determine where an object is displayed inside a form.

```
vbAlignNone = 0        vbAlignTop = 1
vbAlignBottom = 2      vbAlignLeft = 3
vbAlignRight = 4
```

The `AlignmentConstants` are used to set the `Alignment` property of the `CheckBox`, `OptionButton`, and `TextBox` controls.

```
vbLeftJustify = 0
vbRightJustify = 1
vbCenter = 2
```

Date and Time Constants

The `VbDayOfWeek` constants are used to identify specific days of the week in the `DateDiff`, `DatePart`, and `WeekDay` functions.

```
vbUseSystemDayOfWeek = 0   vbSunday = 1
vbMonday = 2               vbTuesday = 3
vbWednesday = 4            vbThursday = 5
vbFriday = 6               vbSaturday = 7
```

The `VbFirstWeekOfYear` constants are used in the `DateDiff` and `DatePart` functions to identify how the first week of the year is determined.

```
vbUseSystem = 0        vbFirstJan1 = 1
vbFirstFourDays = 2    vbFirstFullWeek = 3
```

The `FormatDateTime` function uses the `VbDateTimeFormat` constants to determine how the resulting date will be formatted.

```
vbGeneralDate = 0      vbLongDate = 1
vbShortDate = 2        vbLongTime = 3
vbShortTime = 4
```

Drag-and-Drop Constants

This section enumerates the constants used when performing drag-and-drop operations within a VB project.

The `DragOverConstants` are passed into the `DragOver` and `OLEDragOver` events of controls and forms to indicate the transition state of the control being dragged in relation to the object for which the event fires.

```
vbEnter = 0
vbLeave = 1
vbOver = 2
```

The DragConstants are used as an argument to the Drag method of controls to indicate the action to be performed with respect to the object.

```
vbCancel = 0
vbBeginDrag = 1
vbEndDrag = 2
```

The DragModeConstants are used to set the DragMode property of controls and forms to determine whether a dragging operation begins automatically when the object is clicked.

```
vbManual = 0
vbAutomatic = 1
```

File Constants

The functions GetAttr, SetAttr, and Dir use the VbFileAttribute constants to identify file attributes.

```
vbNormal = 0        vbReadOnly = 1
vbHidden = 2        vbSystem = 4
vbVolume = 8        vbDirectory = 16
vbArchive = 32      vbAlias = 64
```

Form Constants

The constants in this section are used with events, methods, and properties of the Form and MDIForm objects.

The QueryUnloadConstants are used to return how a form is about to unload in the QueryUnload event.

```
vbFormControlMenu = 0    vbFormCode = 1
vbAppWindows = 2         vbAppTaskManager = 3
vbFormMDIForm = 4        vbFormOwner = 5
```

FormShowConstants are used in the Show method to determine whether the form must be dismissed before other forms can regain the focus.

```
vbModeless = 0
vbModal = 1
```

The FormArrangeConstants are used with the Arrange method of the MDIForm object to arrange the windows or icons within the form.

```
vbCascade = 0        vbTileHorizontal = 1
vbTileVertical = 2   vbArrangeIcons = 3
```

The WindowsState property determines the visual state of the form and is set using one of the FormWindowStateConstants.

```
vbNormal = 0
vbMinimized = 1
vbMaximized = 2
```

The StartUpPositionConstants are used with the StartUpPosition property to determine the position of an object when it first appears.

```
vbStartUpManual = 0        vbStartUpOwner = 1
vbStartUpScreen = 2        vbStartUpWindowsDefault = 3
```

The FormBorderStyleConstants are used with the BorderStyle property of the Form, MDIForm, and UserControl objects, in addition to the Frame, Image, Label, Line, MSChart, OLE Container, PictureBox, Shape, TextBox, and Slider controls.

```
vbBSNone = 0               vbFixedSingle = 1
vbSizable = 2              vbFixedDouble = 3
vbFixedDialog = 3          vbFixedToolWindow = 4
vbSizableToolWindow = 5
```

The MenuControlConstants are used to set the behavior and location of a menu displayed using the PopupMenu method.

```
vbPopupMenuLeftAlign = 0       vbPopupMenuCenterAlign = 4
vbPopupMenuRightAlign = 8      vbPopupMenuLeftButton = 0
vbPopupMenuRightButton = 2
```

Graphics Constants

The constants in this section are used when dealing with graphics.

The PaletteModeConstants are used to set the PaletteMode property of the Form, PropertyPage, UserControl, and UserDocument object to determine which palette to use for controls on the object.

```
vbPaletteModeHalftone = 0      vbPaletteModeUseZOrder = 1
vbPaletteModeCustom = 2        vbPaletteModeContainer = 3
vbPaletteModeNone = 4          vbPaletteModeObject = 5
```

The FillStyleConstants are used with the FillStyle property exposed by the Form, Printer, PropertyPage, UserControl, and UserDocument objects, as well as the PictureBox and Shape controls. The FillStyle property specifies the pattern used to fill circles and boxes created with the Circle and Line graphics methods.

```
vbFSSolid = 0              vbFSTransparent = 1
vbHorizontalLine = 2       vbVerticalLine = 3,
vbUpwardDiagonal = 4       vbDownwardDiagonal = 5,
vbCross = 6                vbDiagonalCross = 7
```

The ScaleModeConstants are used with the ScaleMode property of the Form, Printer, PropertyPage, UserControl, and UserDocument objects, as well as the PictureBox control, to specify the unit of measurement when using graphics methods.

vbUser = 0	vbTwips = 1
vbPoints = 2	vbPixels = 3
vbCharacters = 4	vbInches = 5
vbMillimeters = 6	vbCentimeters = 7
vbHimetric = 8	vbContainerPosition = 9
vbContainerSize = 10	

The DrawMode property of the Form, Printer, PropertyPage, UserControl, and UserDocument objects, as well as the PictureBox, Line, and Shape controls, determines the appearance of output from graphics methods such as Line and Circle. The property is set using the DrawModeConstants.

vbBlackness = 1	vbNotMergePen = 2
vbMaskNotPen = 3	vbNotCopyPen = 4
vbMaskPenNot = 5	vbInvert = 6
vbXorPen = 7	vbNotMaskPen = 8
vbMaskPen = 9	vbNotXorPen = 10
vbNop = 11	vbMergeNotPen = 12
vbCopyPen = 13	vbMergePenNot = 14
vbMergePen = 15	vbWhiteness = 16

The DrawStyle property is exposed by the Form, Printer, PropertyPage, UserControl, and UserDocument objects, as well as the PictureBox control, and specifies the line style for output using the DrawStyleConstants.

vbSolid = 0	vbDash = 1
vbDot = 2	vbDashDot = 3
vbDashDotDot = 4	vbInvisible = 5
vbInsideSolid = 6	

The ShapeConstants are used to set the Shape property of the Shape control to indicate its appearance.

vbShapeRectangle = 0	vbShapeSquare = 1
vbShapeOval = 2	vbShapeCircle = 3
vbShapeRoundedRectangle = 4	vbShapeRoundedSquare = 5

The RasterOpConstants are used as an argument to the PaintPicture method of the Form, Printer, PropertyPage, UserControl, and UserDocument objects, as well as the PictureBox control, and specify an operation performed on an image as it is drawn.

vbDstInvert = 5570569	vbMergeCopy = 12583114
vbMergePaint = 12255782	vbNotSrcCopy = 3342344
vbNotSrcErase = 1114278	vbSrcAnd = 8913094
vbSrcCopy = 13369376	vbSrcErase = 4457256

```
vbSrcInvert = 6684742        vbSrcPaint = 15597702
vbPatCopy = 15728673         vbPatPaint = 16452105
vbPatInvert = 5898313
```

Keyboard and Mouse Constants

The constants in this section are used when determining which key was pressed or mouse button clicked.

The ShiftConstants are used in many events such as MouseDown and MouseUp to determine the state of the keyboard when the event occurred, specifically whether the Shift, Ctrl, or Alt key (or any combination thereof) was depressed.

```
vbShiftMask = 1
vbCtrlMask = 2
vbAltMask = 4
```

The MouseButtonConstants are used in many events such as MouseDown and MouseUp to determine which mouse button was pressed when the event fired.

```
vbLeftButton = 1
vbRightButton = 2
vbMiddleButton = 4
```

The KeyCodeConstants are used in the KeyDown and KeyUp events to return which key was pressed.

```
vbKeyLButton = 1             vbKeyRButton = 2
vbKeyCancel = 3              vbKeyMButton = 4
vbKeyBack = 8               vbKeyTab = 9
vbKeyClear = 12             vbKeyReturn = 13
vbKeyShift = 16            vbKeyControl = 17
vbKeyMenu = 18             vbKeyPause = 19
vbKeyCapital = 20          vbKeyEscape = 27
vbKeySpace = 32            vbKeyPageUp = 33
vbKeyPageDown = 34         vbKeyEnd = 35
vbKeyHome = 36             vbKeyLeft = 37
vbKeyUp = 38               vbKeyRight = 39
vbKeyDown = 40             vbKeySelect = 41
vbKeyPrint = 42            vbKeyExecute = 43
vbKeySnapshot = 44         vbKeyInsert = 45
vbKeyDelete = 46           vbKeyHelp = 47
vbKeyNumlock = 144         vbKeyScrollLock = 145
vbKeyMultiply = 106        vbKeyAdd = 107
vbKeySeparator = 108       vbKeySubtract = 109
vbKeyDecimal = 110         vbKeyDivide = 111
vbKeyA through vbKeyZ = 65 to 90
vbKey0 through vbKey9 = 48 to 57
vbKeyNumpad0 = 96
vbKeyNumpad1 through vbKeyNumpad9 = 97 to 105
vbKeyF1 through vbKeyF16 = 112 to 127
```

The `MousePointerConstants` are used with `MousePointer` property of forms and ActiveX controls to specify the type of mouse pointer displayed.

```
vbArrow = 1              vbCrosshair = 2
vbIbeam = 3              vbIconPointer = 4
vbSizePointer = 5        vbSizeNESW = 6
vbSizeNS = 7             vbSizeNWSE = 8
vbSizeWE = 9             vbUpArrow = 10
vbHourglass = 11         vbNoDrop = 12
vbArrowHourglass = 13    vbArrowQuestion = 14
vbSizeAll = 15           vbCustom = 99
```

LoadPicture Constants

The `LoadPicture` function uses the `LoadPictureSizeConstants` and the `LoadPictureColorConstants` to specify the size and color depth of the resulting image.

The `LoadPictureSizeConstants` are

```
vbLPSmall = 0            vbLPLarge = 1
vbLPSmallShell = 2       vbLPLargeShell = 3
vbLPCustom = 4
```

The `LoadPictureColorConstants` are

```
vbLPDefault = 0          vbLPMonochrome = 1
vbLPVGAColor = 2         vbLPColor = 3
```

Logging Constants

The logging constants are used with the `LogEvent` method of the `App` object.

The `LogEventTypeConstants` are used to determine the severity of the event to be logged.

```
vbLogEventTypeError = 1
vbLogEventTypeWarning = 2
vbLogEventTypeInformation = 4
```

The `LogModeConstants` are used with the `StartLogging` method of the `App` object to determine how logging will be carried out.

```
vbLogAuto = 0            vbLogOff = 1
vbLogToFile = 2          vbLogToNT = 3
vbLogOverwrite = 16      vbLogThreadID = 32
```

Message Box Constants

The following constants are used in the `MsgBox` function to specify the style and buttons that are collectively called the `VbMsgBoxStyle`.

vbOKOnly = 0	vbOKCancel = 1
vbAbortRetryIgnore = 2	vbYesNoCancel = 3
vbYesNo = 4	vbRetryCancel = 5
vbCritical = 16	vbQuestion = 32
vbExclamation = 48	vbInformation = 64
vbDefaultButton1 = 0	vbDefaultButton2 = 256
vbDefaultButton3 = 512	vbDefaultButton4 = 768
vbApplicationModal = 0	vbSystemModal = 4096
vbMsgBoxHelpButton = 16384	vbMsgBoxRight = 524288
vbMsgBoxRtlReading = 1048576	vbMsgBoxSetForeground = 65536

The possible return values of the `MsgBox` are enumerated as the `VbMsgBoxResult` constants.

```
vbOK = 1
vbCancel = 2
vbAbort = 3
vbRetry = 4
vbIgnore = 5
vbYes = 6
vbNo = 7
```

OLE Drag-and-Drop Constants

The `OLEDropEffectConstants` are used in arguments passed into the `OLEDragDrop`, `OLEGiveFeedback`, and `OLEDragOver` events to identify the action that has been performed.

vbDropEffectNone = 0	vbDropEffectCopy = 1
vbDropEffectMove = 2	vbDropEffectScroll = -2147483648

The `OLEDragConstants` are used to set the `OLEDragMode` property of controls to specify whether the component of the programmer handles the OLE drag/drop operation.

```
vbOLEDragManual = 0
vbOLEDragAutomatic = 1
```

The `OLEDropConstants` are used to set the `OLEDropMode` property of controls and forms to specify how a target component handles drop operations.

```
vbOLEDropNone = 0
vbOLEDropManual = 1
vbOLEDropAutomatic = 2
```

Resource Constants

The LoadResConstants are used as arguments to the LoadResPicture and LoadResData functions to specify the original format of the data being returned.

```
vbResBitmap = 0
vbResIcon = 1
vbResCursor = 2
```

String Conversion Constants

The constants used in the StrConv function to convert string data are enumerated in the VbStrConv constants.

```
vbUpperCase = 1        vbLowerCase = 2
vbProperCase = 3       vbWide = 4
vbNarrow = 8           vbKatakana = 16
vbHiragana = 32        vbUnicode = 64
vbFromUnicode = 128
```

Window Style Constants

When executing a program using the Shell function, you can use one of the VbAppWinStyle constants to determine the style of the resulting window.

```
vbHide = 0             vbNormalFocus = 1
vbMinimizedFocus = 2   vbMaximizedFocus = 3
vbNormalNoFocus = 4    vbMinimizedNoFocus = 6
```

Summary

In this chapter, I've enumerated many of the important constants used in controls and forms within Visual Basic. It's good practice to use the constants whenever possible, instead of their numeric equivalent, to make your code more readable and consequently easier to maintain.

CHAPTER 23

A COM Primer for Visual Basic Developers

Beginning with version 3.0, Visual Basic began to include support for the Component Object Model (COM) by acting as a client for COM objects. Although most VB developers are familiar with the CreateObject and GetObject functions used to reference COM objects, you might not be familiar with the theory behind COM or its implementation. This is, by most accounts, a good thing and is largely the result of the great work done by the VB development team to hide the details of COM from VB developers while still allowing them to leverage its power and sophistication.

However, because everything in VB (and indeed all Microsoft products) revolves around COM and because creating and using COM objects is the core of many developers' activities, it is essential that you at least understand the basics from a Visual Basic perspective.

To provide this foundation, I'll discuss the big picture of COM and how it relates to Visual Basic.

A Brief History of COM

Although the Component Object Model (COM) has not had a long history, it has been a confusing one. Originally, the concept of allowing one piece of software to access services from another was born from the attempt to allow applications such as word processors to embed or link to data provided by other applications such as a spreadsheet. In this way, a user could work with multiple types of data in their native formats, all from inside the same document. This document-centric view of data became known as *object linking and embedding (OLE)*.

Using this technology, for example, data created in Excel could either be linked into a Word document while still residing in an XLS file or be embedded into the Word document.

NOTE

The initial release of OLE 1.0 was based on dynamic data exchange (DDE) and, although functional, had severe problems related to performance and resource usage that doomed it from gaining wide acceptance.

Even before OLE 1.0 was rolled out, a team of developers at Microsoft had been working on replacing the underlying DDE foundation of OLE with a new component-based technology that was object-oriented and language independent and addressed the issue of interprocess communication. This was largely because Microsoft had realized that creating compound documents is nothing more than one instance of the more general problem of enabling one piece of software to use the services provided by another in a plug-compatible fashion. This technology was christened *COM* and debuted in 1993 with the release of OLE 2.0.

As more and more services were added to COM and it became prevalent in Microsoft products, the company decided to place all the technologies relating to COM under the umbrella term *OLE*. Of course, these new uses for COM, such as creating controls and components, had little to do with linking or embedding, so the term *OLE* ceased to be an acronym and took on a life of its own. This usage found its way into VB in version 4.0, where the ability to create OLE servers and use OLE controls was introduced.

With the rise of the Internet, in 1996 the marketing folks at Microsoft were seeking a flashier name for this technology and hit upon *ActiveX*. This term—although originally retaining a more narrow definition related to Internet-specific features of some COM services such as controls—was eventually expanded to encompass the entire range of COM services. This new usage has been evident in VB 5.0 and 6 with the ActiveX DLL, ActiveX EXE, ActiveX Document, and ActiveX Control project templates. At this point, the term *OLE* once again reverted to its original meaning of object linking and embedding. However, if you look closely, you will still find plenty of references to OLE in the names of core pieces of the COM infrastructure.

As if that isn't confusing enough, the term *ActiveX* is beginning to wane, and the term *COM* has finally reached the forefront. Most developers these days refer to COM components and COM servers rather than use the older *ActiveX* term.

NOTE

Because VB still refers to COM technology using the *ActiveX* moniker, I've retained those references in this book where appropriate. For example, I refer to COM components as *ActiveX code components* and COM controls as *ActiveX controls*.

The Benefits of COM

At its core, COM defines a standard way for two pieces of software to communicate using an agreed-upon set of rules. The benefit of this approach is that as long as a development tool adheres to these rules, it can produce software that uses and/or exposes services to other COM-compliant software.

For an individual developer, this is a godsend because COM does not tie down a developer to a specific development tool or language, giving you the freedom to work in the environment in which you are most comfortable. Fortunately for VB developers, VB is the highest-productivity, COM-enabled development environment on the market. Consequently, VB developers win both ways; they reap the benefits of rapid application development using VB and the ability to use services provided by COM components written by third parties. Conversely, COM components written in VB can be used in other environments, such as Visual C++. In fact, if you think about it, VB's productivity, which derives from its capability to leverage prebuilt components, is a direct result of its tight integration with COM in its use of ActiveX controls and ActiveX code components.

In addition to being language independent, COM also provides an object-oriented paradigm to expose services in one piece of software (a server that houses objects) to another (a client). COM objects can be thought of as packages used to house methods and properties that specify the behavior and state of the object. Although terminology differs, the term *COM object* is often used interchangeably with *COM component*, as I will do in this chapter. However, some authors further make the distinction that a COM component refers to the static definition, whereas a COM object is a runtime instance of the component. In any case, the heart of a COM object is the interfaces it supports. As I'll discuss later, the methods and properties of a COM object are grouped in interfaces that become the contract between a client and a server through which communication occurs.

At the physical level, the fundamental rule that COM specifies is a binary standard for the layout of the COM component. This agreed-upon standard, based on the structure a C++ compiler uses for a class, enables a client to invoke methods and set properties using a series of pointers. Because the way the component is laid out in the computer's memory is specified ahead of time, clients can invoke methods and properties in components compiled at different times and using different compilers. In addition, for in-process components, this makes calling members of a COM object just as fast as calling procedures compiled within an application.

Perhaps the primary benefit of COM is that it provides *location transparency*. Each COM object lives inside a server that can be either a DLL or EXE. These servers can be located on the same computer or on a different computer on the network. As shown in Figure 23.1, this leads to three typical scenarios: COM objects located in DLLs and loaded in the same address space as the client, COM objects located in EXEs on the same computer and communicating across processes, and COM objects running on a remote server and using Distributed COM (DCOM) to communicate. In all cases, the client application can be oblivious to the actual location of the COM object.

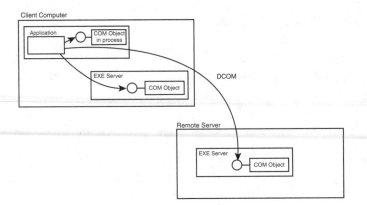

Figure 23.1

COM objects can be accessed in-process, cross-process, and remotely.

NOTE

A slight wrinkle in the architecture shown in Figure 23.1 is that DCOM also allows for products like Microsoft Transaction Server (MTS), where COM objects actually live in a DLL but are loaded in a surrogate process (MTX.EXE) on the MTS server. This allows them to operate as remote objects.

The work of locating the appropriate server and handling the communication is performed by the *COM library,* a set of system services that track the location and identities of all COM objects available from a particular computer. In Visual Basic, this means that a developer can simply use the CreateObject function or New statement to instruct the COM library to find and load a particular COM object. For example, Microsoft Excel exposes its functionality through a set of COM objects. Although Excel always runs in a separate process on the computer, its services can be accessed with code such as the following:

```
Dim objXL As Excel.Application

Set objXL = New Excel.Application
objXL.Workbooks.Add
```

When the Add method of the Workbooks collection is invoked, the call is actually being performed across processes on the local computer.

Interfaces

As mentioned previously, the methods and properties of a COM object are packaged into interfaces. Put simply, an *interface* is a semantically related set of functions, which define the contract between the COM object and the client application. It is the interface that defines the calling syntax of the services the COM object will provide. The main point to be grasped here is that the interface does not specify how methods and properties of an object will be implemented, but instead defines only their signatures. This architecture ensures that interfaces are separate from implementation, which makes using COM objects from different vendors simple. In other words, as long as an object supports a particular interface, a client can call its methods and properties in a plug-compatible fashion. This idea is known as *polymorphism* and is explained in more detail in Chapter 15, "Using Object-Oriented Techniques." In fact, the definition and publication of interfaces is the foundation on which COM-related services popular today—such as the original concept of linking and embedding (OLE), ActiveX controls, and OLE DB—are built.

An interface is typically depicted with a line and circle extending from a COM object, as shown in Figure 23.2. This figure depicts part of the interface for the `clsProject` component discussed in Chapter 15.

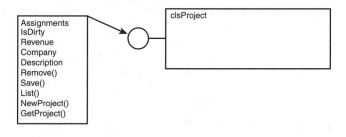

Figure 23.2

An interface is the contract between a COM object and a client application.

For now, the second key point to remember is that after an interface is defined in COM, it should be immutable. In fact, when an interface is created, it is stamped with a globally unique identifier (GUID) called an *interface identifier* (IID). This 16-byte value is guaranteed to be unique across space and time (well, not actually but close enough).

When defined, neither the number of members of an interface nor their data types or return values can be changed. This is required because a client application will rely on the interface for its functionality. By changing the interface, you are breaking the contract with the client. Remember that the client application may not be able to be recompiled whenever you want to change an interface. If changes to the interface are required, the COM specification mandates that an entirely new interface be created. In this way, COM interfaces are also said to be *self-versioning*.

NOTE

Although the COM specification calls for rigidity regarding the versioning of interfaces, Visual Basic relaxes some of these constraints and alleviates much of the work surrounding versioning as discussed in Chapter 16, "Building ActiveX Components."

IUnknown

Every interface in a COM object is derived either directly or indirectly from a special interface named IUnknown. This interface contains methods that handle the housekeeping details of a COM object. These methods appear in Table 23.1.

Table 23.1   Methods of the IUnknown Interface

Method	Description
QueryInterface	Used to provide runtime-type inspection for clients so that they can determine whether an object supports a particular interface. Also, used by a client to navigate between interfaces within an object.
AddRef	Used to implement reference counting for the COM object. Each time a client creates an instance of the object, the AddRef method should be called to ensure that the object does not destroy itself until all clients have released their references.
Release	Used as a companion to AddRef and called when a client will no longer use its instance of the object. AddRef and Release are used to keep track of client references to the objects so that the system knows when the server can be terminated.

For all intents and purposes, the VB developer needn't be concerned with these methods because VB calls them behind the scenes when acting as a client. For example, when an object is created using CreateObject or New, the AddRef method of the object is called behind the scenes. In the same way, when the object is set to Nothing, its Release method is called. The following code results in calls to AddRef and Release for the clsProject COM object.

```
Dim objProj as Consulting.clsProject

Set objProj = New Consulting.clsProject

' Perform some work here

Set objProj = Nothing
```

Similarly, when creating a COM object with VB, the VB runtime implements the IUnknown methods so that the object cleans up after itself after all clients have been released.

The QueryInterface method is used to determine whether an object supports a particular interface and to navigate between interfaces within an object. For example, assume that an object implements both the ICompany and IVendor interfaces discussed in Chapter 15. Using the VB TypeOf statement generates a call to the QueryInterface method of the current interface to determine whether the COM object supports the requested interface. If so, the expression returns True, and a reference to the interface is returned (invoking QueryInterface a second time) by casting an object variable defined for that interface to the existing object variable. After the interface is referenced, one of its members can be invoked.

```
Dim pCompany as ICompany
Dim objVendor As IVendor

' Test to see whether the object supports the IVendor
' interface
If TypeOf pCompany Is IVendor Then
    ' If so, cast a reference to an IVendor object
    ' and set the preferred property
    Set objVendor = pCompany
    objVendor.Preferred = chkPreferred.Value
End If
```

How VB Handles Interfaces

Much of the work that goes into creating COM objects and their interfaces is hidden from VB developers. Within a VB project, COM objects (and usually interfaces) are created when a public class module is added to an ActiveX DLL, EXE, or Document project. As discussed in Chapter 7, "Using Class Modules," class modules can contain methods and properties defined with public Sub, Function, and Property procedures. In most cases, these public members become the interface for the object.

NOTE

Class modules are appropriately named because they are directly correlated with a *COM class*. A COM class is simply a particular implementation of one or more interfaces. In this discussion, a COM class can be used interchangeably with a COM object or COM component.

When a project containing a class module is compiled, VB creates a hidden interface behind the scenes with the name of the class prefixed with an underscore.

TIP

This interface will not show up in the Object Browser because VB always hides identifiers prefixed with an underscore.

At this time, it also publishes both the interface and a reference to its type library (discussed later) in the COM library. In addition, a COM class is created and published in the COM library with its own GUID, called a *class identifier (CLSID)*. When compiled, the new COM object can be referenced in code using a combination of the VB project name and the name of the class module known as the *programmatic identifier* (ProgID). In the example cited earlier, Consulting is the name of the project and clsProject, the name of the class module, so the ProgID becomes Consulting.clsProject.

Although this is the standard approach used in most VB projects and works well when there is a one-to-one mapping between the interface and the class, it is not very flexible. The more elegant COM-compliant technique is to create user-defined interfaces so that the interface can be implemented by multiple classes and a class may implement multiple interfaces. One technique to do this using the Implements keyword is discussed in Chapter 15.

Outside VB, interfaces are defined using the Interface Definition Language (IDL) and compiled using a special compiler called the Microsoft IDL (MIDL) compiler. IDL simply specifies the methods and properties of the interface, along with its data types, arguments, and return values. In addition, attributes of the interface, such as the interface it is derived from and its unique identifier, are also specified. A good way to start looking at IDL is to use the oleview.exe utility provided by Microsoft. Basically, this utility can reverse-engineer the IDL used to specify interfaces installed on your computer.

Although an in-depth discussion of IDL is beyond the scope of this book, an example of the IDL generated by VB for the clsProject class discussed earlier is shown in Listing 23.1.

Listing 23.1   The IDL Generated by VB for the clsProject Class

```
[
    odl,
    uuid(97BA9D13-C1F2-11D2-A076-006008EB5F25),
    version(1.0),
    hidden,
    dual,
    nonextensible,
    oleautomation
]
interface _clsProject : IDispatch {
    [id(0x6003000a)]
    HRESULT Add(
                [in] BSTR pDesc,
                [in] BSTR pCompany,
                [in] BSTR pContact,
                [in] BSTR pPhone,
                [in] VARIANT_BOOL pClass,
                [in] DATE pStart,
                [in] DATE pEnd,
```

```
                    [out, retval] long* );
[id(0x6003000b)]
HRESULT Remove(
                    [in] long pID,
                    [out, retval] VARIANT_BOOL* );
[id(0x6003000c)]
HRESULT List([out, retval] _Recordset** );
[id(0x6003000d)]
HRESULT GetProject(
                    [in] long pID,
                    [out, retval] VARIANT* );
[id(0x6003000e)]
HRESULT AssignConsultant(
                    [in] long pID,
                    [in] long pConID,
                    [in] CURRENCY pRate,
                    [in] DATE pStart,
                    [in] DATE pEnd,
                    [out, retval] VARIANT_BOOL* );
[id(0x6003000f)]
HRESULT RemoveConsultant(
                    [in] long pID,
                    [in] long pConID,
                    [out, retval] VARIANT_BOOL* );
[id(0x60030010)]
HRESULT GetEngagementNum([out, retval] BSTR* );
[id(0x60030011)]
HRESULT ChangeConRate(
                    [in] long pID,
                    [in] long pConID,
                    [in] CURRENCY pRate,
                    [in] DATE pStart,
                    [out, retval] VARIANT_BOOL* );
[id(0x60030012)]
HRESULT GetAssignments(
                    [in] long pID,
                    [out, retval] _Recordset** );
[id(0x60030013)]
HRESULT GetRevenue(
                    [in] long pID,
                    [out, retval] CURRENCY* );
};
```

NOTE

Unfortunately, using user-defined interfaces in VB does not allow the resulting COM object that implements the interface to be used from VBScript and JScript. As a result, you should not use user-defined interfaces when the COM object must be accessible from Active Server Pages (ASP).

Type Libraries

For COM to be an effective tool for publishing software services, developers must be able to see the definition of an object's interfaces at design time. This is the function of the *type library*. In VB, a type library is created when the component is compiled and is included in the binary image. However, type libraries can also exist in standalone files, normally with a .tlb extension.

TIP

Chapter 15 discusses how to create a standalone .tlb file using the Remote Server Files check box of the Project Properties dialog box.

As mentioned previously, the type library—actually accessed as another COM object—is published in the COM library so that development tools can access and view its contents. In VB, the References dialog, accessed from the Project, References menu shown in Figure 23.3, includes a list of all the available type libraries installed on the computer. By choosing one, VB will read the interface definitions and make them available in the Object Browser. In addition, the IntelliSense feature of the code window will be able to check the syntax used to invoke methods and properties.

NOTE

As you will see later, using a type library also allows VB to use a more efficient form of binding when the COM object is called at runtime.

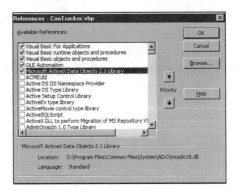

Figure 23.3

The References dialog shows type libraries published on the local computer.

Activation

At runtime, when a client application instantiates a COM object using the CreateObject function or New statement, the COM library is assigned the task of locating the server in which the object resides, loading the server, and returning a pointer for the requested interface to the client application.

The COM library as implemented on 32-bit Windows platforms includes a set of system services (DLLs and EXEs) and entries created in the system Registry for interfaces, classes, and type libraries. The Service Control Manager (SCM, or affectionately referred to as the *scum* and implemented in rpcss.exe) is the component of the COM library responsible for activation. Figure 23.4 depicts this process.

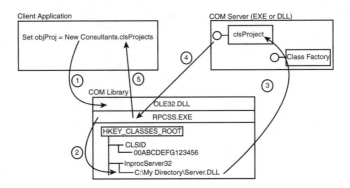

Figure 23.4

The activation process for a COM object.

As implied in the diagram, the ProgID of the COM object must first be translated into a CLSID. This can be done either at runtime by a lookup into the Registry or at compile time if a type library is available. When the CLSID is known, the VB runtime makes a call to the SCM passing it the CLSID when the New statement is executed (step 1). For components that are located on the local computer, the SCM then locates the binary code that implements the server in a Registry key named LocalServer32 or InprocServer32, depending on whether the object should be loaded in-process or out-of-process (step 2). The binary image is then loaded into memory, and an instance of the object is created (step 3). In most cases, the code that actually creates instances of components is located within the DLL. This code is referred to as a class factory and is simply another COM object automatically created by VB upon compilation. After the instance is created, a pointer to the requested interface is returned to the SCM (step 4) and subsequently passed back to the client application (step 5). At this point, all subsequent communication occurs directly between the client application and the instance of the object.

After all references to the object have been released (by calling the Release method derived from IUnknown), the object is responsible for destroying itself.

Automation

As mentioned earlier, COM defines a binary standard for the layout of objects. This structure is known as a *vtable* (or virtual function table) and requires the client to traverse a series of pointers, as shown in Figure 23.5.

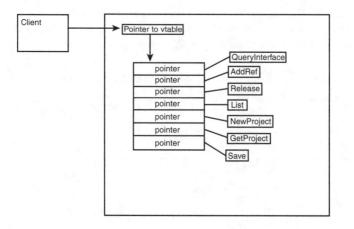

Figure 23.5

The layout of a vtable interface.

Although, since version 5.0, VB has been able to use this native vtable interface, some programming tools cannot produce code capable of this feat. For example, interpreted languages such as VBScript, as implemented in the following ASP code, cannot use a vtable interface:

```
<HTML>
<BODY>
<%
    Set objProj = Server.CreateObject("Consultants.clsProject")
    objProj.GetProject Request.QueryString("Code")

    Response.Write("The project description is: " & _
    objProj.Description)

    Set objProj = Nothing
%>
</BODY>
</HTML>
```

For these types of clients to gain access to COM objects, a technique known as *OLE Automation* or simply *Automation* was developed.

IDispatch

Automation allows simple programming environments to use the services provided by COM objects through what is known as a *dispinterface* derived from an interface named IDispatch. A dispinterface defines a level of abstraction that allows a client to make all its calls to the object through the Invoke method provided by IDispatch. In a dispinterface, only the methods of IDispatch (and those derived from IUnknown) are present in the vtable and not those of the object. Internally, the Invoke method uses a conceptual Select Case statement to execute the requested method using an internal identifier known as a *dispid*.

This arrangement is much simpler because the runtime interpreter for those languages need only know how to traverse the pointers for IDispatch, which can be hard-coded. Table 23.2 describes the methods for IDispatch.

Table 23.2 Methods of the IDispatch Interface

Method	Description
GetIdsOfNames	Maps the names of methods in the dispinterface with an internal number named a *dispid* used to invoke the method.
GetTypeInfo	Retrieves type information for an object that can then be used to retrieve the type information for methods of an interface.

GetTypeInfoCount	Retrieves the number of type information interfaces that an object provides. In other words, if the method returns 1, the object provides type information.
Invoke	Used to invoke a method using a dispid retrieved from GetIdsOfNames.

When using a dispinterface, the client will call GetIdsOfNames at compile time or run-time to determine the dispid of the method that is to be invoked. This dispid is then passed to the Invoke method that actually makes the call. Note that IDispatch is also used to discover information about the data types of arguments and return values from methods in the interface.

Dual Interfaces

Implementing a dispinterface is required when dealing with clients that can't traverse a vtable. However, using a dispinterface adds extra overhead and is much slower than binding directly to the vtable. For this reason, in many instances you will want to implement interfaces that do both. Luckily, VB always implements just such a combination vtable and dispinterface, called a *dual interface*. The vtable for a dual interface is just like that for a dispinterface, except that pointers to the actual methods are added to the end of the table.

Keep in mind that even though an object supports a dual interface, it does not mean that a client will automatically use the vtable implementation. Which method is used depends on how the client is bound to the COM object.

Binding

Binding is the term used to refer to how a client sets up a call to a COM object. The mechanism used affects the overhead of the call and as a result, the performance. The mechanism that is used is determined by several factors, including the way the object was compiled, whether it has a type library, and the syntax used in the calling program.

In VB, there are three types of binding that can occur: late binding and two types of early binding known as dispid binding and vtable binding.

Late Binding

Late binding is used when the VB code declares a variable as Object or Variant. In these cases, the compiler cannot tell ahead of time which CLSID and IID will be requested, so the determination must be made at runtime. A sample declaration, creation, and use of the clsProject object using late binding follows:

```
Dim objProj as Object

Set objProj = CreateObject("Consultants.clsProject")
objProj.NewProject
```

At runtime, VB uses the dispinterface interface and calls GetIDsOfNames passing it the name of the method and then uses the returned dispid to call the Invoke method to execute the method and return the result. Essentially, this means that two calls to the object must be made each time a method or property is accessed, thereby decreasing performance. For objects that reside in a separate process from the client, or perhaps even on a separate server, this greatly affects the responsiveness of the call.

Therefore, late binding should be used only when the requirements of the program dictate that the class of the COM object is truly not known at compile time or when the component containing the class does not provide a type library.

DispID Binding

DispID binding is a form of early binding and is used when the component provides a type library but does not provide a dual interface. In this case, VB uses the GetIdsOfNames method of IDispatch to return the dispid of each method or property called at compile time rather than at runtime. This allows the compiler to essentially replace the name of the method or property with the dispid in the compiled code so that the Invoke method may be called directly at runtime.

To use early binding, the clsProject object first must be added to the References dialog (refer to Figure 23.3) so that its type library may be loaded and used. Second, the declaration of the object must be changed to use the explicit ProgID.

```
Dim objProj as Consultants.clsProject
```

Vtable Binding

This is, of course, the native form of early binding employed by COM and uses an offset into the vtable to invoke the methods of the object.

This method is the fastest way to call COM objects and, as mentioned, takes no more overhead than calling a function in a DLL if the component is loaded in the same process as the caller. If the object being called is out of process or across the network, vtable binding is still the fastest, but the performance gain is not as significant.

When acting as a client, VB will always use vtable binding if the object supports it and the object is explicitly dimensioned with its ProgID. Consequently, the form of early binding (dispid or vtable) the VB compiler uses is not up to the caller, because the syntax is identical, but is dependent on the COM object.

All COM objects created with VB automatically support dual interfaces and provide a type library so that they will be early bound using vtable binding when called from VB using an explicit ProgID.

CreateObject Versus New

When using early binding, there are actually three ways to create an instance of a COM object. All three of the following code snippets for the clsProject object are functionally equivalent.

```
Dim objProj as New Consultants.clsProject

Dim objProj as Consultants.clsProject
Set objProj = CreateObject("Consultants.clsProject")

Dim objProj as Consultants.clsProject
Set objProj = New Consultants.clsProject
```

In all three cases, the component is created using the SCM as previously described. However, the first method is not recommended because the object will not actually be created until the first time it is referenced. This requires the compiler to essentially wrap all subsequent calls to the object in If...Then logic to determine when the object is actually created.

Likewise, the second technique is not recommended because it requires one extra call to the SCM to do a lookup of the ProgID and translate it to its CLSID.

On the other hand, the third technique is recommended because the CLSID of the object can be discovered at compile time so that the process of activation can be as streamlined as possible at runtime.

TIP

Using the New operator to create classes internal to a project is recommended because it instructs VB to bypass the SCM in favor of a private and optimized creation method.

GetObject

As a final note, you can also use the GetObject function to return a reference to an already instantiated COM object or create a new instance initializing it with a file. The function takes two optional arguments: the pathname and ProgID. By setting the pathname to an empty string (" "), a new instance of the object will be created. To create a new instance of clsProject, you would execute the following code:

```
Dim objProj as Consultants.clsProject
Set objProj = GetObject("","Consultants.clsProject")
```

If the pathname is omitted, an existing instance of the object will be returned if possible or a trappable error will occur. If the pathname contains a file, the object will be instructed to load the file upon initialization. For example, to create an instance of Word and load it with a document, you would code

```
Dim objDoc as Word.Document
Set objDoc = GetObject("c:\My Documents\report.doc","Word.Document")
```

If the pathname is specified, but the class is not, the file will be loaded and a COM object created using the association information stored in the system Registry.

DCOM

For COM to be used effectively across the network and enable clients to access objects running on remote servers, a mechanism had to be used to provide the communication. Microsoft chose to piggyback on the existing remote procedure call (RPC) industry specification to create Distributed COM (DCOM). Simply put, DCOM provides the infrastructure to intercept calls to objects, route them to the appropriate server, and return the results to the client application. In addition, DCOM provides security for those calls ranging from client authentication to encryption.

Figure 23.6 depicts this architecture.

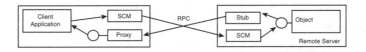

Figure 23.6

Communication between a client and a remote server begins with the client application and uses a proxy and stub with RPC.

As noted in the figure, a proxy and stub are created on the client and server computer, respectively, in essence to trick the client application and the COM object into thinking that the communication is happening locally. The management of these objects is handled by DCOM.

Although the details of the infrastructure are beyond the scope of this book, it is worth describing the way in which a client computer can be configured and the mechanisms used to call a remote COM object.

Configuring the Client

For a client application to call a remote server using DCOM or a component running in MTS, the DCOM client files must be installed on the client computer. On Windows NT 4.0, the files are included as part of the base installation. However, on Windows 9x systems, the DCOM files must be installed separately. The DCOM98 1.0 installation ships as a part of Visual Studio 6.0 and can be installed using the DCOM98.EXE program.

Accessing the Remote Object

Essentially, there are two ways to call a remote object using DCOM: using CreateObject directly or configuring the client using DCOMCNFG.

Using CreateObject

New in VB 6 is the capability to pass a second argument to the CreateObject function that specifies the name of a server on which to run the component. For example, to create the clsProject object on a server named SOLUTECH1, you could use the following code:

```
Set objProj = CreateObject("Consultants.clsProject","SOLUTECH1")
```

When this code is executed, the SCM on the local machine contacts the SCM on the remote server and passes it the CLSID and IID that are being requested. If the remote server can load and create the object, a valid reference is passed back across the network.

NOTE

DCOM uses a pinging technique (every two minutes) to ensure that the remote server is still alive. If the remote object does not respond after three pings, it is assumed to have been destroyed.

This sort of code lends itself well to situations in which the server can be changed dynamically to implement some form of load balancing.

Using the DCOMCNFG Utility

For situations that are more static or to configure a remote object that is used by several client applications on the same computer, you can use the DCOMCNFG utility. This utility is not installed in a program group, so it must be executed from the Run dialog on the Start menu. The resulting dialog appears in Figure 23.7.

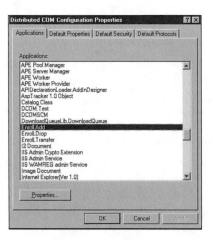

Figure 23.7

The DCOMCNFG utility used to configure both client and server properties for remote components.

As you can see, the application presents four tabs. The Applications tab lists all the components that can be configured to use DCOM. For a component to appear in this list, it must have its CLSID in the list of class IDs under the `HKEY_CLASSES_ROOT\AppID` key in the Registry. The Default Properties tab allows you to set the default communication properties for all the components on the computer, and the Default Security tab lets you set the default access, launch, and configuration permissions. The Default Protocols tab lists the network protocols available to DCOM on the computer.

TIP

If you don't see your component in the list, it might be listed by its CLSID and not its ProgID. To display it as a readable name, alter the Registry key `HKEY_CLASSES_ROOT\AppID\{your CLSID}` and change the Default key that reads `value not set` to the ProgID. Then close and reopen DCOMCNFG.

To set the individual permissions for a COM object, select it from the list of applications on the Applications tab, and click Properties. These properties are stored as values in the `AppID` key for the CLSID of the component. The options that are presented and those you would set differ as to whether you are configuring the client computer or the server.

On the client computer, the primary tab you will be interested in is the Location tab, which specifies the computer on which the component can be found, as shown in Figure 23.8.

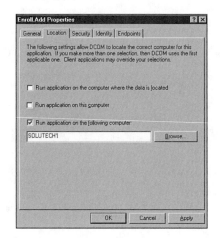

Figure 23.8

Setting the remote server name using DCOMCNFG.

Setting the remote computer name creates a `RemoteServerName` value under the `AppID` key for the CLSID of the component in the Registry.

TIP

This value can be set automatically by an installation program created using the Package and Deployment Wizard. To do so, use the Remote Server dialog in the wizard. Note that you will have to check the Remote Server Files check box on the Component tab of the Project Properties dialog box before compiling the component.

Summary

In this chapter, I presented the history and benefits of COM, as well as defined core COM concepts such as interfaces, activation, Automation, binding, and DCOM.

Obviously, the details of COM are more complex than discussed here, but this should give you the basics that will allow you to be more productive in VB as a result. For further reading, I would recommend *Understanding ActiveX and OLE* by David Chappell, as well as *Programming Distributed Applications with COM and Microsoft Visual Basic 6.0* by Ted Pattison. Both are excellent places to drill down a little deeper into what is surely the most important concept for a VB developer to grasp.

CHAPTER 24

Array Techniques

In this final chapter, you will examine some of the basic sorting and searching algorithms that are useful when dealing with arrays in Visual Basic. In addition, you will look at a common technique for providing type-ahead functionality in a form-based application.

Sorting Algorithms

It is often useful to sort data used internally by an application in order to display it to the user or as a step preceding a search. In this section, I will present the basic sorting algorithms as they are implemented in VB and discuss their pros and cons. In all cases, the algorithms presented are designed to sort in ascending order and to work with multidimensional `Variant` arrays structured in a conceptual table where the first dimension of the array represents the columns and the second, the rows. Obviously, each algorithm can be simplified to use an array with a single dimension or a specific data type.

Multidimensional arrays were chosen because they can represent more data and are useful for storing data retrieved from a relational database. All the sorting functions discussed in this chapter also use a private procedure named `CompMe`, shown in Listing 24.1, to perform the comparison. Abstracting the comparison into a separate function allows the same code to sort the array in either ascending or descending order and perform either a numeric or string comparison.

> ### TIP
>
> If you simply perform less than or greater than comparisons on strings, VB will compare the numeric values of those strings, resulting in a sort that will be case sensitive. In `CompMe`, you will notice that the `StrComp` function is used, where appropriate, because this function is faster and doesn't require the string to be converted to uppercase before being compared.

Listing 24.1   The Compare CompMe Function Used in All the Sorting Algorithms in This Chapter

```
Private Function CompMe(ByVal pArg1 As Variant, ByVal pArg2 As Variant, _
    ByVal pDesc As Boolean, Optional pEqual As Boolean) As Boolean

CompMe = False

' If descending, do a less than compare
If pDesc Then
    Select Case pEqual
    ' If equality is specified, use an equal sign
    Case True
        ' Check whether it's a string to do a string compare
        If VarType(pArg1) = vbString Then
            If UCase(pArg1) <= UCase(pArg2) Then
                CompMe = True
            End If
        Else
            If pArg1 <= pArg2 Then
                CompMe = True
            End If
        End If
    Case False
        ' If not specified, do a < compare
        If VarType(pArg1) = vbString Then
            If StrComp(pArg1, pArg2, vbTextCompare) = -1 Then
                CompMe = True
            End If
        Else
            If pArg1 < pArg2 Then
                CompMe = True
            End If
        End If
    End Select
Else
    ' If ascending, do a greater than compare
    Select Case pEqual
```

```
Case True
    ' Check whether it's a string first
    If VarType(pArg1) = vbString Then
        If UCase(pArg1) >= UCase(pArg2) Then
            CompMe = True
        End If
    Else
        If pArg1 >= pArg2 Then
            CompMe = True
        End If
    End If
Case False
    ' Check whether it's a string
    If VarType(pArg1) = vbString Then
        If StrComp(pArg1, pArg2, vbTextCompare) = 1 Then
            CompMe = True
        End If
    Else
        If pArg1 > pArg2 Then
            CompMe = True
        End If
    End If
End Select
End If

End Function
```

Bubble Sort

The first and most basic sorting technique is the bubble sort. Using this technique, the array is sorted by comparing pairs of elements according to their indexes and swapping them if the element with the smaller index is greater than the element with the larger index. In this way, after one pass through the array, the largest element will have been "bubbled" to the last position in the array. These steps are repeated as the array is again traversed, this time leaving off the last element. In total, the number of comparisons for a bubble sort equals $(n-1)*(n/2)$, where n is the number of elements in the array. For example, with 10 elements in the array, the number of comparisons would be $45 = (10-1)*(10/2)$.

Although the bubble sort slows as the size of the array grows, it is simple to remember and is very efficient for smaller arrays (less than 25 items). However, given the formula above, as the number of elements in the array grows, the number of comparisons grows very quickly. For example, sorting an array with 20 elements takes 190 comparisons $(190 = (20-1) * (20/2))$. As you can see, doubling the array size increases the complexity by a factor of 4. A public Sub procedure that can be included in a code module appears in Listing 24.2.

Listing 24.2   A Bubble Sort Procedure

```
Public Sub BubbleSort(varArray As Variant, _
    Optional flDescending As Boolean, Optional ByVal pIndex As Integer)

Dim i As Long
Dim j As Long
Dim varTemp As Variant

' If the optional index is 0, set it to the
' lower bound (sort by first column)
If pIndex = 0 Then
    pIndex = LBound(varArray, 1)
End If

' Loop through the array using the second
' dimension of the array (the rows)
For i = LBound(varArray, 2) To UBound(varArray, 2)
    For j = LBound(varArray, 2) To UBound(varArray, 2) - 1 - i
        ' Compare the items in the array
        If CompMe(varArray(pIndex, j), varArray(pIndex, j + 1), _
                flDescending) Then
            ' If the first item is larger, swap them
            varTemp = varArray(pIndex, j)
            varArray(pIndex, j) = varArray(pIndex, j + 1)
            varArray(pIndex, j + 1) = varTemp
        End If
    Next j
Next i

End Sub
```

You will notice that the procedure takes an optional third argument that specifies the index of the first dimension on which to perform the sort. This technique makes it possible to sort the array in different ways. For example, the following code retrieves an ADO Recordset and then saves it in a Variant array using the GetRows method. The array can then be sorted on different fields in the Recordset by position using the BubbleSort procedure.

```
Set rsProj = New Recordset
rsProj.CursorLocation = adUseClient
rsProj.Open "SELECT * FROM Projects", cnCon, adOpenStatic, adLockReadOnly

varData = rsProj.GetRows(adGetRowsRest)

BubbleSort varData, False, 2 ' Sort by company
```

Selection Sort

The second type of sort you can implement is the selection sort. The selection sort is actually the inverse of the bubble sort and uses a similar nested loop approach to find the lowest value element in the array. When found, the element is copied to the beginning of the array, and the search is confined to the remainder of the array. This process is repeated until all elements have been placed.

Like the bubble sort, the selection sort is not particularly efficient for large arrays and performs the same number $((n-1)*(n/2))$ of comparisons. A procedure to implement a selection sort appears in Listing 24.3.

Listing 24.3   A Selection Sort

```
Public Sub SelectionSort(varArray As Variant, _
    Optional flDescending As Boolean, Optional ByVal pIndex As Integer)

Dim i As Long
Dim z As Long
Dim j As Long
Dim varTemp As Variant

' If the optional index is 0, set it to the
' lower bound (sort by first column)
If pIndex = 0 Then
    pIndex = LBound(varArray, 1)
End If

For i = LBound(varArray, 2) To UBound(varArray, 2)
    z = i
    ' Iterate through the rest of the array to find the lowest
    ' value
    For j = (i + 1) To UBound(varArray, 2)
        ' See whether the value is less
        If CompMe(varArray(pIndex, z), varArray(pIndex, j), _
            flDescending) Then
            ' If so, j is the lowest index
            z = j
        End If
    Next j

    ' Put the new lowest in position
    varTemp = varArray(pIndex, z)
    varArray(pIndex, z) = varArray(pIndex, i)
    varArray(pIndex, i) = varTemp
Next i

End Sub
```

Insertion Sort

The third type of sort to be considered is the insertion sort. Using this technique, the array is traversed starting with the second element. As each element is examined, it is determined whether the element should come before the preceding element. If so, the current element is picked up, and the preceding element slides into its place. The element that was picked up is then iteratively compared against each preceding element until its rightful place is found.

The insertion sort is more efficient for larger arrays than either the bubble or selection sorts and works especially well on data that is almost in the sorted order. The number of comparisons that have to be made depends on how closely the data resembles the sorted order. The algorithm to perform the insertion sort appears in Listing 24.4.

Listing 24.4   The Insertion Sort

```
Public Sub InsertionSort(varArray As Variant, _
    Optional flDescending As Boolean, Optional ByVal pIndex As Integer)

Dim i As Long
Dim lngPos As Long
Dim varTemp As Variant
Dim lngLB As Long

' If the optional index is 0, set it to the
' lower bound (sort by first column)
If pIndex = 0 Then
    pIndex = LBound(varArray, 1)
End If

' Cache the lower bound
lngLB = LBound(varArray, 2)

For i = lngLB + 1 To UBound(varArray, 2)
    ' Pick up the current value
    varTemp = varArray(pIndex, i)
    lngPos = i

    ' Loop back until the beginning
    Do While lngPos > lngLB
        ' If the element to the left is larger than the current
        If CompMe(varArray(pIndex, lngPos - 1), varTemp, flDescending) Then
            ' Shift the element to left over one
            varArray(pIndex, lngPos) = varArray(pIndex, lngPos - 1)
            lngPos = lngPos - 1
        Else
            Exit Do
        End If
```

```
    Loop
    ' Put the current element into the empty hole
    varArray(pIndex, lngPos) = varTemp
Next i

End Sub
```

Shell Sort

The shell sort is a variant of the insertion sort but uses a skip count to speed the process of getting smaller elements to the front of the array. In other words, rather than start at the second position and make a comparison to the element immediately preceding it, the shell sort starts much further along the array and compares with an item much closer to the front. With each iteration, an insertion sort is performed, and the skip count becomes smaller until the skip count reaches 1, at which time a normal insertion sort is done. The advantage is that larger elements do not have to be moved long distances within the array (one place at a time), as in an insertion sort.

A shell sort is useful for larger arrays that are not necessarily in sorted order, although, as with the insertion sort on which it is based, arrays that resemble the sorted order are preferred. The code in Listing 24.5 shows a shell sort.

Listing 24.5   The Shell Sort
```
Public Sub ShellSort(varArray As Variant, _
    Optional flDescending As Boolean, Optional ByVal pIndex As Integer)

Dim i As Long
Dim lngPos As Long
Dim varTemp As Variant
Dim lngLB As Long
Dim lngSkip As Long
Dim flDone As Boolean

' If the optional index is 0, set it to the
' lower bound (sort by first column)
If pIndex = 0 Then
    pIndex = LBound(varArray, 1)
End If

' Cache the lower bound
lngLB = LBound(varArray, 2)

' Assign the skip count
Do
    lngSkip = (3 * lngSkip) + 1
Loop Until lngSkip > UBound(varArray, 2)

lngSkip = (UBound(varArray, 2) - 1) * 3
```

continues

Listing 24.5   continued

```
Do

    ' Decrement the skip each time through the loop
    lngSkip = lngSkip / 3

    ' Check the remainder of the array
    For i = lngSkip + 1 To UBound(varArray, 2)
        ' Pick up the current value
        varTemp = varArray(pIndex, i)
        lngPos = i

        ' If we've reached the beginning, increment the
        ' skip count, but signal that this is the last pass
        If lngSkip = 0 Then
            lngSkip = 1
            flDone = True
        End If
        ' Check whether the preceding element is larger
        Do While CompMe(varArray(pIndex, lngPos - lngSkip), _
            varTemp, flDescending)
            ' If so, slide it in
            varArray(pIndex, lngPos) = varArray(pIndex, lngPos - lngSkip)
            lngPos = lngPos - lngSkip
            If lngPos <= lngSkip Then Exit Do
        Loop
        ' Put the current value back down
        varArray(pIndex, lngPos) = varTemp
    Next i

Loop Until lngSkip = lngLB Or flDone

End Sub
```

You will notice in Listing 24.5 that the skip count was calculated before the sort to provide a value that, when divided by 3, will produce the index at which to start the sort. Keep in mind that starting the first insertion sort at a higher index provides a greater benefit because it is more expensive to move the value later. The skip count is then divided by 3 with each iteration of the loop until it reaches the lower bound of the array or has effectively reached 0.

QuickSort

The final sorting algorithm I'll discuss is the QuickSort. This algorithm was originally published in 1962 and is generally considered the fastest.

The QuickSort uses recursion to divide the array and sort it in sections based on a pivot value. Basically, the algorithm predetermines a pivot index and then traverses the array in both directions to find the index at which that element should be sitting when the array is fully sorted. Along the way, elements are swapped to ensure that the element identified by the pivot index is always greater than all the elements lower in the array and less than all the elements higher in the array (when doing an ascending sort). When completed, the array is partitioned into two sections around this value (hence the term *pivot*), and the process is repeated recursively.

Although the QuickSort is usually faster, keep in mind that because it uses recursion, there are stack space issues to be aware of and it might not perform as well as other techniques if the elements are already close to being in sorted order. The code to implement the QuickSort appears in Listing 24.6.

NOTE

You can use one more sorting algorithm, known as the Counting Sort. I do not include it here because it sorts only numeric values, whereas the techniques presented in this chapter work for both numeric and text data. For numeric data, Counting Sort is very fast, with little resource usage. For more information, see the article by Rod Stephens at `www.microsoft.com/officedev/articles/movs102.htm`.

Listing 24.6   The QuickSort

```
Public Sub QuickSort(varArray As Variant, _
    ByVal pIndex As Integer, ByVal pFirst As Long, _
    ByVal pLast As Long)


Dim lngPivot As Long

' If the range is valid, sort
If pFirst < pLast Then
    ' Split the array and return the index of the item that is in
    ' the correct location
    PartitionArray pFirst, pLast, lngPivot, varArray, pIndex
    ' Sort the lower portion
    QuickSort varArray, pIndex, pFirst, lngPivot - 1
    ' Sort the upper portion
    QuickSort varArray, pIndex, lngPivot + 1, pLast
End If

End Sub


Private Sub PartitionArray(ByVal pFirst As Long, _
    ByVal pLast As Long, ByRef pPivot As Long, _
    varArray As Variant, ByVal pIndex As Integer)
```

continues

Listing 24.6   continued

```
Dim varPivot As Variant
Dim varTemp As Variant
Dim i As Long
Dim j As Long

' Choose the pivot as the last element in the range
varPivot = varArray(pIndex, pFirst)
i = pFirst
j = pLast + 1
Do
    ' Loop from the beginning of the range until you
    ' find a larger element or there are none
    Do
        i = i + 1
    Loop Until CompMe(varArray(pIndex, i), _
        varPivot, False, True) Or i >= pLast

    ' Loop from the end of the array until you
    ' find a smaller element or there are none
    Do
        j = j - 1
    Loop Until CompMe(varArray(pIndex, j), _
        varPivot, True, True) Or j <= pFirst

    ' If they haven't crossed, swap them
    If i < j Then
        varTemp = varArray(pIndex, i)
        varArray(pIndex, i) = varArray(pIndex, j)
        varArray(pIndex, j) = varTemp
    End If

Loop Until j <= i

' Swap the pivot with the split in the array
varArray(pIndex, pFirst) = varArray(pIndex, j)
varArray(pIndex, j) = varPivot

' Return the index of the element that is now in the correct
' location so that another sort can be done of the two halves
pPivot = j

End Sub
```

In Listing 24.6, notice that the QuickSort actually consists of two procedures: QuickSort and PartitionArray. The QuickSort procedure calls PartitionArray and calls itself recursively to partition the resulting sections of the array.

Performance

Which sorting algorithm you should choose for a given application is highly dependent on what type of data and how much data you will be sorting. To give some basic benchmarks, I ran a very simple test using a two-dimensional array in which the second index of the first dimension was populated with random numbers. I then ran each of the sorting algorithms discussed in this chapter, using a variable number of elements. The timings in Table 24.1 should give you some numbers to consider.

NOTE

Remember that this test uses random numbers, which should be well distributed. For data that is more highly ordered, the results will be different.

Table 24.1 Performance Timings in Seconds Using the Various Sorting Algorithms

Elements	Bubble	Shell	Selection	Insertion	QuickSort
20	< .01	< .01	< .01	< .01	< .01
75	.40	.01	.02	.01	.01
250	4	.03	.28	.17	.02
1000	6.7	.19	4.9	2.9	.08
5000	168	1.3	121	74	.49

TIP

One simple method for obtaining timings at the millisecond level is to use the GetTickCount Win32 API function. It simply returns the number of milliseconds that have elapsed since the system was started.

Searching Algorithms

After an array is sorted, it is often beneficial to be able to search it for a particular value. In this section, you will look at the most often used searching algorithm—the binary search—followed by a variation of the binary search known as the *interpolation search*.

As with the algorithms for sorting, the searching algorithms presented in this chapter work on two-dimensional arrays, with the first dimension representing the columns and the second, the rows. The algorithms work for both string and numeric data and perform string searches without regard to case.

Binary Search

The binary search is perhaps the most popular searching algorithm in use. The concept behind the algorithm is the same as the QuickSort, namely, to divide and conquer. With each iteration, the midpoint of a sorted array is chosen, and a comparison is made. If the search value is higher than the midpoint, the bottom half of the array is discarded, and the top half is searched in the same fashion. This process is repeated until the search value is found or the array can no longer be divided.

In the worst case, the binary search takes n steps, whereas the array contains 2^n elements. A procedure to implement a binary search on an array sorted in ascending order appears in Listing 24.7.

Listing 24.7   A Binary Search Algorithm

```
Public Function BinSearch(varArray As Variant, _
    ByVal varSearch As Variant, Optional ByVal pIndex As Integer, _
    Optional ByVal flPartial As Boolean) As Long

Dim lngLow As Long
Dim lngUpper As Long
Dim lngPos As Long

' Set the upper and lower bounds of the array
lngLow = LBound(varArray, 2)
lngUpper = UBound(varArray, 2)

Do While True
    ' Divide the array to search
    lngPos = (lngLow + lngUpper) / 2

    ' Look for a match
    If flPartial Then
        ' If partial is specified, do a comparison
        ' on the substring because it should be a string
        If StrComp(Mid(varArray(pIndex, lngPos), 1, Len(varSearch)), _
                varSearch, vbTextCompare) = 0 Then
            ' If we've found it, get out
            BinSearch = lngPos
            Exit Function
        End If
    Else
        ' Check whether it's a string
        If VarType(varSearch) = vbString Then
            If StrComp(varArray(pIndex, lngPos), varSearch, _
                    vbTextCompare) = 0 Then
                ' If we've found it, get out
                BinSearch = lngPos
                Exit Function
            End If
```

```
        Else
            If varArray(pIndex, lngPos) = varSearch Then
                ' If we've found it, get out
                BinSearch = lngPos
                Exit Function
            End If
        End If
    End If
        ' Check whether it's the last value to be checked
        If lngUpper = lngLow + 1 Then
            lngLow = lngUpper
        Else
            ' If we get to the lowest position, it's not there
            If lngPos = lngLow Then
                BinSearch = -1
                Exit Function
            Else
                ' Determine whether to look in the upper or
                ' lower half of the array
                If VarType(varSearch) = vbString Then
                    If StrComp(varArray(pIndex, lngPos), _
                            varSearch, vbTextCompare) = 1 Then
                        lngUpper = lngPos
                    Else
                        lngLow = lngPos
                    End If
                Else
                    If varArray(pIndex, lngPos) > varSearch Then
                        lngUpper = lngPos
                    Else
                        lngLow = lngPos
                    End If
                End If
            End If
        End If
Loop

End Function
```

Note that the BinSearch function in Listing 24.7 returns the index of the element if the search is successful and a -1 if the search value is not found. In addition, the function includes an optional final argument that determines whether a partial search is executed using the Mid function. This can be especially useful for string searches such as the one performed in the final section of this chapter. This implementation of the binary search also uses the StrComp function when doing string comparisons so that the search will be case insensitive.

TIP

As with most searching and sorting algorithms, the binary search can easily be rewritten as a recursive procedure in the same way that the QuickSort was done.

Interpolation Search

A variant of the binary search is the interpolation search. Basically, this algorithm uses the same divide-and-conquer approach, but it attempts to make an intelligent decision about where the division should take place. In other words, rather than simply split the array in the middle, an attempt is made to make an educated guess about where the array should be split.

As an example, consider searching a sorted array for the string "Cochrane". Rather than split the array in the middle (which would typically be near values starting with the letter M, assuming an alphabetically even distribution), the algorithm notes that the letter C is in the first 12% of the letters of the alphabet (.12 = 3/26) and uses that information to begin the search in the first 12% of the elements of the array. A similar calculation is made for numeric arrays based on the value of the upper and lower element being searched.

NOTE

In the following implementation, I use the technique described in the preceding paragraph when searching for a string during the first pass through the array only. Subsequent passes use the binary search technique of dividing the array in half. A more complex calculation would be necessary to interpolate in later iterations because, unlike numeric data, additional characters beyond the first would have to be considered to interpolate correctly. Fortunately, the value of the interpolation search is primarily realized in the initial guess.

Of course, the interpolation sort works best for arrays that contain an even distribution of values and is most beneficial for searching large arrays that are evenly distributed. However, searching an array that is unevenly distributed using this technique might actually be slower than the binary search.

The algorithm in Listing 24.8 implements the interpolation search using recursion. Like the binary search shown earlier, this algorithm works on arrays sorted in ascending order.

Listing 24.8   The Interpolation Search

```
Public Function InterpolationSearch(ByRef varArray As Variant, _
    ByVal varSearch As Variant, Optional ByVal pIndex As Integer, _
    Optional ByVal flPartial As Boolean) As Long
```

```
Dim strComp1 As String
Dim strComp2 As String

' Check differently if we're searching on strings
If VarType(varSearch) = vbString Then

    If flPartial Then
        strComp1 = Mid(varArray(pIndex, LBound(varArray, 2)), _
            1, Len(varSearch))
        strComp2 = Mid(varArray(pIndex, UBound(varArray, 2)), _
            1, Len(varSearch))
    Else
        strComp1 = varArray(pIndex, LBound(varArray, 2))
        strComp2 = varArray(pIndex, UBound(varArray, 2))
    End If

    ' Check whether it's even in the range
    If StrComp(varSearch, strComp1, vbTextCompare) = -1 Or _
            StrComp(varSearch, strComp2, vbTextCompare) = 1 Then

        ' Not found, so get out
        InterpolationSearch = -1
        Exit Function
    End If
Else
    ' Check whether it's even in the range
    If varSearch < varArray(pIndex, LBound(varArray, 2)) Or _
        varSearch > varArray(pIndex, UBound(varArray, 2)) Then

        ' Not found, so get out
        InterpolationSearch = -1
        Exit Function
    End If
End If

' Perform the search
InterpolationSearch = FindIt(varArray, varSearch, LBound(varArray, 2), _
    UBound(varArray, 2), pIndex, flPartial)

End Function

Private Function FindIt(ByRef varArray As Variant, _
    ByVal varSearch As Variant, ByVal pLeft As Long, _
    ByVal pRight As Long, ByVal pIndex As Long, _
    ByVal flPartial As Boolean) As Long
```

continues

Listing 24.8   continued

```
Dim lngGuess As Long
Dim strComp1 As String
Dim strComp2 As String

' Check whether we've found it
If VarType(varSearch) = vbString Then
    ' If partial is specified, do a comparison
    ' on the substring
    If flPartial Then
        strComp1 = Mid(varArray(pIndex, pLeft), 1, Len(varSearch))
    Else
        strComp1 = varArray(pIndex, pLeft)
    End If

    If StrComp(strComp1, varSearch, vbTextCompare) = 0 Then
        ' Found it, so get out
        FindIt = pLeft
        Exit Function
    End If
Else
    ' Do a numeric comparison
    If varArray(pIndex, pLeft) = varSearch Then
        ' Found it, so get out
        FindIt = pLeft
        Exit Function
    End If
End If

' See whether we're finished searching
' and still have not found it
If pLeft = pRight Or varArray(pIndex, pLeft) = varArray(pIndex, pRight) Then
    FindIt = -1
Else
    If VarType(varSearch) = vbString Then ' String data

        ' If it's a string, make a guess based on the relative position
        ' of the first letter of the search string
        If pLeft = LBound(varArray, 2) And pRight = UBound(varArray, 2) Then
            ' First time through, so give it a guess
            lngGuess = Int(((Asc(UCase(Left(varSearch, 1))) - 64) / 26) * _
                        (pRight - pLeft + 1)) + pLeft + 1
        Else
            ' Not the first time through, so simply divide
            lngGuess = (pLeft + pRight) / 2
        End If

        ' If a partial compare, search only the substring
        If flPartial Then
```

```
                strComp2 = Mid(varArray(pIndex, lngGuess), 1, Len(varSearch))
        Else
                strComp2 = varArray(pIndex, lngGuess)
        End If


        ' Depending on whether the search string is less than
        ' or greater than the array value, search the lower or
        ' upper portions of the array recursively
        If StrComp(varSearch, strComp2, vbTextCompare) = -1 Then
            FindIt = FindIt(varArray, varSearch, pLeft, _
                lngGuess - 1, pIndex, flPartial)
        Else
            FindIt = FindIt(varArray, varSearch, _
                lngGuess, pRight, pIndex, flPartial)
        End If

    Else    ' Numeric data
        ' Make an educated guess about where to start based on the
        ' relative position of the value based on the upper and lower
        ' indexes to be searched
        lngGuess = pLeft + (((varSearch - varArray(pIndex, pLeft)) * _
            (pRight - pLeft)) / (varArray(pIndex, pRight) - _
                varArray(pIndex, pLeft)))

        ' If the value being sought is less than the guess,
        ' search everything below it; otherwise, search everything
        ' above it recursively
        If varSearch < varArray(pIndex, lngGuess) Then
            FindIt = FindIt(varArray, varSearch, pLeft, _
                lngGuess - 1, pIndex, flPartial)
        Else
            FindIt = FindIt(varArray, varSearch, _
                lngGuess, pRight, pIndex, flPartial)
        End If
    End If
End If

End Function
```

You will notice that the FindIt private procedure is called recursively and passed arguments that include the array, the value to be found, the lower and upper indices of the array to be searched, the index of the first dimension to search, and a flag indicating whether, for string searches, a partial search should be performed. Within FindIt, a calculation is made to determine where the next guess should be made.

To use the `InterpolationSearch` function, you could use the following syntax:

```
' Open a recordset
Set rsProj = New Recordset
rsProj.CursorLocation = adUseClient
rsProj.Open "SELECT * FROM Employees ORDER BY LName", _
    cnCon, adOpenStatic, adLockReadOnly

' Retrieve it into a variant array
varData = rsProj.GetRows(adGetRowsRest)

' Search for the last name = Kight
lngPos = InterpolationSearch(varData, "Kight", 2, False)
```

Note that the last name is identified as index 2 in the first dimension of the array, and a partial search will not be performed.

Implementing Type Ahead

A popular feature in commercial applications is the type-ahead feature typically seen in `ComboBox` controls. In Chapter 13, "Using Win32 API Techniques," I show one technique for implementing type ahead in a combo box using the Win32 API. However, this feature is also becoming popular for `TextBox` controls, as evidenced by the address box found in Internet Explorer.

To implement this feature, you can use the sorting and searching algorithms discussed earlier in the chapter. This provides flexibility because multidimensional arrays can be used to track auxiliary information for the data that appears to the user, not to mention the flexibility of using customized sorting and searching algorithms. For example, assume that an application includes a `TextBox` control for entering the name of an employee. As the name is being entered, an array containing the list of employees pulled from a database at application startup can be searched. With each keystroke, if the text typed in matches the beginning of a name in the array, the `Text` property of the `TextBox` can be changed to include the remainder of the name. In addition, information such as the employee's department and social security number can also be extracted from the array and placed in other `TextBox` controls on the `Form`.

The implementation of this technique includes a public `Function` procedure, `LookupText,` that calls the `BinSearch` function from Listing 24.7 to do a partial search based on the current value of the `Text` property of the given `TextBox` control. If a match is found, the procedure simply selects the remainder of the text (that which was not typed in by the user) and returns the index of the item that was found. This function appears in Listing 24.9.

Listing 24.9   The LookupText Function Used to Perform Type-Ahead in a
TextBox

```
Public Function LookupText(varArray As Variant, _
    ctlText As TextBox, ByVal pIndex As Integer) As Long

Dim strText As String
Dim intLength As Integer
Dim i As Long

' Signifies not found
LookupText = -1

' Get the text to search with and the length
strText = ctlText.Text
intLength = Len(strText)

' Don't search if the length is zero
If intLength > 0 Then

    ' Do a binary partial search
    i = BinSearch(varArray, strText, pIndex, True)

    If i > -1 Then
        ' The text was found
        If Len(varArray(pIndex, i)) > intLength Then
            ' Select the text in the control
            ctlText.Text = ctlText.Text & Mid(varArray(pIndex, i), _
                intLength + 1)
            ctlText.SelStart = intLength
            ctlText.SelLength = Len(varArray(pIndex, i)) - intLength
            LookupText = i
        End If
    End If

End If

End Function
```

TIP

As with all the other procedures in this chapter, this one expects a multidimensional array and accepts as an argument the index of the first dimension to search.

The `LookupText` procedure should be called from the `KeyUp` event of the control, as shown in Listing 24.10. Note that the function is not called unless a letter is typed in the control and that after the function returns, the index can be used to populate other controls on the form.

Listing 24.10   Calling the LookupText Function from the KeyUp Event

```
Private Sub txtEmp_KeyUp(KeyCode As Integer, Shift As Integer)

Dim i As Long

    ' Only search when typing characters
    If KeyCode >= 65 And KeyCode <= 90 Then
        i = LookupText(varData, txtEmp, 2)

        ' If found, populate other controls
        If i <> -1 Then
            txtSSN.Text = varData(1, i)
        End If

    End If

End Sub
```

Summary

Because it is sometimes faster and more efficient to sort and search data cached locally rather than requery a database, this chapter focuses on various techniques to sort and search Variant arrays in Visual Basic. Keep in mind that the choice of technique you apply in a particular situation depends on the number of elements in the array, as well as how the data is distributed within the array.

In addition, you looked at two techniques for searching arrays—the binary search and the interpolation search—and used the binary search algorithm to implement type-ahead functionality in a TextBox control.

INDEX

Symbols

! (type declaration character), 78-79
(type declaration character), 78-79
$ (type declaration character), 78-79
% (type declaration character), 78-79
& (type declaration character), 78-79
@ (type declaration character), 78-79
1stData function, 13

A

AbsolutePage property, Recordset object (ADO), 495
AbsolutePosition property, Recordset object (ADO), 495
abstraction
    Microsoft Transaction Server (MTS), 182
    TreeView control, 182-184
ac Projects (ADO Data Control), 111
accessing
    COM objects, 543-544
    Internet, applications development, 248-250
    remote objects (DCOM), 557-560
    type libraries (COM), 550
    Visual Data Tools, 107-108
Activate event (Form object), 150
activation of COM obj.   1-552
ActiveCommand pro   et object (ADO), 495
ActiveConnection
    object (ADO), *
ActiveControl *
ActiveForm p
    157

C

E

J - K

U - V

W - Z